ON PROCEEDING, NEVER HEEDING

"You have just told the one-and-only Tommy McInally that he knows nothing about football."

On Proceeding is the story of one Glasgow boy's journey into teaching and the priesthood, and his life-long passion for trams and Celtic Football Club. Told through a series of witty, sharp, and at times endearing flashbacks, this is a tale of a life led to the full.

Published in Great Britain in 2013

BILL TOLLAN
ON PROCEEDING

Never Heeding

With grateful thanks for all the many
undeserved kindnesses received
and, of course, far:-
  Findelie Smue (still keep for him!)
  Connie (always wanted to please!)
  and of course
  Zak (quiet well-behaved and
        fun-loving unlike others!)

EIGHTY YEARS A TIM

"The tramp of feet
Along Janefield Street
An excited buzz as they pound.

The turnstyles creak
As the game they seek
Hoping winning goals will abound.

Packed tram-cars sway
Grinding Parkhead way
Fans leap off their steps with a bound.

The whistle blows
On the struggle goes
Is it a match that in fame will resound?"

BACKGROUND

My father was born in the mining village of Barrachnie a few miles to the east of Glasgow. His mother was a colliery employee. She was a "cherry-picker" removing stone from the coal conveyor belt. (You will recall that Bob Shankly began his illustrious career with Junior team Glenbuck Cherry Pickers.)

Grandmother had nineteen children and would be at the cherry-picking the day before a birth and be back at the conveyor belt the day after the birth. Father was a twin. One twin would be in St. Paul's Primary school for half a day while the other was down the pit – then they would change over for the other half of the day. This was legal until 1904. (Sometimes for a joke they would not change over and they said that teacher never twigged the non-change-over.) All this engendered by the poverty of such a large mining family.

AN ARMY LIFE FOR DAD

Disgusted with the horrendous underground conditions he had to endure in Barrachnie Colliery, when he was fifteen years old, my father walked to Hamilton, gave a false age, and was enlisted in the first battalion of the King's Own Scottish Borderers. He was "On Parade" for the great Delhi Durba – which probably beat Barrachnie Colliery!

Later in life, the fact that he had been a regular soldier, enabled him to find a steady job with Glasgow Corporation Tramways, which being a regimented service at the time, preferred to give employment to former regular soldiers, and eventually dad became a motorman in Parkhead Depot.

WHERE THOSE BEETLES COME FROM

My mother was born in the silver boom town of Leadville, Colorado, some 11,000 feet up in the Rocky Mountains, at a time when such as Wyatt Earp and Doc Holliday strolled the streets. Grandmother died and was buried four days later after the birth. (I went over and found her unmarked grave among 40,000 others and was able to place a marker on it out of respect for her.)

Grandfather was told he had only a short time to live, and not wanting to leave his children orphaned in the States came back a rich man but lost his fortune by investing in a Catholic Paisley shoe company which went bust shortly afterwards.

My parents were married in 1917. Supposedly they should have been married in 1916 but my mother's papers from the Annunciation Church in Leadville (which claims to have the tallest spire in the world) were lost with the Lusitania – though how they worked that out I never did discover.

HOW THE DISEASE SET IN

The tale went that one evening during the first week of the marriage dad suggested they go for a walk and the walk took them past Cathkin Park where Third Lanark were playing Celtic. From then on my mother became an enthusiastic Celtic fan and was at many matches home and away until she died aged 92. Even in her nineties she was at Tannadice and Pittodrie. When she was eighty, Sean Fallon was kind enough to bring the players up to greet her in the stand and Billy McNeill did the same to mark her ninetieth birthday and on both occasions she was featured on the front page of The Celtic View. On the day of her funeral I wondered at the route the cortege was taking to Dalbeth Cemetery and noticed as we passed that every flag at Celtic Park was flying at half-mast. Some time later I was consulting our doctor Eugene Connelly – who was also the Celtic Club doctor – and I asked him who had been dead at Celtic on the day of my mother's funeral. He was astonished at the question and replied that they had been flying at half-mast in honour of my mother. So, red-faced, I had to send a belated letter of thanks to the Celtic Board. Blush! Blush.

EARLY DAYS

We lived in a toilet-less room-and- kitchen, two floors up in tenement at 454 Westmuir Street – right at the Sheddings – which gave its name to Shettleston – i.e. the junctions of Westmuir Street, Shettleston Road, Old Shettleston Road and Muiryfauld Drive (the latter being Fare Stage 24 on the then great Glasgow tramway System). Later I was to discover that my father had rejected the offer of a modern semi-detached house in the then being constructed splendid Carntyne housing scheme because it was too far from Parkhead Tram Depot. What a load of trouble and money it would have saved me in later life had he accepted the great offer.

There was a happening on our second floor which greatly puzzled me at the time. In the room-and-kitchen opposite lived an elderly couple. He was an Orangeman carter. But from time-to-time I would discover the old lady living with us instead of in her own place. You have guessed it. When the poor old dear heard that the other half of the Old Firm had been defeated she would flee to us for protection instead of being beaten up by hubby. Sad! Sad! Sad!

But it still happens.

In the next close lived a great friend – a medium-sized Yorkshire Terrier. We got on fine and I admired its happiness though living among the noise, smoke and din of the busy street. But there was an unfortunate person we would meet. He was a poor, mis-shapen little fellow who was not the full shilling. The poor wee man was subject to endless annoyance. One thicko thought it a great joke when he met "Daft Erchie" bringing someone a large jug of milk. He shouted to the unfortunate, "There are holes in the bottom of the jug!" Poor Erchie answered that there weren't any and turned the jug upside down to show the rat. How can one human being treat another like that?

MORE PARKHEAD TALES

In Parkhead St. Michael's School (where you could hear the coffins being made next door!) a newly appointed teacher went to the "Infant Mistress" and complained that she could not get a wee boy in her class to take his cap off. Along went the boss to the classroom and said "You! Get that bunnet aff!" and off the cap came – nae bother.

Earnest young priest trying to get on to the topic of morning prayer asks a class "What does your father do first thing in the morning? Pupil trying to be helpful "Pees in the jaw-boax, Faither!"

(For younger readers: "jaw-boax" = kitchen-sink. Parkheid hooses – like oors – had nae indoor facilities, but!)

STARTING AT SCHOOL

"Is a dove a doo Dad
Is a doo a dove
Is a cow a coo Dad
A sparrow jist a spyug
And is a wall a waw Dad
Is a dog a dug
She's gonny warm ma ear Dad
Instead o' skelp ma lug.

Ma teacher's awfy posh Dad
She changes aw oor names
Wee Shugie now is Hugh Dad
And Jimmy's ayeways James
I 'm scunnered wi' it aw Dad
The way she shoogles words
A must be glaickit no' tae ken
That feathered friends are burds.

Ye lernt me all wrong Dad
Ye called a ball a baw
Yur wife is now my Mother
You said it wis ma Maw
Ah'm no share hoo tae spell Dad
Ah'll niver pass ma test
Whit is this ah'm wearin' Dad
A simmet or a vest.

Ah gave ma nose a dicht Dad
When it began tae dreep
She gave me sich a fricht Dad
A nearly fell aff ma seat
Haven't you a handkerchief
She roared as if in pain
No, a jist use ma sleeve, Miss
And wiped ma nose again.

Ah cawd a mouse a moose Dad
Ah shid hiv held ma tongue

That's manure on yir bits Dad
Nae longer is it dung
It's turnips and potatoes
No tatties noo and neeps
She said I'd ripped ma trousers
When I'd only torn ma breeks.

There's twoch words fir awthin' Dad
They're jumbled in ma heed
Hoo kin a be well-bred Dad
When ah keep sayin' breed
Noo is a crow a craw Dad
Is a bull a bull
Ah'll try to git it richt Dad
I will, I will, ah wull."

Anon.

MORE PARKHEAD MEMORIES

An Orange band was marching importantly down Westmuir Street giving it big licks Little did they know that our lot (some of my near relatives included) were hiding in closes on both sides of the street waiting for them. At the appropriate moment our gang rushed out, seized all their instruments and vanished with them leaving a band standing in Westmuir Street bereft of ability to play on behalf of that pederast William of Orange. Billy Boys well named?

Several times Dad showed me an inoffensive-looking man in Parkhead and remarked with a laugh that that hero could get a free drink in any Catholic pub in Glasgow. One day when the Walk was proceeding at Parkhead Cross, the bold fellow had rushed out of the crowd on one side of the street and dived head-first through the big drum, vanishing into the crowd on the other side of the street.

On one occasion my father was waiting impatiently at Glasgow Cross for the long Walk to get clear. He got fed up, released the air-brake, notched quickly up to top series and took his Standard right through the parade – leaving mayhem behind at Glasgow Cross. The polis obviously were not best pleased with having to deal with the disturbance dad had left behind, came to the house and threatened to charge him with causing public disorder. They contented themselves with using a lot of bad language – no doubt realising that if they had made that charge against dad it would have only caused more trouble in Glasgow.

Being an ex-regular soldier, their language did not bother father at all. When I asked him why he had done what he did he said that he was getting hungry and just wanted home for his meal.

All very ecumenical – I do not think!

Many years later in Edinburgh a motorman was pulled off his platform and murdered with his point iron. Three whole Orange bands were cited as witnesses but of course no-one saw anything. So no-one was ever charged with that murder. Never see that on any of the unsolved crimes programmes.

But was not dad lucky?

I am proud to have been in the same Catholic parish (St. Mark's) and attended the same school (St. Mark's Primary) as the great Labour politician John Wheatley. But! In the early years of the Twentieth Century, the East End of Glasgow Catholics were very much pro-Land Leaguers and there was great frustration and annoyance when some of their leading personalities defected to the ILP and Labour parties, John Wheatley among them. Additionally the Catholic Church at that time attacked Socialism and, sad to say, when the St. Mark's parish priest – Canon O'Brien – would denounce Socialism from the pulpit, John Wheatley would be sitting in the church pews laughing back up at him. This laughing at their much loved priest and his defection from The Land League really inflamed passions among some of the ladies of the parish, and one night they assembled at the Shettleston Road/ Wellshot Road cross-roads and hung up an effigy of Wheatley and proceeded to burn it. Oh! Dear!

And one of those arsonists was my mother!

I was the only survivor of six children so was spoiled rotten. Not only by my parents but all my relatives, friends and neighbours – obviously because they all knew of my mother's tragedies.

I loved the walk down to Celtic Park. We descended into the dip in Westmuir Street (which sometimes flooded curtailing the tram service, and then a row–boat from Hogganfield Loch would carry you across the flood). We would go on up the hill to Parkhead Cross where I would gaze in awe at all the trams negotiating the very complicated tram junctions, with sometimes a tram coming out of Parkhead Depot and reversing to go into service or vice versa. Much later a points-box was erected with a points-man working the points from it to speed up tram passage through the very busy Cross with the points policeman instructed to give the trams precedence. No wonder the Lanarkshire trams would have had to go into the city via London Road – if they had gone into Glasgow as once intended.

Then we went on down Springfield Road to Janefield Street. On all this way we passed an interesting variety of shops and there were three that sold top-drawer chocolates – not the usual Glesca "penny tough jeans". And of course I got my treats. I always felt sorry for the poor souls standing trying to sell PK Chewing Gum for a few pence while I was treated so well.

PARADISE GAINED

At the ground friendly gatemen used to let me be lifted gratis over the turn-style. At one time there was a free gate for the unemployed. Cowdenbeath F.C. got it closed – for in those unenlightened days the terracing gate money was supposed to be shared equally between the competing teams. Though I rather suspect that incorrect crowd totals would be given by the home teams – and of course there were no computerised gates. At Shawfield, for example, the directors had an inspection tour and found that there was one more gate than they knew about – so someone had created a good scam! Was the culprit named Struth? Auld Clyde veteran Mattha Gemmill seemed to think so.

I used to wonder why dad would always make for a certain part of the ground. Only later I realised that that was where he and his pals would gather in front of the old burned down pavilion. In that fire all the existing club records were destroyed.

My god-father cousin, Henry McCartney- a Celtic Park ball boy in his youth along with Jimmy McMenemy's son – gave the club all the Celtic material he had collected. Wonder if it is still at Parkhead?

Usually I would sit on the concrete wall between the cinder track and the terracing – as all us wee yins did. But sooner or later a kindly policeman would make us desist from the practice because of the danger of a fiercely mis-hit heavy leather ball trapping our legs against the concrete.

THE JUNGLE

Older supporters will well remember the "Hay Shed" – notoriously nick-named "The Jungle" – which provided some cover for standing spectators on the narrow strip between the pitch and Janefield Street, At one time an extra charge was made for entrance to the shed and at half-time there would be a mad rush down Janefield Street to get to the goal which Celtic would be attacking in the second half. Us wee yins would do the same if as penalty was awarded at other end of the ground. On one memorable occasion Celtic were unusually awarded a penalty. Jimmy McGrory needed one goal to break one of his remarkable goal-scoring world records. Jimmy kept out of the way at the centre circle but the rest of the team half-carried him up to the penalty spot. He broke away back to the centre circle but they repeated their efforts.

Eventually he gave up the struggle to avoid taking the penalty kick – but merely walked up to the ball and turned a right angle and hit it for a shy. Can you imagine any of the over-paid and over-conceited mercenary imports doing such a humble act to-day?

PHYSICAL AND SPIRITUAL REFRESHMENT

On the way back we would stop at the Italian Trattoria – on the left at the start of Westmuir Street – for a dish of hot peas and then go into Salamanca Street to St. Michael's Church if there was a need for the Sacrament of Reconciliation. (Plain Confessions in those pre-Vatican Two days.) And the Church would be crammed with penitents. Of course if it rained we would try the frequent excellent tram service. Coming back we usually found an east-bound tram reversing on the Springfield Road cross-over. But going to the ground by tram was a different matter as our tram service came all the way down the twelve miles from Airdrie through many places including Airdrie, Coatbridge, Baillieston and Shettleston and usually on match days trams would be full-up at Muiryfauld Drive.

My father always tried to change shifts to get to the match but it was not until the great friend of the trams Sir Patrick Dollan exerted his influence, that GCT tramwaymen were given one Saturday in twelve off duty.

Then there was the notorious occasion when my GCT motorman father was due to come down from Airdrie to go off duty at Parkhead Cross in time for the match. He arranged for my mother to stand at our Westmuir Street close-mouth and he would make an unauthorised stop for her. But did he not forget the arrangement and go sailing on past on top parallel leaving mother open-mouthed as he swept past. The aftermath of that mishap lingered on for years. But when dad (numbered 1940!) was operating Parkhead's No. 1161 – the only GCT car equipped with whistles – he sure remembered to blast them twice when passing our close.

FIRST CELTIC MEMORY

On one occasion I "truanted" from Westmuir Street and wandered up Shettleston Road, tempted to see the friendly St. Bernard dogs that were bred in a garden at the corner of Old Shettleston Road and Fernan Street. (Often wondered what happened to them later during the war.) I was shocked to see a green Citizen bill-poster outside a paper shop on the other side of the road which proclaimed the death of Peter Scarffe. Of course I hurried back to tell the sad news. Must have been able to read before I went to Primary School and did not think that at all remarkable then. But I did not remember the sad John Thomson tragedy happening, though I heard that some of the family walked all the way to Cardenden to be at the funeral – as so many impoverished supporters did from the Glasgow area. It was to be a long time before I managed to reach Cardenden myself and say a quiet "De Profundis" by the great goal-keeper's grave. (Please try to do it yourselves.)

IN THE THIRTIES

I used to look forward to the appearance of an Egyptian, Mansour, who would turn out as a forward in the reserves when his ship was in the Clyde. Because of his religion, Mansour did not wear boots but played with stockings wrapped round his feet. Despite that he sure could hit the old heavy leather ball. He took a penalty against

Motherwell Reserves and hit it straight at McClory their great keeper, who clasped it in his mid-rift but such was the venom of the shot that it carried McClory back over the goal line.

There were some great players in that reserve team most of whom who went on to make up the great first team side of the late Thirties, One of them was a fabulous dribbler called Charlie Napier. Many years later his son was presenting one of his dad's jerseys to the club and I was able to tell him that his dad's nickname among the support was "Happy Feet". His son did not know that and was delighted to hear about it. Unfortunately Napier surprised us all by moving to England. On a return visit to Parkhead McGrory asked him why on earth he had left. "Happy Feet" replied that he was fed up with being called a Papish so-and-so. Jimmy replied that he got called that all the time. Napier is alleged to have responded, "But you are one!"

GREAT TEAMS

The great late thirties team usually went something like this:
Kennaway, Hogg and Morrison; Geatons, Lyons and Paterson: Delaney, McDonald, Crum, Divers and Murphy.

I worshipped them but my father would just laugh and say that they were not a patch on his favourites – the record-making team around 1910 – which he would say went something like: Adams, McLeod and Weir; Young, Loney and Hay, Bennett, McMenemy, Quinn, Somers and Hamilton.

(I later was disappointed to discover that Bennett was one of the few Celts who went on to play for Rangers. I think that Dr. Kivlichan was another?)

Of my heroes, Joe Kennaway was a huge Canadian who was signed from U.S. of A. club Fall River to replace the late, revered John Thomson. On one delightful (to me) occasion he flattened Rangers' great mid-field player Dave Meiklejohn (now he was a player and a half and would be worth millions to-day), and then went on to save the resultant penalty. Great rejoicing among our lot. Joe Kennaway had an unusual claim to fame. He had international caps from three countries, Canada, U.S. of A. and Scotland. (In those days the Scottish League fielded an International team drawn from their players regardless of birth place.) Bobby Hogg came from Royal Albert and was later captain during the war years. He too had an unusual claim to fame. He had a full set of Scottish International jerseys – legitimately awarded though he only ever played once for Scotland. Invariably he would be twelfth man, the selectors preferring Catholic Carabine of Third Lanark to be their right back.

Left back Morrison came out of the pits as so many fine players did in those days. Birkenhead born Willie Lyons M.C., the great Captain, had come to us from Queens Park and was a great steadying influence. Maley called him his Bayard – "his knight without fear".

During the war George Paterson came home on leave from the RAF and scored the only winning goal at Ibrox, much to my delight, as I was behind that goal.

But those forwards defy adequate description. The inside trio of McDonald, Crum and Divers could play intricate close-passing penetrating football worthy of Barcelona's Messi and Eto. Malky McDonald was one of the finest players I have ever seen. He could play a wonderful game in any position in the team and during the war years usually had to fill in all over the place – except goalkeeper. Sharp-shooter Buchan would also play as an inside man. The Cleland Saint – Jimmy Delaney – was a wonderfully fast player on the wing and sometimes at centre. The modern Shevenko reminds me of his style. There were crowd demonstrations outside the SFA offices at Carlton Place if he was not included in the International side. But Jimmy was a bit fragile and you could understand why the selectors hesitated about selecting him.

AN ODD ONE FOR YOU?

Here is one for your pub quiz.

Celtic won a cup competition without scoring a goal throughout the tournament and lost a cup tournament without losing a goal. How come? If teams were equal in goals scored or if it had been a goal-less draw at the end of a match in the Glasgow Charity Cup, then the team with the most corners for them won. If the teams were equal on goals and corners at full time then the first team to score or be awarded a corner in extra time won the match.

A GREAT DAY

But on one glorious occasion The Cleland Saint banged in a hat-trick in the final against the other half of the Old Firm. We urchins danced round the school play-ground chanting:

> "Jerry Dawson never saw
> Where James Delaney put the ba'
> He put the ba' way out of sight
> And poor old Jerry near died of fright.
> He put the ba' way in the net
> And left their goalie in the wet."

This scruff-bag thought we were chanting it to the "Red Flag" left-wing anthem and it was to be many years later before I discovered that the tune actually was a hymn tune they much loved in Colorado – the great German hymn Tannenbaum. (Of course later I was to know that that Delaney chant used to be sung the other way directed about Alan Morton and my father's old friend Charlie Shaw.) Dawson was a top-rate keeper though I think he was on the receiving end of an eight goal drubbing at Easter Road – but that was during the war when all things were possible because of enforced strange team selection.

(Jerry went on to try managing East Fife, but soon gave up because of lack of support for the team in Methil – football supporters preferring to take chartered buses to the Old Firm games from outside Bayview Park itself.)

DISTANT SIGNAL AT DANGER

We would not have risked singing that in the Parkhead streets rather than behind the safety of the school's tall railings. (One of the urchin chants we often sang in the streets to the tune of "A Bicycle Built for Two" was:

> "Amy Johnstone flew in an airyplane!
> Flew tae Melborne and never came back again!
> Flew in an auld tin lizzie
> Enough tae make you dizzie!
> Noo she's in bed wi a broken leg

And a bicycle bult fur two!"

Hardly historically accurate!

I was walking along Crail Street to meet my father at Parkhead Depot, when I was stopped by three much bigger boys who asked me if I was a Billy, a Dan, or an old tin can. Of course I knew very well what was afoot. But I put on a very puzzled look and in my best voice, quietly said that I did not understand the question. They drew aside in amazement and I went safely on to the Depot. Phew!

THE FAMOUS EMPIRE EXHIBITION WIN

In 1938 came the great Empire Exhibition in Bellahouston Park. Little did we know then that soon there would be no British Empire.

A wonderful new class of semi-streamlined large smooth-running and very comfortable double-deck cars called Coronations were introduced by Glasgow Corporation Transport for the occasion. (I was privileged to operate one just built – and smelling strongly of paint and varnish – from Mount Vernon to Uddingston. I was only aged ten! And a few intending passengers took my halting efforts very well.)

There is a Coronation – No. 1245 – needing subsidy to get it running at Summerlee Heritage Park at Coatbridge. Visit Summerlee and see how wonderful a Coronation was as a public service vehicle compared to the buses we have to tolerate to-day.

Additional tram junctions were installed along Paisley Road West and regular tram services ran from the city centre to Bellahouston and of course I rode some of them. Additionally there would be special trams to Ibrox sidings from all parts of the network – even from Airdrie, Coatbridge, Uddingston, Clydebank or Paisley and Renfrew.

What also concerned our lot was the Exhibition Football Tournament. We scraped through this, beating Sunderland after a replay we were lucky to win. Fortunately dad was able to take me to the semi-final v Hearts – who out-played us in the first half. But our good defence held out with Kennaway playing a blinder, and Johnny Crum scored the winner for us in the second half. After the match there were two long lines of trams waiting in the lengthy

Ibrox sidings which had cross-overs at both ends of the tracks. I could not imagine how we would ever get on one as there were crowds of would-be passengers fighting to board every Standard car – the Coronations all being on the proper Exhibition services. However my father picked me up and ran to one with the destination "Shettleston". He shocked me by throwing me on to the front platform of the tram. The motorman did not even look round – so he must also have been from Parkhead Depot.

(Dad once told me that Glasgow Corporation Tramway Department had also wanted to run a tram "specials" relief loop along Janefield Street but Celtic were not prepared to share in the costs involved. Pity. The Partick Depot Celtic supporters used to come across to a Parkhead game on "Wee Baldie" – the Baillie Burt experimental High-Speed tram 1089. For the duration of a game it had to be taken down Tollcross Road and parked on a Parkhead Depot siding. How much more convenient for those supporters (and others) a Janefield Street loop would have been.)

Of course the Exhibition Trophy sits proudly in the Celtic Boardroom as we beat Everton in the final, but dad could not get off to take me to that game. No TV in those days.

WATCH OUT – SPIDERS ABOUT

In the Thirties there would be the annual Christmas Day friendly against Queen's Park. Guess which side usually won the keenly contested match? It wasn't the one in the green-and white hoops. No worries then about a change needed to avoid contrasting hoops. We had never even heard of Baird and TV?

FEAR AND TREMBLING

Then one day father said that he had a great treat in store for me. We were going to see Arbroath v. Celtic on a Football Excursion train and we would be travelling over the Forth and Tay Bridges. That was a shocker for me. A week or so previously BBC had produced a dramatic reproduction of the last moments on the passenger train that was involved in the Tay Bridge disaster.

(During a gale the inadequately designed and poorly maintained four central towers of the Tay Bridge had collapsed just as a Kirkcaldy-Dundee train was passing the bridge central span. Track, engine and train dropped vertically on to the river bed with disastrous consequences. Several attempts were made to lift the 4-4-0 North British Railway engine from the deep but several times it broke free of the slings and returned to stand again on the river bed. Hence when it was eventually successfully recovered and put back into service it was known as "The Diver", and worked in the Parkhead/Shettleston area until the nineteen-twenties.)

I was filled with great fear about crossing the replacement Tay Bridge. But at that age you are desperately afraid not to show you are a thorough coward. Came the day and off we went from Glasgow Queen Street Station. Arriving at the mighty Forth Rail Bridge I was amazed at its size and grandeur. (Much of it was pre-fabricated across London Road from Celtic Park.) I was further amazed by the vast shower of coins that were thrown over the bridge from carriage windows. (I have never discovered the reason for that custom. Does any reader know?) On we went across Fife and I could see the Firth of Tay. My knees started to knock but we slowed down and quite steadily and sedately we passed over the bridge.

(To-day the Tay Bridge is in such a poor state that only one train at a time is allowed to pass slowly over it and as closure looms a diversion route via Perth is prepared. Network Rail will never erect a third Tay crossing bridge and they would like to be rid of the Forth Bridge which is far too expensive to maintain. There would be a national out-cry if they tried to do that. But it is a thought that a diversionary route that has been reinstated via Stirling as far as Alloa will be continued to Dunfermline and Fife.)

A BLACKOUT BEFORE THE WAR

Passing through Tay Bridge station we dived under Dundee and stopped in the darkness for what seemed to me to be ages. Of course I now know that the delay was caused by the need to change engine and crew for the short run to Arbroath. There a surprise awaited me – no doubt pre-planned by dad. Jimmy McGrory – no less – came up to us and shook my hand. Wow! I did not wash that hand for a week. The great man said that he had to hurry off as he could not come to Arbroath without visiting the Earl of Strathmore. I think Strathmore was the father of the consort of the Duke of York and she came from Glamis Castle.

But being a republican – well my mother was born in Colorado – I am not up on royal genealogy. The Duke of York (later George the Sixth of course) – and I was once disgusted to have to be in an RAF Guard of Honour for him – when he was king, opened the newly built Parkhead Depot by operating a Standard car from Parkhead Cross down to the Depot and then re-dedicating, the Transport War Memorial which had been brought up from the closing Whitevale Depot. All this in front of a large parade of GCT Great War survivors (all bedecked with rows of medals) at the Transport War Memorial which had been brought up from the closing Whitevale Depot. The Depot visiting book bears his then used signature of "Bertie".

Last time I looked there is a collection of War Memorials gathered behind Parkhead Garage (as the once great Depot now is called) and the garage was so filthy compared with its tram glory days when it was kept spick and span. (That collection is well worth a visit before a home match at Celtic Park.)

AT GAYFIELD

As for the game itself: Jimmy Delaney had his arm broken in a tackle from Arbroath's left back Becci; Willie Lyon went up to centre and our ten men won 2-1. I slept most of the way back to Glasgow. What a day!

INBHAIR GHARBAIN

Our families (like so many other Glaswegians) were mad keen on holidaying in Girvan as it is called these days – Gaelic having long vanished from Carrick. Far off Durham had an influence there once, too. A pre-twelfth century church in Girvan was dedicated to St. Cuthbert. Wonder where it was sited? Not hidden down in Harbour Lane like the present boring Protestant-like Catholic church for sure.

Being the youngest, if we had football going on top of the Byne Hill, I was the chump who had to drop down the steep sides to retrieve the ball. I suppose it kept me fit. (After the Empire Exhibition closed there was a pressure group created who wanted to re-erect the dismantled tall Exhibition landmark – Tait's Tower – on top of the Byne Hill. Quite a nonsense of course. It would have been on its way to Ailsa Craig after the first gale.) But there is an adjoining Girvan hill much easier to ascend and descend. Thank goodness. It is called the Dow Hill and is the site of a supposed Romano/British/Pictish fort. I have often pondered why I have never heard of that interesting hill being excavated or at least scanned with the modern scanning equipment now available. One sunny day I was perched comfortably on top of Dow Hill watching through binoculars as a Celtic five-a-side played in a tournament on Girvan's Victory Park. Never understood or heard an explanation as to why I was not actually allowed to go the tournament itself. I suppose we were just scraped for cash.

One year we stayed in Girvan with the Mitchell family who had a large fishing boat – the Jean Mitchell – of the then normal Clyde type, and I was given trips out on it. (Of course the Firth of Clyde is now quite fished out and there are only prawn-boats based in Girvan harbour these days.) The kind Mitchells arranged for me to have a trip gratis out to Paddy's Milestone (Ailsa Craig on maps!) as the Craig light-house keepers were being changed and the good old Lady Ailsa was taking out the furniture of the new keepers and then retrieving the furniture of the previous families. I was strictly warned that I had to be of perfect behaviour and keep out of the way. So while the unloading and loading was taking place, I found that there was a good-foot-path right over the top of the Craig and down the other side. So I went over it as fast as I could so as not to miss the return trip! On the other side I discovered a small castle built by the Spaniards and a quarry with railways that produced the granite pieces used to make curling stones at Dailly. I did not know then that there was also down on the shore facing Kintyre what I would also have liked to have visited – the remains of a mediaeval chapel. I have tried and tried but cannot find anyone who can tell me the history of the wee building. Was it perhaps originally the site of an Irish monks' hermitage dating from around Columcille's time? If any erudite reader knows I would be most grateful to be enlightened.

But what a thrilling experience for a wee smout. There are people living in Girvan to-day who have never been across to what is now a protected bird sanctuary covered with thousands of gannets. Much later an eccentric friend arranged for a Lanarkshire bus stop to be erected on the Craig. Do not ask me why the lunacy.

And of course my Glaswegian school-mates thought I was making it all up about that wonderful day.

Sadly there is a German Navy U-boat lying on the sea bottom off the Craig. Doenitz sent one of his U-Boats to attack our Home Fleet at the Tail of the Bank. That boat Commander thought that it was too risky to try to get up the well-protected Firth of Clyde and since he did not want his crew to lose their lives unnecessarily he turned back to his base. He was sacked by Doenitz on his return and a second U-boat was ordered out to complete the mission. That Commander did not want to be sacked so he tried to get up the Firth but his boat was sunk by the duty RN frigate patrolling between Ailsa Craig and Arran. Requiescant in pace.

AHOY THERE!

Then a remarkable holiday began in unexpected fashion. For my birthday I had been given a superb little Clyde Model Dockyard wee yacht named Loch Erne. (Told you I was spoiled rotten.) The very next week we were at Girvan again for our usual annual fortnight there. First morning there, I ran all the way to the small children's boating pond just off the Promenade at the then Bathing Station. I did see that the pond was very busy but was too eager to have the wee yacht make its first sail to care about that. Eagerly I watched it race through all the other boats and ran round the pond to reach it at the other side. As I picked it out a man touched my shoulder and astonished me by saying that I had won a prize and he gave me a box of chocolates. Unknown to me The Express newspaper had been holding a competition at the pond. But was it my yacht's prowess that had gained the prize or the St. Aloysius' College blazer I was wearing? The boating pond and the bathing station are long gone but the Clyde Model Dockyard yacht is still a prized possession.

UP-MARKET BUT ONCE

One year we tried staying in a Boarding House. Either that proved to be too regimented or more likely too expensive. In one war year we could only get accommodation in a council hose below the station. Of course I was not allowed to go anywhere near to the railway on my own, but night after night I would lie awake waiting for an engine that would pound slowly up the 1 in 57 single line out of Girvan towards Pinmore. Did not know it then but later discovered that this loco was a survivor of the notorious River class 4-6-0 express locomotives delivered to the Highland Railway around 1913. They were advanced state of the art engines for their time, but unfortunately proved too heavy for some of the bridges and culverts on the Perth-Inverness line.

By the war years this old timer was in a state of disrepair with new valve gear needed and what I would listen to was its remaining only duty taking back from Ayr a long line of carriages that it had brought from Stranraer to Ayr for cleaning.

MY MOST ENJOYBLE HOLIDAY EVER

On the trams an employee had to take his annual fortnight's holiday in which ever fortnight it was allocated between May and October – for obvious reasons the GCT holidays had to be dispersed. One year poor old dad drew the short straw and could not get his holiday dates changed. He had to be "off" in May itself.

I cleaned his brass buttons for him as usual and we went up to Garnethill to see if I could be off St. Aloysius' College during that given fortnight. How I felt sorry for the way my father was treated. The ill-mannered "county" Jesuit Headmaster did not even stop perusing the papers he was sitting studying but merely replied to the polite request: "Take him off. But do not bring him back." Shocking rudeness – but then we were mere Glasgow "scruff" to some of the up-market "County" Jays. However it meant that I was given a fortnightly season and travelled up and down to the College every day from Girvan by good old LMS Stranraer-Glasgow boat-trains.

ROUND AND ABOUT

It was when I was holidaying with my aunt and cousins in their Henrietta Street hired council house holiday abode that Mr. Hare, the Insurance Agent who off-season lived there with his family, took me with him on his smooth-running Ford B Car as he did his business round through many of the villages adjacent to Girvan. That was my very first motor-car ride. What a day!

INITIALS MARK THE SPOT

Dad was a great one for carving my initials on tree trunks. I did not like that at all. One time we were staying with Uncle John Hughes at Eaglesham. Uncle John drove one of Glasgow's large six wheel battery-operated Cleansing Department lorries and he and his brothers had an up-to-date Hillman which he used on the day war broke out on the 3rd of September 1939 to take us to Strathaven to see Harry Lauder's house. That was my second ride in a motor-car.

But later on the tree-carving day we had gone for a hike around Eaglesham, and, crossing a meadow, dad had stopped and gone over to some boundary trees and carved WMT on one of the trees. During the rest of the week Herr Hess landed in that very field on his unsuccessful peace mission. I have often wondered since if dad was "psychic" or was it just chance he chose that field and tree?

TRAMP! TRAMP! TRAMP!

In those by-gone days people did a lot of walking when on holiday– especially our lot. Every year we would take the train from Girvan up the 1 in 57 and through the narrow tunnel to long-closed Pinmore Station and then we hiked across the hills to Lendalfoot. I remember good farm people coming across to us and offering us drinks of milk gratis. They must have felt sympathy towards Glaswegians. Kennedy's Pass was a frequent destination on the then uncrowded road to Stranraer. But one Summer father really did for me. We walked right along the sandy and rocky shore North to Culzean Castle. Boy, was I glad to get the bus back to Girvan. I suppose all the walking helped me to keep me sometimes fit and healthy?

FORE! AGAIN AND AGAIN

After demobilisation I had another interesting (to me!) Girvan railway remarkable happening. On a Girvan holiday week, every morning, Monday to Wednesday, trying in vain to improve my golf, I would be delayed at the same Girvan Golf Course road hole by a small old man pottering about ahead of me. But on the Thursday he called me forward and apologised for the mornings he had delayed my progress. He made me feel rather small by saying he was 92 years old and in the past had been the Girvan Stationmaster. To this day I am still puzzled as to why he thought that would be of interest to me – as it certainly was. He said that his biggest problem as Stationmaster had been obtaining enough wagons for the Girvan potato harvest. Again, later in life, I discovered that when there was enough wagons for the Girvan potato harvest, there would be so many of them, that paths to Glasgow for their trains were hard to obtain on the Girvan-Maybole-Ayr main line and frequently train loads of fifty potato wagons had to be sent to Ayr via the coastal Dunure-Maidens light railway. The price of potatoes in Glasgow shops was cheaper than in the Girvan premises.

DRIVING UNDER THE GROUND

One night coming from the Empire Exhibition I wondered why we were going to Cessnock Underground station instead of just boarding the excellent Paisley – Airdrie service passing Bellahouston and which would have taken us straight home to Parkhead. It was so I could operate a train on the Underground to St. Enoch's. Wow! When I had managed to stop at each station a kindly Stationmaster would look in and joke "Not him again!" Obviously a treat arranged for wee Glaswegians. Could not happen nowadays to a small delighted boy in our over-regimented Elf and Softy nanny state.

However I was in the driving cab right round the Outer Circle later on in life but did not see the lady apparition that is supposed to appear sometimes in the tunnels between Cessnock and Govan Cross. (The trains drove themselves after modernisation with driver supervision for the doors etc.)

That opportunity was given to me in return after I had explained to the then Underground manager how he should operate the Lanarkshire double-deck replica tram at Summerlee Heritage Site, Coatbridge. Go there and ride it!

END OF THE GREAT EXHIBITION

When the great Empire Exhibition closed, there was not a tram standing in any of the Glasgow tram depots. Every tram was out waiting for the closure if not actually on normal service.

GREAT PRE-WAR ENTERTAINMENT

I remember tremendous entertainment at Hampden Park. We enjoyed watching bicycle polo, elephants (who seemed to enjoy it) playing football and a great fireworks display. Then came the great fireworks of the war – blitzes et al. A terrible time.

SAINT MARK'S PARISH

Our church and school, both named after the first of The Evangelists, was handy. They were just across Muiryfauld Drive, and when I was later doing my student teacher practice, I could wait in the house until the school bell rang, stroll over, and still be in time for the lined-up classes entering the school building.

But as a growing-up youth the Church took up far too much of my time when I should have been doing better home-work or studying harder. There was a fine large group of priests there – large because the St. Paul's Shettleston church house was reckoned to be uninhabitable at that time so the priests of two parishes lived together in great and happy harmony under the mild rule of Dean Kearney. One of them – better be nameless – highly amused us altar-boys by singing Celtic parodies to the earnest holy hymns being sung by the parishioners in the church itself. So I learned a good few of the Parkhead fans' ditties that way. Mea maxima culpa!

One I seem to remember was based on "Hail Glorious St. Patrick" and went something like:

> "Hail Glorious McGrory
> Dear Saint of our Isle
> On us thy poor children bestow a sweet smile
> And now that you are high in the Grandstand above
> On Celtic's green jerseys look down in thy love.
> On Celtic's green jerseys
> On Celtic's green jerseys
> On Celtic's green jerseys
> Look down in thy love.
> In the war against Rangers
> In the fights for the Cup
> With Jimmy at centre the Bhoys were soon up.

Three goals in three minutes
Eight goals in one game!
Great Jimmy McGrory our pride and our fame.
Hail Jimmy McGrory etc."

There was an outstanding Irish priest – a Father Gilmartin – a giant physically as well as spiritually. (On one dark night he was coming back down Old Shettleston Road from a sick call visit when a couple of neds miscalled him from a tenement close-mouth. He left the pair lying senseless in the street. The Police told Father Gilmartin that they would not charge him this time but would he please desist from taking such action again.)

The dark days of the Thirties saw east-end mass unemployment. I would walk the length of Shettleston Road going for music lessons, and at each corner on the opposite side of the road would be the same large knot of decent unemployed men – an uncle among them on each corner. Curiously most of them wore a large white silk scarf as they stood chatting to pass the time. (Sadly on one such perambulation I witnessed a poor soul being killed in a fall off a Corporation bus. Requiescat in Pace.)

Father Gilmartin tried to help relieve the misery of the times by organising a fantastic (to me) annual day-out. At the appropriate time a fleet of reserved Standard trams would come down Shettleston Road and we would clamber on and off we would go into the city.

ON THE PORT ROAD

One year we went from the now sadly demolished magnificent St. Enoch Station right down to and across the lovely Galloway hills to the curious little harbour village of Portpatrick with its ruined castle standing over it. This involved a change of engine and a reversal on the Stranraer single line which interested me no end. Even then I was a railway "anorak". In the early days of the Portpatrick-Stranraer line a service to Stranraer stalled on the steep curving gradient coming up out of Portpatrick. This was not an unusual happening so the keen young fireman was eager to help and asked his driver should he go back and halve the train. The astonished driver looked at him and asked him if he had a saw. There was only one carriage behind the small engine.

DAFFODILS BEWARE

Another great parish trip involving a change of locomotive, took us from the huge Central Station to the fabulous Lake District. The lightly-laid Keswick line from the west coast main-line at Penrith could not take the Midland 4-4-0 Compound engine that had taken us to Sassenach land – so to my great delight two small ex LNWR jumbos came on for another lovely run through Wordsworth country.

Of course thanks to butcher Beeching such LMS destinations cannot be reached by rail in these enlightened(?) times.

MORE AMUSEMENT

A lengthy LNER journey from Queen Street Station caused us to arrive eventually in Whitley Bay, and of course I loved the great amusements I discovered there. That destination I managed to reach later in life despite Beeching's rail massacres, but this time via the magnificent Newcastle Metro system. On that occasion my poor black lab was very upset because dogs were not allowed on the great sandy beach – so I did not linger long on the second occasion.

Another of Father Gilmartin's involved planning efforts took us on a great sail via the Kyles of Bute to Lochgoilhead. Be sure I slept most of the way back on these fantastic days out. And everyone, visitors and locals, were so friendly and welcoming.

Shickelgruber saw the end to our parish enjoyments but Father Gilmartin caused great credit to our Church (and his good self!) by being the only local cleric to go round the air-raid shelters during the war-time air-raids and as a result there were several Faith reconciliations and apologies from bigots (including our own Orangeman wife-beater) for their hatred of Catholics and the Catholic Church.

Father Gilmartin kept me busy. Apart from having a large district of my own to perambulate for the many parish collections, I would be kept late getting home from Garnethill on a Friday thanks to the Mercy nun in the adjoining Convent hardly ever having the week-end Mass hosts ready for collection. And to make things worse he made me i/c altar boys – a choice that did no go down well with them or me. It meant that I had to be there at every service in the church. And there were a lot of them to attend and manage in those days. How on earth did I scrape Highers? Guardian angel again no doubt.

Father Gilmartin tried to show appreciation for my efforts when he was appointed parish priest at St. Patrick's, Old Kilpatrick. He had me down for the day and entertained me with a splendid meal and listening to his collection of Caruso John McCormack and Sydney McEwan records. Never hear them on the media these days – worse luck. I later was fortunate enough to meet Father McEwan with St. Aloysius' College teachers on a day out, and later visited the beautiful church he had built in Kingussie dedicated to Our Lady of The Rosary and St. Columba.

And we enjoyed too the Annual Days Out organised by the Glasgow Catholic Transport Guild. Usually the day out would be by reserved trams to one of the many outlying attractive tram destinations such as Milngavie, Rouken Glen or Bothwell Castle. But one year we travelled through to Edinburgh on a fleet of the old open-stair-case TD1 buses. At Corstorphine terminus there were a number of very tall converted ex-cable cars. And we dined well that afternoon in a St. Cuthbert's Co-operative Society Restaurant.

NO REST FOR THE WICKED

But more parish expectations were to come for me. Canon Dennehey arrived on the scene. He was on the Archdiocese planning committee and he soon had me going here and there all over the place, taking out envelopes and sometimes collecting them for him. His rewards were journeys with him on his business trips on buses around the West of Scotland. He would point out many sites where future churches were going to be built. I never pass them these days without saying a deserved prayer for the repose of the soul of their originator.

On one long bus run to Lanark, he recounted a cracker to me. When he was attached to the then recent parish of Christ the King – which had just been established to serve the vast new up-market housing estate of Kings Park in Glasgow, he would take some exercise by strolling around the beautiful park of the same name (sadly founded by a Glasgow slave-trade exploiter.) Occasionally on his perambulations he would be joined by a retired sea-captain. Christ the King started with a large-looking church house for the clergy and only had a wooden building serving as the temporary church. The sea-captain kept insinuating that that set up was quite scandalous, as the Church for the Lord should have been much better than the house for the priests. Eventually Canon Dennehey had had enough of the ridicule and said to the sea-captain that he was going to tell him the real reason for the large house. He told the man that the Pope of the time, Pius XI, Achille Ratti, had mountain climbing as a hobby and he had always wanted to go climbing in our Highland mountains so the large Kings Park house had been so constructed as a base for the Pope to stay there incognito to do that. The sea-captain was warned that for security reasons he was not to repeat that information to anyone. Of course Dennehey well knew that the sea-captain would blab about a Pope's visit. Sure enough Dennehey was summoned to the presence of the Archbishop of Glasgow and asked to explain why a mere priest had been informed of a Papal visit but an eminent Archbishop had not been so informed. Perhaps His Grace had a good hierarchical chuckle when the true circumstances were explained to him. Or may be that was why my kindly Canon friend was transferred from lofty well-off King's Park to poverty–stricken Shettleston? But at least we had the large green space of wooded Tollcross Park for the good Canon to walk in.

AD MAJORA NATUS SUM

While all that church business was taking place I was – much against my will – pursuing the so-called Jesuit education at St. Aloysius' College, known to us lesser mortals as "Wally Dishes". I suppose that because my cousin god-father and his three brothers had been at Garnethill, my father thought that I had to follow in their footsteps. Oh! Dear!

I started in Primary Five (presumably there was only room in Primary Four for those and such as those?) The Primary Five outfit (I would not deign to use the normal word class to describe it) was supervised by a real old biddy (well to me she was, after the splendid young and energetic teachers in St. Mark's Primary. At St. Mark's I sure was puzzled to be told daily by the great Miss Macnabola that we were praying to Blessed Oliver Plunkett!

Plunking school being discouraged. I had also thought that the words of the hymn "Long may the transport last!" was for my dad's benefit! But you live and sometimes learn. St. Mark's had been an early disappointment to me. First time I entered the starter class I was delighted to see a very large rocking-horse in the classroom. But I never got that much-wanted ride on it, nor did I see anyone else have a shot. Then disgrace. For some school event I was dressed up as Little Boy Bue! Imagine a Tim dressed up as Little Boy Blue! I wept about my shame for days on end. To no avail. Blush! Blush! And blush again.

That College Preparatory Primary five teacher showed me how not to "teach" when I attempted to do that in later life. Mostly everything was done by rote. I can still go round all the rivers and capes of Scotland as we recited them almost every day of our miserable lives in Primary Five. We also repeated the lengthy verses of half a dozen poems that were usually quite beyond my comprehension – no explanation being given about what they meant and their role in history and nothing at all also about their poets' lives and why they had written them. But maybe I had fallen asleep as usual. Of course the "learning by rote" was just so that she could sit undisturbed and attend to her personal correspondence?

Then on one occasion she did what she really ought not to have done. My turn came to go down to the pillar box in Sauchiehall Street and post her correspondence. I was so fed up with her and "Wally Dishes", that, going down Scott Street I was greatly tempted to go and ride Britain's longest tram service, GCT's 26 mile run from Renfrew Ferry to Milngavie. That would have been much better than suffering Primary Five for the rest of the day.

But I knew that my dad – after a long struggle – had managed to give up smoking and had also stopped socialising with his brothers in order to scrape up enough money for my College fees. So I just could not let him down by defecting – much as I wanted to go tram riding.

The Jesuit Head at that time was a weird and wonderful individual (to me at any rate) known to us lesser mortals as "Wuggy". (I never found out why "Wuggy". Can any reader tell me?) He once gave me a superb metal cross with a saint emblazoned on either side as a reward for my Religious Knowledge efforts. (Thank you Saint Mark's! Slates, chalks, Blessed Oliver

Plunkett and all!) Wonder what has happened to that cross? Have mislaid it among my many abode moves. Much later he made me a hero among my pals by giving me double-twelve ferulas for some trivial offence or other. Forgetting homework I think it was. (Only much later in life I learnt that he was dying of cancer at that time – so Requiescat in Pace.) But for a time when I was in Primary Five he would repeatedly appear in the class-room and ask if anyone knew how to make a Maltese Cross. I knew what he was at – being a street-wise east-ender I just sat back and enjoyed the amusement – but parents were going frantic trying to teach their sons how to draw on the blackboard various versions of a Maltese Cross. "Wuggy" was not at all a popular Jesuit when he propounded the answer he wanted. Stand on his corns of course! Some kind of that usual peculiar Jesuit humour I suppose?

But! One of the lay staff did not enjoy a bit of humour, though, thanks to stupid me. I was sitting near the classroom door when a male face appeared round the door and asked me if I knew how to light the gas-ring under a kettle. (No Micro-wave in those unenlightened days.) I said I did. So he told me to go along to the staff-room and do it. So I did that. Some time later the face appeared again but this time very irate, and waved a much battered and distorted kettle in my face. I had not checked if there had been any water in the kettle. Mea maxima culpa yet once more.

And then there was the visit we made down to the MacLellan Art Galleries in Sauchiehall Street to see a collection of modern paintings by Matisse. I could not make head nor tale of them and what they were supposed to be about. Imagine my delight when a week-or-so later it was proclaimed in the press that all the supposedly wonderful Matisse paintings had been hung upside down in the galleries.

OFF TO THE SOUTH SIDE

The move on to Primary Six was much more appreciated by me – though not by most of the class, as teacher Miss Sinclair was of the kindly mothering type. Being usually spoiled rotten at home I did not mind that happening at school as well. No doubt she knew what we had had to suffer in Primary Five.

But! When the war started there were not the necessary air-raid shelters for us at Hill Street, and so we, instead of attending at

Garnethill, had to travel to Miss Sinclair's large mansion in wealthy Strathbungo. This delighted me no-end as now I had two great tram services to ride on – to and from education. Additional joy came when made the great discovery that if I alighted from the 15 Paisley-bound car in Bridge Street and waited a few minutes, along would come on Service 8, No. 1002, best of the several experimental light-weight truck cars that were intended to be exemplars for a fleet to replace the many old and so-worn-out Standard cars. And sometimes its friendly conductor would be Mr. Cairns, the father of a College pupil. He always made sure I was all right. And sometimes the occasional sweetie came my way.

Toilet provision for us was a problem for the good Miss Sinclair. So somehow it was arranged that we go along to Strathbungo Railway Station and perform there. For a time afterwards we were known at Wally Dishes as "the railway boys."

But then when we moved back to Hill Street we discovered that a RAF barrage balloon outfit had occupied "The Pitch" – the playground behind the church where we used to bash ra balls about at interval and lunch times. But the RAF erks looking after things proved to be jovial and friendly to us – in the nicest possible way. And if snow fell we would have most enjoyable snowball fights with them.

More on snowball fights later.

Then we had a happening. We were told that a retired PT teacher had come back to help out because of war-time staff shortages. (More on that too later!)

Unexpectedly we were going to have a PT period. So we trooped expectantly into the gym and assembly hall. A squat wee man awaited us there and told us that he was going to show us how to run properly. (And here was disappointed me well able to run away from the Shettleston polis!) I will refrain from naming that retired expert – except to say that his surname was more than appropriate for a Scotsman. (Send a stamped envelope if you do not get the joke!)

So the great running expert started his running performance – which we were to emulate – but suddenly he dropped unconscious on to the wooden floor. Help was summoned and we were quickly ushered back to our class-room.

Later I was to have confirmed what we all imagined. The poor man was completely intoxicated.

We had no more PT that year.

THOSE TERRIBLE WAR YEARS

With the out-break of war, the great team of the late Thirties quickly faded. Kennaway went back across the pond. Wonder what became of him? Because of travel restrictions and air-raid dangers, a Southern Scottish league was formed with limited attendances allowed. Celtic wages were cut to two pounds. My father had a GCT motorman friend whose son Jackie Cantwell played in our team as a centre-forward when he was demobbed from the Navy. His sister Helen told me that even at that late date he only received two pounds when he played, and two pounds for each time he trained. Players were no longer eager to play at Parkhead. Eventually Crum and Divers went to Morton. (In my later RAF Kinloss days I was to see them playing in Inverness for Morton against Clachnacuddin – but it was a dismal cup-tie affair.) Goalsnatcher Buchan joined Stenhousemuir of all places, and things just went from bad to worse after the travesty of the disgraceful dismissal of the great Willie Maley. I once was in great awe when I passed him as he strolled along Girvan beach complete with a splendid fedora hat. Years later I was friendly with Mr. Maley's nephew and nieces at Glasgow University and they still seethed at the shocking manner of their uncle's break with the club of which he was more or less the creator and back-bone for all those long wearying years.

MANAGEMENT CHANGE

Chairman Thomas White brought in stalwart Jimmy McStay as a replacement. Do not know much about Chairman Thomas White and I certainly was not impressed by his son Desmond when I knew him much later. Rightly or wrongly I suspect White was a bit of a bully at heart. He did not seem to like Jimmy McStay standing up to him. Other Scottish teams had famous players "guesting". Matthews and Lawton would turn out for Morton, Shankly for The Jags. And I was staggered to see the great Frank Swift pick up a wet, heavy leather ball by grasping it using only one of his enormous hands when he turned out for Hamilton Accies. Before the war my father's cousin Frank played in an Accies team that defeated Rangers 2-1. The family story relates that the following week Rangers officials came to the Tollan house in Baillieston to sign Frank, saw the Catholic pictures on the walls and apologised, saying a mistake had been made as Rangers did not employ Catholics. (Like so many West of Scotland businesses of the time.) They offered Frank a fiver to play a trial at Ibrox but a Catholic could not be signed by the club. The Rangers officials were told in no uncertain terms exactly to what use they could put the five pound note. And in those days it was big enough for the suggested purpose. And this was at a time when most of that family were unemployed. One of Frank's sisters had obtained teacher qualifications in the early Thirties but had to wait six years before she obtained a teaching post. (My mother once told me that my dad had worked for sixty years and had never even seen a five pound note.) The long–standing family joke was that Frank's brother Joe was muckers with Rangers star Torry Gillick. They were ferocious gamblers. Ibrox never realised that Torry had been baptised in St. Pat's, Coatbridge. We thought that poetic justice of a kind and would often have a giggle about it.

My father had a conductor listed with him for tramway duties. On the cars Catholic was usually paired with Catholic for obvious reasons. My father's new friend had an honours degree in Maths but could only find a post on the trams. Applications were requested to fill a Tramway Inspector vacancy at Parkhead Depot and my dad mistakenly had his conductor friend apply for the vacancy. The latter was turned down on the excuse that he had failed the Arithmetic test. No need to explain yet again what went on in the West of Scotland in the good (for some) old days.

For some peculiar reason White would not let seasoned guest players turn out for the club, although they would have greatly assisted the young and inexperienced Boys Guild players. Matt Busby even trained at Parkhead and always held a grudge re Celtic, because he never was allowed to play for his team. His headline in The Express on the day before Lisbon was that Celtic had no chance of defeating Inter-Milan. He got that wrong, thank goodness. White tried to persist in turning out cheap young inexperienced Boys' Guild players. (Although one -Willie Corbett – played in a war-time International team aged sixteen and a half.)

McStay managed to bring in centre-half Waddell and goal-keeper Johnstone from Aberdeen and Gillan from McStay's former club Alloa. He signed future stars such as Bobby Evans, Willie Miller and the great John McPhail. I watched Hooky play against us at St. Aloysius' College grounds at Millerston and thought he was quite outstanding, easily the best of the twenty-two. McStay never received the credit he deserved for these signings, just as McGrory never had the accolade he deserved for signing most of the Lisbon Lions. The world can be a hard place.

BACK TO WONDERLAND

In 1940's New Year's Day, a smiling dad came bouncing into the kitchen with a brand-new bottle of expensive whisky. (Not that I got any!) His story was that at a Jamaica Street stop, a RN officer who had been standing behind the Coronation's driving cab watching him operate the car, tapped him on the shoulder and said that he had seen dad's GCT badge number "1940" and, since it was New Year's day 1940, he thought dad deserved a Ne'er Day celebration drink which might bring good luck to both of them. Hope that gallant officer survived the Battle of the Atlantic! Unfortunately in my travels my dad's 1940 badge has been mislaid just like the "Wuggie" metal cross.

As the war deteriorated – Dunkirk et al – our mob moved into Primary Seven A. There was now a Primary Seven B class, taken by a bully of a man. Later he became our much-disliked geography teacher. (Imagine telling us that there was no modern use for mercury! Even stupid me (as he called me once!) knew better! One glorious afternoon (for us!) he stalked into our room putting his just-smoked pipe into his jacket pocket.

We watched in silent awe as a red patch appeared on that jacket. Then flames came from the pocket. Then his jacket caught alight and he fled hurriedly away from a laughing load of pupils. Mea maxima culpa – yet again. But if it had been anyone else we would have given warning in good time. I think!

Our Primary Seven A man proved to be a bit of a mystery to us. We all thought him bit of good and a bit of bad. Junior Moral Philosophy amok as usual.

We discovered that he had two sons of roughly our ages. One was a bit paralysed and the other in our class seemed quite healthy. What infuriated us was when from time to time he would roar at his healthy boy over some minor matter that the wrong son had been paralysed. Not a good comment and we felt sorry for the healthy son. Then for a time he used to baffle and bore me on a Monday morning with a rambling detailed account of a journey he made every Friday to a place called Glendaruel. Had not a clue then where Glendaruel was or why the journey was made each week-end. Later I discovered where Glendaruel was and realised that the week-end tricky journeying was to be out of Glasgow in case of an air-raid and have some time with the rest of his family evacuated to the east side of Loch Long. Must have cost him a bit of money though.

One of the good sides to him was that because Millerston had been occupied by the army, on a Wednesday afternoon we were allowed to travel over to the then extensive Queen's Park Recreation Park ash football pitches for ra kick ba! Another splendid tram ride for me. And if it was inclement weather, very considerately, we were taken into his nearby large house and given board games to enjoy. Our P7A man was great on music and unlike in P 5, he would tell us about the composer of the tunes we were going to sing and about the background to the music. Most enjoyable teaching. Then even came greater amusement – to me at least. Our P7 choir was entered into some Glasgow choir event and we won our section.

Somehow we discovered that we were the section winners because no other choir had been entered into our section. When tackled about that our marvellous conductor just happily proclaimed that no other choir had bothered to enter our section because every other conductor knew that they could never have a choir as good as his! Really! And it was in P 7A I experienced two incredible events in my life.

One dull miserable Winter afternoon we were having our usual bounce game on a good old Queen's Park Rec. ash pitch. We had picked our two sides and as we had lost the toss I was standing beside pal Micky McDonald (his dad was an Underground Stationmaster) who was about to kick-off when I saw that their goalic was still ambling towards his goal pulling on his gloves. I quickly said to Micky, "Just tap the ball a wee bit in front of me." Then I gave the old heavy leather ball as good a biff as I could manage. To my own amazement – and everyone else's – the ball did not go too high but took a low straight trajectory right over that goalie's head and on between the other posts without touching the ground at all. So I now claim the world record for the fastest goal ever scored in a football match!

Now this was not on a school-boy size pitch but on one more towards Junior Football size. Up to that time my much-disliked nick-name at Wally Dishes was "Tilly Wollan" bestowed on me by Billy Ottolini (later Constable Ottoloni of Tobago Street Police Station.) Henceforth during the rest of my College stay I was more often called "Big Bertha". Still a female nick-name but a wee bit better than "Tilly"!

Then the second incredible happening came at the end of term. I was amazed to discover that I was FIRST in Primary Seven A! Wow! FIRST in a St. Aloysius' College class. "Wow!" And "Wow!" again!

I could not get home fast enough to show mum and dad my report card. I had not looked at it in my hurry to get home. But when they read it, what was the comment on the report card?

"Willie could do better if he tried!"

I was sick to my back teeth and thoroughly disgusted when I read that myself. But then came the puzzle. How could I do better than be first in a St. Aloysius' College class?

OBSTINACY RULES O! K!

Be sure that after that slap in the face I did not try too hard in the rest of my Garnethill stay – except right near the end – as I will explain later. Now I was content just to drift along in the middle of results. And so I was for ever being called out into the corridor and lambasted by different Jesuits – no doubt thanks to my Jesuit Scholastic cousin Michael McCartney. The one who irked me most was Father Dukes – the Science principal. He was regularly giving me what for.

Now in Secondary it was normal when starting in third year to take the Science or the Classic side of studies. I had wanted to take Science because I was not too bad at Art and was thinking at the time that I would like to go on to the Adjoining Art School and you needed a science background to do that. (And I still treasure my Art Prizes awarded to me by Donalkd McEvoy – the Arts Master.) But I was called in and told by the inscrutable Jesuit Head Teacher to take Classics or leave! And here was the Science Principal belabouring me when I had wanted to do his Science and not the dreaded Latin and Greek. And of course, again, I just could not leave and risk upsetting my father.

I digress.

BIG TIME BECKONS

After P 7A it was up into "the big school" and a Jesuit Prefect of Discipline to contend with as well as the First Year Jesuit Form master. You were fine with the latter Jesuit if you were one of his scout group. He was a great man for lining us round the class-room and asking Maths or French questions in turn. Of course if you got the answer right you might move up depending how your predecessor had done but if you got it wrong you moved down a place. Be sure that the easier questions went to you know who.

But there was a redeeming factor to First Year life. I was delighted to find that as Millerston was still under Army occupation, instead of going to good old Queen's Park Rec and its ash pitches for Wednesday's football, we now went away in another direction along Paisley Road West to Crookston Road where the Old Aloysians had a large grass football pitch for us to use.

Thank you O.A.s for that life-saver. For as well as the first ever kick-ba on grass, this tram-mad boy now got yet another of Glasgow's wonderful and interesting tram rides.

Service 15 took me out to Crookston and then directly back through Argyle Street all the way to Westmuir Street. Oh! Why did our wonderful politicians abandon the greatest tram system in the world at that time? And these days Tram – or Light Rail systems and Tram-Train lines are being opened all over the world except in Glasgow. And what a disgusting shambles Edinburgh has made of things.

But while I was greatly enjoying our first game on a grass pitch I underwent yet another example of that peculiar sense of humour that infected some of the more eccentric followers of Ignatius. The ball was mis-kicked by an opponent and shot away over the touch-line only to be stopped some distance away by a small dry-stone dyke that marked one of the longitudinal boundaries of the O. A. field. Eager to get on with the enjoyment, I raced away several yards from the pitch and picked up the ball over at the dyke to get ready to take a shy. And what did our not-so-wonderful Form

Master do? He gave a foul against yours truly because he had not said the ball had gone out of play. I ask you. No wonder I was not enamoured of life at Wally Dishes. But the Scoutmaster was to get a deserved (in my prejudiced thinking!) cum-uppance. One of the Fathers I greatly admired and respected was a Father Calnan. (Except when he would not let me and pal Gerry accept an invitation to see the great Atlantic liner Queen Elizabeth leaving the Clyde for the first time. That would have been a memorable moment of history to witness.) When Fr. Calnan became the Garnethill Head-Master he wanted to make use of some large storage cupboards but found them to be fully occupied by masses of Scout equipment. Several times he asked his Scoutmaster cohort to have the cupboards emptied, but his requests were just ignored. So one morning Father Calnan rose early and went down to the Church and celebrated an early Mass. He then went back to The College and emptied every piece of Scouting material out into the middle of Hill Street. Imagine the stramash that caused. And of course it gave me a good chuckle or two when I heard about it. And to this day uncharitable me still has the occasional laugh about that Scoutmaster's embarrassment that day. Good for Calnan.

Despite their 15 or 16 years of training and undergoing the long and arduous 30 day Spiritual Retreats, there could be petty disagreements among the Fathers.

At Garnethill two of the Jesuits had had a disagreement about something or other and one of them knew that the other was "hooked" on iced tea-cakes. So whenever a bakery delivery was made he would be first into the large pantry and remove all the icing from every iced tea cake he could find. And he was .supposed to be an intelligent follower of Christ. Wonder what Xavier and Ogilvie made of his behaviour?

About that time I had a great Birthday present – a Celtic Stand Season. (Possible because so many supporters had gone to the forces that seasons were now available.)

It led me to discover that in the middle of Section D of the Celtic stand there would always be at a home game a huddle of black-coated and black-hatted figures. No need to say who they were. I kept well away from them. They must have been doing a lot of penance in those terrible times for Celtic Football and Athletic Club.

BATTLESHIPS

If I thought First Year at the College was a pain-in-the neck a worse shock awaited me in Second Year. There were two family brothers among the Jesuit Garnethill Fathers. If I say that the Second Year Form Master brother inflicted on us was "Fred" that will suffice to identify him. For most of the time, instead of instructing us on the French language and customs, Fred would indulge himself in a series of never-ending raffles in aid of war-time good causes.

Like myself being on limited pocket-money unlike the well-off pupils with loads of cash to spare, Gerry Tennant and me loaded ourselves with squared Arithmetic paper and would sit and compete with each other at "Battleships" while the endless raffles went on. I reckon that in St. Aloysius' College second year I sank more enemy submarines than were sunk in the Battle of the Atlantic. Of course over the years we pretty-well ended all square – in more ways than one!

Gerry and myself were pianists and we practised playing Schubert's Marche Militaire as a duet – changing over the ends of the piano and going again. We had admired Rauwicz and Lauder on the radio. We used the pianos in each other's houses and I was amazed to discover that Gerard lived in Oscar Slater's old apartment at Charing Cross. Dad had once showed me – from the top deck of a Standard tram – Oscar walking along an Argyle Street pavement.

But one lunch-time I outdid myself. Do not know to this day why I suggested that to occupy ourselves during the lunch-break since we still could not use "The Pitch" for kick-ba that we go off and visit the renowned Kelvingrove Art Galleries. (The Pitch still being RAF occupied.)

Can you imagine the time it took to walk to Kelvingrove and back – never mind having a good look round the Galleries. We were about an hour and a half late in returning! But! Do you know that when we explained where we had been, and why we were so late, we never heard anymore about the episode. No doubt the Jays were quite staggered to learn about some of their pupils having such an interest in historical relics. And there was a most kind relic among them too. A giant of a figure – gentle Father Ambrose.

He had formerly been the Garnethill Greek Principal teacher and the decent old fellow had come back out of retirement to help out with the war-time teacher shortages. Not that I enjoyed Greek too much but his classes were conducted quite peacefully and earnestly and were interesting. He must have been a marvellous teacher in his heyday. At the end of his period, when he had given us a little home-work to tackle, he always quoted Matthew: 6:34 in a slow deep amusing drawl:

"Suffeecient (sic) unto the day is the evil thereof!"

We agreed whole-heartedly of course. He once told us that the name of the Ambrose Light that marked the western end of the trans-Atlantic ocean liner racing course was named after one of his ancestors. Wonder if it was ?

And I liked Father Phillipson – Prefect of Discipline – who once told me, when we were chatting, that he was related to the renowned Lancashire County cricketer of the time – Eddie Phillipson.

And he must have been, because there was a College boy who was quite a proficient cricketer and who was keen to advance himself in the cricket world. "Pip" – friendly nickname that some of us gave to Father Phillipson – fixed him up with a Lancashire County Cricket club contract. But our hero did not last long at Old Trafford. When he came back to the dear green place, "Pip" said he had a good idea about what had gone wrong. There was no–one at Old Trafford who was as well educated as our College hero and so he could never have an intelligent conversation with any cricketer down in Lancashire.

And then there was a fellow Old Aloysian – one James Loughran. He would climb onto the top deck of a Standard car in Dennistoun always panting and exclaiming "I feel I have run a mile!" So he was known to us as "Run-a-mile" Loughran. Instead of wasting his time like me at Celtic Park, "Run-a-mile" would be down at the Concert Centre helping musicians put out their stands and equipment and then during the concert itself he would stand in the wings and ape the performance of the current conductor. A famous German conductor saw him doing just at and took "Run-a-mile" into his tutelage and so the keen James was eventually to become the conductor of Manchester's world-celebrated Halle Orchestra and indeed a remarkable BBC Proms Conductor.

THE HAIR TWIRLER

In third year at The College we came under the tutelage of Form Master and Maths teacher "Gaffer Tam". He was a reasonable type but highly amused us by sitting at his teacher's desk gazing at us plodding away while he continuously twirled his fore-lock.

He had two other brothers in the Society of Jesus. My Scholastic cousin, Michael McCartney, told me an amusing (to me!) tale about them when they were all based together in Leeds.

The two brothers had arranged to go out somewhere together and as the first one went out he placed his name-sign on the hall entry board to "OUT". But he forgot about something he should have told his brother and phoned back and asked to speak to his brother. That brother had just put his sign to "OUT" too but turned and answered the phone call and looked at the entry board and said "Sorry! They are both out!"

The army had vacated Millerston Playing Fields by this time and good old "Gaffer Tam" would be out there to referee our football. His frequent advice was "Get your foot in!" He gave up playing with us when Carntyne pal George Stewart took his advice literally and really got his foot in and injured "Tam". But even better times lay ahead.

ALLELUIA!

At the end of Third Year I covered myself in glory and astonished myself and some of the esteemed Fathers by being one of the very few College boys to win a Glasgow Schools Bursary that year, and so having dad no longer needing to pay fees to have me at "Wally Dishes."

One of the questions that delighted me was in the General Knowledge section of the exam paper. "How many statues are there in George Square?" How many times had I sat on top of the good old 23 car and counted them!

After that great result came out, "Lakey" – Father Lakeland .S. J. – who was to be our French teacher in Fourth Year – stopped me in a corridor and pronounced that I was truly a "dark horse". Of course I did not know what he meant at that time and wondered why he had such a pained expression on his face while he made the pronouncement.

It was about that time that our usual snow-fights in Renfrew Street v. The Art School came to an abrupt end. One not-so-bright Art School student – (probably a "cubist"!) came out on to a balcony high above the attacking College boys and poured a huge copper vat full of boiling water over them and so badly scalding some of the College boys. Of course there was a tremendous rumpus about the injuries occurring and the Fathers in charge of the College got into very hot water themselves for not having put an end to the snow-ball activities long before the disaster happened.

"SANS L'ARBITRE ILS AURAIENT GAGNES!"

("They would have won if it hadn't been for the referee!")

As usual Fourth Year began with participation in the Annual Preparatory Four Day Morning Retreat in St. Aloysius' Church. That year we thought the visiting Jay presiding over the retreat was very good and interesting and most instructive. But we were to cover ourselves in a glory of a non-spiritual different kind from that intended. While the poor man was teaching us to sing the words of that wonderful hymn "Lord for To-morrow and Its Needs", we were watching behind him down the church a small boy who was showing off to us how clever he was by walking up and down a row of the individual church seats and waving his arms at us. Unfortunately for him, he did not see that one of the seats was missing and he suddenly vanished from sight down on to the floor. Of course we burst out laughing and the poor Jesuit thought that we were laughing at him. Oh! Dear! Yet again! More time in Purgatory.

In Fourth Year too we began to get a few football matches against other schools, our "Manager" now being a tall thin Jesuit we called "Soapy" – alias Fr. Griffin. And I played at Hampden Park – no less! But not on the main pitch. In those days Queens Park Secondary played their home games on one of the two pitches that lay alongside the front of the South Stand at that time. Could not have been too bad for I was offered a trial with "The Ants" – St. Anthony's Junior Football Club – but father would not let me try to play Junior Football. Probably a wise decision.

And I have always been most grateful to Fr. Griffin for introducing me a to a new world which I came to love. "Soapy" took us to climb The Cobbler (in Scottish Gaelic Ben Artair) – a mountain of 884m in height located near the head of Loch Long.

Although the Ordinance Survey title this peak as Ben Arthur (an Anglicisation of the Scottish Gaelic), the name "The Cobbler" (which the OS mark as an alternative name) is almost universally used by hill-walkers mountaineers and the local populace. Although a thick mist came down and some of us, remembering advice to follow down a stream if that happened, came down the wrong side of the peak, that great day gave me a love for the hills and mountains which I have never lost.

Thank you Father Griffin.

I did not know much about Scottish mountains in those days but enthralled by The Cobbler thrill I decided to try to reach the top of Ben Lomond. Fortunately I found that there was a good path leading from near Loch to the Summit, so I peched my way up that path and was so pleased with myself when I was about to reach the top. My pleasure was soon dashed for there on the small plateau sat granny with pram and grandchild. Oh! Dear! Again!

I never had any liking for collecting Munros but was certainly attracted to some of the finest Highland peaks such as Lawers scattered with false gold, Stobinian and adjoining More, and I could not but attempt Schiehallion of scientific fame. And as I climbed it there was an RAF fighter speeding hundreds of feet below along the adjoining glen. Brave pilot I thought.

But mostly I was happy enough to ascend and stroll on the convenient and in those days most friendly and smoothly- grassed Carrick hills beneath The Merrick. And of course I occasionally could not resist going to Merrick top to see the marvellous views it provided.

But all that enjoyment could not be continued after the wonderful scientific/engineers had managed to blow up Chernobyl while carrying out one of their unnecessary experiments. Chernobyl radiation fall-out devastated the Carrick hills and it became quite unsafe to attempt them again.

But what a pleasant world the good Father Griffin had opened up for me.

"Lakey" was a first-class French teacher and a great musician with wonderful polyphonic choirs that were a treat to listen to. But he had a dreadful way of starting his class. I suppose it was, perhaps, to waken us all up and make us pay attention. He would start a class by wandering slowly up and down each aisle humming and carrying squares of white paper in his hand. These papers might – or might not be – "Bills". Bills were instructions to go to the Prefect of Discipline and receive the number of ferulas written thereon. A ferula was a mighty blow on a hand with a leather strap containing a steel plate. After a few ups and downs a "Bill" might be dropped on to someone's desk. Cannot remember ever receiving one from Lakey – Deo Gratias.

Lakey liked telling Jesuit-style jokes or riddles. Here are a few:

A Sadducee did not believe in the Resurrection. That was why he was sad – you see!

Q. Who is the most handsome Saint in Heaven? A. St. Boniface.

Q. Who was the last Saint into Heaven? A. St. Justin.

Q. Who are the short-sighted Saints? A. St. Philip Neri and St Peter Canisius.

Q. Who was the cricketer Saint? A. St. Paschal Baylon.

And on and on. Not bad and lightened the war-time day. More about Lakey later.

But it was in a Year Four Classroom on the top floor of the College building that disaster struck. We had had a pretty well wild uncontrolled Religious Class from a retired College civilian clerk who had come out to help fill out the straightened war-time lay-staff (though why did not a Jesuit ever do Religious Education with us?) and after he had left the room, I was at the back of the class-room talking football to friend Walter Butler (A muscular footballer and one of the first producers of Coronation Street.) A couple of mischievous imps at the front of the class had seized a quite large square wooden board and heaved it up in our direction and it landed on top of our heads. Without much thought – unfortunately – we picked the missile up and tried returning it back to the front of the room. But for some aeronautical reason, the board swerved half-way there, veered left, crashed through a large class-room window, and landed in Hill Street. Oh! Dear! Bang went our pocket money for ages as we had to pay for that new large replacement window pane.

LAST OF THE LOT

Fifth year is still a lot of blurred memories as so much happened in it.

On the football side we had more big games with more Schools as we were now in the First Eleven "managed" by the male teacher who was now Head of the Preparatory School. I was to encounter him again later in life under different circumstances. In one game he encouraged me to shoot at goal from even further out than I was doing. I was amazed at that encouragement.

We had to take turns at reading for the Jesuits in their house while they were taking lunch. Did not fancy doing that at all. Wanted to be having my own lunch – greedy me!

And I never made the exalted status of being a College Prefect with associated privileges. Was it because I showed I so hated that reading to the Staff – or more likely because with one punch I flattened to the pavement a fellow class-mate who was jeering and making rude remarks to me as I was trying to marshal Preparatory Department pupils. No matter. I survived.

Then there were the bicycle sagas.

I had always wanted a bike, partly because a cousin used to cycle to Girvan from Glasgow and back again on every Summer Holiday his side of the family held there and I had a notion that I would like to emulate that arduous feat. But of course, again, never did.

While operating his tram my father had seen too many traffic incidents involving bikes and always refused to give me the permission I wanted. So what did nasty me do? I resorted to black-mail and said I would not sit my Highers unless I got a bicycle. Mea, Maxima Culpa yet again. How many additional years in purgatory has that sort of nonsense caused me. So I won my struggle and gained a war-time very heavy Armstrong all steel bike. So now I cycled to and from Garnethill each day – except when it was pouring. And I worked out a route to do that without having to use too many sets and cobbles.

Pal Gerry had a bike, so in a fit of youthful madness, one night after school we decided to cycle along The Western Boulevard and

43

do the twenty-seven miles to Helensburgh. We made better time than expected so went on to Rhu to see the Gareloch. No wonder we had made such good time. There had been a violent gale at our backs pushing us along. What a struggle it was just to get back at all to the dear green place. When I sweated in home about two-thirty a.m., I received a mighty, justly deserved, dressing – down which began, "See you and your bike... etc".

I was not deterred by that stupidity and did long solo circuits out into the countryside, including a trip to Largs via Bridge of Weir and on round the coast to Nardini's and then back inland via the Hayley Brae. I walked the bike up the Haley Brae of course. In those days with little traffic to deter them many popular Cycling Clubs would think nothing of accomplishing two hundred mile trips at the week-end. But not coward me.

More disappointing physical effort was to come.

On the annual Sports Day at Millerston I was first in the 100 yards sprint and in 220, 440, and 880 races came in second to class-mate Mike Roberts who had the great advantage of training with Scotstoun Harriers.

My reward for all that effort was about ten and a half old pence in War Time Savings stamps. I threw them away in disgust. I had been thinking of joining Shettleston Harriers but unfortunately changed my mind. Might have made The Olympics if I had done? Fat chance!

There was a one-off Jesuit who took us most ably for Classics in our final year. He had a proper upper-class English accent that I took to be from Oxford or Cambridge but later I discovered he was in fact a native Dubliner. He was held in high esteem as the leading Mariologist in Britain but later he defected from The Church, and became an Anglican Professor of Divinity in Canada. After he later returned to the United Kingdom he was slowly dying while living in abject poverty, and the admirable Jesuits took him back and looked after him in his final years. Great Christianity in action from The Society.

Later Lakey told me that when he was the Garnethill Head Teacher he had terrible trouble with this Classics teacher. He would see from his Office the great Mariologist getting on his bike ready to cycle away from Hill Street when he should have been taking classes. Lakey would have to race out and catch up with him and give him a written instruction to take his classes. That's when I discovered that obedience only was obligatory in The Society of Jesus when it was given in written form.

NO MORE HILL STREET BLUES FOR US

In our final year at Garnethill the Head Teacher was the admirable Father Calnan S.J.

He fore-warned us about the mistakes going to be made in the forth-coming divisions of the Indian sub-continent into India and the two Pakistans. To this day we are suffering from the after effects of the disastrous decisions that Mountbatten was to make.

Father Calnan had a mo-ped and he used to ask us how to get around Glasgow without encountering traffic lights as he had to mightily pedal hard to get the old mo-ped going once it had stopped.

UNEXPECTED HAPPENINGS!

A bad catastrophe happened to me thanks to an unsupervised bounce game of cricket at Millerston.

Why did I have to try to be a wicket-keeper?

A ball from Donnie Renfrew bounced violently off of the top of the stumps and smashed into the point of my jaw. No expert NHS surgery in those days. All I got from Ballochmyle's supposed top man was the verdict that my jaw was dislocated and I would just have to try and live with it. Thanks a bunch consultant.

Life at St. Aloysius' College was coming to its inevitable end. But a bunch of us College Celtic fanatics had gone down to a game at Rugby Park and that was where I saw, for the first time, an Irish tricolour being waved at one of our matches. The flag-waver was Harry McGoldrick – a friend who became a more than useful solicitor and who helped me out when hard-up me was frantically house-hunting later.

One afternoon Fr. Batley had sidled up to me – not this time enquiring about my "dirty" books – but to say quietly: "Be an Accountant". No chance of that.

Because just before that afternoon Gerry and I had a conversation in which we both big-headedly thought we could be much better Jesuits than some we had encountered at Garnethill. Oh! Dear! The folly of youth again.

45

When I made my application to join the Society of Jesus, the only test question I had from good old Lakey was: "Do you know how to boil an egg!" Well may be not a kettle but an egg was no bother!

I was thoroughly perplexed (as usual) when dad would not sign the necessary release form. Parental consent was needed if an applicant was under twenty-one. I could not understand such a refusal when after all he had been so keen to inflict unwanted Jesuit education on me.

Later after I had suffered the great loss of my father's death, (Requiescat in Pace!) it came out that he had refused to sign the necessary application because he thought I was only wanting to emulate my great cousin Jesuit Scholastic Michael McCartney. But as I have said that was not the reasoning that Gerry and I had had. And I had great devotion and interest in Loyola and Xavier.

But I still can croak the great College Hymn to St. Aloysius Gonzaga too:

> Eia, deo accinamus
> Carmen eucharisticum.
> Et Gonzagae concinamus
> Dignum laudis canticum.
>
> Mundum, carnem superasti
> De inferno triumphasti
> Inclite, inclite,
> Victor tu clarissime!
>
> Sive mundus te tentabat
> Vanas per divitias.
> Sive carnis commendabat
> Sordidas delicias.
>
> Semper victor evasisti
> Hoc te scuto protexisti:
> "Quid est hoc?
> Quid est hoc ad aeterna gaudia?"
>
> Non a recto me vocabit
> Vana mundi gratia,

Nunquam posthac me turbabit
Vana mentis gloria.
Cum Gonzaga sum securus
Dum frequenter sum dicturus
"Quid est hoc?
Quid est hoc ad aeterna gaudia?"

FRIENDS, ROMANS, COUNTRYMEN... ER...

Traditionally Fifth Year finished the Garnethill penance off by putting on a stage performance for the rest of the College. For some reason our lot decided to put on a parody of Julius Caesar.

I had to start the proceedings. (My mother used to say that everyone saw me coming. They sure did this time.)

With a white bed-sheet over my shoulders – representing a Roman toga – I stepped through the middle of the closed green stage curtains. My sudden appearance, dressed in this ridiculous fashion, brought gales of laughter from the younger pupils in the hall.

Good start I thought.

Then I was to start the usual "Friends, Romans, Countrymen"... rant, and by arrangement be interrupted by pal, tall Gordon Smith, peddling like mad down the middle aisle on a little child's tricycle and uttering police siren imitations. I was supposed to catch him and pull him up on to the stage to get on with the proceedings. But he came down much too fast for me and I missed him completely and instead of just the trike going on under the stage he went under the stage structure with it. That brought further gales of laughter from the assembled pupils, but big Gordon could have been badly injured. Fortunately the would-be polis was not even scratched. He too must have had a good guardian angel.

Sitting just a few feet away from the nonsense was a new Rector who had only arrived at Garnethill the previous day. From the look on the poor man's face it was obvious that he was wondering what a peculiar world he had entered into.

So that was my inglorious vale to St. Aloysius' College as I thought at the time. But there was another disaster to follow at the usual end of Fifth Year Retreat at the Jesuit Retreat House at Craighead. Waiting for business to start, one of our not-so-bright specimens booted a large rubber ball down a long corridor and toppled a large statue of Our Lady which smashed to pieces when it hit the tiled floor. And it was definitely not "Big Bertha" but I better not say who the culprit was. But then came real life. We left Garnethill happily on the Thursday but on the following Tuesday we were at the funeral of one of our class-mates. Over all those years Liam had been a very pleasant, friendly, and quite unobtrusive member of our group. None of us knew that he had always had had a heart condition and that heart condition had killed him after leaving the College.

Gordon Smith took us for runs in his father's large, posh Lanchester.

And on one occasion coming back along The Boulevard he was desperately trying to get it up to 100 m.p.h. He became quite angry that he could no get it beyond 93 m.p.h. on the speedometer. 93 m.p.h. was more than enough for me sitting beside him in the front of the careering vehicle. No speed limits and no seat belts either in those days.

REQUIESCANT IN PACE AS ANOTHER GOOD FRIEND IS LOST

Another good pal at St. Aloysius College, and later at Glasgow University was Jack Gilroy. A nephew of Jimmy McStay, Jack was a Scottish school-boy internationalist and his uncle kept pestering him to sign for Celtic. Jack was more interested in preparing for university and a B. Sc. course. Eventually Jack gave in and reluctantly signed. The following week McStay turned up at Parkhead only to find McGrory behind the manager's desk. No doubt White considered he could dominate gentleman McGrory more easily than McStay.

So Jack Gilroy only managed two reserve games out of position after being demobbed. But he used to annoy starving me. (Still rationing thanks to that miserable Stalin-loving creature Sir Stafford Crisps who thought that rationing was good for the rest of us while he luxuriated on his vast Oxfordshire estate.) Jack was always complaining about getting chicken every day with the club at Ferrari's Swiss Restaurant at the top of Buchanan Street. Jack went on to play for almost every Scottish Second Division club. He had the unfortunate habit of telling his manager how his tactics should have gone or how badly made or washed were the strips and stockings. Jack could often tell me Second Division scores in advance of the Saturday of the games as allegedly there was at one time a Second Division game-fixing racket (to cheat on the then once popular fixed-odds coupons) led by a Catholic player who better be nameless. Jack's great passion was running the school team of St Patrick's Secondary, Dumbarton. One time Jack became over-heated and was suspended for two years by the Scottish Schools Football Association. Then came tragedy. On a cold Winter's day Jack was driving down a hill near Bearsden, when he saw that two cars had skidded on the icy road and collided. Jack stopped behind them to render assistance. But after he had stopped, the car behind skidded into Jack's car. Jack got out of his car but the broken steering wheel shaft had penetrated his heart and he died beside his car. The strange thing about the events was that the driver of the car ahead had been one of Jack's school team players and the driver of the car that killed him was also a former player of Jack's. It is a strange old world.

I still try to remember to say a profound De Profundis for him and all my other deceased Aloysian friends. .

PARKHEAD POST WAR PESSIMISM

The closing years of war-time football were shocking. We would be doing quite well against the Old Firm and then Duncanson or Williamson (who always seemed to get leave from the services at the appropriate time) would humble us yet again. And this despite the great performances of Willie Miller in goal.

About this time we had a centre-forward who better be nameless. A week before an Old Firm game, he took practice penalty after practice penalty and always "scored". On the day of the game he missed a penalty – but of course.

In those days of a heavy wet leather ball players would line-up just along the outside edge of the penalty box. At Shawfield one wet day, our hero did that but turned to see where the goal-kick had gone. The ball struck him on the back of the head and bounced back past the Clyde goalie Cullen for a goal. The general opinion was that that was about the only way our hero would ever score a goal. Poor lad.

There could be occasional interest generated.

Powerful Joe McLaughlin once burst the back of the net with a shot – as later did winger Paton. But I suppose the poor war-time condition of the nets contributed. We thought things would look up after the war ended. But the situation had gone too far downhill on field and off (ground state was deplorable) thanks to that hard-to-understand Tom White way of running things. We did win the Victory-in-Europe Cup. Then came the great fiasco of the Victory Cup itself. In the final we drew the first game. The re-play developed into the biggest farce to hit Scottish football. And there have been many such occasions. Guess which club was usually on the receiving end! The game details have been recorded many times. Suffice to say the ref. M.C. Dale was clearly in an unfit condition and we quite unjustifiably finished with seven men. And two of these were limping injured. Despite letters of support from opposition players, our three ordered-off men were harshly treated by the SFA. But of course. An attempt had been made by some idiots to attack Dale during the second half but they were obviously so intoxicated too that they could not catch or hit him. In those days supporters were not segregated, and next to me one of our Irish support lifted a too vociferous fan bedecked in red, white and blue by the throat, and asked him did he want to walk out of Hampden or be carried out. The offending loud-mouth quickly diverged himself of his Rangers colours and ran off – once his feet had touched terra-firm again.

It was a pouring wet night. I was wearing dad's heavy-issue black motorman's raincoat and stumbled very upset, along the way to Parkhead. I had just turned from Dalmarnock Road into Springfield Road, when I realised that my father was the motorman on a service 30 car on the right, turning from Dalmarnock Road into Springfield Road. I travelled all the way up Springfield Road on the front platform of the car as I sobbed out the sorry tale.

Players would come and go. One excellent player came and left – leaving us puzzled. James "Jimmy" Sirrell joined the club from Renfrew Juniors in December 1945 – shortly after he left the war-time Royal Navy. Just as my dad's motorman friend's son Jackie Cantwell had done then from Glenboig St. Joseph's. Sirrell made his debut in a Regional league 0 – 0 draw at Dumfries. Tall and slim he was a determined forward and showed great skill and energy and commitment and could really upset defences. To our surprise he was transferred away to Bradford Park Avenue in April

1949 supposedly because of being injury prone. He had scored twice for us in eighteen games. Later he was to become a celebrated Notts County manager and to-day there is a stand named after him at Meadow Lane.

Old-timers were tried and failed. Expensive Kiernan was brought in from Albion Rovers and Bogan from the Hibs but little was achieved. Eventually McDonald left for Brentford and Delaney to Manchester United (allegedly because of gambling debts he owed.) I saw the Cleland Saint at outside–right for Carey's Man U team against Everton at Goodison, but he was only a shadow of the great player he had been. Later I was to see him playing for Falkirk and I had my last sight of him standing in a queue on a wet day waiting to enter the ground for an away match and he looked very down-at-heel in a most shabby rain-coat. I shouted to him that I wished he was playing for us in this match and he gamely shouted back that he wished he was too.

Then there was the episode of another great redeemer from the east who was going to be our saviour. He better be nameless, for he would continually turn up of a morning medically unfit – much to the disgust of the Parkhead gatemen.

We had a great arrival eventually, friend Gerry McAloon from Belfast Celtic. He once told me that the U. S. of A. team that defeated the supposedly mighty English was largely composed of Belfast Celtic players. (It was the general belief at the time that the Irish Catholic Hierarchy had asked Belfast Celtic to close down to try to reduce bigotry tensions in the Six Counties.)

With Gerry at inside forward, centre Jackie Gallagher was, for one season only, the leading League goal-scorer. Jackie had two other claims to fame. Reputedly he would run from Bellshill to Celtic Park for training and then run back to Bellshill. And he once sang "Beautiful Dreamer" superbly well on the radio. That effort made me jealous – for everyone rightly tells me I am a hopeless singer.

YOU'LL BE SORRY

I thought I had escaped from the Parkhead misery. But the escape was to be brief. My Wally Dishes pal, Gerard Tennant and myself were called up under the war-time emergency programme. We both opted for the Navy but RN was not recruiting so RAF it was.

51

We had had the good old Air Training Corps at Garnethill with teachers pretending to be RAF Officers. That gave us amusing moments when they issued wrong commands which we promptly obeyed to create utter chaos. Small minds of course. But we had events that scared me stiff too. A first flight from Prestwick sitting in the co-pilot's seat of a De Haviland Rapide bi-plane: climbing up and down the sheer-faced rungs on the vertical hull of a Woolworth Carrier on the Firth of Clyde. (Often wondered later if that carrier had been the Dasher that blew up off Arran: requiescant in pace.) Being in the ATC meant that our service number started with a 3 – instead of the normal 2. I was awarded 3093291! Still remember that as we had loudly to proclaim it to the Pay Master on pay day.

I arrived at Padgate square-bashing centre in the harsh Winter of 1946/1947, with departing erks giving rude signs and shouting "You'll be sorry!" But I wasn't. I enjoyed the training, strange fellow that I am, especially the cross-country running. I was surprised to find out how good I was at it. One day, on fatigues, I was shovelling a large mass of coke from one end of the heap and then discovered friend Tennant was doing the same at the other end.

I lost one of my nine lives. We were doing grenade-throwing practice. The fine corporal in charge handed a live grenade to the first in the queue – a moron from Dumfries. I was second. The corporal looked at the Dumfriesian a couple of times, then took the live grenade from him and replaced it with a dummy grenade. The dope threw it straight up in the air instead of out of the trench, and it landed right between my feet. Phew! Pause for thought-gathering and thankful prayer. Guardian angel again.

A well as many practices with the ancient Lee Enfield .303 rifle, we had practices on Bren and Sten machine-guns. The latter war-time emergency machine-gun was a proper menace and could take fingers off if great care was not exercised.

In that severe winter of '46/'47, the situation in the camp became grave, and long hut after long hut filled up with diphtheria cases and eventually the camp ran completely out of fuel. So we were despatched home. The train from Warrington took twelve hours to get to Glasgow and the train had neither food nor heating. Spoiled youth of to-day do not know how well off they are. Priority was being given to coal trains and our train would stand so long in loops that the engine had to be taken off and go to a depot for crew change and a new supply of coal and water.

I had just returned to Padgate after the great freeze when I heard that chairman White had died. We expected that the capable Colonel Shaughnessy would be his successor – which would have been great – but Robert Kelly had wangled his election to chairman by getting a mass of proxy votes from an Irish widow. The misery that woman caused us. Away we went into madness again.

One Saturday afternoon about three-thirty, dad saw Jimmy McGrory and trainer Alec Dowdalls walking on Tollcross Road. He stopped his tram and went over to the pair – whom he knew quite well – and asked them what on earth they were doing on Tollcross Road during match time. Resignedly they explained that for the umpteenth time they had carefully selected a team for a match and Kelly had come into the dressing room just before kick-off and put up his version of what the team should be. And so it was to go on for far too long.

PER ARDUA AD ASTRA

Well! May be. But we poor erks had a much ruder version we used to chant in unison. Better not print it here.

As the course for me at RAF Signals Yatesbury was not ready, I was posted to a Maintenance Unit at Whitehouse Common, on a hill above Sutton Coldfield, where the local TV transmitter is now situated. This was largely a waste of time as far as the Airworks was concerned. Daily floor sweeping made me begin to think that Latin and Greek were not so bad. Expensive American high grade machine tools would walk out of the camp despite a large contingent of RAF Police. No doubt they were involved too in some way. I kept well out of that. The Catholic Sacred Heart Church in wealthy Sutton Coldfield was a splendid, richly adorned edifice. But unfortunately no chaplain came to the camp. I soon discovered the delights of the extensive Sutton Park with its miniature railway. And I was impressed to come across a bus stop in the main street saying that buses for Villa Park or St Andrews left there on match days. So I saw a few games at Aston Villa. (They were then nick-named, even by their supporters, as Aston Vanilla, because they were easily licked.) The Birmingham City ground lay next to a large railway complex and was heavily bomb-damaged. There was a lot of publicity about Villa bringing in a match saviour from Wales – a centre called Evans. But I am afraid that like Kiernan et al. he did not impress – nor did the standard of the Villa football.

We made the discovery that Wolves were playing Liverpool in a Championship decider and that in the Liverpool team was a Fagan in the forward line. We hoped that it might be the Fagan who had played for us. (Yes! There were other Tims in the camp. We get everywhere.) So we proceeded to Birmingham's Snowhill station and took a GWR train on the interesting twenty minute ride to Wolverhampton. Of course it was the Fagan who was to become the wonderful Liverpool manager. This was Stan Cullis, Wolves and England captain, playing his last match. But, tough on him, Liverpool won the match and League Title and we Tims were not at all popular with the Wolves fans because we had been cheering for Liverpool.

I managed to get to Glasgow most week-ends to see a match if Celtic were at home. But of course I might as well not have bothered so poor were our lot.

On one occasion, I was standing as usual in the early hours of a Saturday morning on a platform of Carlisle Station, having come off the Birmingham express that ended at Carlisle. Anxious to get to Glasgow to prepare to get to the Celtic game, I was waiting impatiently for the early morning local that stopped at all stations on the old Sou'West main line to St. Enoch's through Dumfries and Kilmarnock. A scenic line – delightful – but not if you are in a hurry to get to Parkhead. To my great surprise the over-night Express Sleeper from Euston to Central stopped right in front of me. Usually it raced on through while I would be wishing I could be on it. But that morning there must have been a need for a loco or crew change. So naturally I dived on to the train through the first available door. I had just regained my composure when a haughty train steward grabbed me and tried to throw me off the express, stupidly shouting that the train did not stop at Carlisle so I could not board it. Hard to believe now, but St. Aloysius' College and the RAF PT Instructors had me fighting fit in those days and I easily threw him aside and told him I had a Travel Warrant and I was on a stopped train and he certainly was not going to be allowed to throw me off. At that point he decided that discretion was the better part of valour and departed. So I sat myself down and enjoyed a much swifter and more comfortable journey from Carlisle to the Celtic match than I had expected.

DING! DING!

Being a tram fan I was able to explore the remaining routes of the once vast Birmingham and Black Country narrow gauge system. I was mightily impressed with the smooth-running of the bogie car on the long run out to Rednal where I had gone to see the notorious Lickey railway hill.

During the late thirties we had staying with us in Westmuir Street an impoverished and homeless, distantly- related family from America. I knew that they had moved to Coventry so I took an impressive trolley-bus ride out the Coventry Road and then a Midland Red bus into Coventry. At one of the stops made in Coventry there was a stationer's shop on the other side of the road so I alighted and went across to it. I asked there if they happened to know anything of the family I was looking for. Hard to believe but the family were in the very house next to the paper shop. What a co-incidence. However I was only grudgingly received. C'est la gemme!

TO THE FRONT "SALUTE!"

But then came a blow. Before I could move to RAF Yatesbury, all surplus bods like myself were commandeered to provide a Guard of Honour for Royalty returning from a jaunt to South Africa. Sassenachs were overjoyed, but this republican was not a happy bunny. One consolation was that we moved to the permanent RAF station at Uxbridge. Here the accommodation and food was of a much higher standard than anything that had gone before. I was able to explore London (always worth a visit) travelling in by two different Underground services and even by a suburban GWR tank engine train from the GWR station. In those supposedly unenlightened days a shilling bought an all-day tram ticket. So I went through the double-deck tram tunnel up to Highgate on a couple of occasions and journeyed on the massive great Feltham trams on the lengthy ride out to Abbey Wood. I also had a day exploring the city with Gerry Tennant whom I met at Victoria bus station. I decided to go to see a friendly between England and

France at Highbury, and unbelievably walking to the game alongside me was another Wally Dishes pal, Tommy Madden. Tommy Madden had several times taken me to away games on the back of his 1926 AJS Big Port motor-bike, illegally using paraffin for fuel as petrol was strictly rationed. The international itself was a bit of a hoot. We still shoulder-charged goalies in those days but apparently the French did not, so every time Mortensen, or whoever, shoulder-charged the Frenchie in goal, he would drop cowering to the ground, causing the crowd to roar with laughter. I believe that these days goalies are over-protected – taking much of the fun out of football. That rule needs amending. After all, football is supposed to be a contact sport. Nowadays players grapple and wrestle with each other in the penalty box with impunity. But touch a goalkeeper... The other thing that needs urgent renew is the present idiotic and confusing off-side rule. A trial match was once played at Hampden without any off-side rule applying. We all thought that an improvement, but unfortunately Stein put the kybosh on such a change being introduced. As the great Shankly put it: if a player is on the pitch – then he has to be interfering with play. Surely that is correct.

ATTENT –SHUN!

Then we were loaded on to a long special tube train and on the way into London we passed tube train after tube train filled with police. I thought "What a waste of resources that could have been used for fighting crime." Eventually, after much hectoring, we were lining Fleet Street and I was in front of The Catholic Herald office. That was the first time I discovered that then great Catholic Weekly. Next we were marched down to The Embankment and there I was standing to attention for ages, and I would have loved to actually see the large E1 and E3 bogie trams thundering past just behind my back. Some bods collapsed and were carried off. I thought about faking a collapse but then decided I was not going to let Scotland down. Eventually the royal carriage arrived and we were ordered to present arms. I was saying a few choice words under my breath but was shocked at what I saw. The royal party looked absolutely fed up and bored stiff. Bertie was made-up to the nineties. I did not know then that he had been a heavy smoker and was in the final stages of cancer. (My cousin, Michael McCartney, was told in the Jesuit novitiate to take up smoking as it was good for his health! Needless to say, he did not last out the then 16 year period Jesuits had to undergo before ordination.) I then mused on the fact that royal jaunts had prevented the heavy armour addition – badly needed by the Hood – and lying on the quayside, being fitted. So had royalty caused the deaths of 1,000 sailors and given the Bismark a shocking victory?

Eventually I was able to take a GWR express to Chippenham and then the idyllic little pannier tank engine push-and-pull train up to Calne – The Calen Flyer -. From there I hiked down to RAF Yatesbury.

YATESBURY

"In a camp at Yatesbury miles from anywhere,
Sits a lonely airman combing icicles from his hair.
And dreaming of her exotic kiss,
With frozen hands he writes her this:
We won't be home at Christmas
They've stopped our Seventy Two."

(Erks' chant – with apologies to Lillie Marlene)

Yatesbury was the very large RAF Signals Instruction camp in Wiltshire, and came as a very pleasant surprise in several ways. Tommy Madden was there doing a radar course and had his AJS Big Port. (And class-mate George Stewart would come over from RAF Compton Bassett to visit.) We explored around the pleasant Wiltshire area. The great Avebury standing stones complex was explained to us in great detail. We visited Gordon Richard's stables and, but of course, Tommy insisted in trying to ride his motor bike up the historic Silbury Hill mound. It was far too steep for that. I used to chuckle at TV investigations of the Hill which would find nothing. I thought they might have found bits of Tommy's bike. This was the famous Denis Compton summer and we were delighted to be able to help local farmers in those largely pre-mechanised farming days. I loved the friendly horses. By and large life in the camp was interesting. There was the sometimes dangerous task of qualifying as RAF electricians and wireless mechanics. Try starting a huge stand-by Diesel by hand. Beware broken arms – as sometimes happened – or researching a high voltage transmitter. We were taught to chant in unison such good advice as:

"Alas he closed the circuit-breaker.
Now he's with the undertaker!"
"Care and caution are essential
When you work with high potential!"
"Make sure the juice is off before
You open the transmitter door!"

But we had plenty of enjoyable recreational activities. Soccer, rugby and even hockey matches were organised for us.

The village of Calne was a pleasant enough place. What scared me about it was the number of people who had bits of fingers missing. The vast Harris food complex was there. I decided then and there never to have a pork pie again.

The first Saturday we were at Yatesbury we decided to walk up to Calne and take the bus to Swindon to see Swindon play. We entered the main street only to see a green bus leaving in the distance. We asked some passers-by when the next bus for Swindon left. There was a bit of a discussion and then they thought it might be on the following Wednesday. So that was Swindon out.

One of the disadvantages of being a young teen-ager during rationing days was always being hungry. The camp had a large food hall. I always tried to be in there as early as possible, gulp down the meal, then race round and join on to the tail of the queue to obtain a second helping. I even managed a couple of times to have three meals at one go, and this despite RAF police being stationed at the mess entrance to prevent that sort of thing happening. Even then I would sneak in to the deserted cooking place at night and look into their vast urns to find discarded pieces of pork or meat or whatever among the remaining gravy.

On overnight guard duty at the main gate I would see the Duke of Edinburgh (imagine a Danish/Greek with that title – what a world royalty is!) He would be whizzing by on the Bath Road in his expensive white sports car. Lucky old him. Muggins would be standing freezing. You can bet that this republican did not present arms as he passed

There were one or two untoward happenings. In one of the lecture rooms was an enormous Canadian made VHF transmitter/receiver. I had been dying to see it working. But when the day came and the lecturer went to instruct us on it, it would not work. The lecturer (and us) found that the whole expensive innards had been stolen and only the case was left. Then there was a wretched Warrant Officer, who, at reveille (06:00 hours!), would stride importantly through our hut banging his heavy cane on every metal locker door. We hated that. But one of the comrades fixed that abuse. He gathered into a box a pile of broken valves and took the box of broken valves to the Station Group Captain and complained that the Warrant Officer had broken all his valves by banging on his locker door. The furious warrant officer had to pay for all the valves and valves were expensive in those days. He never banged on locker doors again, and we then had a peaceful rise from slumber. Later I was to see that same W.O. refereeing Rugby League matches on TV when Rugby League was a proper working-class sport and not the rich money-making business it has become.

Then disaster struck. Almost. We knew that if Celtic lost their league match at Dundee on the Saturday they could be relegated. Imagine. Celtic relegated. Shock, horror! We were due week-end passes and Tommy had been saving petrol and paraffin and agreed to take me to the match. But when he went to give the bike a trial run he discovered that all his accumulated fuel had been stolen. Some jokers stole the large RAF flag that flew over the sacrosanct parade ground – so all leave was cancelled until the flag was returned. Of course it never was. I could not travel to Dundee by rail without an RAF pass, so I went AWOL and hitch-hiked. In those days everyone would stop for a person in uniform who stuck his thumb out. I seemed to be doing well, and various lifts brought me to Newcastle-under-Lyme. I had not a clue where that was, and was walking through a very busy main street when I spotted two RAF Police on the opposite pavement checking RAF personnel for their passes. I thought that I had had my chips and that jankers awaited, for if I continued they would cross the road and stop me and if I would turn back they would know something was up and come after me. I had just decided to dive into a shop I was passing when a large brand new Jenson-Healy limousine pulled up and the driver asked me if I knew the way to Glasgow. Did I not! (Actually I didn't!) My Guardian Angel or Brother Walfrid was looking after me. But another of the nine lives gone. In those days expensive brand–new cars were delivered personally from factory to purchaser and I went past the RAF Police up into Scotland in great luxury. Wow! As it turned out we won the Dens Park match despite John McPhail having two perfectly good goals chalked off. And as it also turned out the way other results went that Saturday we would not have been relegated even if we had lost.

For Dens Park there was a football special tram siding and at the end of the game I dived on to one of the waiting trams and headed back on the long journey to Wiltshire. It is believed that most of the Dundee tram-workers were Catholic as the jute mills would not employ one of us, so maybe that motorman was as pleased as I was? The lads had covered up for me and I was tired but able to restart the course on the Monday. Then came the passing out. I was astonished that I had received good reports and high placement in the order. And after all the time I had wasted at Wally Dishes perusing the hated Latin and Greek, thanks to the miserable Jesuit head who would not let me into the science side which I had wanted to do.

Having become proper RAF wireless mechanics we were now able to put the coveted "sparks" insignia on our sleeves and we were allowed to put down three places to which we would like to be posted. I was watching all the Scottish boys putting down for places like Bishopbriggs, Turnhouse, Leuchars, Prestwick and so on – so thought I had no chance of a Scottish posting, and I put down Hong Kong, Gibraltar and Southern Rhodesia. You've guessed it. The other Scottish bods all were posted to the North German plain. I was posted to Kinloss. I had never heard of the place and I did not know where it was. I thought it was a misprint for Kinross because I knew that there was an aerodrome there. Though I was to arrive at Kinross eventually, as I will relate later.

KINLOSS

I packed up and took kit-bag, Lee-Enfield rifle, great-coat and gas mask on to the wonderful Calne Flyer and went down to Chippenham. Here I was horrified to learn of the assassination of Ghandi. GWR took me to Paddington. I had never been up the LNER east coast line to Edinburgh and Glasgow. (Yes! I was breaking my journey to Morayshire to see a match – but of course!)

So I rode the tube to Kings Cross. Big mistake. The LNER train consisted of twenty-three of Gresley's long splendid carriages and was packed – even in the corridors. I thought the Pacific engine would never manage to get such a load through the Copenhagen tunnels, but of course the splendid Pacific took us away nae bother. I had managed to squeeze me and all the gear into an end corner of a front coach. I was very hungry and when we stopped in Grantham station I dived into the station tea-room. I had just started to sip a cup of tea when the engine whistled and the train took off. I belted out and despite the protests of the platform staff swung on to the last coach as the train gathered speed. It was impossible to get up through the packed corridors and I was worried stiff about the Lee-Enfield .303. At the next stop I raced up the platform and what a relief it was to see everything just where I had left it at Grantham. Guardian angel again (?) but another of the nine lives lost. Phew!

The journey on the Glasgow Buchanan Street to Forres line went smoothly and I was impressed with the way the LMS "Black Five" 4-6-0 ("engine that won the war") took the long train over the old Highland Railway gradients to Drumochter Pass summit. Forres station had an interesting triangular lay-out.

But it was a tedious hike down to RAF Kinloss.

Kinloss was a Coastal Command 18 Group Maritime Operational Conversion Unit aerodrome with the best weather available record in the U.K. and was then in use to train single-engine pilots to become multi-engine pilots using ex-war-time Lancaster bombers. The Command motto was "Constant Endeavour". And so it was at Kinloss. 24/24, Lancasters would roar over our Nissen hut billets, clearing them by only a few feet – or so it seemed at the start of my stay. I had so become used to GCT trams clattering over The Sheddens pointwork that eventually I never really noticed the tram racket. And so too it came about also that eventually I never noticed the low-flying bombers overhead.

It was Lancasters from Kinloss and Lossiemouth that had destroyed the Tirpitz with Tallboy heavy bombs. On signing in I discovered that I was the only Ground Wireless Mechanic and would be held responsible for all electrical equipment, the VHF transmitters and receivers in Station Headquarters, Flying Control, and Runway Caravan Control – as well as the land-lines to a VHF

Direction-Finding Station two miles away and a "hush-hush" UHF Direction- Finding Station four miles out. (The latter was one if the chain of Ultra High Frequency D/F Stations that located the U-Boats of Doenitz during The Battle of The Atlantic.) What? A Tim like Me? Jings!

There was a flourishing Catholic Society on the Station. In Forres itself there was a small but beautifully- presented Catholic Church — St. Margaret's — built by Bute. Only about two dozen local Catholics attended Sunday Mass — so we would go along when possible. Forres was real Presbyterian (but relations with our church and priest were excellent and if the tiny Catholic Parish organised anything it would be well supported.) But on The Sabbath! Wow! Forres would be deserted — with every blind on every house window firmly drawn. Yet! Yet! Come Sunday night and our camp cinema would be packed with people from Forres. They were never seen coming by road past the mysterious hieroglyphic-covered Sueno's pillar, but obviously trekked down to the camp through the fields. Strange business! Strange form of religion?

On match day for Forres Mechanics football outfit, the pipe band would parade up and down the main road (Yes! The main road!) for half- an- hour or so, then turn and pipe its way down to the football ground followed by the mass of would-be supporters. I had a vision of an Irish band starting at Bridgeton Cross and leading the Celtic followers along London Road to Kerrydale Street.

I soon discovered that the main hotel in Forres put on a High Tea on a Sunday afternoon and you could get all you could eat for only a shilling and sixpence. And this at a time when folks back home were on starvation rations — thanks to that wretched Cripps. It was also easy to cycle round the adjoining farms, where they were pleased to see us and sell RAF bods eggs and even ducklings, so I would stock up if going down to Glasgow at the week-end to suffer a game at Parkhead.

There was a well-stocked NAAFI in the camp but we much preferred going to a Church of Scotland canteen for home-made scones etc., and where the grey-haired old dear would make such a fuss over "her boys". No wonder she fussed over us. Much later she was sent to prison for embezzling the large sums of money that should have gone to the C. of S. Notice how I am always on about food in those Stafford Cripps needless austerity days.

GET OUT OF BED. HERE COMES THE AIR-VICE MARSHAL!

Again better not to print the rest of our chant.

Whenever the grape-vine mysteriously informed the cook's department that an unexpected Air Vice-Marshall inspection would be going to take place, the food in the mess suddenly improved. (Though to be fair it was not too bad normally – if you liked venison and rabbit.) Stored decorations and improved cutlery would appear on the tables.

Sunday Church parades were held once a month and when the religious part of the shebang would begin, non-Anglicans like me could turn and march to the edge of the parade ground and stand with our backs to the chaplain's proceedings. That would be quite ridiculous of course in these ecumenical days. The Flight Sergeant i/c the parade drills thought it amusing to bawl out "Fall out R.C.s, Parsees, and all the other arses." I was not for having that – so on one defaulters day I went into the very pleasant Australian Group Captain V.C. and complained about the insult. Jings! The Group Captain got it stopped at once. Though why did all the moustaches also at the parade not have done that before?

I came to realise that because I had all the Daily Inspections to perform, I could quietly absent myself from Parades. Normally I would be away on my twelve mile cycle through the lovely Morayshire countryside– which I quite enjoyed. I was a great believer that if something was working then do not fix it. So I would just look into the DF stations, ask if all was serviceable, have a cuppa with the Direction Finding crews, then find a cosy hedge and go behind it and read a book till I was sure the Parade nonsense would be finished and it was time for lunch. A great life really. But on one occasion the weather must have been inclement so instead of the twelve mile cycle I just went down to the latrines, went into a cubicle and started reading. My peaceful time was disturbed when I heard the sounds of a commotion getting louder outside and I realised that the inspecting Air Vice-Marshall was going to inspect the latrine I was in. The cubicle doors were only about four feet in height so there was always a gap at top and bottom. I left the cubicle door partly open and hunkered on the lavatory seat – so that feet and head were not protruding. To my amusement the great man stood right outside my cubicle door and announced jovially: "This place looks like a proper shit-house." His cohorts laughed "Ha!" Ha!" in agreement. I nearly fell off the seat laughing.

NO FEAR OF RADIATION

Our long-range giant transmitters were out beside the old historic fishing port of Burghead – called The Broch by locals, possibly because of the remains of its Pictish dry-stone wall protection origins. We were invited over there for a meal. But I was quite upset and horrified when the NCOs there demonstrated that they, and the families living with them, did not need any outside electrical power. Their lamps could be lit by radiation from the huge transmitters.

A LEG-PULL OR PLAIN CARELESSNESS?

One fine morning I had a call to say that the "hush-hush" UHF Direction Finding Station was not working at all. I had been instructed that if that happened I was not to attempt a repair but to call the Boffins at the Air Ministry in Whitehall who would come up to see what needed to be done to get the important piece of equipment operational again. I pondered. Then I decided to cycle the miles out to the UHF hut to see if I really had to contact the Air Ministry. Breathless from the hastily ridden four-mile long cycle journey to reach the UHF hut, I opened the door. And immediately I saw that the duty crew had not in fact plugged in the set to the mains. I plugged it in and it worked first time. I said nothing but demanded the usual cup-of char. To this day I do not know if they were really having me on because I was a Catholic or whether it was a Regular v Conscript thing or that they were just plain stupid. On the cycle back to base I thought it was for the first reason and was thankful that my good old Guardian Angel had looked after me yet again. Imagine the consequences for me if I had summoned the Boffins up from the Air Ministry for a set not plugged in. I made no report on the matter.

BEWARE THE IDES OF...

But even more serious things happened too – though I can smile at some of them now. I was cycling under the wing of a white-painted Coastal Command Lancaster when all the bombs fell off and landed beside me. I have never moved so fast on a bike before or since. No doubt the bombs had not been primed but I was taking no chances. Often we would be sitting at the Runway Controller's Caravan at the start of the runway in use and we would be having the time of our lives watching the poor attempts of the trainee pilots trying to properly land a heavy Lancaster bomber. Sometimes the approach would be so bad that the Lanc would bounce right over our Caravan and we would have flung ourselves flat on the grass outside. On one occasion a squadron of Fleet Air Arm planes was coming in from Lossiemouth and were landing with customary FAA precision one after the other. We noticed an elderly civilian slowly cycling round the peri-track. He ignored our flashing red lamp and shouted warnings and waves-off and cycled straight through the landing Seafires. It was a miracle he was not decimated (Jude must have been getting over-time) but crossed the runway pedalling on slowly right through the landing squadron of planes. I wondered what those marvellous Fleet Air Arm pilots thought of our carelessness or at least of the carelessness of the elderly cyclist.

As a Catholic I am not supposed to believe in superstition but what about this series of dreadful "co-incidences" that happened on the 25th day of month after month?

Coming into land, a Lanc crashed on the hills behind the camp: next month one of our Lancs crashed down at RAF Waddington: one flew into the sea: for some reason: another was using the bombing range at Tain and must have been too low for the bombs blew his tail up and he crashed into the range: there was a humorous incident that might have been fatal. A Flying Officer prune was promoted to Flight Lieutenant. We had a Spitfire that was used to make practice mock attacks on our trainee Lancs pilots. The prune took it up o one evening to celebrate his promotion and performed all sorts of aerobatics. I was out on the grass round the perimeter tracks trying to improve my golf and watched him. Coming into land the Spit, he forgot he was not landing a big Lanc. Lancs were dropped on to the runway from twenty feet. Unfortunately for the show-off he dropped the Spitfire on to the runway from twenty feet. The undercarriage collapsed: the tail came off: then the wings: then the engine dropped away and that marvellous prune was left sitting in his cockpit which went on sliding down the runway at great speed .and ended up too far away for me to help. I just laughed and laughed – although obviously the consequences could have been serious. Then came real tragedy. I was up in Flying Control doing my checks and realised that a Lanc was having difficulty trying to land in a cross-wind. It overshot four times and then tried for a fifth. Do not know what happened, but this time it veered right and climbed vertically into the stall position and fell over and came straight down into the camp with engines at full power and I could see the poor pilots pulling on the controls in vain. It went straight into our fuel depot only a couple of hundred yards away. I saw the obnoxious Parade Flight Sergeant plunging into the flames to no avail. I forgave his insults there and then. Do not know why he did not receive the gallantry award he deserved. I then turned and was amazed to see the Officer i/c Flight Control standing with his hands in his pockets quite unconcerned, and I had to go in and tell the clot that the Lanc had crashed. Unfortunately there had been nineteen personnel on board as a trainee Radar course was being held on the Lanc. All our planes were diverted to Waddington and needless to say yet another crashed down there. (I was twice offered a flight in a Lanc but I thought Lancs were death traps and would not have set foot in one – even to go and see the Celtic.) The following week after the terrible crash we slow-stepped day after day with rifles reversed as coffin after coffin was paraded to Kinross railway station. Approaching each 25th you could feel the shocked apprehension in the camp. Then came Battle of Britain Day with all the staged pageantry and mock bombing runs. I saw my first jet and was surprised at how small it was compared with the giant Super Fort that had also paid a courtesy visit. Then came the 25th and to everyone's relief there had not been a crash. Bet you have guessed it. That Meteor jet crashed at Leuchars.. Later there was the tragic HMS Truculent sub disaster in the Thames estuary and one of the Kinloss Lancs was ordered to go down to Rosyth and take navy divers down to Chatham to make rescue attempts. The Lanc crashed before it reached Rosyth.

66

THE CHURCH RETURNS

All bods had cycles. So a few of us would go off of an evening exploring the district. So what Shakespeare play started:

Act One: Scene One: A Camp near Forres,

"Double, double
Toil and trouble!
Cauldron, boil, and cauldron bubble!"?

O.K. Clever clogs. You knew it was Macbeth.

And there was a Witches Cauldron! At Findhorn. It was a fish and chip shop.

So we would usually stuff ourselves there before setting off on exploration. (Yes! Food rears its ugly head yet again!)

We visited the extraordinary Culbin Sands on occasion. The Sands were useful to film producers who wanted to do desert scenes. There is a complete village buried under the inundation from the sea-coast and it was said that sometimes the spire of the village church would emerge from the shifting sands and occasionally its bell would be heard ringing. But we did not experience those phenomena. Last time I was up there I found that an attempt was being made to re-forest the Sands.

Muggins was looking at a detailed survey map and spotted a ruined priory just over the hills behind the camp. So off we went. It was a bit of a climb at first and I was not too popular, especially when AC2 Cameron lost control going down a steep hill, crashed into the fence the other side of a t-junction and went flying head-over-heels into a field. I was amazed and very relieved that he was not injured in any way. We arrived at the site of the priory at dusk and found that the very tall and massive protective wall circling the ruins had been broken down in places. We scrambled over one of the openings and the rest went left so I decided to turn right. I turned the next corner and there was a Benedictine monk walking towards me. What a shock. I thought he was something pre-reformation. But he greeted me in true Christian fashion and I realised he was for real. In the corner of the apse a little group of monks were grouped under a tarpaulin. It transpired that they had arrived that very day, April 13th 1948 to re-found what was once a monastery of the Val des Choux Order founded by Alexander II in 1231, and we RAF clots were their very first visitors. They too made us welcome, as Benedictines always do to their visitors. All gave some of their valuable time to us but the "guest master" was really The Bursar – Dom James McHugh from the Greenock area. I have always thought that visit was one of my greatest achievements – 7-1 and Lisbon aside – of course. And you will know that Pluscarden Monastery (not priory now) has been a great blessing to Morayshire.

One night I was listening to the football results and the announcer said: Celtic Four! Great I thought! Then he pronounced with some blue-nose amusement: Clyde Six! Not so great.

Coastal Command treated us so well that I have always thought Kinloss spoiled me for life. I was never to experience such marvellous treatment again – except perhaps from Glasgow Corporation Transport.

FORE!

Wednesday afternoon was recreation time. I would take my golf-clubs (all four of them – I laugh at all the massive accoutrements I see coming out of car boots at the Girvan Golf Course starter's car park: by the time some modern golfers sort themselves out to start – they could have completed a couple of holes). and do my best on the Forres course. It was a beautiful hilly course. I recommend it to anyone lucky enough to be holidaying up there. But one day I stopped playing. From the top of one of the course hills I saw that a Highland Games was in progress below. I had never seen such an event so sat down and watched. Needless to say I was in stitches at the efforts being made over tossing the caber. The competitor would be striving with all his might trying to heave the great tree trunk, while a knot of judges would be scurrying hither and thither trying to judge the caber fall without the huge object crashing on to them.

But one Wednesday I was very naughty. No flood-lights in those days and the Tims were playing that afternoon at Pittodrie. So I went AWOL that morning and caught the train for Aberdeen. Needless to say we lost yet again. (I went at least ten times to Pittodrie before I even saw us draw a game.) I walked despondently back to the old Joint Station, saw that the indicator board showed the morning train to Inverness would leave from a certain platform and discovered its coaches stationed there. So I walked up toward the front of the engineless train, climbed into a carriage and enjoyed the sleep of the unjust. I was rudely shaken awake by a blue-coated minion of the law who shouted at me that I could not go to sleep on a train. (Of course I could go to sleep anywhere any time – in those days.) I showed him my ticket to Kinloss. But the moron dragged me down the platform and shoved me into a YMCA at two in the morning. I say moron because the clown never thought to ask to see my non-existent RAF pass. Later I had another two run-ins with Aberdeen policemen and I do not think the word decency was in their Highlander make-up. Probably just did not like Glaswegian scruff! Anyways I waited until I thought the coast was clear (or rather that polis had gone away somewhere) and just went back to the Joint Station and back on to the train and went to sleep again. The lads had covered up for me and I slipped back into RAF routine on the Thursday morning – nae bother. Then a great surprise awaited me. A very kindly and decent Squadron Leader wanted to promote me to sergeant but as I had only ten months left before demob he wanted me to agree to do a year instead of the ten months. And what did this idiot say? I did not want to miss a year at University which I would have done by agreeing to serve an extra two months. I still kick myself over that reply because the very next week the Berlin Airlift started and all demob was deferred for two months. So I did my year as an AC2 plonker instead of an important sergeant. And you will probably realise that if I had agreed to that offered promotion I would have a bigger pension to-day.

As it was we had difficulty in stopping an enraged aircraftsman buddy who was proceeding with two large cans of petrol to set some Lancs on fire in protest. Later in life I was amused to find the same idjit had become a secondary school teacher in an east side of Glasgow school. Better not to name him.

Then came another most pleasant surprise. Volunteers were wanted to attend a Moral Leadership course at Rainhill, by Liverpool. Of course I jumped at the chance to see the famous trial ground where Rocket established the success of the steam locomotive. (By this time a second ground Wireless Mechanic was at Kinloss. so there was no objection to my participation in the Course. The powers that be were probably glad to get a candidate and be rid of me for a spell.) An added joy for me was to be able to travel by a Liverpool Green Goddess tram (they were eventually to end up in Parkhead Depot- no less!) out as far as the junction where the St. Helen's trams used to come in. I then hiked the remaining distance to Rainhill. The Jesuits there were a pleasant surprise after some of the "County" mafia at Wally Dishes. We were treated like proper human beings. As well as interesting theological and philosophical talks and discussions, we enjoyed football – but of course – and the Jesuits arranged some fabulous tours round historic Catholic Lancashire sites. The recusant places and stories from Penal times were fascinating. The Jesuit church in Borough Road, St. Helen's (the most Catholic town in England) has a wondrous carillon in its steeple. Well worth a trip after you have savoured the Blackpool tram rides to see the famous illuminations. After the Course I was completely hooked on Lancashire, St. Helen's Rugby League Club, and of course, The Red Rose at Old Trafford.

ALL GOOD THINGS COME TO AN END

(As a motorman said when his tram reached Airdrie terminus.)

I often played monopoly with John McLean – a Scouter from Paisley who ended up as parish priest at Stranraer. John was a most useful and helpful friend as he worked in the Station Orderly Room. I had discovered that on demob ("Roll on the Nelson, the Rodney, Renown! You can't sink the Hood but the B***** d went down!" we would chant in unison) it was possible to receive a Travel Warrant to any part of the British Isles. The catch was that you had to have a relative living there. I knew that the farthest place in the British Isles I could reach by rail was Dingle in County Kerry. There was a narrow gauge line to Dingle from Tralee. I persuaded Gerry Tennant also to obtain a travel warrant for Dingle as he was being demobbed at the same time. Then panic stations all right. A Warrant Officer (big cheese in those good old days) rushed in and asked me whom I knew in Dingle. Oh! Oh! We had an assistant priest in St. Mark's in Glasgow's Muiryfauld Drive called Fr. Lyne. I had served his very nervous first Mass there. And I was quick- witted enough to remember that his uncle was the parish priest in Dingle, so I confidently said "Canon Lyne". "Oh! I wish I had known that before now." exclaimed the W.O. "I am from Dingle!" Collapse of not-so-stout party.

NOT GOOD AT HOME

At that time things continued poor at Kerrydale Street. Kelly continued to over-rule McGrory who did not seem to have the will to oppose him and the problems were confounded by the respect each had for the other. Some of us will have to spend extra time in Purgatory for irreverence as we knew the dreadful forward line of the time as "The Five Sorrowful Mysteries," Mea maxima culpa. And this when Hibernians had that "Famous Five." And the Home of the Broc had "The Iron Curtain". The once very dependable Miller was no longer reliable in goal. Bonnar was brought in and that helped a little in defence. An International coach (first time we had an official coach?) Hogan was brought in, – at the age of seventy – but of the players only the legendary Tommy Docherty bothered to learn from him and consequently built a career from his advice. One time Tommy stayed opposite us at the junction of Shettleston Road and Westmuir Street and we had watched his progress through Boys' Guild and Shettleston Juniors. On week-end leave I had seen one Charles Patrick Aloysius Tully take the great Ian McColl and his side to the cleaners. But Charlie da Tull was away in advance of most of the Celts he played with apart from Docherty and Big Hookey McPhail – but the latter was playing with a badly injured ankle. More on Charlie later. And I had, of course, managed to get to Tannadice – the sloping dilapidated ground of newly-promoted Dundee United (formerly Dundee Hibs) only to see us go down 4-3. But that is the way it was in the Kelly/McGrory regime.

MY FIRST EVER SUIT AND HAT

But off we erks went to West Kirby to be demobbed. Oh how I was sure later that I should have made a career in the good old RAF. At West Kirby it was lashing wet but we were determined to visit the near-by Blackpool Tower so we boarded a really decrepit old double-decker bus. I was afraid we would not make it up even the slightest of gradients but the driver struggled manfully on. I did not envy him. As we alighted at one of Blackpool's three railway stations a Saloon tramcar came in from Fleetwood. Poor motorman. I did not envy him either. Although wearing heavy rain-cover he was absolutely drenched. Anyway off we went in the rain down what looked like a main street. We came across an over-weight blue-coated minion of the law puffing himself to death in a door-way so we politely asked for directions for the Tower and were greeted in return by a coarse volume of verbal abuse. We queried his abuse. Why were we getting it? "What the so-and-so do you think I am standing under?" Oh! Dear! He was. The Tower was closed and unlit. Next day I received my first-ever two-piece suit: a lovely soft hat (green but of course!) shoes and a change of other clothing. So no more "shite-hawks" (erks name for the albatrosses) on our shoulders.

ERIN GO BRAUGH

Gerry Tennant and yours truly set off from the Broomielaw on a Burns-Laird boat for Belfast. We did not want to go by train from St. Enoch's to Stranraer as that would have meant changing at both Stranraer and Larne to reach Belfast. The crossing was fine but when we alighted at Belfast I put my foot in it as usual. I clean forgot we were both wearing our Green and Gold Old Aloysian ties and approached a gun-toting RUC officer for directions to the station for Dublin. What a glare I got in return. The Irish rail track gauge is five foot six compared to our four foot eight and a half inches and there was a massive six-axle dining car on the train. We sat down for breakfast and Gerry was annoyed when the charming waitress brought kippers. Gerry moaned that I had promised great food in Ireland – not kippers. But then followed a sumptuous five course repast. Wow! Had never seen anything like that before. (There I go – food again!) After a very smooth ride we changed trains in Dublin and went South towards Cork – then changed for Tralee. Alighting there I asked a porter when the next train left for Dingle. The response came: "Glory be to God, sir. (Me! A sir!) The last train for Dingle left twelve years ago!" Well not quite. The occasional long cattle special negotiated the dilapidated line with great difficulty. But all was well. The decent authorities accepted our travel warrants for the Dingle bus service. I was delighted to see an emblem of the Sacred Heart prominently displayed at the front of the bus. I imagined the riot that would have ensued had that been on a Yellow Standard going to Bellahouston. Telling a friend later about the religious badge being displayed she said that one time travelling in the Republic they were held up for a time at a cross-roads because the policeman was reciting the twelve-o'clock Angelus. Mrs. Long (owner of our Boarding House) and everyone else in Gaelic-speaking Dingle made us thoroughly welcome despite the fact that they knew we were RAF Reservists. We hired bikes: climbed Mount Brandon and went out to the historic Blasket Islands to see the ruins and stood amazed at the height of the breakers lashing the cliffs over at Caherciveen on the other side of the bay. We laughed when we discovered at night that every other corner house in Dingle became a shebeen. All too soon our splendid holiday was over. We boarded the express for Dublin and the announcement came that we were going to run non-stop to the Capital as there would be a special behind making all the local stops. The reason for the special soon became clear as at every station we raced through, there was a crowd of seminary students waiting for their train. There wouldn't be theses days. The Burns Laird cattle boat from Belfast to the Broomielaw sure stank to the high heavens. But I was now on the verge of a new episode in my life. Fingers crossed and many Hail Marys.

VIA VERITAS VITA

Is the motto of Glasgow University and translates as The Way, The Truth, and The Life – abridged version of "Jesus says: I am the way. The Truth and the Life: no one comes to the Father except through Me." (John 14:6.)

The University coat-of-arms is the same as Glasgow's with the addition of a lectern supporting a book of learning (a bible perhaps?). Glasgow University was founded by Bishop William Turnbull in 1451 after James II obtained the necessary Papal Bull from Pope Nicholas V. It is the fourth oldest in the English speaking world – the oldest University in the world being Bologna probably founded around 1088.

I liked the University hymn. If only it was lived up to. But in too many cases unfortunately not. As we will see:

Gaudeamus igitur   While we are young, let us rejoice
Juvenes dum sumus   Singing out in gleeful tones

Post jucundem juventutem	After youth's delightful frolic
Post molestam senectutem	And old age so melancholic
Nos habemus humus	Earth will cover our bones
Vita nostra brevis est	Life is short and all too soon
Brevi finetur,	We omit our final gasp,
Venit mors velociter;	Death ere long is on our back;
Rapit nos atrociter;	Terrible is his attack;
Nemini parcetur.	None escapes his dread grasp.
Vivat academia,	Long live our academy,
Vivant professors,	Teachers whom we cherish,
Vivat membrum quodlibet;	Long live all the graduates;
Vivat membrae quaelibet;	And the undergraduates;
Semper sint in flore!	May they always flourish!
Vivat nostra societas,	Long live our society,
Vivant studiosi;	Scholars wise and learned;
Cescat una veritas	May truth and sincerity
Floreat fraternitas	Nourish our fraternity
Patriae prosperitas.	And our land's prosperity.
Alma mater floreat,	May our Alma mater thrive,
Quae nos educavit;	A font of education;
Caros et camilitones	Friends and colleagues, where' ere
	they are
Dissitas in regions	Whether from near or from afar
Sparsos congregavit.	Heed our invitation.

But not for a while yet, as the Berlin Crisis meant I had to wait the best part of a year to become a Glasgow Yoonie Undergraduate.

The father of class-mate and very decent friend, Gordon Smith, (he who once tried to get us up to 100 m.p.h. in a Lanchester on the Dumbarton Boulevard but could not quite make it – the follies of youth!) owned a transport firm, Universal Transport, operating heavy lorries on the Glasgow, Dundee, Aberdeen run so I was generously given the post of despatch clerk/telephone operator in their premises on Alexandra Parade. Not that I knew much about what I had to do but soon learned some of the ropes – especially from their helpful foreman. I once asked him why the firm did not use trailers and was horrified at the story which emerged. Mr. Smith and his two brothers had started the business after the First World War using ex-military equipment and his two brothers had been killed in trailer accidents. Trailer was not a word to be used around Universal Transport. Later the firm was nationalised and Mr. Smith was well-compensated: for his premises, his fleet of lorries and his goodwill. He told me that he had never been so well-off in his life. He bought (after a struggle) the large Flying-Boat hanger at Largs and installed it in his petrol station beside our premises on the Parade. And he also bought a former Air-Sea Rescue Motor Launch.

At that time there was a big waiting-list for a newly designed bang up-to-date open-topped sports car. One morning a beaming Mr. Smith arrived to show off his new Austin-Healy Sprite arrival. Unfortunately he parked it behind one of his lorries that was getting orders from me. For some reason the Aberdeen driver returned to the lorry and decided to reverse back up to the lorry garage and so went straight back over the once proud sports-car thoroughly wrecking it. Oh! Dear! I had seen cartoon characters jumping into the air and filling it with unrepeatable expletives and now poor Mr. Smith did just that.

Eventually came the start of University years that were to lead me almost to do a Mr. Smith repeat performance. I was to discover that Latin was a compulsory subject for even an ordinary M.A. degree, and that the Latin professor (seriously miscalled the Professor of Humanity) wanted the standard of Latin at Glasgow to be better than the standard pertaining at Oxford. One of our friends (better be nameless) wanted his M.A. so that he could go into the Church of Scotland ministry via Divinity (for which an M.A, was necessary). He had passed in every other subject on his M.A. course but failed in Latin. Consequently our pal obtained a pass in Latin from St. Andrew's University and asked Glasgow if that would complete his degree that he desperately needed. He showed us the letter he received in return. It simply said; "You, more than most, must realise that the standard of Latin at St. Andrew's University is not to be compared with the standard of Latin at Glasgow University." And it was signed; Christian J. Fordyce, Professor of Humanity, Dean of the Faculty and Clerk of the Senate. So the unfortunate would-be minister had no course of appeal.

Despite splendid commemorative gates being installed in 1951 to mark the five hundredth anniversary of the foundation by Bishop Turnbull. Professor Fordyce, Professor of Humanity (huh!) could tell White Father students that they had no right to be sitting in front of him in his protestant University. So what chance did poor me have all those years away from school and a Jesuit mis-educated Catholic to boot. Nevertheless there was a flourishing Catholic Society and Chaplaincy. The top-drawer chaplain was Fr. Ryland- Whittaker S. J. He was a highly qualified surgeon in his own right and his father had been a Professor of Surgery at Edinburgh University, yet he was disgracefully completely ostracised at Gilmorehill. (Later in the Orkneys he was charged with theft because he had hung on his Youth Club wall a piece of discarded fishing-net given to him for that purpose.) Bigotry rules in Scotland O. K.! But he was better regarded after he saved the life of a valuable injured bull.

A Paisley friend went across North Africa with The Eighth Army. He did a four-year honours course – Double Latin and Greek. Towards the end the Greek Professor told Bert that his work deserved a double first class degree but Fordyce was reluctant to give a Catholic a double-first. So Bert went through life with only a second- class double. So much for serving your country. Bert's younger brother Leo was a bit of a genius and was at Gilmorehill aged sixteen. He easily graduated in Medicine – but being Catholic, he could not get into practice in Scotland so he emigrated to Canada where he became a Professor of Medicine at a Canadian University. Scotland's loss of course.

HOPE SPRINGS ETERNAL

We thought things at Parkhead were going to improve when "Spam"- alias Pat McAuley – ran riot against the other half in the first of our League Cup section matches. But as was usual then, we started the section well, but never qualified. "Spam" did not stay long with the club either. One ray of hope was an incredible able and cool goalie, George Hunter, from Troon. He made some impossible saves. But his health deteriorated and he did not last. But we did manage to win something: the Glasgow Cup!

"Twas a sunny summer's day

In the merry month of May.
And Rangers Celts did play
In front of Danny Kay.
To great football Celts did treat them.
And the Glasgow Celtic beat them.
Where?
Over at Hampden.
Where?
Over at Hampden.
Where?
Over at Hampden
In front of Danny Kay.

You should have seen McPhail.
He made the Rangers quail.
He made them turn quite pale.
To great football John did treat them
When the Glasgow Celtic beat them.
Where?
Over at Hampden.
Where?
Over at Hampden.
Where?
Over at Hampden
In front of Danny Kay."

(Danny Kay was the most publicised American comedian of the time and he had kicked off in the Final.)

Charlie Tully was a hoot!

At Falkirk, in a packed ground (Delaney was in the Falkirk team) he moved a policeman's raincoat out of the way, took a corner-kick and scored direct from the corner. Or we thought he had scored. But the silly ref made him take the kick again. So he put the ball in direct again and this time the goal stood. On another occasion a Falkirk player was taking a shy in front of their vociferous stand. Tully looked round. Saw the ref was not looking and kicked the Falkirk player on the shins. The stand crowd roared. The ref looked round and only saw a beatific Tully standing in front of the shy-taker, so turned away again. So Charlie repeated the performance. I thought the stand roof was going to lift off.

There were always crowd problems at Falkirk. On one occasion a spectator in a bright light green blazer was arrested and marched round the ground to the stand. The media made a big hullabaloo about miscreant Celtic supporters. Too bad that when the case came to court he was a Falkirk supporter wearing a local firm's sports blazer. On another occasion at an all-ticket cup-tie I watched a gateman taking in match tickets and passing them out of the back of the box to an accomplice who then handed them over the boundary wall to another accomplice who then sold them again outside. No wonder Brockville was usually over-crowded.

Then there was the match at Cathkin where again Tully saw the ref was not looking at him – the ball being away up-field. Tully booted Aitken and then threw himself down rolling and yelling in pretended agony. The ref turned round and put Aitken off. So simulation is not new. When he could get away with it Tully would amuse us by taking corner-kicks from the edge of the penalty box instead of the corner flag but of course officialdom soon twigged that scam. Another – apparently legal – trick, was to take the ball from an opponent and as the latter turned away, Tully would shy the ball off the back of his opponent and scoot off quickly with the ball. The Glasgow Weekly News always had a Tully joke feature. 1950 was a Holy Year.

And Celts went out to Roma and played a friendly against Lazio. Some friendly. John McPhail was ordered off! The Weekly News reported that Tully had an audience with the Pope who then took him on to the Angelus balcony over-looking St. Peter's Square. When they appeared the crowds shouted up "Who is that with Charlie da Tull?" More years in purgatory for me.

But perhaps they will be reduced because to go on pilgrimage is not simply to visit a place to admire its treasures of nature...

For three of us – led by Tommy Madden – the other was Arthur McQuade, a quiet class-mate from Albion Street behind St. Mirren's ground in Paisley – and who later had a Consulting Room in Harley Street – made a crazy decision. We bought a used Norton 350 c.c. motor-cycle combination and went off to see the Pope. (The Art School was even crazier. They bought a second-hand double-decker bus to make the Roma journey. But the last I heard of it, it was lying u/s in a used bus site and never turned a wheel towards Italy.) The A1 was not even a dual carriageway – apart from a short stretch past Doncaster. The Channel Ferry was a converted war-time corvette and the bike was loaded on to it by crane.

We discovered that the French roads chosen were largely rough pavee – and fractured our petrol tank. (I discovered later that the rough roads were supposed to slow down a German invasion. Well they certainly did not slow the Hun but they sure slowed us.) I watched with great interest tiny one-deck trams running in and out of the centre of Dijon. Going over the Mont Cenis was a great achievement. Then disaster struck again in the Ligurian Alps. The twisting and turning road (no Autostradas then) did for one of our war-time poor quality tyres. And a hole blew in its cover. We were passing a little mountain village which occupied only the steeper side of the road. Soon a friendly crowd gathered and two carabinieri, with large rifles slung, rode up on beautiful horses. The cry went up "Luigi!" "Luigi!" And youths were sent scrambling up and down the steep hill-side in all directions. We wondered what on earth was going on. Then we saw a giant of a man striding down a hill-side. He was dressed in a complete hunter's outfit and, of course, came with rifle slung. The crowd cheered his arrival and we felt as though we were in an Italian opera. We explained our problem to the great man. He smiled and beckoned us to follow him with our bike. We entered a garage and Luigi went to one of the walls and took down a cycle-repair outfit. We expressed the opinion in no uncertain terms that that was not going to solve our blown-out tyre problem. He laughed, repaired the offending inner tube, then took out a huge hunting knife, went over to a tyre hanging elsewhere on the garage wall, sliced a chunk out of it, folded it up with his massive hands, tied it together with string and shoved it against the gaping hole in our useless tyre. Luigi blew the tyre up for us, put it on our bike and smilingly refused lira offered by us. He clapped us on our backs, the crowd cheered us off and we went all the way to Roma on that "repaired" tyre. Unbelievable. Of course in Roma we bought a proper tyre.

Roma was a lovely city then. It had fine tramway systems which appealed to me. As well as the city system ATAC, there was the narrow gauge AcoTral which went out some sixty miles to places like the health spa of Alatri and industrial Frosinone. And Stefer was standard gauge to Urbino and Castel Gondolfo. Roma Nord was also a standard gauge light rail line to Civita Castellana and far off Perugia. It had its own terminus where it was amazing to see UK built trains shunting under battery power only.

My God-mother Helper of the Holy Souls had advised me that Roma had a tram that went both ways. That had puzzled me. Why should she have made a point of saying that when Glasgow had trams that went both ways? We discovered that she meant a splendid circular service that took us easily and cheaply to some of the historic places we wanted to visit. ATAC was progressive in those times. It had designed and built the first single-deck class of articulated trams in Europe. The very first of the class was destroyed in an allied bombing raid, as the work-shops and depot adjoined Termini Station approach tracks and marshalling yards. It was always amusing to travel on one of the fine smooth-running artics. There was a painted instruction behind and above the motorman's head "vietato parlare guidatore" – (it is forbidden to speak to the driver) – yet there was always a little knot of Romans gathered round the motorman blethering away in great enjoyment. ATAC had developed great plans to go underground in the historic centre of Roma but were never allowed to do that, presumably for archaeological reasons. Vienna saw the plans and did it in Vienna where I saw it all later during several visits to the Austrian capital. Then one night I really covered myself in glory. We had climbed up Marian Mount to see Roma by night and continued over the top and down to a main road. An old-fashioned little single-decker came hurtling down towards the city centre so we signalled for it at a fermata (tram stop). The motorman stopped obediently but the harassed conductor was not for us boarding, saying several times "Deposito San Paulo!" At least that is what I thought he was saying. We were going back to a guest camp near to Basilica San Paulo and I knew there was a large tram depot there. So I persisted in boarding. The conductor gave up and stepped aside. The motorman quickly notched up and we swung smartly into a tram depot. The crew airted rapidly off and we were left staring at a white–tiled depot wall. Another Tollan howler. Never told the old man that one.

As many of the main places of historic interest we could manage to fit in were visited. In the catacombs of S .Calixtus on the Appian Way, (not to be missed if you are in Roma) a kindly monk was showing us around underground and telling us fascinating items of interest. In The Gallery of the Popes we were joined by an ignorant American (I am half-American – so no anti U.S. slur intended) who kept interrupting repeatedly drawling arrogantly "How do you know that?" So unfortunately the fascinating tour was cut short when the monk decided he had had enough of the Yank. We wondered at most of the important sites – the basilicas: The Pantheon: St. Peter's and the Sistine Chapel and The Lateran et al.

The class-mate, Donald Renfrew who had burst my jaw, – later to become an auxiliary bishop in Glasgow – was at the Scots College, so of course we went to the Scots College to try to meet him, only to be told by a porter that the Scottish students were now resident at their summer farm out at San Marino. We went there next day, only to find the students had gone into Roma for some reason – so we never did meet up with Donnie in Roma. I did not mind, as I enjoyed the tram trips – but of course. We thought we had better see the Pope before returning home, and he was staying at his summer residence at Castel Gondolfo. The journey to Castel Gondolfo by Stefer tram fascinated me as the motorman had to use a "chopper" controller instead of the more normal swivel-handle one. We passed the Stefer Depot on the Appian Way and there in the sidings were some "imperiale" (double-deck cars) but we were not to see them running. We had to wait for a couple of hours before Pius XII appeared on his balcony- and of course the Italians were ecstatic. Personally, I could not see what the fuss was all about. He looked like a frail, unwell and tired old man. He had been the Nuncio to Germany and supposedly had closed down the German Catholic Party to help Shickelgruber obtain power – presumably Hitler being thought a lesser evil than communist U.S.S.R. – and he had not publicly condemned The Holocaust.

We calculated that we might have just enough money left to get us back to the Channel. (There was a limit on the amount of cash that could be taken out of the country at that time. I used to wonder who had won the war.) So back over the 7,000 foot Mont Cenis pass we went again and heaved big sighs of relief on reaching Modane. Here an irate Sassenach woman was berating a lounging French youth for not opening a bus door for her. Being a polite Glaswegian (some of the time) I went over and opened the door for her.

She told me I spoke very good Anglais pour un homme Francais. I enlightened her re my birth place. Parkhead rules! O. K.! The pavee did for us again and we lost the side-car mud-guard but by that time we were past caring. We had one day to reach the Channel and we had no food and no money. Not an Adam Smith among the trio. Alongside where we camped for the last time was a field full of turnips – or so we thought. We pinched one for next morning's breakfast. You have guessed it again. It was a sugar beet, so three bedraggled starving youths boarded the converted corvette again and dived for the restaurant.

BACK TO THE GRIND

When I tried the first term Latin paper at the Yoonie I was astonished to find I had gained an unexpected 75/100. But the African next me was awarded 98/100. I blurted out in amazement, "Is your name Horace?" "No! Me Onopotonaki", came the reply. I took a long time to live that joke down. Most of the University subjects were not too bad, although I had to obtain permission from my parish priest before I could be allowed to attend the Moral Philosophy part of the course. That is the way the Church ruled in those unenlightened (?) days. But the Latin exam at the end of the year was horrific. There were six papers on different subjects to pass ands several times I would scoosh five of the six and fail a different paper each time. So it was an almost hopeless struggle for me to scrape a degree. Oh how I wished I had stayed in the good old enjoyable RAF. But life went on.

THE CRAZY GANG!

At Christmas we would work for the good old Post Office as a sorter or delivery man as required. In the Summer, as I will relate, I worked as a tram conductor out of Dennistoun Depot. I really enjoyed that way of meeting lots of people.

We had a good group of friends, most from Paisley, and we had enjoyable outings on bikes around Gleniffer Braes or excursions to Luss or Aberfoyle. Financially my old class-mate, George Stewart, came to the financial rescue too.

His dad was a Sheriff's Officer and I had known Mr. Stewart as a small boy when I adored him because he had shown me a fat note-book in which he had entered every contentious referee decision that had gone against Celtic and every contentious decision that had favoured the other lot. And there were plenty of them. Mr. Stewart needed to have someone delivering Legal Notices for him. Several times I did journeys like starting at Cowcaddens and visiting every house and close and side-street from there right up to Maryhill Depot. Of course I met with much abuse and unanswerable queries but at least it kept me fit. I was appalled at the conditions in slum tenements especially in Lyons Street and could understand the anger.

UPSTAIRS ONLY!

But then I was day-dreaming along Sauchiehall Street and admiring a lovely red-head when I heard my name being called from on high. I thought the deity had been reading my lascivious thoughts, but then realised that it was a fellow student calling my name from the back window of a blue standard tram on service six. He shouted that they were starting students at the Glasgow Transport (formerly Tramway) Corporation head office in Bath Street. So I did a quick about turn and .eventually found myself a conductor in Dennistoun Depot. I have described my own and my father's GCT experiences in "The Wearing of the Green" (thoughtfully published and sold for £12 by Adam Gordon, Kintradwell Farm Cottage, Brora, Sutherland, KW9 6LU; tel. 01408 622660; e-mail: adam@ahg-books.com). Suffice here to say that we had a rather notorious Service Seven – Millerston to Bellahouston – known as "The Yellow Peril" because one time the sides of the trams on that service had a yellow band painted on to help illiterates recognise which route the approaching tram was supposed to be on. The service never went into the centre of Glasgow but crowds of passengers came on and left in Dennistoun, Bridgeton, Gorbals and Govan. This meant more work than on other services for the conductors and conductresses – hence the Yellow Peril sick joke. Service Seven was used on match day either to Ibrox or Parkhead. We only had the old Standard cars and if one was over-loaded and groaning at the springs or properly loaded according to the rules, it was easy-peasy to appreciate which team that tram's conductor supported. On one occasion a car had jammed with a broken axle on one of the tight Craigton Road railway bridge curves and when we arrived at Bellahouston terminus we obviously could not return to Govan so an inspector directed us to proceed on along Paisley Road West to regain our proper route at Paisley Road Toll. When we pulled up unexpectedly at Cessnock, motorman Hammy Brown applied his hand-brake and alighted and crossed to the pavement gutter where he stood with his head bowed and heavy rain-coat open. When he returned I asked him if he was feeling all right and was told he was fine but that he would was not going to pass that place without paying his respects. So I knew we both supported the same team. We students passed the motorman's examination but the blinkered short-sighted Union would not let us operate the trams although there would be several trams standing unused in depots at the rush hours. No wonder would-be passengers stopped trying unsuccessfully to board packed-out trams and turned to the motor-car instead. Unions often cannot see the wood for the trees. And as is well known, senseless union militancy landed us with over-long Thatcher rule.

PARADISE REGAINED ?

We thought things were going to improve at Parkhead however. The massive giant from Sligo – with the massive accent – Sean Fallon – started to appear in the team. Sean turned out to be a true gentleman and a great asset to Celtic and Scottish Football. As usual we were out of the League Cup to Motherwell after qualifying for the later stages, but we had revenge in the Scottish Cup Final. Tully had run riot against a fine Raith Rovers team in the semi-final which we scooshed 3-1 despite a Boden own-goal.. I had always wondered why the likes of McNaught and Maule were not brought to Parkhead. The Final was a dismal affair. It really dragged on but McPhail as usual came to the rescue with our solitary goal. We had had our revenge on Well and the Scottish Cup came back home to Paradise at last. Unfortunately – as usual in those days – promise soon faded. Partly there were lots of injuries to blame.

SOME AMUSEMENT FOR A TIME

Meanwhile the social side of Yoonie life was enjoyable. For starters I no longer needed to go up to the Shettleston Wash House and pay for a bath. There was lots of tennis at the University Sports

Ground at Anniesland. On one occasion after tennis I became annoyed at one of the players going round the dressing-room throwing pails of water at others. I quietly pinched his shirt and held it out to him like a matador. He threw a pail of water at the shirt and queried why I had not pulled it away and it had been soaked. He never ever spoke to me again after I informed him that it was his shirt. Chortle! Chortle!. I became quite proficient at golf on the Union snooker tables. This was when each player had a different coloured ball and the white was used in turn to advance your colour round the pockets while the others might try to stop you.

A TRUE PANTOMIME

Of course our Yoonie gang could not refrain from one of them organising something a bit out of the ordinary from time to time.. One Christmas an eager-beaver booked us into one of the top boxes for the Pavilion panto. (You will know that irrepressible Charles Tully – when in trouble with a ref asked him if he would please refrain from sending him to the Pavilion as he had been there the previous night.)

During the Panto one of the comedians on stage as well as high in our box – turned and looked up, pointed to us, at us and asked the rest of the audience if they would applaud the toffs high up in the box. Red-faced, I wished I had brought my green-and- white Celtic scarf with me so that I could have waved it back. That certainly would have caused one of the celebrated Arthur Montford's great stramashes. I think that was the time they delighted me – at least by happily singing:

"SHUGGLE, SHUGGLE SHUGGLE!
CLANG CLANG CLANG!
SHUGGLE SHUGGLE SHUGGLE
BANG! BANG! BANG!
SHUGGLE SHUGGLE SHUGGLE
CLANG! CLANG CLANG!
ON THE ROAD TO AUCHENSHUGGLE IN THE
MORNING!
BUT IF YOU EVER GO TO THE TRAM DEPOT?
WILL YOU EVER FIND US?

OH! NO!"

And, but of course, we never ever dreamt that the time would come when we would not be able to go to The Rye Field on a Glasgow Standard Mark Two bogie car ever again, thanks to the motor-loving politicians of the time, a provost who had shares in India Tyres Inchinnan, and powerful railway trade unions.

FORT AUGUSTUS

Some student friends had an uncle who was Head of the then Fort Augustus Boarding School. The good-natured Benedictine invited us to come up and camp on the Fort Augustus Abbey grounds. We were only too eager to do that. So up we went and pitched camp as invited. We wondered why monks would keep appearing and gaze at us on their territory. It transpired that the Benedictine Head had not told his community about his invitation to us.

While we were staying there the monks decided to celebrate the Feast of Our Lady of The Snows by appropriately celebrating Mass on the top of Britain's highest mountain – the massive Ben Nevis – all 4409 feet of it. Of course we went off down to Fort William to take part in their Mass long before the monks' departure. Nevis may mean cloudy but as we trod up the narrow path to the ruined observatory at the summit it sure was misty. It was only on my next couple of visits to the top on clearer days that I came to realise how dangerous that path actually is with steep precipices bordering its north side.

The fit monks sped past us during our ascent and had actually started the Mass by the time we reached the top.

The Abbey itself was a most impressive building – built by Bute for the Benedictine community. Since it had to close with the loss of the Boarding School (owing to the demise of the British Empire), various suggestions have been made as to its future use, but nothing has been achieved so far.

A local lady would sit in her high garden with a pair of binoculars, desperate to see Nessie. A former pupil had presented an elephant's foot to the monastery. So one night two of the monks went out with the elephant's foot and stamped tracks all over the woman's garden. Next night the poor soul was in Fort Augustus village excitedly telling everyone that Nessie had been in

86

her garden. Wonder what Benedict made of that? And I wonder what he made of our efforts at

SANCTA MARIA ABBEY NUNRAW

In 1946 Cistercians had returned to White Castle grounds at the foot of the Lammernuir Hills once owned in pre-Reformation days by White Cistercian nuns..

The monks had issued an appeal for volunteers to dig the foundations for a new Abbey building, so nothing loath, off went a pal and my-self.

We were highly amused when at Haddington Station one of the would-be trench diggers had to ask for our assistance to get his suit-case down from the luggage rack. This man was typical of the many free-loaders who descended on the Abbey for free board-and-lodgings and who were unable or quite uninterested about the muscular effort needed to dig through the extremely thick and heavy Lothian clay filled soil. So the monks had to clear out the free-loaders by making a charge for board and lodgings.

The guest master was most friendly to us and told us tales of their early days after arriving at Nunraw from Mount St. Josephs, Abbey at Roscrea.

In their early Nunraw days if a local from Garvald met a monk walking down a country road, the local would jump over a hedge to avoid contact with the Cistercian – another of the Knox bequests to Scotland.

But in the first harsh Winter after the monks arrival, the conditions were so bad that even road communication to Garvald was impossible. (The Gifford and Garvald Light Railway had become impassable – being blocked with snow-drifts.)

With Garvald's food supplies running out, the good monks went down through the ice and snow to Garvald bringing milk and bread for the villagers.

After the locals had received that kindness, they showed more help and friendship for the Abbey.

A GREAT OPPORTUNITY MISSED?

Then we had another glaring example of West of Scotland bigotry. The SFA secretary was a dictator type by name of Sir George

Graham. Note the Sir. That said a lot. On one occasion the Scottish International team and officials were travelling back from London to the dear green place and a waiter passed the players with a tray of whiskies. Torry Gillick stopped the waiter and enquired who the whiskies were for. On being informed, Torry took the tray from the waiter and passed the whiskies round the players. Needless to say that Torry never received another International cap after that bit of mischief.

Bully Graham decided that it would be great sport to attack Celtic for flying the Irish Tricolour at Celtic Park on match days. He ordered it to be taken down. This was great meat for the anti-Celtic side of the media and the coverage went on and on. Celtic responded that the flag had been a gift form the president of The Irish Free State (as it was then). It was also pointed out that there was an Irish emblem – the Harp – carved into the stone-work of the Easter Road stand. Would that also have to be removed? Personally I have always regretted that Bob Kelly did not take that opportunity to take us into the English Leagues. Anti-Celtic sentiment was to continue to simmer among the SFA officials for a long time. They seemed to ignore the fact that after all they and Graham were supposed to be servants of the clubs. It took someone with the back-bone of the great Fergus McCann to finally shoot them down for a time with the threat of legal action.

Then there was the Festival of Britain which was designed to lift spirits after the depression of the war years and their aftermath. Glasgow Corporation decided to join into the spirit of The Festival by holding a special cup competition named The St. Mungo Cup. We had a titanic struggle to get to the final with Sean doing his valiant efforts as a centre and win this supposedly great trophy. But when the St. Mungo Cup was examined in the Celtic Trophy room it was soon discovered that the hard-won cup was in fact second-hand and had once been a Provan Gas-Works Trophy. Ye Gods. What a bunch in the Corporation. Our club offered to purchase a proper replacement trophy – but of course that would never do.

Players came and left Parkhead as usual. "Spam" going was a surprise. Wee Bobby Collins came in as a bit of an accident after a dispute with Aberdeen over the signing of another player. He had a great reputation. But I, for one, felt he only turned it on when he felt like it. May be I do him an injustice. The player I thought fantastic – but as usual he did not stay long – was fair-haired Jim

Walsh from Alloa – who had scored a hat-trick in the cup-winning run. At that time the other half vaunted their impregnable "iron curtain" defence. On a marvellous occasion Walsh ran forward with the ball nut-megged centre-half Willie Woodburn (who was later to be suspended "sine die" for continuous foul play) then did the same to captain and full-back George Young and went on to smash an unstoppable shot past international keeper Brown.

But once when he was coming along London Road on a good old Service Nine Mark two bogie car which was heading for famous Auchenshuggle, Jim jumped off the tram as it cruised past Kerrydale Street, (Did we not often jump on and off moving trams in Glesca! Of course it was a common practice.) Unfortunately a Celtic Director was motoring behind the tram and witnessed the incident. Walsh was called in, severely reprimanded, and heavily fined for what he had done. Whatever happened to turning a blind eye? Perhaps that is why Jim Walsh did not stay long with us?

Then long-striding smooth-football playing expert Willie Fernie also began to appear. What an attractive player to watch!

A MESSIAH IS FOUND

Something had to be done about the poor showing by our reserves. I had once taken a 15 tram up to Coatbridge to see us playing Albion Rovers in a Cup match at Cliftonhill. I was very depressed when we were two down at half-time. However we finished by winning three – two. Their centre half, one Stein, was held accountable by the Albion Rovers Board for their second half loss of three goals, because the story went about that he had asked them what was the bonus for wining the tie and had been told there wasn't one. The story continued that three times big Jock had lifted his leg and let the ball past and each time turned towards the Board and laughed. And so he was transferred to Welsh club Llanelli who were spending a lot of money in an unsuccessful attempt to enter the English Leagues. Our then chief scout was Gribben from Baillieston. After Llanelli's failure in their objective, Gribben suggested bringing back Stein to play with our reserves and have them learn from an experienced player. Not long after Stein came, regular centre-half Alex Boden was injured and Stein was drafted into the first team as an emergency replacement. But of course he was such a fine player that he kept his place in the first team until an ankle injury suffered against Rangers brought his playing days to a close. When he returned from Wales, a cousin of ours had helped him move into the adjoining house in Burnbank. It turned out that Jock's dad was violently anti-Celtic and when Jock started playing regularly in the first team, Jock's poor mother was to be seen wandering around Burnbank asking passers-by if they knew what the Celtic score was as her husband would not allow her to listen to the Celtic commentary on the radio. The family name was properly Lowenstein and they were part of groups of miners brought in from Lithuania in the nineteen-twenties to keep down the wages of Scottish mine-workers. Obviously they were regarded as "black-legs". As a young man Stein was buried under a fall of stone in Bothwell Castle Colliery and had to be dug out by other alarmed miners who rushed to the scene to assist in a rescue attempt. No doubt such an experience had a marked effect on his mental attitude. It was not unusual for Lithuanians to be brought into Scotland to do heavy manual work. For example, a group of Catholic Lithuanians were killed in a traffic accident on the old Glasgow and South Western Railway.

NO COMPASSION

Then more tragedy for us. Jackie Millsop died during an unsuccessful appendicitis operation. A two-minutes silence requested to mark his passing was shockingly disrupted by hooligan supporters of the other half of the Old Firm. And of course that hooligan element in modern times persisted in insulting us with their twisted rendering of "The Famine Song".

CROWNING GLORY

A surprise awaited us at the end of another woeful season in normal competitions. To mark the Coronation of Elizabeth the First of Scotland and the Second of England, (do wish they would get that right!) the special Coronation Cup tournament was held. We really did not have a right to be there on merit though Neilly Mochan coming in from Middlesbrough made some improvement. Strangely the rather eccentric Robert Kelly was not a fan of Neil who was to be too often not selected. We had brought in an African-American named Gil Heron too – but he never made the grade, unfortunately – only managing a few first team games. Although the tournament was to be a great success financially (realising about half-a-million) there was preliminary controversy over the original miserable proposed remuneration for the participating players who included stars such as Simpson, Milburn and Brennan of Newcastle: Rowley, Aston, Byrne, Pearson and Carey of Manchester United and so on. Perhaps our Springburn scribe best summed up the event from our point of view?

"Said Lizzie to Philip as they sat to dine
I've just had a note from a good friend of mine.
His name is Big Geordie he's loyal and true
And his nose is my favourite colour of blue.
He says that the Rangers are right on their game
And asks for a trophy to add to their fame.
We'll send then a trophy that they're sure to win.
Said Philip "Look out lest the Celtic step in!"
Said Lizzie to Philip "They don't stand a chance!
I'm sending my Gunners to lead them a dance.
With Celtic defeated the way will be clear
For a trophy at Ibrox in my crowning year!"
Alas for the hopes of the royal true blue
For Celtic beat Arsenal and Manchester U.
And Hibs in the final and lo and behold!
All Hampden was covered in Green, White and Gold.
Said Lizzie to Philip when they heard the news
"A blow has been struck at our loyal true-blues.
How can we beat Celtic and put them below?"
Said Philip to Lizzie "I really can't say.
For Celts have won cups now for many a day.
If we're to beat Celtic we'll have to deport
The bold Glasgow Irish their loyal support!"
Then lift up your glass to the old Green and White
Who strive at the football with all of their might.
A credit to Scotland wherever they play.
May Glasgow Celts flourish for ever we say."

Of course I doubt if the then Royals were ever aware of the Old Firm at all. I was in the North Stand at the Final and have never seen such a wonderful display as Willie Fernie turned on in the first half. It was breath-taking. But their Famous Five of Smith, Johnstone, Reilly Turnbull and Ormonde (what would they be worth in our present-day-market?) really got going in the second half and it was a desperate backs-to-the-wall effort for us to hold our winning position. But another unusual member had arrived in the Parkhead Trophy Room.

VALE

My Gilmorehill sojourn came to an end at long last. I was sorely to miss all the student fun, playing in Joe Beltrami's team, and especially Charities' Days when gaudily adorned students took over Glesca on one Saturday in the year and especially the trams. There was a special regulation ordering tram crews not to allow students with collecting cans on our "caurs" – but of course the tram personnel were too wise to try to enforce that daft (literally!) ban and they all enjoyed the fun too. There were King Farouks and Marx Brothers ad nauseam and one Charities Day my piece de resistance was to wear my hill-climbing gear, climb a lot of scaffolding at Charing Cross and then spend ten minutes or so changing the tram points at Woodlands Road with an ice axe until a blue-coated-minion-of-the-law ordered me in a friendly tone to desist.

Before the afternoon football match it was the done thing (for me anyways) to go on to the pitch before the game and obtain the ref's tossing-up coin for my can. They too never seemed to mind. But there was an occasion when one did mind. One of the girls (better not say who she was – she might batter me -kept dodging round the Shawfield terracing erratically blowing a loud whistle that unfortunately matched the sound of the match referee's. That continual disruption to the game did not go down too well!

A year after graduation I was in the dimly lit University library perusing their railway books when I became aware of a shadowy figure standing beside me. I glanced round and my knees began to knock when I saw it to be the dread Christian J. Fordyce himself. I was absolutely staggered when he uttered the words: "I wish I had known, Bill, when you sat in front of me that you were interested in trains!. Your life would have been very different!" I also wondered why he knew my user name. C.J.F. went along the shelf and showed me a book he had written on The West Highland Railway. Another one of life's missed turning points.

PREMIUM ERROR?

My cousin god-father was Deputy Manager of the then prestigious Royal Insurance Company's Glasgow office and was hell-bent on me entering his enhanced promotion scheme for that company. He flew into a rage when I said doing that held no interest for me and I intended to join the teaching profession. He ranted and roared at me for about twenty minutes or so yelling red-faced abuse such as those who could not do taught and teachers were the lowest form of animal life and so on – until his sister Agnes came in and ordered him to desist. I never told him that one of the reasons why I wanted into teaching was that teachers had a five-day working week which meant I could get to away games – which I would not have be able to do in an insurance position. Another foolish decision? Read on.

I used to wonder why I could be shunted up to my cousins' house in Ardmillan Street in Carntyne at week-ends. I came to realise as I grew older that the reason was to get me away as much as possible from the smoke and dirt generated by Beardmore's steel-works adjacent to our Westmuir Street tenement. In fact Beardmore's howitzer shop was just across Shettleston Road from us and was the occasion for a fatal tram accident when, in fog, one of their heavy lorries was reversing unprotected into the howitzer shop and a Coronation tram ran into it. I suspect that the motorman had been looking at his time-board as was usually the case when coasting down that part of Shettleston Road, but that may be doing the unfortunate motorman an injustice. The tram's conductress did not so what she had been told to do in the event of a tram accident, namely to pull down the bow-collector from the over-head and so disconnect the tram from the overhead electricity supply which was around 660 volts d.c. The courageous motorman escaped injury in the collision but re-boarded the car in attempt to rescue passengers but was fatally electrocuted.

On one occasion when I was a youngster my Godfather told me that he had been down at Dumfries trying in vain to persuade the Administrator of the Galloway Diocese Cathedral- St. Andrew's – to take out property insurance. The following week-end I was again at Ardmillan Street and my god-father said that I would not believe what had happened during the week. The Cathedral in Dumfries had burnt down and, of course, he thought that it was un-insured. But was it? The good people of Dumfries were not best pleased that the Bishop's Chair was moved to Good Shepherd, Ayr. I believe that the ex-cathedral towers still stand.

Of course one of the many inadequacies of seminary training was that there was no instruction at all on the reality of dealing with the material problems of life. No doubt that because the instructors themselves were ignorant of Domestic Science etc.

Visits to my aunt and cousins in Carntyne's Ardmillan Street were very pleasant and enjoyable before the war, despite Barlinnie Prison walls looming in the background. You could walk up past a farm and might see a pair of lovely Clydesdales ploughing a field. After enjoying the "tramp! tramp!" enclosed passage at Ruchazie, there would be the blacksmith's shop to look into, and then it was down round Hogganfield Loch to the Robroyston rhubarb fields. I only recently discovered that rhubarb prefers special climate conditions to grow well – as it did in Yorkshire too.. Must have been a special climate around Robroyston as there were acres of flourishing rhubarb there. Here too there was "the quarter-mile" footbridge over the fields to Robroyston station on the main-line out of Buchanan Street Station to Perth and the north. Often there would be an ex-Midland railway heavy 4P 0-6-0 tender engine to watch from the bridge as it shunted the hump in Robroyston goods yard. From Robroyston Station a line zig-zagged up the hillside to Robroyston T B Hospital from where it continued away in the distance to a modern-looking colliery at Barmulloch. Occasionally I saw a wagon of coal being pushed and pulled up the zig-zag to the hospital but I suspect the Barmulloch colliery was closed, as I never saw anything on that part of the mineral line.

A thing that puzzled me at the time was that sometimes I would be sent away up to the green-houses at Craigend to purchase tomatoes. I would wonder why tomatoes were not bought at the local shops but me not to make reply – me just to do or die on the long trek to Craigend Nursery and back. Of course later the penny dropped. I was sent out of the way so that I could not over-hear private family matters being discussed.

Visitors to my cousins' house were interesting too. Their next door-neighbour was a police inspector who was always niggling at me to make the polis my professional career. No chance of that happening of course. Then there was a massive Mr. Henderson who was part of the LMS wreck crew at Polmadie motive power depot. I was always intrigued when Mrs. Kinnear called with her beautiful daughter Olive. Olive's grandfather was the once redoubtable Celtic full-back Gerry Reynolds of Maley and Carfin notoriety. Unfortunately by war-time there was a problem with poor old Gerry. He could not understand about sweety-rationing (like me) and would cause trouble in sweety shops when refused his treats. Mrs. Kinnear had to muster as many sweety-ration coupons as she could manage to obtain from friends and go round local sweet shops depositing them there so that poor old Gerry could get his sweets treats nae bother. Surely enough the world is a peculiar place. I was to encounter Ruchazie, Robroyston, Craigend and the Henderson and Kinnear families under different circumstances many years later.

HOPE TRANSFERRED AGAIN

As well as our clear-out from Gilmorehill, there was a clear-out from Parkhead which seemed to bring success. Our friend Tony Hepburn went – along with such as Hunter, Rollo and Mallan. A long-awaited double came along. The League was won by an astonishing margin of eight points and in a gruelling Scottish Cup final typical brilliant play by Willie Fernie saw Sean Fallon (but of course) score the winner. Pity that as usual we were hopeless in the League Cup. But like our initial professional careers in Education, Celtic success did not continue.

THE BLIND LEADING THE BLIND

I found myself with a group of ex-service men at Jordanhill Teacher Training College. We ex-servicemen found that College a place not best suited to our experiences and taste. I will not name names for obvious reasons. For starters we were put off psychology for life by the psychology lecturer. He obviously was a Freud fan as he came complete with typical Freudian beard and Freudian notions. He treated us like a Primary school class of wee weans and that did not go down too well with us ex-servicemen. Each class would start with a roll-call. Imagine grown men having to say "present" when their name was called. Eventually even the Freudian worshipper came to realise that there were fewer with him as the "presents" had indicated. Someone would always call "present" when an absentee was named. So what did the not-so-bright chap do? Pass round a class roll to be signed. Unbelievable stupidity. Of course Lawrie Reilly, George Young , Charlie Tully et al would apparently have attended his lecture. One of the psychology books we were supposed to have studied was by a Vernon Traill. Needless to say we had a non-existent Vernon Traill sit the end of term paper. And he passed. Much cause of mirth among us.

Then there was the poor lad who tried to interest us in teaching Nature Study. (No! Not that kind! Worse luck!") He would have us ex-servicemen out doing tree-bark rubbing and such activities that would be of immense help in a place like Parkhead or Anderston where there were neither trees nor country-side. One of our bored lads amused the rest of us for the best part of two periods by insisting, that, of all things, gold fish could live without being fed. He might have said that they pass loads of excrement – as mine certainly do.

But our betes noires were the two ladies who were elocutionists. (How did I manage all that radio talk at Kinloss without being able to speak clearly?)

Most of the time was spent by each of us giving a lengthy speech in turn. Three guesses what I spoke about. There was a large muscular lad from Barra and he used to spout lengthy stories about Highland paranormal happenings which left the ladies enthralled and the rest of us splitting our sides.

Of course at this supposedly top-drawer College of Education we were never told anything about autism, dyslexia or child abuse.

But one morning a fit of madness descended on us. The magnificent Jordanhill building had two massive staircases. (Which reminds me that a Christian Brother once told me that his order had ordered built in Singapore a large new secondary college. When all the Asian-type scaffolding surrounding construction was taken down it was discovered that they had forgotten to put in any staircases. We should talk. When our St. Augustine's Secondary was opened it was discovered that no teachers' staff-rooms had been provided.)

For some peculiar reason the elocution ladies made use of a lecture-room on the ground floor and a lecture room on the top floor. Scouts were placed in position and when the duty lecturer made for the ground floor room we belted up the other stair-case to the top one and sat there. Then when she decided to come up to the top we ran down to the bottom room and sat there. And so it went on for most of the period. We were a shower who were brought to earth with a severe bump. The College had arranged for us to spend a day at an approved school which had better be nameless for we thoroughly disapproved of what we saw there. We papists had a Marist Brother who was supposed to see us through a Catholic Exam which we had to pass to be allowed to teach in a Catholic School. We asked him to arrange for our group to visit St. Mary's Approved School in Bishopbriggs. He gave us a day for the visit but when we turned up in Bishopbriggs on that day they knew nothing about our coming although they made us welcome and let us see all that they did for the unfortunates under their care. All our group were much more impressed with St. Mary's than they had been with the previous approved school visited. And that pleased me no end. Next day came the earthquake. The Jordanhill College Director was a very fine person whom I greatly admired. – H.P. Wood. (When we played badminton according to the then rules we would call out "H.P." instead of "wood!". Small things amusing small minds no doubt.) The Director told us that we were all being thrown off the teaching course. He had turned a blind eye to our previous misbehaviours – such as absenting ourselves to attend football matches and so on, but he could not have a whole group not attending for a whole day. Eventually he accepted our explanation about what had happened about the Bishopbriggs visit, but warned us we were on our last chance re our nonsenses. My opinion now rated the Marist Order at Zero, and of course later we were to find teachers in Catholic Schools who had no qualifications of any kind and most certainly did not pass any religious exam. I could name several who even became Head Teachers. So much for those of us who spent our lives and energies in Academia. Eventually H.P. decided that enough was enough and to our great relief we were put out into the world of teaching at Easter instead of having to drag on for another session to the Summer recess. No doubt there was great relief in the illustrious halls of Jordanhill too. But why on earth did I not then go back to the good old GCT and become a qualified motorman? Which I would have loved being. Another of life's stupidities?

AN APPROPRIATE DAY TO START

And as you might expect, I started as a teacher on April the First – more fool me.

SWIMMING TOGETHER

So they sang at Eton. My problem in Glasgow education was just to keep my head above water. How I used to wish that I had stayed on in the RAF where I had been so happy. After the war Glasgow had built half-a-dozen up-to-date schools that were design to be emergency hospitals if that was needed. They were beautiful buildings and even had a small indoor pool! Of course British designers being British designers, it was soon found that the electrical installations in these schools were in fact at least faulty if not down-right dangerous and all the wonderful terrazzo flooring had to be drilled up to be able to get at and replace the offending electrical work. My first appointment was to one of the hospital schools, St. Martha's, Balornock.. But that was too good to be true. When I arrived all apprehensive on the First of April, I was met at the entrance by an old Yoonie friend, Tom Walsh. He explained that the appointed head had a continual medical problem and that an assistant head was actually running the school. Tom was going into the Janitor's House to phone that assistant head with the message that Jack House of the Evening Times was doing a series on the new Glasgow Schools and was coming that day to visit St. Martha's. Tom vanished into the janitor's house and a small boy brought the assistant head to me. When he was at St. Mungo's Academy that assistant head had the habit of seizing something from a pupil and shouting "praeda!". Praeda being a Latin word for booty. So his nick-name among the Academy pupils was Old Praeda. At least that was the censured version.. During the war that teacher was up at Girvan station intending to go back to Glasgow. When the train from Stranraer came down the single line from Pinmore and pulled up in Girvan station, it was packed to the gunnels with servicemen – as long-distance trains usually were during the war. Our hero was frantically running up and down the platform trying to see how he could board the train, when a smart young officer ran up, stood to attention, saluted, and said "Come with me Mr. Praeda, Sir, and I will get you a seat." The officer had been a pupil at St. Mungo's and thought the teacher's surname was Praeda!

The Assistant Head had just started to speak to me when yet another boy ran up and told him he was wanted on the phone. The Assistant Head excused himself and went to take the phone-call. He came back all excited saying that Jack House was on the phone and was coming that day to do a feature on the school. (Jack House did feature articles for The Glasgow Evening Times – such as walking round the city boundaries etc.) Later I discovered that the poor A. H. had had boys out at various bus stops waiting to guide the non-existent Jack House to the school. Note that girls did not feature in those non-equality days. More about more serious non-equality in Glasgow education later. I had been allocated a class and class-room in the original school for the area – St. Bede's on the Red Road – a ten minutes walk away from the new school. (St. Bede was to inhabit my life later too!) Obviously the splendid new building was for those and such as those. Now but one of the several annexes of St. Martha's, St. Bede's was one of the pre-war wooden schools. My situation could have been a lot worse. The staff was welcoming and pleasant, meadow larks sang over the scrubland outside, and I could see much railway activity on the mainline out of Buchanan Street and its junctions, and on the old Caledonian eastern loop-line. (Occasionally an old Jumbo 0-6-0 would struggle to find its footing on the loop-line gradients and I pitied the harassed crews struggling to make progress.) But education as such was not going to be easy-peasy. Bill McLennan and myself were to try to educate 100 pupils between us for the best part of four years.

A few years ago a prominent Labour woman berated the teachers of my time for not doing an adequate job. She did all right for herself, ending up as Governor of a Dominion. But if she was so interested in education (?), where was she when we had the great post-war teacher shortage and over-crowded post-war schools? (And I was six years teaching before I had the weekly wage that I had received as a GCT conductor.) But those children in my first class were great. They were very well- behaved and were all tryers. Sad to say, now I grieve because as I said previously Jordanhill had not informed us at all about child abuse or the various children's' mental problems such as autism and dyslexia that are well studied now.

So what has all this to do with being a Celtic fan you will be asking. Stick with me. I discovered that in that huge school no teacher was looking after the football team. So I dived in and displaced the not-too pleased janitor who had been doing a good job with the team. Eventually we had two teams in different sections of the Primary School leagues and each year both teams would win their sections but only one was allowed to go on and win the Primary School Championship for three years running. Boast! Boast!

We had pitch difficulties of course. I got into trouble with the superintendent of Springburn Park for complaining to him about the terrible ash pitches the boys had to play on. No use telling that block-head that Edinburgh school teams played on smooth grass. I discovered that we could use the pitch in the "poor house" in Petershill Road and that went well until the Boys' Guild discovered that too, came in after us, and did a lot of material damage – so playing there was out. More of that Boys Guild misbehaviour later. We then used St. Roch's Juniors ground in Garngad. (Older trams had Garngad on their destination screens – Coronations and Cunarders had Royston for the same cross-over!) Would you believe that that pitch could have a burn running down across the middle?

HARRY! HARRY!

One sunny lunch time I was standing on the school veranda and started to admire the football skills of a wee fellow who was the only boy in the playground wearing shorts. When the afternoon bell rang I spoke to him and asked him if he would like to play in one of the school teams on the following Saturday. He said he did not want to – so I left it at that. At the end of the year his father gave me a dressing-down for not insisting that he played. I pointed out that it was not in my make – up to make a pupil do something he did not want to do. The pupil's name? Harry Hood! So I was known for a while round Glasgow as the clown who did not play Harry Hood in his school team.

Of the many fine players we had had, I only heard of one who made it professionally. Our centre-half was an excellent player and extremely well-behaved pupil – John Parkes. Later I heard that he had been with Arsenal and had been released by them, so I approached Jimmy McGrory who took him on at Celtic Park. Later I asked Billy McNeil about John's progress at Parkhead and was staggered by the reply. McNeill said that Parkes was far too nice a person to make a good professional footballer.

Then a happening. I believe that one time Glasgow Education Department had spent an awful lot of money opening a Primary school for a planned housing scheme that was never built. Thereafter G. E. D would not open a Primary School until the associated housing development had been completed. Consequently pupils from a being- constructed housing area were bussed to an existing Primary School. (This led to small bus owners becoming quite well-off. Bussing children around Glasgow was so profitable that old double –deckers were coming from all round the place to get the owners' hands rubbing. There were even the aforesaid old double-deckers coming to Glasgow each day even from as far away as Perth.) Our happy existence at St. Bede's Annexe in the Red Road (where the extremely high tower blocks were later positioned) came to an end with the bussing-in of pupils from far-off Garthamloch. Their Head Teacher installed himself in the former H. T. room next to my class-room. Previous to his coming I would answer the telephone in the room next door as the call would usually be for me about football arrangements. Now the message would come and this self-important person would not come next door to me to deliver the message and a pupil (yes – a boy again!) would have to run all the way down from the main building. Eventually I had had enough of the nonsense and decided to teach the H. T. a lesson. But before that on one occasion he came flying red-faced into my classroom and I wondered what I had done wrong this time. But it was not me. That H.T. had gone into one of his teacher's classrooms and asked to see the male teacher's C2 writing books. (The specially-lined C2s were kept for a good-writing practice only.) The boss had inspected one and picked-up a second one and the male teacher asked if he was going to look at all the C2s. The Head said he was. Whereupon the teacher had said then you better take over the class and airted rapidly yont leaving behind a stunned H.T. I could hardly contain my mirth. That ill-mannered, ill-disciplined teacher was teaching in another school next day – such was the then teacher shortage. I was to come across him much later when he would enthral females with his wonderful tales of having been an RAF pilot – when I knew for a fact that he had at best been a Corporal in the Argyle and Sutherland Highlanders. Our own ill-health H.T. (who would stupidly boast that he had once been an active member of the IRA – as if) – had the custom of calling a staff meeting for three o'clock on a Friday – so we would be away up on a bus to the main building before three o'clock and usually the beaming H. T. would be sitting on the bus clutching his brief-case. When all the main building staff and the staff from the various annexes had assembled that H.T. would say "No competent business? Then let us go home." Of course it was a great grievance among the Garthamloch staff that they would be assembling at ten minutes past four waiting for their buses to take them to Garthamloch while we would be home or elsewhere by that time. So come The First of April and that morning I sent a message round the Garthamloch class-rooms that their buses would be coming at three o'clock and on no account was there to be any delay in getting down to the Red Road to meet them. Of course come three o'clock there was an impatient line of pupils and teachers waiting the non-arrival of their buses and that pest of an H. T. was tearing his hair out. He was more respectful to us others after that episode, but many more years in Purgatory for me.

Sadly, years later I heard that he had been walking along Paisley Road West with his wife when a large wheel had detached itself from a passing lorry, had mounted the pavement and caused him serious injuries from which he died. Requiescat in Pace.

Taking fifty energetic pupils for whole day after whole day, week after week and month after month was a mentally tiring business. In those good old days in Catholic Schools we would soldier on from August right through to Christmas with only an occasional Holyday of Obligation day off and even then we had to be back to sort the pupils out in their particular Church at their Children's Mass .Usually when I got back to Westmuir Street I would dive exhausted into the front room and immediately fall fast asleep on the couch. Occasionally my mother's older brother Joe McGranaghan would be in the living room and he clearly resented that I would just greet him and then disappear. I confess that possibly we were both a bit odd. I could not for the life of me understand why he would walk all the way from Shettleston to Paisley and back on a Saturday when we had had that marvellous Airdrie-Paisley tram service passing through Shettleston.

OLD NICK APPEARS

There were odd occurrences at St. Bede's. One Winter's morning we were hard at it, when, without warning, a huge tongue of flame and a grimy figure suddenly appeared in the middle of the class-room. The pupils all shrank in terror. Me too! Me too! A wee girl later said she thought it was the devil appearing. Me too! Me too! But it was only a plumber who had been sent under the school with a blow-lamp to keep the water pipes from freezing.

No doubt that idiot thought it a good joke to play. But what if a child (or me) had had a heart attack?

Then there was the occasion when boys were on each others backs jousting with others in the field behind the school. One crashed to the ground and split his leg wide-open from knee to ankle on a piece of glass.

I wrapped the flapping length of skin into place, bandaged the leg as best I could, and took the boy down to the Royal Infirmary on a number 16 bus. (We never thought about 999 and an ambulance in those unenlightened days.) After about an hour and a half wait, a young doctor came out and asked me to come in and see his handiwork. This I was not keen to do but he insisted saying that he now had the Royal Infirmary record as he had put in 25 stitches. That boy was off for several weeks, Yes! And the first day he as back he was at the jousting again. When I had finished with him he did not do it a third time.

But we had amusing moments too. All bored and tired in our staff-room on a near end-of-Summer-term afternoon, one of the teachers said to me, "Ask your class what a wharf is. Someone will tell you that it is a wee man." Thought it would be a waste of time. But after afternoon prayers I asked the class if anyone knew what a wharf was. Most twigged it was a trick but the smout of the class immediately jumped up and said, "Sir! A wharf is a wee man with a wee hat, a wee jacket, a wee waistcoat, a wee pair of trousers and a wee pair of boots – and a lantern. And he goes out at night." The class were stunned but I said "Mr. McShane would like to know that. Go and tell him!" After the wee fellow went out, the class dissolved in mirth and we listened to wee feet running along the wooden veranda. A door opened and then there were roars of laughter. Back came the lad as proud as punch. I asked, "Did you tell Mr. McShane what a wharf was?" "Yes Sir!" "And what did you tell him?" "I told him that a wharf was a wee man with a wee hat, a wee jacket, a wee waistcoat, a wee pair of boots and he has a lantern and goes out at night." I said, "But you forgot about his wee pair of trousers." "So I did!" he shouted. And before I could stop him he was off running along the wooden veranda again. And again my class dissolved in mirth and again we heard a door opening and then gales of laughter again. Back the lad came as pleased as punch and I left it at that. At the Monday morning interval I said to McShane "I would never have believed that the joke would work." He asked "What joke?" I said about the smout telling you about what a wharf was." He said the smout had not gone to his class. Later I discovered a teacher who was furious with me. He said that he had just managed to settle his class down for the afternoon's work when the door opened and a boy came in and started the rigmarole about what a wharf was and his class was uproarious with laughter. He then complained that he had just settled the class down again when the boy reappeared and shouted that he had forgotten his wee trousers. Again his class had roared with laughter and he had had to try to settle them down for a third time. Wonder how many extra years in Purgatory that episode will get me?

OFF TO RA GEMME!

We teachers had fun too. No-one had a motor car – so getting over to Hampden after school for a late afternoon/evening match was difficult. A load of us had managed to get down to Castle Street, trying to get to the Scottish cup semi-final replay against Airdrie. We were milling about wondering what to try next, when an empty coal-lorry pulled up and the driver shouted that he was going to the match. We climbed on to the empty platform and stood, unprotected, all the way over to King's Park. No Health and Safety in those unenlightened days, and an accident could have cost St. Martha's most of its male staff. Big Hookie's two goals saw us through to the Final. And of course we drew the first Cup Final match against Clyde and then lost the replay. It has to be said that the referee was faultless. That in fact was his surname – Faultless. Clyde were a fine strong outfit then. There was the celebrated postman internationalist Harry Haddock at left back and the great players Anderson, Robertson and Ring among the forwards. I seem to remember we had previously let winger Ring go. I had taken the school hand-bell to one of the games and, ringing it too vigorously, the bell came apart and the round brass resounder flew up in the air and, coming down, hit a supporter on the head. I thought he took it rather well. More Purgatory for me. I also had a noisy wooden rattler in those days.

Meanwhile that original unfit H. T had been dismissed for his too many absences and unfortunately his Assistant Head (Mr. Praeda!) was also dismissed for not reporting the Head Teacher's absences. An example of the problems an unfit H.T. could cause was when some parents told me that they appreciated my football efforts and they were putting on a big concert to raise money for me.

The week of the proposed concert I was asked how many tickets I had sold. I had to say that I had not seen any concert tickets. The organiser said that was strange because he had given all the tickets to my Head Teacher to be sold. Investigation discovered that the tickets were still sitting in the Head Teachers desk – untouched. We teachers ended up having to scrape up money to re-imburse the parents' expenses.

I thought that I would be O K with the new Head because I had played (well at least turned out!) in his football team at St. St. Aloysius' College. But that did not turn out to be the case. Eventually I had the dread HMI crit. As we had had such big classes we had only basically concentrated on English and Arithmetic – which was all we really had time for. I was dismayed when the feared H.M.I. requested the class to say some poetry for him. As usual Our Lady came to my rescue. (I am a great believer in the efficacy of The Memorare.) We had not done any poetry. Inspired, I said to the class please recite "Bring flowers of the rarest". When they had said it beautifully, the poor old H.M.I. beamed and said, "Thank you! That was really lovely. I had not heard that fine poem before!" Phew! Relief all round.

Good job I had thought of the May Day hymn to Our Lady.

THANK THE BERGAMO POPE FOR THE SECOND VATICAN COUNCIL

Another test always tried my patience – which you will have gathered has little depth. Annually we were subjected to a religious examination. This would usually be carried out by a young priest who thought he was the bee's knees etc. I soon twigged that instead of questioning the class on the set religious syllabus and record of work, he would ask questions about anything else. So, of course, I made sure we had covered most things outside the syllabus as well as the syllabus itself.

Then we were subjected to the "confessions" scandal. To this day some priests will not use the correct description "Sacrament of Reconciliation". St. Martha's covered several parishes and we would have to march the unfortunate children all the way uphill to Immaculate Heart of Mary church in Broomfield Road. This was no joke in inclement weather. The church would be packed with hundreds of children and their teachers – trying to find pews with space for the confession queues and there would be priests here there and everywhere. Just a nonsense of course. There is absolutely no reason why they could not have had their Reconciliation sessions in each school. I tried to have that done – but with an absentee head I could get nowhere.

Then when our turn came to be in the main building we tried to give our pupils as much enjoyment as we could of the amenities they had missed by being in an annexe which did not have recreational facilities. One of the know-all assistant priests made an official complaint that we were not teaching the children properly. He had been seriously injured in a car accident and we had been praying regularly for his recovery. Hmmm!

I discovered that the class-room I had been allocated in the main building had no crucifix and that that applied to all the classrooms in St. Martha's school. The story went that since the school served several parishes, the parish priests could not agree about paying for crucifixes. (Later in life I wondered if that had been the real reason for disagreement. There had been the Jansenist heresy in the church. Jansenism proclaimed that Christ only died for the good. Their crucifixes had the arms of Christ not extended horizontally but almost vertically. When the French Revolution occurred the Jansenists, who were centred on the Port

Royal Convent in Paris, fled to Maynooth. Hence the Irish clergy big- stick approach to life. Be good or else! The West of Scotland was infected with this approach brought over by priests the Irish Bishops did not want. I had had my eyes opened at St. Aloysius' College. Before his untimely death Tom Winning was going round his churches ordering Jansenist crucifixes to be replaced. I now wonder if a dispute over Jansenist v Orthodox crucifixes was at the bottom of the non-supply of crucifixes to St. Martha's School?)

I bought an orthodox crucifix for the class-room with my own money.

HOPE GOODNESS WILL BE REWARDED

Every year we would have a week at the Corporation's Residential School at beautiful Aberfoyle. Hope the geniuses who thought the splendid idea to get Glasgow children into the countryside were suitably rewarded in this world? They certainly will be in the next.

Mornings were given (officially!) to lessons – the afternoons meant recreation – usually a long walk exploring the countryside. One of the gang had the super idea of having a friend arrive pretending to be an important high-ranking detective from Scotland Yard. The classes lapped up his tall tales – and we had to arrange fort him to return the following year – by popular demand. But one week things were not so happy. .A boy from a Clydebank Catholic school went missing. We were all out searching the untamed countryside for him – pupils as well as teachers. I was worried in case we lost one of ours too. Eventually it was discovered that the boy had gone to the main road, thumbed a lift, and a thicko lorry-driver had taken him to Glasgow – without bothering to inform anyone. Of course we could not miss going to Loch Katrine and having a ride on that wonderful old steamer "Sir Walter Scott" – still now over one hundred years old and still taking tourists to enjoy the wonderful beauty there with mountains and streams reflected on the waters of the loch. When we returned to the coach and did the usual safety number check we were one short. Jings! A couple of us raced back towards the steamer pier full of apprehension. To our relief we found our missing smout wading in the so-called "magic wishing pool" and stuffing his pockets with as many of the good-luck coins that he could find. Phew! What a relief!

BONNIE MORAY

In my first Summer we had a fortnight's holiday camp at that most pleasant spot Garmouth at the mouth of the Spey. Garmouth was where Charles II landed in June 1650 after swearing to abide by The National Covenant and The Solemn League and Covenant.

In the days of sail, the mouth of the Spey once saw seven shipyards building in all some three hundred ships, including Clippers and Cape Horners, but the coming of iron ships killed that marvellous industry off. We saw no signs around Garmouth that such yards had ever existed. The weather was marvellous and pupils and teachers were treated like royalty. The children kept asking why the local people were being so nice to them – for example taking them into gardens to show them peacocks etc. We teachers were given the freedom of their nine-hole golf course. But did not we have to walk across the magnificent railway bridge over the Spey to try our luck on the Spey Bay Championship course. After our puny efforts, wee were howfing it back to the railway and saw the steam from a train heading north. We ran as fast as we could but only managed to rush on to the platform to find the train had departed. A lady came out of her office and asked us if we had wanted to board the train. We replied that we would just walk back across the bridge. But she dived back into her office, took out a red flag, waved it and blew a mighty blast on her whistle. To our amazement the train halted halfway across the bridge and reversed back into the station where the guard was kind enough to descend and help us up into his van, and back across the bridge the train went. And do you know we did not have train tickets. Could not happen these days on our crazily- organised railways and with all the nanny state Health and Safety palaver. That line is long closed and though the rails have been removed it is possible to repeat our walk across the bridge.

After Mass one Sunday at St. Mary's in Fochaber a lady raced up to me. I expected a complaint about something but instead she complimented me on the marvellous hymn singing by our pupils. She said she was originally from Glasgow and she missed the great singing there as no-one could sing quite as well as Glasgow children. Wow!

One teacher went exploring into the hills. Way out in the countryside he came across the large eighteenth church in Presholm dedicated to St. Gregory. Staggered, he asked a local why on earth there was such a large church there where there were so few inhabitants. The reply also staggered him. There used to be a great many Catholics living there. He asked when that was and was told "Before The Reformation!"

THERE WILL ALWAYS BE HOOLIGANS

And you have guessed it. The wretched Boys' Guild had to do what we did – as usual. They badly damaged the nice little Garmouth school and wrecked the school library. So the local authority naturally never allowed their school to be used as a holiday camp again.

DAS CAPITAL!

Next year we tried Musselbrough. The accommodation and food were good but our boys were not allowed to play football on any of the available grass pitches, much to everyone's disappointment. I did not care much for our pupils seeing the fraudulent mock auctions that were generally taking place on the beach. But at least I managed a ride on one of the ex-Manchester "Pilcher" trams that Edinburgh had brought in. I was very disappointed in it. No wonder Manchester got rid of them. Despite its modern look, internal accommodation was very cramped and crowded – much worse even than our old past-their-sell-by-date Glasgow Standard cars.

Then there was the alarming Arthur's Seat episode. We walked the pupils all the way to the top to enjoy the great view from the 800 foot high basalt volcano plug. I doubt if King Arthur had been there – though we showed the pupils the remains of an ancient fort. A shock awaited when we regained ground level. The usual safety count showed that we were one pupil short. I was afraid he might have fallen over Salisbury Crags. We searched and searched to no avail. And I even wondered about the various ponds. You can imagine our relief when we returned to the school and found him comfortably ensconced within. Phew! Apparently as our crocodile departed he had dived into a sweetie shop and coming out did not know where we had gone – so just went back into the school and waited.

A MODEST GENTLEMAN

The following year the school tried Aberdeen's Torry district. While they were enjoying football on the beach a young man approached and asked if he could join in too. He came most days to take part in the football and when return was being made to Glasgow, he asked if the school would be back the following year. And sure enough he joined in the following years too. His name was Denis Law!

TRANSPORT PROBLEMS

I first travelled up to Balornock by taking the good old 23 tram to High Street – then trolley bus up to Castle Street: then the 16 Robroyston bus to Petershill Road. As well as being expensive, this took about forty minutes if I was lucky with connections. (I did not mind the interesting trolley bus ("whispering death" to Glaswegians) part – as sometimes a single-decker would appear. The then General Manager E.R.L. Fitzpayne had tried these single-deckers as they were much cheaper to operate. However they usually ran pretty empty as Glaswegians never took to the rear entrance – front exit idea – as with the modern experimental tram 1004 – nick-named "The Blue Devil" because of its two-tone blue colour scheme. (When Fitzpayne came as General Manager he did not like the GCT colour schemes and wanted everything to be painted light blue. It was gently pointed out to him that that would not be a good idea in Old Firm city.) The public naturally disliked the few seats and a lot of standing room in the single-deckers, so just waited for the next double-decker. A plus was that the conductor was comfortably seated at the interior rear of the single-decker bus instead of standing on an open platform. The biggest problem (apart from the cost) of doing the Parkhead-Balornock return journey by GCT, was in fact the return journey. There was little bother in getting back to High St./Duke St. but there the 23 tram coming from the city centre would often be full. Sometimes I would have to take a 30 to Parkhead Cross and walk home from there – and even going on down to Glasgow Cross usually meant having to wait for a short-working 15 to reverse on the Trongate cross-over. So when the weather was reasonable, I would cycle along Old Shettleston Road, cut through lower Carntyne and Riddrie and past Provanmill Gas Works. Next the problem would be passing Blackhill safely. This was a notorious housing scheme. Occasionally there might be a couple of policemen standing on each corner – which made it fairly obvious that there had been a prison break-out. A Police Inspector once told me a couple of his Blackhill experiences. He only once had a complaint from one Blackhill resident about another. The complainant was upset about the noise coming through the wall from the adjoining flat. Knowing he was dealing with Blackhill, the Inspector gathered a posse comprising of a sergeant and ten (repeat ten!) constables and went to investigate. He found that the next-door neighbour was a scrap merchant and the noise was occasioned by the scrappy's horse being stabled in his bath-room. British Rail stopped sending freight over the old Caledonian/LMS east of Glasgow loop-line which passed Blackhill. The Blackhill mafia would have a unit in the marshalling yard marking the vans they wanted to raid: then as the slow freight passed Blackhill, rails being greased with butter to slow it, a unit would jump on the marked wagons and cut the locked bolts, then jump off: then the next unit would climb on board and throw off the goods they wanted to plunder: another gang was ready to pick up the booty and scamper rapidly off. A plus passing Blackhill was seeing the remains of the once very busy Monkland Canal boat lift that helped to avoid the long delays caused by using the lengthy Blackhill chain if canal locks.

KEEPING TIME

With all my efforts to be at Balornock in time it was irritating- to say the least – to have a Head Teacher standing at the school gates watch in hand and uttering criticism such as "What is wrong with you young teachers? You are only getting here as late as five minutes to nine!" I thought I had solved matters. (Later poor Bill McShane was rushing up steep Balgrayhill from the Springburn tram to be in time for his class – which had four sets of twins in it - when he took a heart attack and collapsed and died. I think I can say that after that episode I never once complained about any teacher being late.)

Getting a loan from my aunt and cousins I bought a very cheap 1936 Ford Eight for a few pounds. Its spare wheel was mounted outside on the back. It had no heater and had an opening windscreen for air-conditioning with hand operated wipers. When I purchased it, the heap used more oil to the mile than petrol, but eventually I scraped up enough money to put in a re-conditioned engine. But it was not to be the solution.

One of the girls came from Sandyhills and I suggested that she should take "the penny bus" (single-deck service 30 from Carmyle to Riddrie – usually operated by the most modern buses) to Carntyne station where I would pick her up and give here a lift up to Balornock. All went well for a while but the morning came when she was not on the bus. Service 30 ran at twenty minute intervals and I knew that if I waited for the next bus we would both be about ten minutes late for school. But I knew that if I did not wait then she would be over an hour late in getting up to St. Martha's. So I waited for her. Next day the boss came storming in – raging that I had been ten minutes late the previous morning. For once I kept my cool and tried to explain the circumstances to him and that I did not want the Sandyhills girl to be an hour late etc. All I got was the warning to concern myself with myself and not someone else etc. So I told the unfortunate girl that I would not be able to wait for her next time she missed the bus. Sure enough, only three days later she was not on the bus – so off I went to Balornock. Next day the boss was back raging at me that I had caused the Sandyhills teacher to be over an hour late through not waiting for her. Again I tried to be patient and explained that I was only carrying out his previous instructions. But he would not cease the storm. I decided that enough was enough and after school I went straight to the Education Office in Bath Street and explained I needed an appointment to a school nearer home. There was no delay, and immediately I was told to report to the new school in Barlanark for next school year. Appropriate that the school being opened was dedicated to St. Jude – my favourite recipient of prayers for the Celtic. (A frequent occupation for the idle youth of Barlanark was to roll objects down their steep railway embankment in efforts to hit a passenger train ascending the gradient from Shettleston towards Garrowhill Halt. Later I had been making the long journey home to Garrowhill from Mallaig after a sailing holiday, and a large child's pram (fortunately sans l'enfant) came down into the former LNER 2-6-2 tank engine at the head of our local. I had to sit a few minutes from much needed food while the enginemen struggled for over half-an-hour to free the pram from the locomotive's valve-gear.)

When my transfer papers arrived in St. Martha's that H.T. was quite incredulous that I should want to leave a school where I had been doing so well etc. etc. This time I did not keep my cool and replied that I found it impossible to carry out his contradictory instructions. He said that I took life too seriously – which was news to me. I had been told by "Baldy" (Fr. Leo Batley S.J.) several times that I was far too frivolous!

WRONG COMPASS READING FOLLOWED

Then came a surprise that confounded me. The H.T. said that there were three vacancies for teachers at St. Aloysius' College and he had arranged for me to go and see the Jesuit Head about filling one of the vacancies. This I did – and of course was taken to the cleaners by that Jesuit Head who said that there was an urgent need for me to go to the St. Aloysius' College Preparatory School as there was a class there that had been allowed to get out of control and needed sorting out. When I had done that he would have me in place in the Secondary the following year. I fell for the lie. No wonder my mother always berated me saying that that people saw me coming! Full events in the next chapter. I pointed out that I had already agreed to start at St. Jude's and could not just disappear from there and leave them a teacher sort – so I would have to wait until St. Jude's had a replacement for me before I felt I could leave Barlanark.

St. Jude's was only a one SMT bus ride from the stop opposite us in Westmuir Street, so travelling became much easier and I sometimes walked home from Barlanark for the sake of some exercise. It was interesting to be part of the official preparations for a school opening and as when there was an RAF Air Vice- Marshall inspection in the offing, all sorts of decorative additions appeared in the school which would disappear immediately after the opening. Naturally I had to start a football team but we had no equipment, so I organised a raffle which raised so much money that I gave half the proceeds to the Infant Department for their needs.

When I went into Lumley's Emporium to purchase the football strip for St. Jude's School, the pleasant shop assistant who helped me choose a strip was none other than one of my great Celtic heroes – Johnnie Crum!

I felt pleased with life – then into the classroom stormed a red-faced parish priest – – who demanded to know who I thought I was organising a raffle in his parish without his permission. That Parish Priest was a bit of a sad case. I suppose it was no joke opening a parish in a new housing scheme. But he had the habit of prowling round the outskirts of the school peering in windows and sometimes cowering down not to be seen. The Head – liked that boss a lot – had enough of the spying and when Fr. B. did his cowering act under the window of the H.T. office, the window opened and the contents of a tea-pot was poured over the priest. Great hilarity duly ensued.

After a few week's, a replacement arrived for me. I was astonished, surprised and very embarrassed to be given a small presentation before I left and some very complimentary remarks came my way. Amazing.

So it was off to begin a new episode in my life. It was not to be an enjoyable one. But it started in an unexpected way. Celts' form went as usual, much up and down like the proverbial yo-yo. There was a League extension to eighteen clubs. We would be top of the League but finish fifth or thereabouts usually. Normally in the League Cup we would be going strong, beat the other half of the Old Firm and then unexpectedly lose to them. This of course was often down to the erratic nonsense of Kelly interfering in team selections – though one Old Firm defeat that occurred was down to an ankle injury that finished Stein's playing career.

THE HEART OF MIDLOTHIAN

Unusual things tended to happen in games v. the Jambos. There was the marvellous Tully/McPhail goal before a record crowd at Tynecastle – one of the greatest goals ever. Between them their long-distance passing had ripped apart the home defence. And in another game Mike Haughney scored with two penalties and we still managed a defeat. But the weirdest ever was the 1956 Cup

Final. I could not believe it – as Meldrew might have uttered – when the team selection was announced. One of my former altar boys from St. Mark's – Craig- was a complete novice on the right wing, with Haughney –our regular full-back inside him. Incredible and hard to understand. It was always said in Edinburgh that Hearts would never win The Cup as long as the trams ran up and down Gorgie Road. Well! The Gorgie Road tramway was abandoned (shame!) and Hearts won the Cup.

There was some recompense the following season when at last we managed to win the League Cup – but only on a replay after a goal-less draw v. Jags at Hampden.

And we were to repeat the performance in one of the all-time great Celtic victories. I was to start at John Ogilvie Hall – the St. Aloysius' College Preparatory School- on the Monday, so before the 1957 League Cup Final, George Stewart accompanied me to find out where the school was. We discovered it was in Camphill Avenue in Langside and was basically a converted large mansion with a dining hall attached. That part of Langside was known as the Little Vatican – because as well as the Jesuit presence, Marists , Helpers of the Holy Souls and Carmelites were there on adjoining premises.

Later I suggested to the boys that just occasionally instead of punting a ball about for half-an-hour they might consider going to the nine o'clock Mass in the Carmelite Convent. And some did. What happened? The holy Carmelites banned the John Ogilvie boys from attending that Mass. And it is supposed to be Christianity! (More on the latter later!) Much later, "Lakey" (Fr. Lakeland S.J. – the French Master who had, as I said, taught me such phrases as "Sans l'arbitre ils auraient gagne!" "If it had not been for the referee they would have won!") was to tell me that when he was the Garnethill Headmaster he had gone to the Jesuit Provincial and asked for money to buy the whole of Langside Hill. Lakey's plan was to have a circular single-deck college running round the perimeter of the hill and enclosing playing fields. One of the reasons for his plan was that he had been so fed-up with the time being wasted by some-times boozed-up teachers travelling out mid-week to the College Sports ground at Millerston. It would have been a great idea. Later still the Jesuits bought a farm (think it was co-incidentally called Millerston) on the Busby-East Kilbride Road at the edge of Busby with the notion of moving the whole College caboodle out there – which would have got the College premises all together and away from the very unsavoury Garnethill area. But the concern of parents re travelling difficulties to that far flung south side of Glasgow put paid to that plan too.

DIES MIRABILIS

After exploring Langside we walked down to Hampden for the 1957 League Cup Final in confident mood – as ever. But we had reason to be confident. The Billy McPhail/Sammy Wilson partnership was doing well and also up front we also had such great players such as Neilly Mochan (though it has been alleged that Kelly did not play him as often as he should have done as Kelly never really forgave Neil for having been convicted for driving without a proper Driving Licence) and Charlie Tully, while Fernie, Evans and Peacock made for an excellent mid-field line-up. Before the start we had a tremendous resounding rendering of the national anthem from one end. After the result I used to wish it would happen at Old Firm games again – but of course it never did. The details of the 7-1 wonder victory have been recorded many times so no need to repeat them again here. Allegedly their downfall was the playing of new centre-half, Valentine, who had been signed from Queen's Park for £6,000. Q.P. being an amateur club all that money (quite a wealthy return in those days) was pocketed by Valentine personally and, supposedly, he used the cash to purchase a farm in the Perth area – so in that case he would not have been too bothered by the result. I always drink a toast to him on Valentine's Day and all true Celts should do the same in my opinion. It did not help them either when forward Murray had to limp all through the second half. I was dying to see the highlights of our quality-filled side on the BBC Sports programme. I should have known better. At that time BBC Scotland had a real second-rate sports production. Their usual commentator was one Peter Thompson who was not a patch on STV's much admired (and justly so!) Arthur Montford of "stramash" fame. (I had been a great Paisley Pirates ice-hockey fan and used to devour his father's ice-hockey column in the Evening Tines.) Thompson had started as a hanger-on at the Scottish BBC Sports facility which had occupied the old Black Cat cinema site at the corner of Springfield Road and Dechmont Street – a few strides down Springfield Road from

Parkhead Cross. As a boy I was never allowed to go to the Black Cat cinema as it had a reputation for being flea-ridden. Thompson had worked his way up to being the commentator via being the tea-boy and general curmudgeon, to being the Sports presenter. Came the League Cup highlights with Thompson all simpering. I wondered why at the time in view of the score. At half-time came the shock. The unapologetic Thompson explained that they could not show the high-lights of the second half as a camera man had forgotten to take the cover off his camera. So did BBC Scotland only have one camera at the match? Years later the story was propounded that the pictures from Hampden had to be were transmitted to London where they were photographed and the highlights sent back to Glasgow and that it was a London incompetent who had forgotten to take the cover off his camera lens after half-time. Too busy with his cup of tea or perhaps something stronger? And this in 1957. Unbelievable if true. Thompson then gave a verbal summary of the second half including the gushing acclamation of "a glorious goal from the golden head of Billy Simpson". No gushing admiration for all those glorious goals of ours. Letters of complaint about the second-rate BBC Glasgow Sports productions to the Director-General of the BBC of course received the standard "passed on to the persons concerned etc." reply. Pass the buck! Pass the buck! But they must have had a drip effect because eventually one night the Sports studio had been slightly upgraded in the sense that two large TV screens were in situ behind Thompson. He simpered as usual and said – and I kid you not – that we were now going to watch highlights of the match between Tottenham Forest and Nottingham Hotspur – repeat "Tottenham Forest and Nottingham Hotspur" – and he turned to watch the screen on the left behind him and the game came up on the other screen! That seemed to have finished Thompson's BBC career. But then there was some jiggery-pokery (but of course) re the appointment of his successor, but I will not go into that one. After the fabulous seven-one victory we thought that we were in for a few great seasons but as usual that great eleven did not last. For example: my mother was speaking to Billy McPhail and he told her that he was not interested in playing football but wanted to open a restaurant instead. His departure finished the career of Sammy Wilson (who had totalled up 32 goals that season) just as the career of Jackie Gallagher went downhill

when the superb Gerry McAloon left. We ended third in a league
we might well have won and were knocked out of the Cup again by
that fine Clyde team. The next season we were back to usual
mediocrity and as well as Billy McPhail, the wonderful long-striding
Fernie and Bobby Collins had both gone. I often wonder if the
Collins transfer came about because of what happened in a home
match against Clyde. The Shawfield Management and Celtic were
very friendly in those times and towards the end of that season The
Bully Wee were involved in a dangerous relegation battle. Clyde
came to Parkhead and it was obvious that the Celtic side were
taking it easy during the game, obviously being content to draw the
match and not leave Clyde pointless. But somehow or other in the
second half wee Collins managed to accidentally score two goals.
The looks of disgust he got from other Celtic players each time and
at the end of the game said a lot about what had been arranged to
happen.

AD MAJORA NATUS SUM

(I was born for greater things) was the motto imposed on their
pupils by the Jesuits, their own motto being Ad Majorem Dei
Gloriam (for the greater glory of God). Was I born for greater
things? Judge for yourself. My supposed one year at the College
Preparatory School turned into 13 years – despite repeated requests
for the original promise of an appointment in the Secondary
School as I desperately needed the mortgage money etc.

When I first went to Langside I searched the grounds in vain
for a Neolithic Bronze Age standing stone dating from between
2000 and 1400 BC that I mistakenly thought to be there on the hill.
But the two metres high cup-and –ring marked stone had been
removed to the Kelvingrove Art Galleries in 1902. So I was a bit
late in looking for it in the grounds of John Ogilvie Hall.

A fine member of the John Ogilvie Hall staff was the lay-
teacher in charge – Tom Burke. He was very considerate of my
having to take care of my aging mother and tried to arrange my
"free" periods to help me out (when the class was having P.E.,
Music, etc. from their specialist instructors). The normal time-table
started at 09:30 and ended at 15:30 – so the normal day was not
onerous and some days Tom would arrange the specialist periods
so that occasionally I would not need to be at Langside until 10:30

hours and might be able to leave at 15:00 hours or perhaps sometimes even to have a longer lunch break which would allow me time to dash home to see if all was going well there. Like me Tom was a red-hot Tim and we would go down to Hampden together if there was an important match happening there. It was on one of these occasions that we heard for the first time the Glasgow Celtic anthem pinched from Belfast Celtic. (It was the belief then that the Irish Bishops had requested Belfast Celtic to close down in an attempt to reduce sectarian violence in the six counties.)

BREAK FOR FOOTBALL

Sometimes on the way home after school I would look in to Barrrowfield to watch the Celtic third team playing a match. On one occasion it was against the other half of the Old Firm and when I went into Barrowfield I was staggered at the amount of violence taking place on the field. Players were literally kicking lumps out of each other and I wondered at the incompetence of the referee. Poor Charlie Gallagher was caught up in the middle of an ongoing melee and put his hands out to prevent serious injury and that clown of a ref ordered gentle Charlie off. Or was he just a clown? (In an evening game at Parkhead – not long after substitutes were introduced, Stein decided to replace Gallagher near the end of the match. Poor Charlie was trudging despondently towards the pavilion and somebody in the stand wondered why Gallagher was being substituted. One supporter, John McCabe, another teacher at John Ogilvie Hall, loudly replied that Charlie had to go to his Children of Mary meeting. The stand dissolved in laughter but poor Gallagher obviously heard the comment and, red-faced, hung down his head after looking up at the stand.)

MORE TROUBLE AND STRIFE FOR ME

If Tom Burke was a great person to work for, the then Jesuit Head Teacher was another kettle of fish. I had believed that the Jesuit system to be a very sensible one – no member of the Society to hold a position of authority for more than three years. After that he moved on to a different position. But time after time our Dennistoun hero went to his superiors and sought and was granted re-appointment as Head of the College for yet another three years. Poor gentle Fr. Manning S.J. hung about for some years waiting to succeed as Head Teacher but of course that never happened. (Manning's family were great beneficiaries for the church, One example was the giving gratis of the land for the church in Kinross.) The Jesuit Head was the type of boss we all have had to put up with at some time or another – domineering and quite unable to accept any judgement other than his own. He first infuriated me by an act of sheer bloody vandalism. Outside my class-room window stood a marvellous auracaria (Chilean Pine). Myself and the class delighted in watching tree-creepers going about their business as they amazingly worked their acrobatic ascents and descents up down its trunk. One year, on returning after the Summer holidays the auracaria had been cut down – without any consultation with us simply because one of the old biddies had wanted that done. And of course the Jesuit Head should have been prosecuted as the vandalism had occurred in a preservation area. Then one day he amazed me by handing me a book of coloured paints and said that I could have the class-room re-painted in whatever colours I wanted. I should have known better. I picked a colourful scheme to replace the original dreich greys I had inherited and looked forward to a brighter future after the holidays. Of course when I returned to start next session the room had been re-painted in the original dreich greys. When, extremely disappointed, I challenged the Jesuit Head about the failed promise, he just shrugged and said he did not like the colours I had chosen and walked away. There were several playgrounds at John Ogilvie Hall – all open to the elements and without any form of shelter. Tom Burke had tried and tried to have some shelters provided for the boys – as the weather could become very wild on top of Langside hill. The Jesuit Head kept saying he had plans in hand. But for ages nothing happened. And then something certainly did. But never a shelter appeared for the boys. Tracy decided to have a new and very modern square block erected. On the ground floor was a much-needed chapel that could – as far as size went – comfortably accommodate the school. On the upper floor there was a class-room and an art room – with a stock cupboard between them. Sounds good, does it not? But it was not at all excellent. The Jesuit Head Teacher had gone to the same wonderful architect who bankrupted the Glasgow Archdiocese with his over-expensive but unusable Cardross seminary. First of all there was a long delay as the builders had to wait for some expensive bricks Coia had ordered from London but which were in short supply. Of course within a few weeks of these wonderful bricks being in situ they started to drop their facings and this wonderful modern block became an eye-sore. The Jesuit Head had been advised several times not to install the then fad of having heating elements within the floor planks. But of course he knew better. Soon some parts of the floor heating did not work and in any case the chapel was still too expensive to heat and the Jesuit Head repeatedly turned down the rheostats whenever he visited Langside. Another fad of the time was for buildings to have flat roofs and the building continually leaked. Every time workmen had to gain access to the roof, they could only reach the roof hatch by climbing on the stock-room shelves. Consequently the shelves were continually being broken with expensive replacements needed. On one occasion I was there when the Jesuit Head was complaining to Coia about the fact that the drains installed on the roof were too highly placed to allow water to run off the roof. The Jesuit Head actually seemed to fall for Coia's explanation (very lame in my opinion!) that they were placed "high" so that there would always be a pool of water lying on the roof which would act as "insulation". Unbelievable. The teacher in the new class-room asked a boy to open a window as the room was becoming too hot. As the pupil opened the window the window hinges gave way and the teacher had to rush over and pull back the boy who was dangling out of the window. So thereafter the windows in that room could not be safely opened. Then a key broke in a lock and a replacement could only be obtained from Hong Kong! And I am not making all this up. And poor Tom Burke never got his playground shelters.

I tried to help the shelter problem by setting up a games room in the disused attic for use at lunch time – when he could be there. . As well as the usual board games, with pupils always checkmating me at Chess, we eventually had a moderately-sized Scalectric track which was thoroughly enjoyed by everybody – including me! Of course that Jesuit Head did his expected rant when he discovered this. "Who gave you permission to use the attic, etc.?" But I was well used to his narcissus personality by that time.

Then there was the great storm. I think it was about 1963. Many trees in the grounds were down. A woodman came in and asked for permission to look at the damage and then came back and offered to pay £3,000 to remove the wreckage, admitting that there was one very rare tree he would like to have. Of course the know-all Jesuit refused that excellent offer but instead paid a firm £3.000 to take the timber away. And £3.000 was a lot of money in those days.

The biddies were always narking at me to take on something extra – as if I did not have enough on my hands trying to look after the aging parent. I admired the Apostleship of the Sea and other charities but mistakenly thought that the best thing I could do to stop the continual pestering was to try Rugby. Wally Dishes was no longer a proper soccer school as it had been in my time. In the early fifties St. Aloysius' College had played Clydebank in a Scottish Schools' Cup tie at Clydebank and our fellows had been subjected to being pelted with rivets and also suffered serious foul abuse. Rightly the Jesuits said to the Schools Association that they had an obligation to look after the welfare of their boys and they requested that The College be in a different section of the league from Clydebank the following season. Of course that reasonable request was ignored and so the College went over to Rugby despite many protests about that decision. Parents were concerned about the well-known after-match misbehaviour among certain Rugby players. There had been an element on the College staff pushing for Rugby as the school game anyway and that nonsense from The Schools Football crowd played right into their hands. The pro-rugby lot were led by one Forester whose favourite trick was to dangle a class miscreant out of an open window by the heels and ask the class should he let the boy drop. And this from at least a story high. Later when the Jesuits had dragged the extremely frail Cardinal Grey through to Garnethill for an ordination, Forrester thought it smart to introduce himself to the aged tottering old man – who had to be supported by two other clergy – with the comment "Sure I went to the same school as you, your Eminence. For a game of Rugby, your Eminence." (The Cardinal had gone to Fettes College – like Tony Blair. Obviously modern history was not a strong point at Fettes. Three times we had to pull out of Mesopotamia but Blair went in for a fourth time.) Thanks to great help from the marvellous Gerry McDonald – the top P.E. man at

Garnethill and Fr, Granger-Banyard S. J. – who had responsibility for games etc. – John Ogilvie Hall soon was pretty proficient at Rugby. When necessary we could put out three fifteens. At one time we had fixtures home and away with Belmont House at Newton Mearns, and Scotus Academy in Edinburgh. But Belmont House came to feel it was undignified for their older boys always to be beaten by our youngsters and pulled out of the fixture. Unfortunately Scotus Academy was a failure in Edinburgh and it closed down. But we had excellent relations with Leith Academy, Glasgow High School and our good friends at Hutcheson Grammar. (More about Hutchie later.) Glasgow Academy was a different kettle of fish! We exchanged post-match hospitality with the other schools and of course we gave post-match hospitality to the Academy but that hospitality was never returned. They always had some petty excuse not to do that. Then there was the great afternoon when all three of our teams defeated all three of the Academy teams at Millerston. (We heard afterwards on the grapevine that their Arts Teacher who was responsible for their teams received a severe dressing-down for allowing the College to whack them.)

I was as pleased as can be, but when I was having my tea the phone rang. Without any polite introduction (toujours la politesse not being in the Jesuit Head's vocabulary) I was straight away assailed by the charge "With your customary lack of consideration for those under your charge you shot off from Millerston and the boys were left to their own devices." In vain I pointed out that I had in fact seen off all the rugby players and that in any case Joe Kenny (one of the J.O.H. staff who greatly assisted me with Rugby matters) and Fr. Granger-Banyard were still in the pavilion awaiting the arrival of the Old Aloysian rugby players who were expected for their training session.

Never ever received the slightest apology for any of several of that Jesuit Head's vicious comments about me.

Should have insisted on him putting them in writing and then taken him to court – of course. But financially I was still desperate to get a post at Hill Street as had originally been promised.

Eventually the story came out. One bright specimen had gone into the Police Office – which was directly across Cumbernauld Road from the College playing fields – and said the teacher had gone away and left him and he was totally lost. All the Police had to do was to cross the road to the pavilion with him to check his tale. Instead two Police Officers put him in a police car and drove him across Glasgow to his Newlands mansion. Too bad that there was a direct bus service from Millerston to Newlands! And they say our Policemen are wonderful. When they got to the door of the house it was opened by an au paire who promptly collapsed with the shock of seeing the sibling with two Policemen. She had to be rushed to hospital. All my fault of course. I should never have taken on Rugby. That was far from the only time a fabrication was made about me and believed by that Jesuit Head.

Although there was the time when I justly landed in big trouble over the Rugby. We were playing Glasgow Academy at Anniesland and rather than have our hired bus take every player back to Langside before starting off for home from there, I asked the players if they were all sure how to get home directly from Anniesland. And of course they so all assured me. Should have known better than believe all of them. One bright specimen found himself marooned in Cambuslang and did not know how to get to his home town of Coatbridge from there. And at eight p.m. his frantic parents had to get to Cambuslang to rescue him. Too bad there was that excellent Blue Train service directly from Anniesland to Coatbridge and he could have been straight home in well under an hour. Yet at Balornock I could say to intelligent pupil Andrew Lynch to have the football teams to anywhere in Glasgow on a Saturday and he would have them there and back nae bother. And at John Ogilvie Hall we were supposed to have la creme de la crème! Some of them more like ra soor-mulk kids!

Eventually the long suffering Tom Burke took a coronary standing right beside me. I had often wondered why he had put up with Tracy on his back for such a long time. To my astonishment I was put in temporary charge of John Ogilvie Hall apparently because I was the longest serving male teacher. I then had many an up and downer with the Jesuit Head but I could not have cared less as I knew I would not get that appointment full-time anyway and in any case there was no way I would have wanted to be permanently subservient to that narcissus and his whims.

DID IGNATIUS REALLY INTEND THIS?

We were several times at the bed-side of the dying Warden of John Ogilvie Hall – "Baldy", Fr. Leo Batley S. J. He was rather a strange person for this boy from the East end of Glasgow to deal with. As I intimated previously, when he was at Garnethill he had the habit of sidling up to you and whispering questions such as "How are your dirty books coming along?" Of course in those innocent days I did not have a notion about what he was up to.

In his death throw the poor man would be continually shouting about some youth drowning in a river and what he should have done about it. Very sad to listen to. At Garnethill he used to set week-end essays with such titles as "It" or "Then" or such puzzlementa. I would sweat over trying to do a page or two on these abstractions and find out on the Monday that Donnie Renfrew (later to become an auxiliary Bishop in the Glasgow Archdiocese) would have completed twenty or more pages – which Baldy would call rubbish and just rip them up. I once asked Baldy why, try as I might, I always only received a C+ each time. He replied that he never ever bothered to read my efforts. So much for Jesuit mis-education.

His replacement as Langside warden was more interested in trying to decipher Runic/Pictish inscriptions than anything else. After his first celebration of Mass for us he complained that he did not want the pupils singing all these modern hymns at his Mass but wanted them to do plain chant. So I spent a year teaching the school plain chant and eventually they could sing the whole Mass beautifully. But! You have guessed it. Back came the Jesuit Head to celebrate a Mass for us and afterwards ranted red-faced as usual and said he never wanted to hear that rubbish again at his Mass. See Jesuits… Guess who never took singing practice for the school again.

SAD SAD SAD

Yet, as I previously indicated, my favourite cousin had joined the Society and as a scholastic was at Mount St. Mary's College, near Sheffield. For some reason, which the family could never discover, (Jesuit secrecy no doubt) he and his class were involved in a Ministry of Food experiment to see the least amount of calories a person could live on. Seems strange the Jesuits would allow that to happen? Michael McCartney developed Bright's Disease as a result. When I was at RAF Yatesbury I would hitch-hike across to Heythrop College near Chipping Norton to be with my dying cousin.

On one occasion I was being driven in a smashing sports car and we were running alongside a very tall estate wall which went on for a considerable distance. The kind driver who had given me a lift saw my amazement at the size of the wall and explained that the estate belonged to Sir Stafford Cripps – the Stalin admirer – who, after the war, had wee weans and the rest of us on rations "because it was good for us", while he enjoyed the products and luxury of his large estate. Another lift saw me on a country road and approaching a tight bend. As I followed it round I realised that the road was crossing a railway over-bridge. I looked over the bridge parapet and to my astonishment there was a station with the name-boards "Adlestrop"!

I have always loved Edward Thompson's great poem. And, believe it or not, as he described on his unexpected train stop, all the birds of Oxfordshire and Gloucestershire WERE singing around me. Wow! And Wow! Again.

Michael McCartney had not completed the number of years required as a scholastic before a Jesuit could become a priest. The week of his death permission came from Roma to have him ordained but he was far too weak by that time.

But it was not all doom and gloom at Langside. Life had its uplifting occasions

CHA-CHA-CHA GLASGOW CELTIC!

We had merry Cha-Cha-Cha celebrations for every great Bhoys victory. (Cha-Cha-Cha consisting of Champagne, Chablis and Chartreuse. No wonder they were such merry occasions.) Life at Langside had other uplifting moments too. And away from school our family gatherings would resound to many Celtic choruses. The one we really roared out cum gusto was:

"Putting on the agony
Turning on the style
Watching the old Celtic

Winning by a mile.
We really had to chuckle
We really had to smile
At the Glasgow Celtic turning on the style.

Big Billy is the Captain
Wee Jimmy on the wing:
Murdoch, Chalmers, Auld
Make we fans all sing:

Simpson, Craig and Gemmell
Defensive wall so stout.
Glorious Lisbon Lions
Greatest without doubt.

Putting on the agony etc. etc."

Sadly our chorus leader died. He had picked up a piece of shrapnel on a D-Day beach and eventually it moved inside his body and killed him. A great guy and friend and a great Celt. Requiescat in pace.

Good old Lakey had come back to Glasgow after a stint of being the H T of an important English Jesuit College St. Ignatius, Enfield. His previous spell as "Wally Dishes" HT must have been met with approval by his Jesuit superiors.

Now he was living in a mansion The Society had purchased at Temple, by Anniesland. He tried in vain to discover if the name "Temple" had had associations with The Order of Knights Templar.

Of course Father Thomas Lakeland S, J – alias "Lakey" – had to be invited to John Ogilvie Hall to preside at the Langside "end of year" prize-giving. First prize to be given out was the Primary Four award for Religious Knowledge. I saw the old well-known customary gleam of devilment come into Lakey's eyes. He asked our pupil what his surname was – knowing it full well. "Church, Father", said the earnest wee boy. "Are you related to the One, Holy, Roman, Catholic and Apostolic Church?" asked Lakey, with an amused grin at the assembled group of teachers. "No Father!" came the expected reply. Asks Lakey, "Have you heard of The One, Holy, Roman, Catholic and Apostolic Church?" "No Father!"

replied the bemused winner of the Religious Knowledge Prize. The ladies had furious looks on their faces while we males could hardly stifle our laughter. Oh! Dear!

DEUTCHSLAND UBER ALLE!

In my first class at John Ogilvie Preparatory School there was a German boy Grotz, who on his arrival with us knew no English at all. Yet by the end of his first year he far outshone the rest of the class.

ITALIA GRANDE!

Another two boys were Italians – surnamed Bezoari. Their father was the Italian vive-consul in Glasgow. Signor Bezoari liked Glasgow and the College so much that at the end of this normal tenure he would be off back to Italy bearing largess to have his Glasgow stay renewed. That decent man always saw that if there was an Italian team playing in Glasgow I had a complimentary stand ticket from him. There was the occasion when Roma scored at Ibrox and only one man stood up in the Ibrox main stand and applauded the goal. That hero (coward me remained seated) was the late Jimmy Farrell (R.I.P.) a director of Celtic.

REJOICE AND BE GLAD! ALLELUIA!

Mr. Farrell was also on the College Board of Governors. He must have been really fed-up with me because every time we met I would be moaning at him about the hopeless Kelly regime at Parkhead. I had gone up to Garnethill to pick up some stock wanted at Langside and happened to encounter him in the College building. He once told me that when he was with Celtic in Moscow, with Chairman Kelly and others of the Celid Board, they had circumnavigated Red Square dropping Holy Water from bottles under their coats. The watching KGB (or whoever) could not work out what they were up to. Before I could get into my usual moan, he silenced me by saying that I would not have to moan at him any more because Bertie Auld and Jock Stein were coming back to Parkhead. (Bertie had been transferred away by Kelly because on one occasion Auld had missed the team bus for an Edinburgh game and although he had beaten that bus to Edinburgh with his car, the eccentric Robert Kelly was not best pleased.) I went into the first bookie's I came to going back to Langside and put a fiver on Celts winning the Cup. The odds were 9-1 against so I sure cleaned up when they did take the Cup through beating Dunfermline in the Final thanks to the two Auld goals and McNeill's great header. With John McCabe we also had a good cricket team on the go and could hold our own with the minor sides of some of the local Western Union clubs. There was a cricket professional living in an adjoining street but of course the Jesuit Head would not allow us to have him in to coach our promising lads. But then, without any courtesy to us we discovered that a member of the secondary staff had taken over our fixtures and that was that.

SHORT RESPITE

There was a year when the Jesuit Head was an absentee – d.g. – and "Wee Bella" – Fr. Greenwood S.J – took over the running of the school. He was much more reasonable and open to suggestions and we could do things that we could never do under that previous Jesuit Head Teacher – such as coming second over-all in the Glasgow School Sports at Scotstoun. Of course the returnee Jesuit Head was enraged about that on his return. I remember "Wee Bella" being terribly upset at the demise of his favourite football team Accrington Stanley – a demise which afterwards was shown need not have happened – though Stanley have now been resurrected and are doing well.

VIVE LA BELLE FRANCE!

For a number of years Fr. Greenwood organised a College three weeks stay in La Belle France. The French had the "Comitie d'Acceuil"- which was an organisation which arranged the use of schools for holiday purposes. This was to help defray the cost of keeping the school support staff employed during the school holidays.

Fr. Greenwood used that excellent idea to give staff and pupils a taste of continental life. After three days in Paris we would go down to Grenoble. Fr. Greenwood chose Grenoble because to go further south the climate would be too hot and north of Grenoble we would not be able to enjoy a Mediterranean- style situation. During our three days in Paris we would visit the usual famous sites – though I personally would ride around the city standing like so many Parisians on the open back platforms of the autobuses and try to look into as many railway stations as I could manage. (I was a great devourer of the S.N.C.F. magazine "Le Chemin de Fer".) But for the boys the first Parisian target was, of course, the Tour d' Eiffel and there would be a competition to see which boy would win the race up the stairways to the top. We old men would wait for the lifts, of course, and usually the boys would be at the top long before us. We twice disgraced ourselves at the Pantheon – the memorial to French anti-Catholic heroes of the Enlightenment. Once we had a good football match going there and on another occasion one of the guides insisted on taking our party down into the catacomb: this despite Fr. Greenwood's protests. He had a good idea what would happen. The proud guide stuck out his chest and proclaimed "Ici repose Jean-Jaques Rousseau, l'homme de la nature et de la verite!" and was greeted by a very loud raspberry from the boys We were hurriedly ushered out. One night our bus was stuck in a traffic jam and we were belatedly crawling through Montmartre and the boys loudly cheered every lady-of-the-night we passed. Poor Bella was sure red-faced. On one visit during a time of civil unrest over de Gaulle's policy of decolonisation in North Africa there was an artillery piece mounted on top of the Arc de Triomph. Our boys could not wear their caps or blazers around there because the College eagle was regarded as "Germanic" (well it WAS Austrian) and war-time memories were still strong.

HAUTE-SAVOIE

Grenoble is a lovely city surrounded by high mountains and so is nick-named the Capital of the Alps. The capital of the Isere Department is dominated by the Bastille crag which was fortified in the past as a defensive position. Its summit can be reached by a busy cable-car system and so it is easy to obtain a wonderful aerial view of the city of about 150,000 inhabitants. For the first years we stayed in an enormous modern boarding-school Lycee des Aux Claires (so called because it is situated between the River Isere and the River Drac). It had two full-sized hockey pitches on the roof and then two full-sized indoor hockey pitches on the top floor. There were two staff rooms each having accommodation for one hundred teachers. (When St. Augustine's Secondary was opened in Glasgow it was realised, somewhat belatedly, that no staff-rooms had been provided in that "modern!" school. See architects...)

When Lycee des Aux Claire was built in de Gaulle's time it was regarded as a white elephant but eventually was packed out with boarders from the surrounding country-side. The Head Teacher told us that being a Catholic in the French Education Service was difficult and that in order to become a Head Teacher she had to attend Mass etc. some place where she was not recognised. There was an up-to-date Olympic swimming pool in Grenoble. We made good use of that. But exploring one of the more disreputable parts of the city we found The Celtic Bar. I kid you not. However that establishment was as seedy as the area and had some tough looking customers so we never ever made a return visit. While talking to a shop-keeper he was ecstatic about Scots and also the RAF. He said that during the war a whole squadron of American Flying Fortresses had tried to bomb a near-by river bridge but had only succeeded in wiping out a village two miles away. Next day a single Lancaster had flown low up the river, dropped one bomb and destroyed that target.

Above Grenoble lies the Vercors plateau. It was a centre of Resistance to the Nazis and the Germans had mounted howitzers in the valley below and shelled all the villages on the plateau. When Fr. Greenwood took us on a bus tour through the Vercors, in each village we would see a large blue plaque proclaiming how many of its inhabitants had been slaughtered by "le Salle Boche". But Fr. Greenwood's bus tours could go to happier places. Especially popular were runs through the mountains to Die and the Dieois region and over the Col du Lautauret and the Col du Galibier. Captain Scott trained at the latter pass for his ill-fated and ill-prepared attempt to reach the South Pole. At one bend in the path Jimmy Gordon (then the College Greek teacher and later boss of Radio Clyde and Scottish Tourist Board) would lay out a large "7-1" in case any supporter of the other half of The Old Firm might also come panting up the path and be suitably dismayed. One afternoon we were playing the boys at football in the large school playground and Jimmy tripped and broke an arm. The Head

Teacher's young daughter took us along to a doctor's surgery in a large block on the main street. Jimmy and the girl went up in a lift to the surgery while we waited anxiously for a long time for their return.

At long last the lift came back down and when the doors opened there was Mr. Gordon with one arm in a sling and the other holding up the young girl who had apparently fainted. Jimmy took a long while to live that escapade down.

We liked to go on a long day's trip to Annecy in the Haute-Savoie. Annecy was once a centre for Calvinism which moved there from Geneva but later the Bishop there was Saint Francis of Sales. It was a great experience to climb up to the high Basilica of the Visitation and pray at the tombs of Francis of Sales and his correspondence friend St. Jeanne de Chantal and then have a superb panoramic view of Annecy and its magnificent lake.

BEST LIQUEURS BY FAR

We also looked forward each year to a journey up to the Grand Chartreuse to see the mother house of St. Bruno's Order of Carthusian monks. Grand Chartreuse is in a most desolate position over 4,000 feet up in the mountains. Usually the Grenoble bus company provided a "mountain" bus which had counter-pressure brakes and was driven by a trained mountain-experienced driver. One year that bus and experienced driver was not available but in order not to disappoint les Ecossais, an ordinary coach was provided. Descending the severe gradients from Grand Chartreuse the over-worked brakes, and consequently the coach, caught fire. We had a long wait until rescue climbed up to us and we were disappointed at not being able to make the usual visit to Voiron where the different blends of Chartreuse are produced and consequently we missed the usual free sampling of the liqueurs.

TROP BEAUCOUP DE SIRENS

Then one year Lyce des Aux Claires was not available and we were placed in an old school – Henri-Quatre. It was a dismal building long overdue for demolition and was right in the centre of Grenoble. But the food was tremendous. For the first five meals we had the potatoes cooked in five different ways. I thought I was in paradise. But then the usual food-ignorant took over and the boys asked the cooks to provide frites for each meal. I do not mind chips but not at every meal please. But that school's position in the centre of Grenoble finished Fr. Greenwood's excursions to La Belle France. Night after night the sounds of Police sirens screaming filled the air and was too much for Fr. Greenwood's nerves. Additionally, on the over-night stop in Paris on the way home, one of the pupils was brought in by the Gendarmerie for some minor offence or other.

TORBAY SUMMERS

Next Summer he had found a boarding-house in Paignton and for several years we had some of the junior Collegians there for a few weeks. Paington was over-crowded with cars, but it was pleasant to go along to breath-taking Goodrington Sands instead. One lunch-time we were returning back to the boarding-house and saw the double-deck service bus coming behind so we raced to the stop ahead. When we had all boarded the bus, the diver left his cab and came round. The boys were alarmed and sat in unusual silence because in Glasgow if a driver did that it usually meant trouble ahead. But the Devonian was as pleasant as could be and smiled and said that we were in Devon to enjoy ourselves and there was no need to run to a stop to board a bus. All we had to do was signal we wanted to board the bus and he would pull up and stop where we happened to be. The pupils were stunned at that courtesy and could hardly believe it.

Of course we always had tours of Dartmoor and did the circle – bus to Taunton and Totnes – then boat trip down to Kingswear – and steam train back to Paignton. To-day the smashing Paignton – Kingswear line is a superb preserved steam operation. Not to be missed if you are in Devon. Brixham, Buckfast, historic Kent's Cavern and Babbington Caves were also visited and on one occasion Tom Burke himself was on holiday at the magnificent Queen's Hotel over-looking the harbour in Torquay. Do not think he really appreciated our calling. One year we "inspected" Ark Royal at Devonport.

EUROPE CALLS AGAIN

But I had itchy feet and ran trips to Loyola to see the home of St. Ignatius and to Mantua to visit the home of St. Aloysius. On the way to Loyola, we saw the small lonely chapel standing in a field – only some kilometres south of Paris – and it marks the northern limit of the Saracen invasion of France from Spain. – an invasion which only terminated there because of illness and our cold climate – much as the first siege of Vienna had ended.. In Spain we stayed at Fuentarrabia just over the border from France. Our driver knew that diesel was cheaper in Spain than in France and so he would not fill up in France. We ran out of juice between the two Customs posts and the Custom Officials from both countries were in knots at the sight of all the boys and teachers pushing the bus into Spain.

I enjoyed the coastal narrow-gauge line from Bilbao to the frontier. It has recently been modernised. I truanted to Lourdes and, while impressed by the scenery, was not at all impressed by the commercialisation of what is supposedly a holy place. Nor did the church at Loyola impress. Huge blocks of solid silver acting as altars. Ugh! At Fuentarrabia a glass of wine was only three and a half pesetas and we thought that a bargain until we journeyed in-land. There a glass of wine was only one and a half pesetas. So visitors at Fuentarrabia were being ripped off- just as Girvanites used to do to the crowds that came down from Glasgow. The long journey down through France to Spain was pretty tedious and uneventful but on the return journey we arrived at night to a hotel on the banks of the Loire river. There were some steps leading down into the river and did not one boy race right down the steps into the Loire and a courageous adult had to dive into the river to rescue him. A narrow escape.

And the journey to Mantua was full of incidents. I always issued a letter to parents of those coming on the holidays advising that sums of money for the pupils' enjoyment must be given to adults and not to the boys themselves. A stupid grandmother had handed her grandson £50 in cash just as we set off and at a rest stop in the north of England the clot of a grandson boy had sat on a wall and counted the money and then became confused and left the £50 on the wall. I thought we would have had time to go back to recover the money (a large sum for those days) but that proved not to be the case. We did not find the money and in the narrow roads down to East Anglia it became obvious that we were not going to be in Felixstowe in time for our booked ferry to Zeebrugge. I dropped one of the drivers off in Colchester with instructions to phone Felixtowe and ask them to hold the ferry for us. I knew the ferry company would do that if asked. But thicko driver spent his time phoning round Glasgow to try to find someone in Glasgow to phone Felixtowe. We arrived at the ferry port just in time to see the ferry pulling out. So eventually we arrived at our hotel in Beule – outside Bonn hours and hours late – but the wonderful people there were all in splendid uniforms waiting for us with a marvellous meal. And what happened? As might be expected, the Glasgow ignoramuses turned their noses up at the fine repast and only wanted chips as usual. A few rude words were quietly said in their ear-holes and that decent hotel staff were not insulted. I could have stayed in that hotel for ever instead of moving on as planned, because the hotel was right next the turning circle and depot of a tram line from Bonn. Bonn then being the West German capital. Our next over-night was at another superb hotel on the shores of Lake Lucerne. On the way to that hotel we visited the comprehensive Lucerne Railway Museum (do not miss it if in Switzerland) and enjoyed the rack railway from Vitznau to the top of the Rigi mountain. The panorama from the top of the mountain was more than impressive. It was breath-taking. Then it was on to see the William Tell statue at his native Altdorf and over the St. Gotthard Pass to Italy and our Milano stop. There were no Swiss road tunnels down the St. Gotthard then. We could see our hotel in Milano but it was surrounded by a one-way system but our driver could not find the correct way to it off the circular perimeter road and eventually gave up and drove the wrong way down a one way street to it. The over-night stop was adjacent to the marvellous cathedral, opera arcade, and vast railway station. Great places to inspect. Of course, still proud of my tramway father, I stood in awe at the procession of Peter de Witte trams following one another on the nearby streets – as our beloved Glasgow trams used to do. I knew that a modern underground line had just opened so I went down to the near-by station to have a ride. And lo! And behold! There was one of our boys sitting in the carriage I had entered. I thought him to be quite an enterprising chap who should do well in life. Of course I told his editor father about the episode when we returned to Glasgow but he was quite unconcerned – although things could have turned out to be serious. The summer was very hot and several times Police stopped our coach on the journey from Milano to Rimini because we were running with the passenger door open. So it was a great relief to reach Rimini and the coast. But on the outskirts of Rimini we were stopped again by a Police motor-cyclist. But this time he was there to guide us through the crowded streets to the hotel that awaited us. Rimini was an enjoyable happy place but the same could not be said of Mantua. I found it depressing – if not down-right oppressive. Unlike my experience with most Italians (who generally loved Scottish people) those we met in Mantua were not at all welcoming and treated us with great suspicion. We even had trouble trying to gain access to the Gonzaga church and even postcards were brought from under the counter with great reluctance. I was glad to be away from Mantua. I suggested to the bus company foreman who was our coach driver that we could returns from Italia via the Simplon Pass instead of going back over the St. Gotthard Pass. He was agreeable. The ride over the 5.000 foot Simplon was nothing as intriguing and complicated as the St. Gotthard had been but the panorama gave us the most marvellous views. We descended to Realp. Straight ahead was a vast precipice with a road zig-zagging up it. I was relieved that we would not have to tackle that dangerous climb. But of course we had to. This was the notorious 8,000 foot Furka Pass. On the outer extremities of each hair-pin bend the front of the coach would be overhanging the edge of the precipice. Phew! Some years later, the owner of the bus company purchased a new Jaguar, and he and his wife did the grand tour of Europe. On his return he said to his bus foreman that he had been over the most terrifying climb he had ever experienced. It was the Furka Pass. His employee laughed and said the he had been over it years before with Bill Tollan. What the owner said about me can not be put in print. Over the Furka we alighted and walked into the tunnel that had been driven into the vast Rhone Glacier. After another delightful evening at the Hotel Sternau by the Lake Lucerne beach near Vitznau, we travelled on to Germany. Here what could have been a great tragedy nearly happened. We had stopped at a service area for break and when we re-loaded I was tired and for once I did not personally count that all the boys were on the bus but relied on each of the adults telling me that the group of boys for which they were responsible were all on board. After we had travelled for more than an hour towards our next hotel stop, the hue and cry arose that one of the boys was not on the bus. I was not too concerned, thinking that it was an old joke that the pupils were playing and that in fact they had performed the trick of hiding the boy under a seat to fool their supervisors. But it was only too true. We had left a pupil behind at the last service area stop. A frantic search eventually provided a used straw with the name of the service area and a telephone number. But at our German Hotel no-one there spoke fluent English and none of our party had fluent German. Adults went round the little German town and eventually a party was discovered with whom we could communicate and who kindly agreed to phone the service area to ask them to look for the missing boy. An off-hand message came back to the effect that our boy was not there. We phoned again courtesy of that decent German and insisted that they make a full and proper search of their service station, including the dining area. This time they came back to say that they had indeed found him sitting alone in the dining area. Phew! Relief all round. The German Police were superb and they collected the errant boy and put him on a train for Mannheim. (On the way to Italy the German Police had stopped our coach and quite politely told us that at a service area some of our boys had discovered that our shillings worked the German one mark machines and would we please see that it did not happen again.) We went to meet the designated train at Mannheim and I was mightily impressed with the guard of the train who would not let us have custody of the pupil until he was properly satisfied that we were the authentic people to whom he should hand him over. It transpired that as our coach was loading at the service area the errant boy had decided at the last minute to avail himself of the lavatory facilities and when he finished relieving himself found the coach gone, so he had simply gone into the dining area and sat there for hours.

GREAT JIMMY AGAIN

The sons of Celtic and Scotland Doctor Fitsimmons and Jimmy McGrory were pupils there and James Hubert Edward McGrory played well in our rugby sides and the great Mr. McGrory and a daughter would come and help with pre and post match activities, for which I was very grateful and proud.

At the time of the great 7-1 victory Sputnik was all the wonder of the world and our Celtic scribe composed the following parody:

"Twinkle, twinkle little Sputnik.
How I wonder at your neat trick.
Up above the world so high
Doing zig-zags in the sky
But how on earth can anyone sleep
As you go 'Bleep! Bleep! Bleep! Bleep!'?
Telling all the Tims in heaven
Rangers One and Celtic Seven!"

Unfortunately for some seasons Satellites would have no great Celtic news to spread until Jimmy Farrell's prediction came to pass and Stein and Auld lifted our spirits.

AGMs GONE MAD?

My pal George Stewart was in the Inland Revenue and was posted to Whitehaven and he would let me have his proxy vote to attend Celtic A.G.M.s There were never more than about a score of shareholders attending and they were pretty dismal affairs with Bob Kelly sitting there smirking all the time. I could not stand pompous White and I shot him down on one occasion. That season we stand season ticket holders had had to pay to go into a League match in order to be able to purchase a stand ticket for a Cup game. I asked him why we had to suffer that costly indignity. He denied that had ever happened. I took the offending tickets from my pocket and quoted times, dates and games and politely called him a liar. He then became flustered and red-faced and spluttered that he had done that because season ticket holders were too big for their boots and he had wanted to teach them a lesson. All this after saying he had not done such a thing. You can imagine my opinion of White's character was not too high. I noticed that Kelly was rather pleased with White's discomfort and wondered what had caused the fairly obvious ill-feeling between them. (Much later White complained at a Directors' meeting that too many complimentary tickets were being handed out and said the costly practice should stop. Stein kept quiet at that meeting but before the

138

next home game went to the Stand season ticket gateman Jimmy Henaughan and asked him when a complimentary ticket was presented would he please ask the person presenting the complimentary ticket who had given him it and to write that name down on the back of the complimentary ticket. Stein collected all the complimentary tickets from that game and at the next Directors' meeting, when the matter of too many complimentary tickets being given out was raised again by White, Jock produced that collection of named tickets, counted them and showed that it was complainer White himself who had given out about forty such tickets. Collapse of stout party. There were no flies on big Jock.) On one memorable occasion Kelly was asked why winger Frank Brogan had been transferred away. The answer staggered us all and showed what a real draw-back Kelly was to our old club. Frank (and I thought him as fine a player as the legendary left-winger Murphy of pre-war seasons) was apparently only good for scoring goals. Could you imagine that being said of a modern player? Repeatedly Kelly was asked about bringing Stein back as manager and would deliver the same reply. Stein was not a suitable person to be dealing with young players and the club had a better man in Sean Fallon. (Of course eventually Kelly had no option but to bring Stein back after a threatening mob surrounded his car at the ground.) One of the matters Kelly knew about was what had occurred before the shocking two-nil loss to Dunfermline in the Scottish Cup Final replay of 1961. Dunfermline was a team that had previously never managed to defeat us. On the evening before that replay, Dunfermline manager Jock Stein, match referee Phillips and Celtic's Peacock were ensconced in Stein's Burnbank house. When questioned about such an inappropriate meeting, the lame excuse was that the trio (all members of the same Lodge) were sorting out tickets for the match. My cousin, who lived next door to Stein, reported the meeting to Kelly and Peacock never had another season at Parkhead. No wonder season after season was so dismal with Kelly at the helm. That Irish widow had a lot to answer for.

DISTANT SIGNAL AT GREEN

Eventually things for me took a turn for the better – or so I thought at the time. I unexpectedly was offered the position of

Assistant Head at St. Conval's Primary School in Pollokshaws – which meant more of the much-needed cash – in case I had to put my mother in a nursing home. I did not know where that school was and the John Ogilvie Hall staff laughed at my stupidity. They took me out to the front door of the old mansion and pointed St. Conval's out to me on a hill over-looking Shawlands away to the west. Be sure that I left my domineering Jesuit Head red-faced and spluttering when I said a fond adieu to him. After a long wait of some thirteen years he had told me he had that place for me in the Secondary department at Garnethill. I presumed that was just some sort of face-saver as he must have heard about me leaving the College staff.

Then there was the saga about Blessed John Ogilvie's proposed canonisation.

The Jesuit Head Teacher wanted a hymn composed for John Ogilvie Hall to sing in order to honour the expected coming Saint and the arrangement was made that "Baldy" – Fr. Leo Batley S J would put the words together and then great musician Lakey – Fr. Thomas Lakeland S J – would compose the words. Poor friend Lakey brought three musical versions for the proposed hymn and, unbelievably, none of them fitted Baldy's complicated words. So Lakey had to put together a fourth stanza version to fit Baldy's awkward words. We did sing our own version for a while but then were told to revert to the Archdiocesan hymn to Ogilvie:

The Ogilvie Hymn

On the battlefields of Scotland
In the hour of victory,
There was heard the cry of heroes
"Ogilvie, an Ogilvie".
Gallant son of gallant fathers
It was thine as theirs to fight.
But with gates of Hell contending
Thou didst die for truth and right.
Blessed martyr, thy example
Will our strength in weakness be,
Hear our cry in times of peril,
"Ogilvie, an Ogilvie!"

By the scaffold all undaunted
Strong in grace we see thee still,
Looking up serene and smiling
With a firm unconquered will.
It is thy bright hour of triumph
Like Our Lord on Calvary's cross,
Victory is thine in dying
Endless gain in seeming loss.
Blessed martyr...

Blessed martyr, hear thy children
Be our guide and shew the way.
Make us strong and keep us steadfast
In the warfare of today.
Looking down from heights of glory
See in us thy kith and kin,
Teach us thy strong trust in Jesus
That we too may victory win.

PILGRIMS PROGRESS

Annually we joined in the John Ogilvie Memorial Walk from the
Glasgow Tolbooth (where he had been imprisoned) up to
Cathedral Square, and every year that unfortunate misguided so-
called clergyman, Hassan, would be standing glowering hate at us
from a side street. He would be attired in black top-hat, coat-and-
tails and boots with a bright orange vest and white breeches and
also fiercely clutching a large riding crop. We had a bit of a laugh
about him when one year the big white horse in Dumbartonshire
that was ready for him to ride as Grandmaster of an Orange Parade
was painted overnight with green stripes and so the poor beast
became a Celtic horse instead.

Last I saw of the poor fellow was many years later at the foot of
Roma's Spanish Steps, where, looking very much down-and-out, he
was sitting playing a shabby set of bag pipes to try to gain a few
liras. But that sometimes is the way of the world?

YO-HO-HO! AND NO BOTTLE OF RUM!

University friends' dad had a launch that had been one of the Dunkirk small boats and had a plaque affixed to honour that effort. On a number of occasions he was kind enough to give us an afternoon's expedition from Bowling down to The Tail of the Bank or up into the Gareloch This made us keen to sail further. With everyone in full-time employment there was no need for temporary summer jobs and the gang took to exploring the waters of the west coast of Scotland and as many of its sea lochs as we could navigate. We would charter or borrow a yacht and eventually we had managed to sail all round Mull and all round Sky. One regret we had was that we never dared to cross to Barra. We were always concerned in case a storm arose that might prevent us returning in time for our jobs restarting after holiday time. It was always a joy to start our cruising by the pleasant trip from Bowling down past the Tail of the Bank to our normal first anchorage in the safe mooring of the Greater Cumbrae's Ballochmartin Bay. Here it was delightful after the hectic life of Glasgow to see the string of fairy lights along the Largs promenades and listen to the pleasing sounds coming across the water. Then we would head for Ardishaig and the Crinan Canal as we did not have the courage to tackle the treacherous waters off the Mull of Kintyre. One sunny morning we were cruising pleasantly along doing just that when a destroyer came racing towards us doing its thirty odd knots. Although we were under sail, that captain or officer of the watch made not the slightest effort to give us a wide berth but came hurtling past about 200 yards off. One of our crew was anxious to observe the normal courtesy of dipping our red ensign to the ship's white one but I was much more concerned about staying afloat. I did an emergency turn to port —regardless of the danger of a swinging boom – and put our bow into the enormous destroyer wake. One minute all we could see ahead was the clear blue sky. Then we were staring at the greeny-blue sea. And so it went on till we had cleared the devastating destroyer wake. Phew. A narrow escape. My opinion of the Royal Navy fell to zero.

One worry about the passage of the Crinan Canal was the reckless behaviour of the skippers of puffers. These morons would sweep round the numerous canal blind bends at a rate of knots and there was no way they could have known if the canal ahead was clear for their careless speeding. On one bad occasion to avoid a being wrecked in a head-on collision we put the helm hard-over and ended up off the canal in among some trees and bushes. We were not best pleased. Of course the selfish puffer bonehead made no effort to come back and assist with our strenuous re-floating efforts. One glorious morning we were locking-out at Crinan with four other yachts and the boss of one asked me where we were heading for. I mused that we were thinking of Iona but that to avoid the notorious Corryvrechan (White Witch) whirlpool between Jura and Scarba we intended to go north round Scarba then across.

He said that the tidal situation was just right for taking the much shorter passage between Scarba and Jura as Corryvrechan would be fairly peaceful. As it turned out it was stirring only fitfully to starboard as we passed it by, and we were relieved. But then to our complete dismay we saw a large tidal wave looming ahead. There was nothing we could do but put our bows into it and hope for the best as a twenty foot high wall of water crashed over us. Fortunately we staggered through in good order and I mentally said a prayer of thanks to the shipwrights who had done such a good job putting the yacht together. There was a flat calm beyond the tidal wave and when we had recovered our wits and shaken hands all round, we saw a small red object in the sea over towards Mull. Being young and full of curiosity we thought we had better see what that was, thinking that it might have been a large buoy that had become adrift. We soon saw that in fact it was a man rowing in a small dinghy trying to tow a cabin cruiser. And that the red object we had spotted was I fact the storm sail of his yacht. He asked me to come aboard to meet his wife and two small children and indicated his dilemma. The cruiser had an eight cylinder in-line Thorneycroft engine and clearly the engine crank-shaft had broken because two pistons were projecting up through the cylinder head. That must have been a frightening experience. We could not leave the poor chap there so we towed his disabled craft over towards Mull then past the Torran Rocks of R.L.Stephenson fame and round into the Sound of Iona.. There was no safe anchorage for him there so we continued up round the North-west tip of Mull and down into the safe sheltered anchorage of Bunessan Bay. The poor chap had the decency to offer me £350 salvage money – which was a hefty sum in those days but the crew agreed with me that we had been only too pleased to be of assistance and glad to have been able to help him in his time of need. We wished the poor chap and his family well and then piled into our own small dinghy and rowed ashore for refreshments and discussion of a remarkable day. We asked for our usual tipple of rum. Sorry no rum available. No brandy nor whisky neither. In fact no spirits of any kind available in a Mull pub made the day even more remarkable. A few months later the news was in the press that that pub manager had been jailed for consuming all the pub's stocks of spirits himself.

It was remarkable how without fail each Summer we would pull into a remote jetty or anchorage and there would be a Wally Dishes' boy in his College blazer watching our performance. This happened at the old slate quarry port of Easdale. It is an interesting place on the Firth of Lorne about fifteen miles south of Oban with no road access to the mainland yet it has the famous Clachan Bridge across the Atlantic to Seil Island. Apparently in Hanoverian dictatorship days no-one in Highland tartan dress was allowed south of Seil Island so the bridge was also known as the barrier to the wearing of tartan. The place sometimes is called "Clachan" and sometimes "Truish an Truish" (The House of the Trousers).

As often would happen when we tied up or moored at a remote spot an old-timer would row up for a chat and give us some of his own sailing reminiscences. Our Easdale friend had an amazing account. When the large Easdale slate quarries were flourishing, this chap and a mate would sail their large engine-less heavily slate-loaded schooner from Easdale to Glasgow's Broomielaw and back via the notorious Mull of Kintyre. (No Crinan canal for them!) . He said it was quite easy. (Could not see that myself!) They would simply use an ebb tide to get down to the Mull and then an incoming tide would take them up the Clyde to the Broomielaw. And then they used the tides to return to Easdale. The tough old-timers did that for a pittance no doubt. When you consider what self-comforting politicians and wealthy bankers get away with these days...

There was a much taller tale told one day when we were sheltering between Ulva Island and Mull. This old fellow was full of local tales and when we asked whether Staffa was inhabited he joked and said "Only by sheep!" But he continued that on one occasion he and his pal were doing a bit of poaching on Staffa when they saw a tourist launch coming out of Iona Sound. They went down to the beach and met its arrival. Supposedly our friend stepped forward and pronounced that he was the Provost of Tobermory and his friend joined in with the statement that he was the Sheriff of Argyle and they were not allowed to land on Staffa. "And behold they turned and went back to Iona.". Could not believe a word of that, of course, but it was amusing. Usually it was not possible to enter Fingal's Cave because of the heavy swells coming off the Atlantic but on only one occasion there was a flat calm and it was possible for me to skull our wee dinghy into the very famous cave itself. Not many can say they have done that. (I have requested that Mendelssohn's wonderful Hebridean Overture is played at my funeral. Hope in fact that they remember to arrange that. I will be watching!) We liked going into sheltered Dunstaffnage with its castle. It was handy to stroll into Oban from there to obtain the necessities of life. A favourite resting sheltered anchorage was in a bay at the mouth of Loch Duich opposite the famed Eilean Donan castle. There would also be anchored there a very large beautifully turned out schooner. We never saw it sailing. Then one summer the two crew of the schooner called us over and invited us to come aboard and have a look around. The interior was as magnificent as the exterior. The great yacht belonged to the Wills family (of cigarette notoriety these days). The two friendly lads had the job of maintaining it down at Greenock during the winter months. Then they would navigate it up to Loch Duich where it would lie peacefully during the summer months. Very occasionally one of the Wills' families would remember the yacht and come up for a week-end's sail. But apparently that was a very rare event. I thought not a bad job to have. Lucky old them! On adjacent green banks sloping down to the sea lay a number of deserted large white ship's life-boats in good condition. Apparently they were from a torpedoed vessel. We had thoughts about buying one for our own use but as they say hell is paved with good intentions and we never got round to doing that.

PENNY PLEASE!

We would be very naughty when we moored off Tobermory. We had to be careful about that because for a time there were navy divers trying to find a supposedly sunken Spanish galleon from the

145

ill-fated Armada. We had no toilet facilities on the boats so at Tobermory we would nip in to one of the large hotels, find a bathroom and have a good and welcome scrub down. Usually we just had a sea plunge for that. We had a good laugh one time. One of the crew was sitting in the cock-pit reading a paper while he was performing his number two effort. A holidaymaker rowed up in his oarie-boat, clung on to the side of the craft and had a long conversation with our hero. The visitor never realised what was going on. We were splitting our sides in the cabin as we watched. But we had less pleasant happenings.

On one occasion we had run out of drinking water so we anchored off Staffin and went ashore to a pub to ask for a supply of water. We sat unattended for a long time and then we were told that there was a water shortage on Skye and that they could not spare us any water, A water shortage on Skye! Unbelievable! But at least we could see the wonderful Totternish peninsula with its amazing series of rock formations and we walked across to the standing stones at Eyre. There were other times when we got it completely wrong. One of the crew had to get back to Glasgow so we moored off Mallaig in a flat calm and we rowed ashore doing a couple of trips in our small dinghy. After seeing the West Highland train off on its wonderful scenic journey, we stayed too long having refreshments and a good natter, came out and found a howling gale had arisen. Our yacht was heaving and tossing and tugging at its anchor chain. A most alarming sight. Despite the incoming high waves we just had to get out to save the boat. And we did what we would not normally do. Everyone packed into the wee dinghy and by some miracle we managed to struggle through the high seas to the boat and clamber aboard – which in turn was not easy. There was another time we had to over-load the dinghy. We had ventured up to the top of the long and twisting Loch Sunart in order to visit Strontian village of nuclear fame. There was a warning in the sailing club hand-book about the dangers of gusts of wind swilling up Glen Tarbert from Loch Linnhie and sweeping over the crest of the hills down into Loch Sunart.. So we doubled the length of the anchor chain we normally laid out and thought that was a save enough precaution. We walked round the shore road and up into the pub at Strontian. The pub regulars were interested in our arrival but thought we were the crew off a large yacht and asked us how the owners treated us. After a most pleasant and enjoyable evening we made our farewells to the pub regulars and walked back down to Loch Sunart where we were shocked to see our boat heading to sea down Loch Sunart. Clearly it had dragged its anchor. We raced to the dinghy, piled on regardless, and then rowed like mad to catch up with our errant craft. Fortunately we got aboard before it ran aground or went out into the Atlantic.

PANTIES SHORTAGE?

On one of our last trips before marriages and the arrival of children put an end to our sailing expeditions, we were coming back through the Crinan Canal and I had gone ahead to assist the operator of the opening road bridge with his manual efforts. It was a warm sunny day and one of the girls was wearing a white silk blouse and navy blue tennis pants. The canal bridge man sidled up to me and asked me was I off the boat that had Miss Scanty Panties aboard.

Of course we all sat for the Yachtmaster's Certificate and after we had each gained it the friendly CPO in charge of the courses invited us to apply for a RNVR commission. But none of us did. Another of life's opportunities missed.

But then we marvellous sailors nearly had a bad tragedy. A place some of liked visiting was the Lake of Monteith. (The only Scottish Lake because the Dutch map-maker of the time mistook a local's pronunciation of "laigh" – meaning "low-lying" – for "Lake".) Menteith is low-lying because it is on the northern edge of the great Scottish Lowland Fault. The great attraction for us there was the fine hotel which provided excellent food at a most reasonable price and then it was possible to hire rowing boats to cross the Lake to its largest island – Inchmahome – and walk through the ruined Augustinian Priory that had been built there in 1328 by one of the Comyns. But one night we lingered too long enjoying Inchmahome and trying to row back we encountered a fierce storm. We could only go forward gingerly bit by bit – trying both to progress to safety and trying frantically to avoid being swamped. That night Lake of Monteith proved even more terrifying than our Mallaig ordeal.

MORE ALARMS AND EXCURSIONS

Until 1943 Parkhead was served by the splendid 22 mile long tram service 15 which ran from Airdrie through the city beyond Paisley to Elderslie. The maximum fare then was only two old pennies and children like me travelled at half-fare. So it was very easy for me to travel on service 15 to games at Broomfield, Cliftonhill, Paradise, Ibrox and Love Street and so I did. (And up to 1932 Abbotsinch – no less –was served by that single-line tramway that ran from Paisley's Gilmour Street centre past Love Street!)

But as I said before, our team's performances matched those awful days for the world. But I lived in hope. In 1943 Transport Manager E.R.L. Fitzpayne (he who had wanted all our trams painted light-blue) decided that he did not want service 15 trams delaying traffic while they turned right from Jamaica Street into Argyle Street, so he made all service 15 trams from Airdrie now run straight on along Argyle Street to new large double – track sidings at Anderston.

I had always wanted to walk through one of the by that time closed-to-traffic vehicular tunnels under the Clyde at Stobcross. Celtic reserves were playing the other half of the Old Firm at their ground So one night I took a tram to Anderston Cross sidings and walked down to one of the Finnieston tunnels, ran down a long spiral stair-case and found that the tunnel, instead of carrying Clydesdales and their carts, was now almost filled with giant water or perhaps sewage pipes. I plodded on underneath one and climbed to the surface again at Mavisbank. Although I made the best time I could – fit as I was in those good old days – it took me longer than I had expected to reach Cessnock and the giant east stair-case of Ibrox Park – later scene of that terrible second Ibrox crowd disaster.

(The earlier Ibrox 1902 disaster was said to have been because of inadequate crowd control that had led to the over crowding of the new West Tribune Stand. The overcrowding proved too much for the new stand's wooden flooring which collapsed under the undue weight, Many spectators fell forty feet and 25 were killed (requiescant in pace) and 517 injured.)

Puffing to the top of the extremely high terracing staircase, I was astonished to see our reserves being allowed to kick theirs off the park. I was even more astonished to watch our centre-forward (as they were called in those unenlightened times) missing open goal after open goal from inside the six yard box. I came home and pronounced that that was one reserve who would never make the first team. Oh yes? His name was Stevie Chalmers – which shows what I know about football.

That second Ibrox disaster cause considerable embarrassment to that priest-golfing friend of mine – Kerryman Father Lyne. He was at the match and went back to his church house disappointed with the score draw but quite unaware of the crowd disaster happening on the giant stair-case. A journalist cousin in Dublin – knowing that Father Lyne would have been at the match – phoned him and asked him what had caused the disaster. Father Lyne said that we had just scored a winner with a few minutes to go when Harry Hood had taken a very poor shy that had allowed them to score an unexpected equaliser. Of course it was the scoring of that unexpected equaliser that had caused fans descending the giant stairway to turn back and try to get back to the top and colliding with a mass of fans descending. Poor Father Lyne took a long while to get over that bad mistake.

Father Lyne used to train at Parkhead and when during the dreadful war years Celtic were unable to obtain a much-needed new hoops strip, he brought a new strip for the club from Dublin. I liked it very much and have always thought that it was far more attractive-looking than the simply second-rate second and third strips the club perpetrates these days for money-raising purposes.

Fr. Lyne's Dublin strip was white with short green sleeves and had a large green shamrock on the front.

I have always been very saddened that no great credit has ever been given to Jimmy McGrory and Sean Fallon for signing most of the Lisbon Lions. There is no part of the fine Celtic ground named after him. Nor after the great Willie Maley neither. Very strange omissions in my opinion. What do you think?

Transport experts used to come from all over the world to experience and travel on our superb Glasgow tramway system. But thanks to internal-combustion-loving politicians and political activity by railway trade unionists our much-loved tramway system was destroyed and had gone by 1962. The excuse was that instead we were having suburban rail lines round Glasgow electrified. But when these over-vaunted electric trains started running there were serious design faults found with them and several broke down and caught fire. The main problem was the difficulty of changing over while running from the open-air twenty five thousand volts in the external overhead to the erroneously planned much reduced voltage in the reduced overhead clearances in Glasgow's tunnels.

Our third team were playing away at Dumbarton so I thought to experience these new "Blue Trains" for the first time, by travelling on an Helensburgh train from Garrowhill (where we were now living) to Dalreoch – which was the station for Dumbarton's Bogside ground.

It was fascinating being able to sit behind the motorman and watch the track scene unfolding ahead. (Though later, many motormen would pull down a secluding blind and prevent that enjoyable experience happening.) That night the weather was wretched with gloomy driving rain and Bogside lived up to its name. The pitch was a quagmire and the terracing was not much better. We were three down at half-time and I was thinking I was a complete idiot standing there. I felt even more despondent when we came out for the second half, for there in the side was the little red-headed ball boy from the front of the stand. I thought we must be scraping the bottom of the barrel, and thought about going back to the train there and then. But the little the red-head ran amok – very surprising on that dreadful surface – and we won the game despite being so far down at half-time– much to my astonishment. On enquiry I discovered that his name was J. Johnstone. And we all know what came after that initiation.

At St. Aloysius' College we were allowed to wear long trousers on entering fourth year. Do not know if that had anything to do with it but from that time my very tolerant parents allowed me to go by train to away matches if I had enough pocket money saved for that purpose. I particularly enjoyed the train journeys to Edinburgh, Dundee and Aberdeen being a "Steam anorak" as well as a tram and Celtic fiend. Going to Edinburgh I would steam spot passing Haymarket m.p.d. sheds. There as well as some of the famous Pacifics of the then LNER named after great race-horses, I watched out for the old NBR 0-6-0 Goods engines that, on coming back from war service in France, had been given commemorative names of that time such as Mons or Foch or Aisne. To-day Maude – No.673 of that J 36 class – has been wonderfully preserved and runs trains which visitors can travel on at Bo'ness.

The usual train from Queen Street for a match in Edinburgh was the ten minutes past twelve departure. One Saturday I entered a compartment and sitting there was one of the old mad bunch from Jordanhill Training College. I said I had not realised he was a Celtic supporter. Her said he wasn't, so – rudely, I suppose – I asked him why then was he going to Edinburgh, He said he was going to see The Secretary of State. I thought he was up to another of his old leg-pulls. But sadly he was not. He was on his last appeal before being kicked out of the teaching profession. His Partick Head Teacher wanted him removed from the teaching profession as he had persisted against the Head's orders in teaching calculus to Primary Five pupils! Do not know how this last appeal went but imagine that the powers that be would not be very sympathetic. I did say earlier we were a mad lot at Jordanhill.

If the Edinburgh game was at Tynecastle the obvious thing to do was to alight at Haymarket where that train always stopped and just saunter along the short distance to Tynecastle. However on a couple of occasions I stayed on to Waverley and climbed up those awful steps to Princes Street and then over to St. Andrew's Square from where "Football Special" trams could give me a wee Edinburgh tram ride to Gorgie Road. When the match was at Easter Road I would usually go there via St. Mary's Cathedral. Apart for praying for the dead and others and for forgiveness for my sins, I liked to stand on the Cathedral steps and watch how skilled the Edinburgh motormen were in negotiating a short length of single track in Palmerston Place that had obviously been deliberately installed to prevent the front of the Cathedral being blocked if the double-track had passed it. The pathetic mess made of modern Edinburgh tramway construction was not so considerate of the need not to obstruct the Cathedral frontage.

When the Pope's "fore-runner", Archbishop Marcinkus, visited the Cathedral and entered the sacristy he said he could not see any toilet facilities and asked where they were. The administrator opened a door and said that the toilets etc. were at the other end of a tunnel that ran under the sanctuary to the other side of the building because that was where the water supply pipes and drainage sewers were. Marcinkus complained that having the Pontiff walking underground to the toilets would not do at all and that if the administrator wanted the Pope to come he would have to put in a toilet facility at the sacristy. The alarmed administrator fled to Cardinal Gray about the demand and said that it would cost a fortune to do what Marcincus wanted done. Gray said that if the Pope was to visit the cathedral then no matter the expense involved there would have to be a toilet in the sacristy. So one costing some £3.000 – complete with gold fittings etc. – was installed in the sacristy. At the due time of the Papal visit, four minutes were allowed for John Paul II to make use of the expensively installed facilities. But he did not want to – so that everyone stood in the sacristy twirling their thumbs for four minutes. Whatever happened to the poor man at the gate?

CLIPPITY-CLOP!

One time we were swarming down a street to Easter Road and on our left at an opening into some waste ground a poor fellow was doing his best to gain a few coppers by performing a one-man-band act. I was just thinking he was doing rather well when a pompous mounted police sergeant pushed his horse up through an annoyed crowd and bawled down at the musician to stop playing. But the one-man-band-act went on playing and to everyone's delight the bully's horse started to dance to the music. The red-faced minion of the law turned his animal and went away in great embarrassment. We all cheered the horse. No doubt that bully took it out on the horse afterwards. I always thought that in those unenlightened days that the police did not have too much to bother them.

LOST CAUSES

On a couple of occasions my aunt Agnes slipped me a ten shilling note, so that I was able to take an earlier train to Waverley and ride some of the excellent Edinburgh tram routes. I did the Granton circle and also went to Joppa by the round-about service via the docks and came back by the direct route to the GPO. And on one fabulous occasion (see why later) I even had enough money to treat myself to lunch, eating beside a little string orchestra. I really thought I had arrived.

Returning from Edinburgh matches I used to take the semi-express from Waverley that journeyed to Glasgow via Bathgate and Airdrie and dropped me at Shettleston. (At the time of writing this line is being re-built and electrified after the 1982 ridiculous closure and lifting of track between Bathgate and Airdrie.)

Dundee gave me the chance to have short tram trips up to Dens Park and, as I said earlier, once I had a ride on a football special from the Dens Park football siding down hill to the city centre. Dundee once had the great idea of restoring and rehabilitating the long run from Lochee through Dundee centre to Broughty Ferry. (The latter place once had its own tram system. When the Broughty crews were holding their Annual Day Out, the Dundee tramwaymen would come in and perform the Broughty duties!) Modern fast PCC style cars were to be purchased as was done in places such as Den Haag. What would they give to have such a modern light rail system to-day?

There is a belief that the Dundee motormen once had a "day out" on the Glasgow system and were amazed that Glasgow motormen could sit down while operating a tram. But I have never found a picture of this event. If you have one or know where one is, please be kind enough to let me know.

Unfortunately the nationalisation of electric power supply in the U.K. meant that a uniform charge of three and a half old pennies per unit was then the rule with no allowances. This increase in the cost of electricity meant that the idea of an improved Lochee-Broughty Ferry light-rail service had to be abandoned, as it then became cheaper to operate buses.

Once I was walking back from Pittodrie to the Joint Station in Aberdeen and saw that the tram depot at King Street had been completely re-furbished and absolutely shone in the sunshine. I looked in, and seeing nobody was there and that all the trams were out on duty, I trespassed right through the depot full of admiration, and with the thought that the admirable Aberdeen tram system had a bright future. Unfortunately not. With nationalisation the Granite City lost its cheap supply of Hydro-Electric power, and with it now being cheaper to run buses in Aberdeen, the whole system was abandoned. Yet Aberdeen had had a small fleet of some of the largest and finest trams in the U.K. I managed one trip on one and was mightily impressed.

After two smaller stream-lined cars were built by English Electric, Pickerings of Wishaw built the large splendid bogie cars. Sad to say not one was ever preserved. The enterprising Blackpool manager came up to see about taking the stream-liners to

Blackpool. A story – probably fictional – was that the Blackpool manager, being a portly gentleman, could not enter the narrow driving cabs. More probable is that the reason for Blackpool not taking the superb cars was their size (they could only run on certain routes in Aberdeen) and they required two conductors. On its older cars, Aberdeen had different "coloured" trams for each different route served – because of the number of would-be passengers who were illiterate in early tram days – as in Glasgow. On my first visit during the war I saw some of the trams were painted all brown. I thought then that was because of a war-time shortage of paint. But in fact it was an additional "coloured" route band that Glasgow did not have. There were also ex-Nottingham and Manchester trams in service. There were two ways to reach Pittodrie by tram. Busy Service Five went on along Queens Road to Hazlehead but there was a turn-off loop for football specials that took cars right behind the Pittodrie main stand. I once watched fed-up motormen on the old green open-fronted hand-braked cars – only used for special workings – stopping their cars by just running into the one in front. No wonder they looked rather battered. A more interesting tram route was service Nine which ran from Castle Street to the Sea Beach terminal not far from the Pittodrie terracings. This route went via Constitution Street and wound is way through narrow passages between harbour sheds and even had its own small sub-depot.

I probably enjoyed the three hour train ride to Aberdeen more than some of the second-rate Celtic displays there. If you sat on the right hand side of the carriage a train-spotter like me could have good sight of the old Caledonian (then LMS) St. Rollox loco works. (St. Rollox is another version of St. Roch and an old church dedicated to St. Rollox was demolished there to make a station for the Garnkirk-Glasgow railway when it first entered Glasgow in 1831.) Next we would slowly climb past Balornock sub-shed: Stirling might produce a mixture of LMS and LNER locos: named LNER 4-4-0s like Morayshire (now preserved at Bo'ness) might be there with their LMS counterparts.

But Perth was a bit special.. There, after the LNER and LMS sheds was the old Highland Railway one. So with three motive power depots, Perth always had a great variety of engines to be "spotted". Later I was to like Perth station for another reason. Coming down to Glasgow from Kinloss, the Inverness- Forres –

London night express (which I used to take to Coatbridge Central) would stop for a lengthy engine change and it was possible to race up from the platform to a fish and chip shop on the over-head road bridge and buy a large fish supper. As I indicated before, I was always hungry in those days of rationing.

Aberdeen itself would have the occasional engine off the Inverness line as well as other LMS and LNER engines. On one occasion, after a Pittodrie match, a game of Solo started as we left the Joint Station. The kitty was not won until I managed it just as we rattled over the points into Buchanan Street Station. I grabbed the three pounds fifteen shillings (a week's wage for most in those days), leapt from the slowing carriage, and made a bee-line for the 23 tram before the other three disgruntled Solo players could react. I could not tell my father about that good fortune because he had several times warned me against playing cards on a train. But as I indicated earlier it meant that I could later afford that lunch in Edinburgh at Patrick Thompson's. Sometimes the team would be on the train – and occasionally both sides of the Old Firm. It was sad to experience that their team always travelled first class while our lot travelled third class (or second class as it became).

SPECIAL TIMES

Then there were the mostly enjoyable football special trains. Prices were very cheap – only a few shillings return. Surprisingly the more enjoyable rides were on the specials to Cartsdyke Greenock for the Morton games. There always seemed to be "happenings". One time Celtic centre-half McGrory was in one corner of a compartment and I was sitting in the corner opposite. A "know-all" in the compartment started boasting to everyone that he was a great pal of McGrory and the Celtic player said this and did that. Of course he was quite unaware of the player's presence with us. McGrory said nothing but looked across at me and we both just quietly shook our heads. On another journey back from Cartsdyke we had one of Arthur Montford's "stramashes". Celtic's left-winger at the time was Alec Byrne., He was a very skilled and fine footballer. But, how shall I put it? He was not best suited to the rough-and-tumble match we had just seen on Cappielow's usual mud-heap. (And they prided themselves on being "The Pride of the Clyde!") One upset passenger in the compartment voiced a disparaging opinion about Byrne but in quite uncomplimentary terms. An irate fellow passenger literally jumped to Alec's defence and pleaded that he was a good husband who treated his wife and family very well. I wondered what that had to do with ability on the field. And so did others – only vocally. Strong unrepeatable language was hurled at each other by the protagonists until we reached Glasgow Central. There I opened the carriage door and leaving them to it, I airted rapidly yont from the dispute – being a cowardly, cowardly-custard blanc-mange pudding as usual.

But there was to be a much greater confrontation off a Greenock Morton special later. A friend started as a cleaner at Polmadie motive power depot. Supposedly in the good old days of the London, Midland and Scottish Railway Company, Catholics were largely employed at the former Caledonian Polmadie shed, while non-Catholics were started at Corkerhill – the former Glasgow and South Western Railway m.p.d. No doubt there was a fear of a Catholic/Protestant confrontation on the driving platform. (Glasgow Corporation Tramways also tried to keep Catholics with Catholics and Protestants with Protestants on the trams.) As was the order of promotion on the railways, a cleaner eventually would be promoted to "passed cleaner" (which meant he could start learning to fire steam locomotives and after over 300 firing turns he would be promoted to fireman). (After the same number of driving turns a "passed fireman" would become a qualified driver.) My friend had only done a few firing turns on short-distance freights when, unexpectedly, he was rostered to be the fireman with a passed-fireman as driver, on an Orangeman special to Larkhall from Central Station. My friend had never been up the line to Larkhall before (he had been the other way on a short goods train) and, not wanting to let his passed-fireman driver down, he had too much coal in the fire-box when they arrived at Larkhall. The Parade Master was astride the obligatory white horse on the road over-bridge awaiting the Orangemen off the special train. But as these were streaming up through the station to join the parade assembly, the loco steam safety valves erupted and a massive plume of white steam shot up in front of the over-bridge. The alarmed white horse reared and threw the Grandmaster on to the roadway. The Orangemen thought the train crew had done this deliberately and started to come back down to attack them. Seeing what was about to happen, the signalman had the good sense to change the station starting signal from "on" to "off" and my friend and his driver were able to pull away from the danger. When they arrived back into Central Station with the return train, my friend heaved a sigh of relief that his first firing turn on a passenger train was over, but as they pulled into one side of the platform, a special train from Cartsdyke, full of Celtic supporters, pulled into the other side of the platform and the obligatory green v orange pitched battle developed on the platform and my friend and his driver had to seek shelter under their engine to avoid the flying missiles. My friend always said that he would never forget his first "passenger" firing turn.

We had a Catholic friend who was a driver attached to Parkhead motive power depot. He was surprised when he and his Catholic fireman were rostered to take an Orangeman special from Queen Street Station to Helensburgh. The pair rubbed their hands in glee and set off "hell for leather" with the special over the twisty line to the Firth of Clyde. They made a record time but there were a lot of very queezy Orangemen by the time Helensburgh was reached. Of course they were hauled over the coals for what they had done, but they could not have cared less about that, and had many a laugh about it afterwards. But I have often wondered what the shed-master was up to picking a couple of Catholics for an Orangemans' Special?.

We made a more peaceful and railway interesting singular journey to a cup-tie at Brechin. Our special pulled up at Bridge of Dun – north of Montrose. The Black Five came off and an old veteran Caledonian Jumbo 0-6-0 buffered up in its place and propelled our excursion up into the spacious Brechin terminal station. (There had been many proposals for a through station in Brechin but all the ideas came to nothing. To-day Brechin station is the fine headquarters of The Caledonian Railway Preservation Society. Unfortunately they had to move their splendid collection of preserved railwayana from Brechin itself down to the safety of Bridge of Dun. Thank you do-gooders for all the present-day yobs.) The cup-tie occasioned first sight of the famous Brechin hedge with which I was to become better acquainted in later years, and of course, we sure sampled the genuine splendid Forfar bridies. For the game we were packed into the small terracing space behind the East goal. At half-time the prominent Evening Times sports writer of the day "Alan Breck" (R.E. Kingsley) pushed his way through our jeering mob and left the ground. (No doubt to the nearest pub!) He never returned, yet a full account of the game appeared in his paper under his banner. (Of course later it became clear that it was quite common for a reporter to have a report printed on a sporting event which he had not in fact attended. The celebrated cricket correspondent of The Guardian, Neville Cardus, was well known for producing comprehensive and interesting accounts of cricket matches he had not attended.) Oh! And we had an easy victory. Weir scored twice and then Big Hooky and there was no reply. Glebe Park had known worse. Brechin had lost three pre-war games in one season by ten-nil in each. But as usual in those days our cup "run" soon ended, the Dons putting us out 1-0 at Parkhead in the third round.

ROUND THE BRIDGES

A fascinating football special was to Dunfermline for an evening game. I wondered at our route taken from Buchanan Street. We headed for Falkirk Grahamston but turned north before then and crossed the Forth by using the Alloa rail swing bridge. (Long since dismantled.) Then we proceeded through Alloa (only recently got a passenger service restored) to Dunfermline. After the match the excursion proceeded forward and to my delight we crossed the Forth Bridge to make our return to Glasgow. If such a journey were possible to-day, rail anoraks like me would be paying pounds for the wonderful circle tour instead of the few bob it cost us. There were other stations visited and unusual journeys made on the good old football specials.

For a while a station for Hibs matches was tried on the Portobello-Leith goods line behind the Easter Road terracing. A special for a Somerset Park match would go to Newton station outside Ayr.

Often we would use a normal service train for away Games. Flemington Station was most convenient for Fir Park. (After it closed I had a remarkable evening walk from Motherwell's Station to Fir Park for a reserve game. That spring evening blackbirds were giving the most tuneful big licks in every garden on the way to the ground. T. Gemmel was in the stand that night hurling continuous abuse at the match ref.)

Then there was the awful display of hooliganism by our hoodlums at Hamilton West station. The crowd had started to make its way to the station when we were five goals down at Douglas Park. Then some sort of recovery was made by our stiffs and as each goal – up to four- was scored supporters (huh!) started to run back to the ground to see the finish of the game. Mayhem ensued in the streets of course, and when the Glasgow local pulled into Hamilton West station, in many cases over-excited fans did not bother to open the carriage doors but dived head-first through any compartment window that was open. Quite shocking. I saw the same thing happening to a lesser extent at Falkirk High. The Edinburgh-Glasgow express had burst out of the tunnel and barely stopped when some were going into the compartments head-first through the open windows. The elderly driver on one of Gresley's great LNER 2-6-2 mixed traffic engines looked back in amazement and disgust. Should have asked for a ride on his footplate – of course

DOON HAMERS

Then there was an eye-opener for youthful me at any rate. On a Saturday I had been down to Dumfries by special train where we lost three-one (as usual) and when I got a 15 tram back from St. Enoch's station I dived into St. Mark's Church for reconciliation (or confessions as the sacrament was carelessly called in those pre-Vatican Two days). To my unbelief, before I had got started, the redoubtable Father Lyne (an All-Ireland Gaelic Football star who trained regularly at Celtic Park) asked me " How did we do to-day, Willie?" This was the first time I realised that despite the separating screen between confessor and penitent they well-knew who the penitent was. I also wondered how he knew I had been at the match. And of course I afterwards tried to make my confession where I was more likely not to be known, for that had been a real shock to the system.

IN THE KINGDOM

And there were the visits to Stark's Park. What a horrible ground Raith Rovers had. We would be packed into the narrow rectangular covered enclosure. I did not mind that too much, for behind the open back of the enclosure I would see smashing green LNER locomotives belting past full blast. But we had an amusing afternoon on one occasion. For our edification and delight the Rovers had provided the entertainment of a Boys' Brigade Pipe Band doing its stuff on the pitch before the game. No offence to anyone but I am not mad keen on pipe bands of any kind at the best of times. But entertainment came when the band started to perform American Army Band manoeuvres. But without American precision. Eventually they started parading round the pitch centre circle in single file and as the circumference became narrower and narrower they eventually mobbed and crushed the bandmaster who was standing on the centre spot. Of course this caused great cheering from the enclosure.

Then it was realised that doing his TV commentary from a gantry above us was Archie McPherson no less. Access to this shaky structure was by means of a single long ladder. Our bright specimens took away the ladder and left the TV party marooned. Eventually another ladder came and this time it was protected by a blue-coated minion of the law. (In Garrowhill our garden was adjacent to that of Magnus Magnusson and Archie McPherson also lived in Garrowhill. He had been Head of Swinton Primary School. One afternoon I went into Arthur Reilly's as usual for my butcher-meat. Arthur and I often went to away games together. That afternoon Arthur told me that he had just had Archie McPherson in and Archie was in a very distressed state. He told Arthur that he had always been a great Rangers fan but Waddell had just banned him from Ibrox because of some comment he had made during a commentary.)

NEW TRAVEL

One tremendous non-rail excursion took place and this was the first time I had ever travelled on a motorway. This was going to Liverpool for the second leg of the Cup-Winners Cup Semi-final in which the referee afterwards admitted he had wrongly disallowed what would have been a fine winning goal by Bobby Lennox.

Then there was the sickening let-down by Aer Lingus. Before the semi-final with Dukla Prague, John McCabe and myself were convinced that we were going to win the European Cup and we chartered their then most modern plane – a BAe 111. But on the week before the Final, someone in the company realised that now because of the great demand for places to Lisbon they could obtain much more money by chartering it to some other party and charging more than they had charged us. They stuck us on an old DC-6B four-engined prop. One first flew in 1951. Well-wishers who were at Glasgow Airport to se us off said afterwards we were the only plane that did a low-level take off. On board there was great discontent because the liquor supply soon ran out. The pilot told us that the only time he had carried more rowdy passengers involved once flying whaler crews across the Pacific. He said it was a beautiful day with no bad weather reports anywhere nearby. His plane started pitching badly and he was puzzled why this should be. On investigation he found that the seamen had lifted all the cabin seats and stacked them at the back of the plane. They had put on their heavy sea-boots and were placing bets on who could slide farthest down the plane. We certainly were not up to doing that.

It was the Feast of the Ascension and the very friendly Portuguese said that they had never seen so many men at Mass. Going into the ground there was much amusement that there were no ticket turn-styles but everyone sobered up a bit when we saw mounted cavalrymen lined up with slung rifles. No wonder no turn-styles were needed. We had hardly taken our seats when a very large portly Italian seated immediately in front of us turned round and said that he was very sorry for us wasting our time and money coming. We naturally asked why. The answer came that for an important game such as this, Italians always "arranged" the referee. Did not work on that occasion, did it! The second half had just started when a very excited gent disturbingly tried to scramble into a seat behind us. He loudly proclaimed that he had been told at Glasgow airport that the flight would not arrive in Lisbon in time for the start of the Final but he had been most determined to see some of the match. Just as he finished his proclamation he missed his footing, slid down under our seats and knocked himself unconscious on the concrete tier. Last we saw of him he was being stretchered away. So the poor soul did not see much of the Final. No doubt he proudly proclaimed later that he had been to Lisbon. He sure had!

We were walking away from the ground and approaching a t-junction, when the Celtic team bus full of excited, red-faced, laughing and standing players came down to our road. We had never seen, and probably never will see again, such a wonderful sight. Of course we all ran cheering alongside the bus until it sped away. At the airport frantic officials were just packing the crowds of supporters on to the first plane available but somehow we came back on the old three-rudder DC-4B. I have always had one regret about that visit to Lisbon and that is that I never had the chance to have a ride on the amazing tram route 28. If visiting Lisbon do not miss experiencing that remarkable route.

And Engelbert Humperdink, no less, sang for us a parody on his famous Eidelweiss song:

> "Lisbon we know
> Was all aglow
> At Celtic's great endeavour!
> Green and white
> Stein's delight
> In Paradise for ever!"

If only!

ALL NOT WELL

Then I really covered myself in ignominy. I arranged for a bus to go to the great match at Leeds – the first leg of the 1970 European Cup semi-final. I was promised a brand new bus – so I presumed that all would be well. But it turned out that the "new" bus did not come in time and we were sent off on an old second-hand bus which, incredibly, had a double gear-box. Whether it was the incompetence of the driver or the state of the bus, but it packed up before we reached Carlisle. The bus company representative on the coach was one Michael Kelly (yes! that Michael Kelly). Do not quite know why he had to be there at all but in any case he did nothing about obtaining a replacement bus and me and all my disgruntled friends had somehow to make our own way to Leeds. I took a long time to live that disgrace down.

A Jesuit from Garnethill did an amazing job in the stand leading our fans in song and imitating Henry Wood. Of course George Connelly sent us ecstatic with that first minute goal. But alas a second European Cup should have happened but did not and poor George became a very psychologically disturbed young man and his Celtic career did not develop as a well as we all expected it would do.

At the time of the Final I had been called for jury service which was most disturbing and to make matters worse I was "named" on the day of the Final but was rejected by the defence counsel as not suitable to his taste. Yet I had to sit there while the sad Final was on.

OUT OF THE FRYING PAN INTO THE FIRE!

St Conval's Primary School was attached to the Parish Church of St. Mary Immaculate, Pollokshaws. The school could not have its name as St. Mary's as there was an earlier school of that name in Glasgow. The main building was one of the ubiquitous Edwardian era substantial red-sandstone primary schools dotted around Glasgow. I found the infant department of the school to be in a detached primitive mid-Victorian building. More of that later.

St. Conval, a disciple of Kentigern, settled at Inchinnan (the conjunction of three rivers) around 497. His "chariot" a stone on which legend has it he sailed from Ireland, can be seen beside the Renfrew walk-way.

(Legends have many Celtic/Breton saints sailing about on stones. Wonder what they really were up to? Probably they were just using wicker baskets?)

After the staff at John Ogilvie Hall had laughed at my ignorance as to the whereabouts of St. Conval's School, big-hearted Tom Burke told me to be off and see the head of St. Conval's school.

NO WELCOME ACROSS THE VALLEY

So about ten minutes later I was at the Pollokshaw's School knocking on the H.T.'s door and looking forward to having a happier chapter in my life. Boy was I wrong. The H.T. turned out to be most unwelcoming. I was given a most frosty reception. Her first comment was that I should have been there two days ago. Politely, I tried to explain that I had only received the appointment letter some twenty minutes previously. No reply to that came, but she pulled out a foolscap page of instruction from the Education Department concerning the parking of teachers' cars. On no account had they to be driven across a school playground in order to be parked. She asked me where I had parked and I said in the driveway adjacent to the dining hall. She told me to follow her out to my car and then ordered me not to park there but to drive across the playground and park in a pupils' shelter. And so it was to go on. Reprimand after reprimand came for supposed misdemeanours. One I well remember was because I was standing around dismissal time, supervising a well-behaved class going to the cloakroom for their belongings and I was thinking T.G.I.F. Her nibs had crept up behind me and asked the usual favourite question, "And how long have you been teaching, Mr. Tollan?" This time because a girl had taken her school-bag with her from the class-room to the cloak-room and back. Big deal. And such niggling went on and on. A teacher had not turned up for the class opposite – so I organised the start of the morning for my class and the other one. Of course I had the usual rocket for doing that and was told to mind my own business etc. The teaching staff too obviously had a thing about me because I had been so long in a private school. But I could accept and understand that. One of them was an aunt of legendary James Craig of Lisbon penalty shock to my system. Later she told me that dentist Jim was leaving Celtic because of an ankle injury. He had married a daughter of Jimmy Farrell and they later went out to South Africa. But that did not work out because of the long distances involved in away matches with Mrs. Craig being left behind in their house staffed with coloured servants.

I was late in discovering one of the causes of that Head Teacher's obvious dislike for me. At that time the Glasgow Education Department would not allow women to be heads of a Primary School if the school role went over five hundred pupils. In that case a male head was put in instead. There were several cases where after a woman head had retired from a school, the next head would find that the school role might be over six hundred pupils, no less, or even more, the woman head having falsified the role return in order to keep being head of the school. A ridiculous situation of unjustified sexual discrimination, of course.

I had only been a short time at St. Conval's when a councillor friend phoned and asked me how I was getting on and what I thought of the Pollokshaws' school. I replied that I thought Catholic councillors were a disgrace in allowing Catholic children to be in such a dangerous and unhealthy place as the mid-Victorian building they were in. (There was a tower full of guano right up the side of the class-rooms which each had a door opening into the guano-filled tower. The class-room walls were very hot from the ancient heating system.) My friend replied that he would have my job for my insulting remark about Catholic councillors and slammed the phone down. Ho! Hum! But he then went to the house of the school janitor who did not live at the school (more on that janitor later), and obtained the school keys and went up and inspected the infant building. He phoned me later that night and apologised for his previous reaction to my comments and said that my criticism of Catholic councillors was more than justified. He wasted no time and shortly had a score of high-heid-yins from the Scottish Office, the Scottish Education department, the Glasgow Education Department and the leaders of Glasgow Corporation gathered together in Pollokshaws to inspect the Infant Department. They opened a door and found that the thicko janitor had allowed a Scout group to fill the room completely with all their tents and camping equipment. And this was adjacent to the furnace room and the walls against which tents etc. were lying were quite hot from the adjacent furnace room. They were all horrified and tut-tutted and continued to tut-tut when they inspected the rest of that awful building. They at once agreed that speedy action had to be taken and very swiftly plans were drawn up and the construction of Glasgow's very first open-plan school was completed in the main school playground. When the open-plan replacement was announced, the Head Teacher called a staff-meeting and indignantly proclaimed at great length that she had been trying for a long time to have something done about the disgraceful building without any success and now somebody had succeeded where she had failed. Of course she glared at me. I just laughed and admitted being the culprit.

When the open-plan building was complete the Head resigned from teaching as she wanted nothing to do with it. Would you believe (and I am not making this up) that after her retirement "do "the man-hating Headie asked me to run her back to the school. I reluctantly did so because I suspected that something untoward was coming my way. At the school I parked outside the dining hall where I had parked on my first day. That retiring Head Teacher exploded in rage and told me to drive across the playground and park where she had instructed me to park on my first day there. Unbelievable.

A REAL LADY

My first lady Head Teacher was replaced by the wonderful Mrs. Malloy – who was everything that the previous one was not. We got on like a house on fire.

But we had had appointed at the same time a sad wee Infant Mistress – as the Head of an Infant Department would wrongly be described in those unenlightened times. She had tried three times to be a nun but no convent would have her.

On the new stair-case joining the new and old parts of St. Conval's there was a landing with a large shelf below a window. The over-devout Infant Head would have a large holy statue standing on the shelf. But then the more down to-earth Mrs. Malloy would see that, and she would take it down and replace it with Father Christmas or something more amusing for the Infant pupils to laugh at. And there would always be the amused question raised in the Staff-room at Interval times: "What's on the shelf to-day?"

Mrs. Malloy had a parrot which she brought in occasionally to show the children. Then the bird became a bit worrying. It was taken to a vet who said that it was just dying of old age. Mrs. Malloy had not realised it was over ninety years old. She purchased another parrot after the old one died but unfortunately it did not take to life in Newton Mearns. The vet said that it had been too long in the pet shop and was lonely and sorely missed its former pet shop company. So Mrs. Malloy got a wee dog. But I had moved on by that time, although we still kept in touch socially.

I mentioned the original janitor earlier. I knew he was not the full shilling. He had wonderful tales such as going out into the yard and directing lost pilots to Glasgow airport and man-handling and throwing out a police-inspector who had come in to complain about balls being kicked over the fence into his garden and so on. Daft story came after daft story. He went eventually, and I thought we had been given a decent replacement.

But Mrs. Malloy would be away one afternoon in the week on Education Department committee work. Soon sharp-eyed pupils were telling me where the janitor had "planked" bottles of spirits in various places around the school so that he could have a good booze-up on that afternoon. Of course I had to reveal this too to Mrs. Malloy. So one afternoon she pretended that she was away to her meeting but came back an hour or so later with two officials from the department and they found an inebriated janitor. To my dismay they took him straight out into the street, asked for his uniform cap and jacket and that was him dismissed. It transpired that he had received two previous warnings, and one of them was a final one, about being found drunk on school premises during pupil hours. Altogether it was a very sad business to be involved in. But there were other janitor problems to occur in my school life later.

When I went to Pollokshaws there were two tower blocks in Shawbridge Street of the same design as Ronan Point. After the gas explosion disaster there, the Shawbridge Street tower blocks had been closed to have all gas fitting removed but had gradually begun to be filled up with residents again. One afternoon one of our wee boys was receiving the customary dressing down for being late back for school. The wee soul burst into tears and complained that they lived on the top floor of one of the thirty-odd storied tower block. When he went home for his lunch he found that the lifts in the tower block were not working so he had to climb all those stories up a stair-case. His mammy had sent him for a loaf, so he had to go down all those flights of stairs on his wee feet for the loaf and then climb back up again. Then he had to go down the staircase again to return to school. And here he was getting a row for being late. Poor wee fellow. Those tower blocks have now been demolished.

At St. Conval's two parents told me two different stories about being ostracised. One was a police detective. During what he thought was going to be a routine investigation the suspect pulled a gun and shot dead his colleague. He said he had fled the scene and hid in a cupboard to avoid also being killed. But for doing that he was then ostracised by his former police friends. The unfortunate parent asked me was he really supposed to tackle the gunman bare-handedly as he was not armed himself? The other case also shocked me. One of the parents was a video-tape editor by profession. He applied to join the BBC and had his "Board" in London. On joining the Glasgow BBC, he found that there was no

Catholic employed there and that they did not want a Catholic among them. And this in 1970. So they would not even speak to him and made life among them as unpleasant as they could.

It was about this time too that Archbishop Tom Winning pointed out to the Glasgow Education Department that although there were more Catholic pupils than non-Catholic in Glasgow schools there was no Catholic in any promoted post in the Education Department itself. Tom said that unless that situation was remedied he would go public on the matter. So eventually one was appointed but the high-heid-yins in the Department then went out of their way to put him in as many embarrassing situations as possible, and to make his life with them as unpleasant as could be arranged.

Of course I had tried to run a football team. (There was not one organised there when I went to the school.) They were pretty dismal footballers. I tried and tried to gee them up. On occasion at lunch-time I would have the would-be players gathered together in the playground and on a memorable afternoon I was trying to show them how to kick a football properly with some force. (One of my Wally Dishes nick-names – apart from the obvious one of Tilly Wollan was as I said, the more acceptable one of "Big Bertha") I was shooting across the playground but one effort went off course and right through a class-room window. So much for Big Bertha accuracy. That gave them a laugh – but neither the H. T. nor the class-room teacher.

One Saturday we were playing Langside Primary and all during the first half, one of their parents was being a real pain-in-the-neck with much shouted abuse, at times at me – the referee. At half-time I went over to him and told him that if he did not modify his obnoxious behaviour I would have him ordered out of the ground. I could have done that as he was on our private property. After the end of the game one of our parents wondered that I did not know who that offender was. He told me I had been dealing with one of Rangers' Danish Internationalists. I replied that if I had known that I would not have waited until half-time to deal with him!

OPPORTUNITY MISSED

About this time two of my friends – both highly respected in their professions – one an engineer – one an architect – went round the main football grounds in Europe and produced a wonderful plan for a superb modern second stand at Parkhead. But the short-sighted Celtic Board of the time would not even look at the plans – with egoist White saying that supporters wanted to stand at the matches not sit. What an opportunity missed. We had to wait for a more enlightened owner – the great Fergus McCann – to have much needed ground improvements for the ordinary spectators. About then too, Martin Buchan, recognised as one of the best full-backs in the U. K., became available and I was properly dismayed when Stein made no effort to sign him. It made me wonder how long we were going to stay at the top if players like that were ignored.

OPPORTUNITY GAINED

Then came the request that I apply to be put on the list for Head Teacher interview. Little did I suspect what was to come as a consequence? Never really had any ambition to take on the responsibility of taking charge of a school. I found that thought profoundly frightening. And I knew of friends' wives who would not let their husbands go forward for headships, but the fact that my mother was aging and there was the possibility of having to find money that I did not have, to let her get into a nursing home, won the day.

TWO INTO ONE WILL NOT GO

Eventually I was asked to attend for interview at the Glasgow City Chambers no less. The City Chambers is an awesome building. Well worth a look if you have not been inside. The interior architecture is magnificent. It was completed by architect William Young in Celtic's famous year 1888. When I discovered that co-incidence it gave me a little confidence for what lay ahead but that confidence was soon shattered completely. Trying to be a good cit, I waited at the bus stop in Clarkston Road for a bus into the city. Unlike in the good old tram days, when a Service Five tram into the city would have speedily appeared, I waited and waited. Ambulance after ambulance racing towards Clarkston passed by on the other side of the road. My knocking knees knocked even more.

It was, of course, the day of the Clarkston shopping block gas explosion when twenty poor souls lost there lives.

My nerves were not assuaged at the City Chambers. I was directed to the first floor and was dismayed to find a score or so candidates like myself milling around, all quite disconcerted, and showing it. Listening to the chatter I soon discovered that the large assembled group of councillors had chosen one of their number to do all the questioning and that the question that no one apparently could satisfactorily answer was what to do if one of your lady teachers was in trouble. I did not have a clue either. The councillors' spokesman kept throwing me into dismay by keeping mis-pronouncing St. Aloysius' as St. Aloisius'. I wondered if this was deliberate to test my reaction so I ignored the insult. Then came the sixty dollar question – what to do if one of my lady teachers was in trouble. I knew perfectly well what he meant but I had made up my mind about a response. I was silent for a moment as though the question was unexpected. Then I adopted a puzzled look and said I supposed we would have to do our best to find out who had given her the child and try to have him do his duty and stand by her. The assembled crowd of councillors roared with laughter and the red-faced interviewer indignantly spluttered away that was not what he meant. I do not remember much else about the interview as I was splitting myself too, mentally, at the interviewer's unexpected, and dismayed panic reaction. Unfortunately, and very sad to say, I had to deal with exactly that dilemma later on.

I had presumed that my levity at the City Chambers had ruined any chance I had of further promotion and I was not too worried about that because life under Mrs. Malloy at St. Conval's was going very well indeed.

So it came as a quite unexpected surprise when only a short time after that City Chambers affair, I received a letter appointing me as Head Teacher of St. Augustine's Primary School in the north side of the city on the Monday of the following week. I thought at first one of my pals was conning me but it proved to be a genuine letter. I had friends who were teachers in St. Augustine's Secondary School in Milton so I knew it was not a terribly bad area to be at – though a good travelling distance from Muirend where we were living. (When St. Augustine's secondary was officially opened it was discovered that not even one staff-room had been provided for the teaching staff. Not as bad though as when the Christian Brothers had had a large multi-story school built in Singapore. When the customary bamboo scaffolding enveloping the edifice there was removed, it was realised too late that no stair-cases had been put in the building. See architects...) I was musing on how best to get to Milton but a couple of days later another letter arrived from the Education Office appointing me Head Teacher of St. Philip's School in Ruchazie on the Wednesday following Monday's day of appointment to St. Augustine's. Completely perplexed, I phoned the Education Department and asked them if they really wanted me to go to St. Augustine's and take charge there for three days and then remove myself to St. Philip's School?

BACK TO THE OLD STAMPING GROUND

Ruchazie was once a model housing scheme but a not so-bright councillor decided that was not good enough and that it would have to have its share of the less well-behaved families. So it went rapidly down-hill. Remember the notorious ice-cream wars murders? And that was only one of the crimes committed in the scheme when I was there. There were murders committed too in adjacent Hogganfield Loch Park.

A small but very memorable incident occurred when a brand new replacement telephone box was erected where as a boy I used to watch the blacksmith at work shoeing horses. We discussed how long it might last. Some optimists thought two days. In fact it was demolished in two hours. So much for the Ruchazie community spirit.

I was to discover that since the adjoining Craigend housing scheme was in the process of being completed I also had to look after a school there. (As I said previously, Glasgow Education Department had once built and opened a school for a housing scheme that was never built – so they naturally were determined not to be caught that way twice so future schools would only be officially opened when the appropriate housing scheme was officially completed.) I was saddened to see that the Craigend school was on the site of what used to be the very large tomato glass greenhouses. As I also said previously, when I would be staying with my aunt Agnes and my cousins in Carntyne's Ardmillan Street and they had something to discuss that they did not want me to hear I would be hurriedly sent off to the Craigend tomato place to purchase tomatoes. That I did not mind as I could saunter along and see what was going on in Gartcraig Farm and possibly admire the ploughman's magnificent Clydesdales horses ploughing a field. That farm site was to become the Corporation's Gartcraig bus garage. Loitering on the wooden bridge over the Monkland Canal, I might watch a boatman cutting away weeds and certainly be entertained by a hard-working black water fowl. Then I would divert to the embankment beside some football pitches where we had once buried my pet canary and pay my respects to it, for I had been devoted to it. Next I would go slowly along a lovely narrow road lined with my favourite silver-birch trees. Now all that was gone. To make my distress even more profound, the Craigend school was in the Motherwell Diocese with all that that entailed. Two different religious syllabuses for pupils from two different dioceses sitting in the same class-room. No way to solve that dilemma. Then it became only too clear that the antediluvian Irish parish priest in Ruchazie would not allow the priest from the Motherwell parish into St; Philip's School to assist with the then wrongly titled "Confessions". Should have been "Sacrament of Reconciliation" of course.

I was never much in favour of the routine of going to that Sacrament being imposed on children. No wonder so many left the Church when they grew up. I use the word "antediluvian" of that Ruchazie Parish Priest advisedly – though "obscurantist" might be an even better description of him. On one occasion after a school Mass he stormed into my office and said he never wanted such rubbishy hymns sung at one of his masses again. Where did such nonsense as "tell prisoners that they are prisoners no more, tell blind people that they can see, and set the down-trodden free" come from? I thought inwardly "from the Psalms you old ignorant fool", but held my peace.

I tried to assuage the great anger coming to me from the teaching staff about the Ruchazie parish priest's treatment of the Craigend priest by suggesting that the next time there was a summons to send pupils for the Sacrament of Reconciliation, they only send Ruchazie children. But he had sat and counted his penitents and again he came storming into my office complaining that I had not sent him all the children as he had requested. As gently as I could manage, I pointed out to him that he was breaking

Canon Law by depriving penitents of the choice of confessor where that was a possibility. "You have committed a Mortal Sin" came the shouted response. I asked him why I had committed a Mortal Sin? "Because lay people are not allowed to read Canon Law", was the quite ridiculous retort. I asked him how we were supposed to know what Canon Law said if we did no read it. "That is for me to tell you", came more nonsense. Shaking my head in disbelief I thought "and this is supposed to be Christianity."

I tried to resolve the whole Glasgow-Motherwell affair by having the Glasgow Archdiocese Education Representative out – a fellow Celtic supporter and widower – Fr. Coia. But I was to discover later that he had done absolutely nothing to help. There was an assistant priest attached to St. Philip's Parish and we sometimes shot off together to away games after four o'clock. This was the start of the troubles in the Six Counties and when we returned from a game late on there would be an unmarked police car watching what went on in the parish. Phones were also illegally tapped. This was common practice at all Catholic parishes in the West of Scotland at that time.

That poor assistant priest had ambitions to be the next Sydney McEwan and to further his cause he had his picture published on the front page of The Daily Express singing an aria but dressed in his full Mass regalia. This did not go down well with Tom Winning and my fellow Tim received the father and mother of a dressing down which left him in a most depressed state.

To try to cheer him up a bit, I bought two expensive Stand seats for an International World Qualifier game against Czechoslovakia at Hampden – principally because Celts Hunter, McGrain, Connolly and Dalgleish were in what turned out to be the 2 -1 winning team. Without consulting me in any way the Ruchazie p. p. arranged a parish meeting for that same night and ordered me to attend. I told him I had a previous engagement. He contacted the Director of Education who phoned me and ordered me to attend the meeting. I pointed out the circumstances and replied that I was not going to waste to expensive stand tickets as I had not been consulted about the timing of the parish meeting. I heard no more about it from the Director of Education but the p. p. told his parishioners that by not attending his meeting I showed that I could not care less about his school. (There was a Director of

Education who believed that all teaching staff were on 24 hour duty!)

TB STRIKES

One pouring wet night my assistant priest friend discovered the school janitor lying unconscious in the heavy rain. The alcoholic was rushed to hospital be the emergency service and there it was discovered that he had a virulent form of Tuberculosis. So for three weeks we had a T.B., testing team trying to test everybody connected with the two schools. Eventually they gave up and when I asked for the results of their searching – as far as it had gone – they informed me that they had identified thirteen cases of virulent T. B. in the schools. I expressed my shock and horror but was told that was what they would have expected to be there anyway in the 800 plus pupils and staff. That did not cheer me up any because I then thought of all the teachers in Glasgow (including me!) who might have been leaning over virulent cases of T. B. without being aware of the fact.

NOT OPUS DEI

Two representatives from the Daily Record turned up one morning and explained that they were following up a complaint from one of our parents to the effect that there were several uncovered valve and other openings in the school playground. I said that there certainly were. The proper cast iron covers had been stolen by local scrappies and even replacement wooden covers made out and put on by the janitor had been taken too. So they put a camera down one of the open holes and we arranged for a wee girl in school uniform to stand over the hole peering down into it and they took a picture of her looking into the hole. The story accordingly appeared in the Daily Record and as expected I had an irate call from the Director of Education asking me did I not know that I was not allowed to contact the media about a school matter without his permission. As politely as I could muster, I replied that in fact I had not contacted the Daily Record but that it had been done by a concerned parent and I explained to him all the circumstances that had brought that about. I had no more criticism from the Department but they arranged for a more speedy replacement of the missing covers than the Clerk of Works had previously bothered to arrange.

I previously had had an up-and-downer with this clerk of works. After the war Glasgow had constructed ten all-glass schools because of the then shortage of suitable building bricks. St. Philip's was one of them. They were awful buildings – either too hot in the summer or too cold in the winter and of course the glass walls started at ground level so the bottom windows were easy targets for thugs and vandals and stupid children. I walked round the St. Philip's school as soon as I could manage the time to do it and was horrified to find that several ground- floor panes of glass were completely missing from infant classrooms. I was able to enter a classroom through one empty window space and exit via another space. I tried repeatedly to have the appropriate clerk of works to come and see me but all my efforts were ignored and I did not even receive an acknowledgement of any kind to any of my messages. So I wrote to the Director of Education (he must have loved me!) about the situation and pointed out that I could not be responsible for an insecure school and that the clerk of works would not respond to my messages. A day later I was trying to have a discussion with teachers about the problem of teaching science in a primary school when the meeting was rudely interrupted. All hot and bothered and red-faced and sweating, the missing clerk of works appeared and shouted at me that I had almost cost him his job. I took him into the corridor and told him in equally forceful terms what I thought of him and his refusal to respond to me and that he had got the come-uppance that he deserved for his ill-manners. (I suspected that there was a bit of sectarianism in his ignoring me.) No doubt the teachers had a good laugh at our expense. The wretch tried to excuse himself by saying that they had given up on the task of repairing our school windows. (I knew that unbreakable glass had been tried in schools but the vandals had soon discovered that they melted away under a wee bit of heat.) I pointed out to him that he knew perfectly well that a square metal panel could be placed where there should have been a glass window and that he had better get on with the task of so securing our school and pronto with it. And of course that was eventually done.

POOR RELATIONS

Another problem with St. Philip's School was that it shared the grounds with Ruchazie Primary with no protection between the schools. Repeatedly I would come across wee girls sitting crying because they had been physically bullied by bigger boys from Ruchazie Primary School. And of course the wee girls never gave me a name. I tried tackling the other Head Teacher about the bullying problem but he was in his final retirement year and could not have cared less about anything. So I contacted the Office to see if they could provide a remedy. I should have known better. They contacted the local police and three guesses what action the police took? They arrested some of our boys for dropping litter. I say I should have known better because years before, the Jesuits had complained to the police about what sometimes happened in the Garnethill streets outside St. Aloysius' College and that was the police response there too. They arrested College boys for littering the streets.

A parent came to me several times and said she had a complaint that neither the police nor the local councillor had tried to deal with. Eventually I suggested that she tell her M.P. about the problem. I got an irate call from that Labour M.P. asking me who I thought I was telling one of his constituents to contact him. Unbelievable, but it happened. Are M.P's only there for the money and expenses they receive?

SEARCH PARTIES OUT

Then one afternoon a frightened mother appeared and said that her infant son had not returned home from school at the normal time. The police responded rapidly and had a massive turn-out going from house to house and entering each searching for the child. By six p.m. the missing child had not been found after some three hours of intense police activity. It then transpired that the child had been in a school-friend's house all the time and the occupants had been too frightened to let the police know they had the missing boy. The Inspector in charge of the search came in and astonished me by requesting that I make another pupil go missing. He laughed at my alarm and said that during the search they had discovered three houses stacked with stolen property. Another search would be very welcome.

PEACETIME BLACK OUT

However one long-standing difficulty that really annoyed the police were the street lights being switched out at night – time and time again. Eventually it was discovered that a disgruntled sacked employee of the lighting department had given a master key for the lights to a ten year old pupil (not one of ours!) and the afore-said boy had been having the time of his life going round Ruchazie turning off street lights after street lights. The joys of housing scheme life.

WHO WOULD BE A HEAD TEACHER?

When I first entered the St. Philip's School I looked for the Head Teacher's room and had a shock when I entered. There was a gent in a smart suit sitting there clutching a brief-case. I thought "Not an H. M. I (Her Majesty's Inspector) before I can even draw breath." But he was not an H. M. I. The Office had sent him as an additional teacher. What a ridiculous posting I thought when I heard his story. He had been running his own private school in Southern Rhodesia and here he was in the wildest part of the east end of Glasgow. I sent him up to the Craigend school to help with our Primary Seven classes there. This arrival brought the number of teachers on staff to eighteen. Me: four assistant head teachers: and thirteen teachers: three of the teachers were retired ladies who had come out to help in our crisis – and two of them were mothers of teachers on the staff who had answered their daughters cries for help: .the combined schools role was over eight hundred pupils. What a situation – which was not helped by one of the assistant heads being one of the worst hypochondriacs I have ever had the misfortune to meet. Repeatedly off with some obscure non-existent disease – on return the medical encyclopaedia would be devoured and another mysterious non-existent disease would be thought up and so there would be more absence.

Another problem was that one of the Infant Mistresses (as they were called in those unenlightened days) followed orthodox infant spelling practice while the other followed something called the

Initial Teacher Alphabet. Her teachers' hated it and we could never find enough text-books for them.

I soon learned that it was a good idea to double back unexpectedly from Craigend if St. Philip's thought I was up there. Several times I would find one of the St. Philips's assistant heads nicking off early and standing at the bus stop. Then there was the embarrassment for us both of me having to order her back to the school. I would of course have agreed to her leaving early if she had had the courtesy to ask me first. The replacement janitor (an ex-train driver from the age of steam) had to be watched too. On one occasion I was to find him with half-a-dozen other janitors having a card game and booze-up in one of the classrooms during school hours.

I knew that one of the Fathers McKelvie brothers had been running a school football team but search as a I might I could not discover what had happened to the team jerseys. Some time after I had moved on it was whispered to me that one of the school auxiliaries, who had been a class-mate of mine in St. Mark's Primary School, had actually stolen them.

Oh how I longed for the good old enjoyable days at RAF Kinloss.

Shortly after my first arrival at St. Philip's I encountered a gentleman poking round one of the dark corridors. I asked him what he thought he was doing. It turned out that he was the Director of Education whom I had never met and he had just visited the school to see how I was getting on. Oh! Dear! Tollan boobs again. But he turned out to be quite friendly, even giving me a Masonic handshake – which made me wonder how many Catholic Head Teachers might be in the Masons.

Towards halfway through the school year, the local councillor (whose father had been like mine a GCT motorman) held a ward meeting at which she foolishy announced that there was no teacher shortage. Usual politician blah of course. But our over-worked teachers heard about this and erupted even worse than usual so I had no other choice but to put nine of our classes on part time – which of course I was quite entitled to do.

At the end of the year the Southern Rhodesian gentleman left – which did not surprise me. He asked me for a reference. I am not keen on giving a signed reference at the best of times but all I could honestly say about him was that he had been in charge of a

Primary Seven class in our Craigend School for one year. Shortly, later on, that reference was returned to me covered in large marker-pen scrawls saying what he thought about me, the school, the Education Department and Glasgow in general. None of it very complimentary! I had a wee thought and filed it away. Sure enough, later, a letter came from the Department requesting a reference for him. I replied that he already had been given the reference enclosed and this was how it had been returned. I heard no more from the office but presume they had some amusement too.

BIG CHANGE COMING

At the end of the school year came a huge surprise. My friend in the Department phoned me to say that the Education Department were going to officially open the school in Craigend and did I want to stay on in Ruchazie or go through the bother of opening a new school. Was I glad to have the chance of being shot of that Irish priest – an uncharitable thought of course – so I plumped for the chance to be the first head of the brand new Craigend school.

I felt that that made up a wee bit for a disappointment that had followed with my appointment to St. Philip's School. The Education Committee in their wisdom had said that we were to be one of the first schools in Glasgow to be issued with pupils' computers. Quite an enlightened proposal. But a full Corporation meeting turned the idea down – rubbishing computers and saying that they would only ever be an expensive waste of time. See some politicians…

I had a parting present from Celtic before leaving Ruchazie. A player – who better be nameless – crashed his car into our school railings on Gartloch Road and allegedly fled the scene, leaving a girl passenger injured in the car.

I said to my friend in the Department before leaving that one of the St. Philip's female teachers would make an excellent Head Teacher and I was more than pleasantly surprised when she actually became the head teacher at St. Philip's.

WHAT'S IN A NAME

Bobby Murdoch had gone to Middlesbrough bad ankle and all.

Years previously my mother and myself were at a reserve game at Parkhead. A few seats along from us were two gentlemen. One was very agitated and was biting his nails the whole time. My mother, being my mother, moved along beside him and asked him if he needed medical attention as there seemed to be something amiss. The poor chap explained that his son was playing his first trial for Celtic and he was anxious that he should make the grade. He need not have worried. Many years later Bobby Murdoch told me that the other man with his father had been the teacher from Our Lady's High School who had recommended him to Celtic.

But now Celtic were obviously going to be on a downward slope. Although Bobby Lennox scored his 250th goal in a 6 – 1 thrashing of East Fife at Methil when we won the League, and none other than Harry Hood scored a hat-trick against the 'Gers in the League Cup, Dundee won the League Cup and we went out of Europe in that notorious tie against the thugs of Athletico Madrid.

David Hay was to leave after his serious injury and loss of wages dispute with Stein. When the new school session began the Irish parish priest in Ruchazie discovered that I was no longer Head Teacher of "his" school and told his parishioners that I was a traitor who had betrayed him and them. Wonderful Christianity again of course!

But his parishioners were to "betray" him too. Because of several "disturbances" at parish social centres, Tom Winning had ordered all the parish social centres in his Archdiocese to be closed down. Accordingly the poor old Ruchazie parish priest tried to close his but his parishioners refused to do that. There was a consequent court case, and it was ruled that since the licence for the premises was not in his name he had no legal right to close the place down. So off he went away back to Ireland in a huff. Meanwhile I had to re-organise things between the Ruchazie and Craigend schools, moving the Craigend pupils out of Ruchazie to Craigend and the Ruchazie pupils out of Craigend back to Ruchazie.

Having sorted that mess out it was obvious that the Craigend school was over-crowded and that as usual we did not have enough teachers.

I even resorted to stopping at shops and asking the employees if they happened to know of any teachers that were not teaching and explained why I was asking. If they were kind enough to help out I

Some of the back-court gang I loved to play with.

With solemn mum. But what am I plotting?

First Communion show-off with extended family.

Dad on left with highly entertaining twin - Uncle Jimmy.

Pa and me.

Ma and me.

Nag and me.

Well I made buck house.

And I still hate dressing up.

St Aloysius Jesuit House.

St Mark's primary school.

The Sheddens.

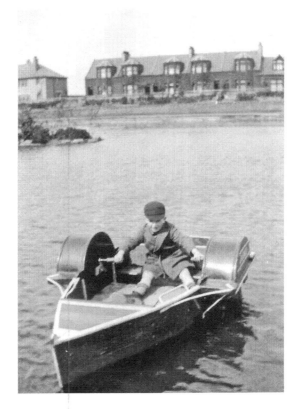

Girvan - the boating lake.

Girvan - Byne hill.

Girvan - on the shore.

Girvan - Nag.

Girvan - golfing.

Girvan - Pa in Victory Park.

Girvan - PS Waverley.

RAF moral rearmament course led by the excellent Rainhill Jesuits.
(Be sure that I visited the site of the famous Rainhill trials!)

Some of the air wireless mechanics; the poor old erk on the left was a ground wireless electrician/mechanic. Guess who?

Coastal command station Kinloss personnel.

Me clowning on Dingle beach.

Dingle.

Yatesbury erks.

Tommy Madden with his 1926 AJS Big-Port.

VHF Controller and me.

TEACHER

Left to right: Jimmy Gordon with his broken arm in a sling - then Greek master; later ran Radio Clyde and Visit Scotland. Lady is headteacher of the school we usually stayed in - Lycee des aux Claires - so-called because it stood between rivers Isere and Drac. Then Paddy Maguire, science master. And on right, happy Gerry McDonald, kind friend and marvellous college rugby coach, then later became head PE teacher at St Roch's secondary. Great and wonderful organiser of the holiday is the cleric in the group, Father Greenwood SJ; at that time he was very distressed by the extinction of his favourite team - Accrington Stanley!

St Aloysuis' College - Paris pupils.

My suffering souls: class Ogilvie six, 1961-62.

John Ogilvie Hall - Dover 1967 pupils.

John Ogilvie Hall - Paignton pupils.

St Rose of Lima School - building presentation at opening.

St Rose of Lima School - audience at opening.

Skipper.

Sailing away.

Crinan canal.

Garrowhill garden.

The pontiff always looked at the person behind. Was he looking for a possible assassin?

Who is the smartly-dressed chap on the left? Unusual for him!

Arriving at Nemi in Joseph Corcoran's car.

Wonder what the joke was?

Some of our Beda year. A Beda year normally started with 32 candidates for the priesthood but usually only eight or nine out of the beginners became priests. Out of our 32 one died and twenty-eight were ordained priests. Have often wondered why that came about? Our priest-preparation director was Fr Brian Michael Noble - fifth from the right - great man who became Bishop of Shrewsbury but suffered severe illness there. I often wished I had gone to Shrewsbury instead of Dunkeld.

Innerpeffrey Chapel once held tombs of pre-Reformation bishops flat on its floor, but a concrete floor has now been laid over them.

St Columba's Church - Birnam.

Our Lady of the Sea - Tayport.

St Bernadette's - Tullibody.

Kinnoull hill.

Train from Dundee from Kinnoull hill.

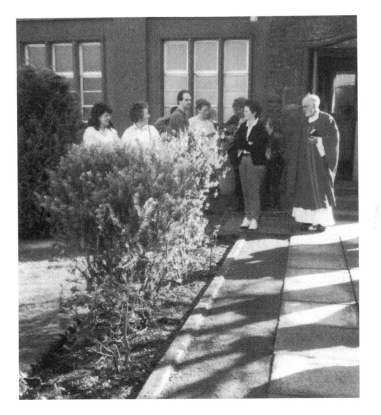

Palm Sunday at St James', Kinross.

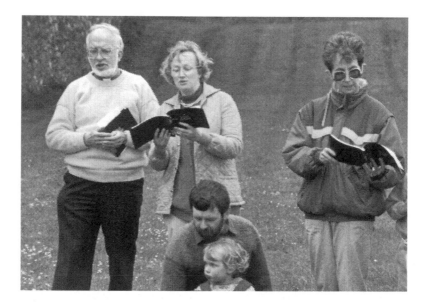

Hymns outdoors at Loch Leven.

Churches Together at Kinross: poor Jimmy the woof would rather have been chasing the local wild deer.

Kinross Academy musicians generously performed for us at Kinross House.

THE CHIEF OF CHAPLAINS
UNITED STATES NAVY

takes pleasure in presenting this

CERTIFICATE OF APPRECIATION

to

Father William Tollan

In recognition of loyal and faithful service to
God and Country through   outstanding contribution
of time and talent to the religious community at

Chapel of Faith

Edzell, Scotland

Date: 30 September 1992

David E. White
Chief of Chaplains

OPNAV 1730/1 (22-93)

Certificate from the US navy at Edzell.

The 'hidden' seminary at Scanlan.

Hospitality in the CR Smith suite at Celtic Park.

COLORADO

Denver and Rio Grande narrow gauge railway - Loco 583.

Approaching the Rockies. Buffalo in the distance. This was Codi country.

With Holly and Eileen.

Inside Annunciation Church.

The plot where grandfather had his profitable hardware store.

Grandmother's grave.

A section of the standard gauge line between Leadville and Climax is operated as a passenger excursion railroad called the Leadville, Colorado and Southern Railroad.

Tourist train heading for Climax.

With owner Bill Sibley who with wife Marjorie were so gracious with me in Colorado.

To the Alpine tunnel - Alpine tunnel sign. Alpine tunnel is a 1,772 feet narrow gauge railroad tunnel located east of Pitkin, Colorado on the former Denver, South Park and Pacific Railroad route from Denver to Gunnison. At an elevation of 11,523 feet, it was the first tunnel constructed through the Colorado Continental Divide, and according to the US Forest Service "remains the highest railroad tunnel and the longest narrow gauge tunnel in North America." However, it did not last long in service. Construction began in January 1880 and was scheduled to last for six months but instead dragged on till July 1882, and the line was abandoned in 1910 due to minor damage in the tunnel. Now the tunnel is sealed shut and the remaining trackbed serves as a trail for hikers and off-road vehicles.

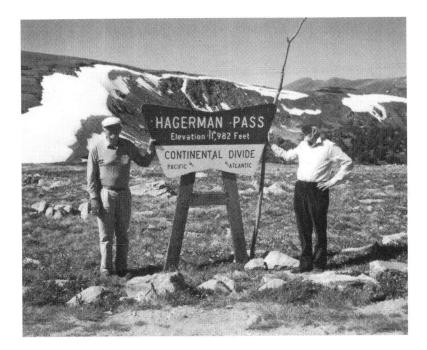

At Hagerman pass on the continental divide. Hagerman Pass, elevation 11,925 feet, is a high mountain pass that crosses the continental divide in the Rocky Mountains of central Colorado.

Georgetown Loop - shay-type locomotive of kind designed especially for use on temporary uneven lumber tracks. Note absence of coupling rods. The Georgetown Loop railroad was one of Colorado's first visitor attractions. This spectacular stretch of narrow gauge railroad was completed in 1884 and considered an engineering marvel for its time. The thriving mining towns of Georgetown and Silver Plume lie 2 miles apart in the steep, narrow canyon of Clear Creek in the Rocky Mountains west of Denver. Engineers designed a corkscrew route that travelled nearly twice that distance to connect them, slowly gaining more than 600 feet in elevation. The route included horseshoe curves, grades of up to 4%, and four bridges across Clear Creek, including the massive Devil's Gate High Bridge.

Woodstock. On 10 March 1884, Woodstock, Colorado, was levelled by an avalanche and was never rebuilt. Six children died in the boarding house and seven others lost their lives to the white death. A train which had stopped there for refreshments was climbing the other side of the valley and crew and passengers were horrified to see the tragedy happening. It was only guessed that the rumble of the train or the whistle broke the snow loose from high above and sent it down the mountain.

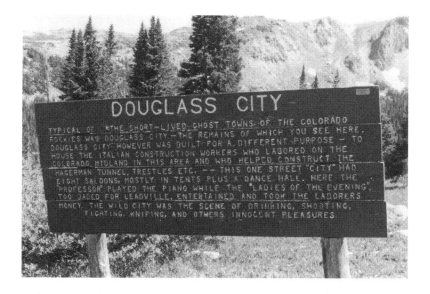

Douglass City sign. Douglass City sits at an elevation of 11,000 feet , high in the majestic Rocky Mountains. The town was built to house Italian workers who were helping to build the Colorado Midland Railroad. There isn't much left to remember the town by, but there is just enough that it's easy to imagine what had been here. The frames of some cabins still remain, and there is a sign posted in the area that states that the city had eight saloons, a dance hall, and a professor who played the piano while the ladies of the evening (who apparently were fed up with the 'city life' in Leadville) entertained the immigrant labourers as they emptied their pockets much quicker than they'd earned the money in them. The real question is, how did they get the piano all the way up there? I can't tell you how many times I've imagined their journey up those rugged mountains on horseback and wild burro, awkwardly carrying the backbreaking piano up a narrow and brutal trail.

In October 1859, prospector Jim Taylor panned some gold from Willow Creek, and carried it back to camp in a tin cup; he named the valley "Tin Cup Gulch". For years the areas was the site of seasonal placer mining, but no year-round communities were established, partly because of the danger of Indian attack. In 1878, lode deposits were discovered in the area, and the town of Virginia City was laid out in March 1879. By the 1880 census, the town had a population of 1,495. Virginia City was incorporated in August 1880, but confusion with Virginia City, Nevada, and Virginia City, Montana, caused the residents to change the name. The town was reincorporated in July 1882 as Tin Cup. Early Tin Cup was a violent place. Town marshal Harry Rivers died in a gunfight in 1882, and marshal Andy Jameson was shot to death in 1883. The town population declined when the mines were exhausted. The post office closed in 1918, and the last town election was held in 1918.

TRAMS

Artic on short-working turn-back at P. Vittoria Emmanuel.

Stanga at Porta Maggiore - Roma's main tram junction in my time there.

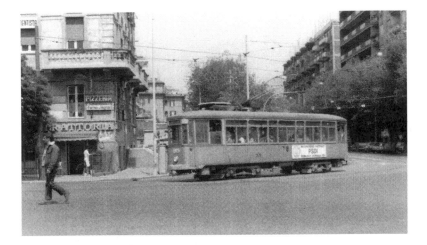

MRS car outside Trastevere station.

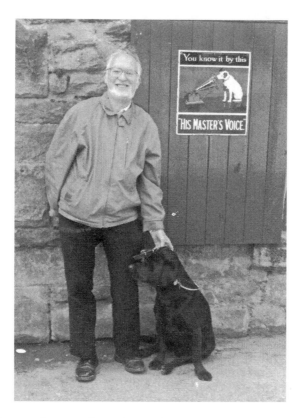

With Jimmy the woof at the national tramway museum, Crich, Derbyshire.

Operating 1017 (Photographer - A Gordon).

Dressed up for Adam Gordon's book "Wearing of the green".

Me and a cup of tea - Summerlee.

Tramway village - 1282.

My favourite motorman and fellow, Tim Hamilton Brown, takes the crowd east (Photographer - W Guthrie).

Last tram and personnel leaving Dennistoun depot to go to
Dalmarnock. This coronation ran via the forbidden-to-coronations
sharp curve at Parkhead Cross. I suppose that was the equivalent
of putting two fingers up to the thicko politicians of the time!
(Photographer - W Guthrie).

Coronation on Argyle Street.

Standard car at bottom cross-over in Dennistoun terminus sidings.
Note bow collector is not touching the overhead.

Coronation car at Bishopbriggs terminus (Photographer - W Guthrie).

PALS

Jimmy the Woof with friends - what a great character he had.

Jimmy the woof in the Ochils.

Freckles was the first springer spaniel from CR Smith. A grandparent of the dogs was the champion dog at Crofts one year. This was the cleverest - Freckles - died of weed-killer poisoning, only six. I wept buckets. Probably spread by a stupid council gardener. Loved his ball.

Connie: this was Connie. Came after spending four years in a ghillie's cage. Died this year through old age on Queen's Jubilee day so could not get a vet to come to help her final moments. Loved picking up golf balls and once caught and brought me a hare; and a herring; and hedgehogs and birds and snails galore.

Zak: replacement Zak came in the autumn. Loves foraging and zig-zagging like the proverbial mad march hare. Previous to coming, lost the sight of one eye through losing a lens cap. Has a tremendous pedigree but is unable to reproduce. But very obedient and we get along fine.

would go to the teacher's address and try to persuade the teacher to come and help and would even say that if they chad a small baby or child to look after the school auxiliaries would take care of that problem for them. Despite all my repeated efforts I only succeeded in persuading one good-natured soul to come and join the teaching staff.

To try and help out I started to take a class for half-a-day and was consequently struggling to cope. The Craigend school was semi-open plan, the idea being that some of a class could be outside their given class-room working in an open space and as a consequence the class-rooms were on the small side especially as the class roles were on the large side. Most of the teachers did not go for the outside idea at all, so the wee class-rooms became very much over-crowded.

Then I received an order to go to a meeting with the Chief H. M. I. for Scotland. I protested that things were in a desperate state in my school staffing-wise, and my absence would make things worse. But I was told I must obey that order – or else!

At first I split my sides laughing internally at this Inspector for he was a complete double for Arthur Askey with all Arthur's extraordinary put-on actions. I thought the clot might also have gone on to do Arthur's silly songs, jokes and dances and even utter the famous "I thank you!"

I wondered what strings had been pulled to make this buffoon the Chief Inspector for Scotland. He had his pet Head Teacher with him – obviously from a school in a very posh area, for the Inspector started to lambaste us in his audience for not running our schools as properly and well as his "star" did. Our critic went on to tell us that we did not delegate this that and the next thing to our assistant heads as his pet did and as we ought to have done. I had had more than enough of the nonsense he was spouting, so I stood up and told him he did not know what went on in our schools. My assistant heads were teaching full-time and I was trying to help out with our teacher shortage by taking a class also when I could. I pointed out that we were so over-crowded that to get from a classroom door to a teacher's desk I had to ask pupils to move their desks out of the way. He shouted at me that he would have my job for my impudence in interrupting him. I pointed out that he had not hired me so that he could not fire me. He angrily responded that he would have an inspector out to inspect my school on the following Monday. I said I would look forward to that and that the visiting inspector would be very welcome.

So first thing on the Monday a quite pleasant, younger inspector came into my office and began by saying that I did not do my cause any justice by exaggeration. I said nothing in reply but ushered him into school corridor and invited him to open any class-room door of his choice.

He went to the first door, opened it slightly and peered in. He quickly closed the door and came back into my office. So you were not exaggerating, he said, shaking his head. I agreed smiling.

Then followed a remarkable question. He asked me how he could obtain a season ticket for Celtic Park!

For some strange reason, no Inspector ever came near me nor my school for the rest of the time I was a school head!

NO TAILOR'S DUMMIES?

Another of my many difficulties emerged. The Craigend parish priest wanted a school uniform- which I did not think was a bad idea. But he wanted it to be purple and could not be persuaded otherwise. I knew that a uniform in the colour of purple would be more expensive than a uniform in any other colour and I had no wish to inflict such unnecessary expense on our working-class parents. I had an outfitter in and went over prices and materials with him but thought that he was chancing his arm a bit and would prove to be far to expensive, so I fished around various sources and found an outfitter who could supply purple uniforms at a more reasonable price than the first man. So the new supplier got the uniform deal and then when he discovered that, the first outfitter blew his top with me because he had not received the deal after all his initial effort.

SEALED AND SETTLED

But I had other things on my plate too. Frequently I had to be involved in friendly meetings with the builder's Clerk of Works and the Education Department Clerk of works (not that Ruchazie one!) over finalising various details about the school building. Then came the day when I was told I could not attend their final meeting. Fairly obviously a financial deal was in the making between them but clearly the school was about to be finally officially opened and I was relieved that that was going to happen at last.

WHAT IS IN A NAME

Unexpectedly, I was tipped off that because of my efforts to get the school going, I would be given the privilege of naming the school.

The adjoining Motherwell parish church was dedicated to Saint Dominic but because Glasgow already had a school named after St. Dominic in Castlemilk, that title could not be used to avoid confusions arising. John Ogilvie had been used previously, but I have always admired the heroes that took our Church in Scotland through the Reformation and Penal times. Ninian Winzet and Quintin Kennedy confounded Protestant Reformers with words, but a long line of Apostolic Administrators such as Thomas Nicholson and James Gordon risked their lives and made arduous journeys throughout wildest Scotland to administer sacraments and encourage the few other priests to do the same.

For intending priests who could not manage to reach Scottish seminaries abroad, hidden seminaries such as Scalan and Lismore and Preshome were contrived.

The longest serving Administrator was George Hay who soldiered on all through the dark Hanoverian days. So I wanted George Hay to be remembered by the name of the Craigend school.

When the Englishman, Bishop Thomson, phoned me to ask what name I had chosen for his school, I said "George Hay" and began to explain why. But he irritated and annoyed me by interrupting with a long-drawn-out sarcastic Sassenach drawl: "Surely you know, Mr. Tollan, that a school has to be named after a saint?" I said that I certainly did not know that had to be the case, but he better name the school himself. Silly old short-tempered me. Obviously I could have given everyone a laugh by naming the school St. William – after St. William of Perth who was martyred at Rochester while on pilgrimage to Roma, or St. William of York, the saintly archbishop who was probably poisoned. (Later this English Bishop Thomson named one school after homosexual John Henry Newman and another after a Pole – John Paul II. So much for a school having to be named after a saint!)

183

The name he chose appalled me – St. Rose of Lima. Apparently she was the choice because she had been a member of the Dominican Third Order. I was appalled because this strange lady was from a very wealthy family and she had decided to be a hermitess living at the bottom of her wealthy garden. (Wish I could have been a hermit living at the bottom of a wealthy garden away from all the slings and arrows of outrageous fortune!)

How do you explain that one as an exemplar for the tough weans of the wildest part of the east end of Glasgow?

But that name was to give me an unexpected good laugh. After the name of the school was known I went to attend a Head Teachers' meeting. On my entry the whole assembled crowd stood up, cheered and clapped, and shouted: "Here comes old Roses' Lime Juice! I thoroughly enjoyed the good joke.

Then came the formal opening of the school. The contractors invited me to choose a large picture for the school and my father having worked on the Glasgow cars – and me also – I selected a view of a large red Standard Bogie Car Mark Two on GCT service 9. That choice of course went down like a large lead brick with the rest of the staff and I had to endure a lot of vocal objection over my choice. Not that that bothered me. What bothered me was the ceremony of opening the school.

The huge Strathclyde Region had taken over the Glasgow Education Department and in the platform party for the opening ceremony were to be, as well as the Archbishop of Glasgow and the Bishop of Motherwell, a load of high-heid-yins from Strathclyde Region and Glasgow Corporation – too many to be on the actual platform so that the first two rows of seats facing the platform were to be part of the platform – if you see what I am getting at.

When I tried to become involved in making the seating plan, I was told in no uncertain terms that the seating arrangements were to be arranged by Strathclyde and had nothing to do with me.

Unfortunately the Craigend Parish priest and his cohorts were placed in the seats facing the platform and not on the platform itself. For some time after the opening I was repeatedly assailed by the parish priest and his associates for insulting him and them because I had not put them on the platform itself, and they just would not accept that I had had nothing to do with the seating arrangements.

In fact I felt very sorry for that parish priest. The architect of his church, in a not so wise idea, had provided the church with an all-aluminium roof which was taller at one end and sloped down into a lower upward curve at the other. Of course youths from all over the place came to climb on to the roof and enjoy the marvellous free giant "shute". It was a proper nightmare for the parish priest.

WHERE OH WHERE HAS MY LITTLE DOG GONE?

On a Holiday of Obligation the whole school was sitting in the next-door Church waiting for Mass to begin. We waited and waited and waited, but there was no sign of the priest appearing to celebrate the Mass for us. As usual it was all my fault, and I was getting the darkest of dark looks from the teachers who had the difficulties of having to keep their classes in good order. I had not a notion where he was. Not in his house, hall or sacristy for sure, was all I could establish. Eventually the long delay was explained. His good old dog had been standing at the door of the church wagging his tail in friendly greeting for the arrivals and the stupid first teacher had grabbed the poor animal, opened an adjoining cupboard door and shut the friend in there without bothering to tell anyone. The frantic parish priest had been away going round Ruchazie and Craigend and Hogganfield Loch Park looking for his missing pal.

PLACE YOUR BETS PLEASE!

The take-over by Strathclyde meant that to equalise all the School Summer Holiday arrangements throughout the huge Region, Glasgow Schools received an extra week's holiday. For the first time ever, I was able to enjoy Ascot Week on the Television. In those days I was keen on the then ITV Seven and the each-way sixpenny Yankee (you picked four horses and put them into trebles and doubles and an accumulator) a harmless bit of fun which made the race-meeting on TV much more interesting. Of course you had to study the form and that too was interesting for a stupid mind like mine.

That Ascot week I, quite amazingly, cleaned up £84 with my wee sixpenny bets. Did I not bless Strathclyde Region! (Many years previously – when I was having to cope with the domineering Jesui Head Teachery, the seven horses I had picked for my ITV Seven all won. But two of them had been entered in different race meetings from the ITV meeting . When that happened then was that you went on to the favourite in the ITV race they did not race in. I am not making this up. Six of the horses won O K, but the other favourite I had to go on came to the last fence about twenty lengths ahead of its field AND FELL – depriving me of about £94,000. And I had been looking forward to telling the bullying Jesuit that there was a vacancy at John Ogilvie Hall. C'est-la-gemme!)

ONE OUT ALL OUT

When I was at Craigend there was a lot of teacher unrest and annoyance at their low pay and having to cope with shortage of staff – and rightly so.

But at Craigend there was one teacher who was about ten or twelve years older than the rest and who had been in previous employment before becoming a teacher. I often wondered why she had done that. She had the younger teachers by the nose and when an official EIS strike was called they would not take part – although EIS members – but then she would have them out on unofficial strike just to cause more chaos. This did not please me as I was getting unnecessary trouble and bother. So I told them what I thought of their irresponsible actions. That made me most popular.

LONG HAIR DAYS

But one of the young girls was an excellent teacher and she asked me if she could organise a school football team. Naturally I was all for that but she then said that one of the Primary Five girls was by far the best footballer in the school and could she play her in the team. I said that I had no objection to that happening but I thought that she would run into trouble from other schools and the Schools Football Association and there would also be the problem of toilet facilities etc.

I suppose it was because of the fashionable long hair of those days but the girl played in the school team and there was never a squeak of protest about it.

That fine teacher had previously wanted to be an Air Hostess but on her application was found to be one and a half inches below the minimum height required. Then to my dismay the minimum height requirement was lowered and she decided she was going to try again. I tried all I knew to dissuade her but she was determined and so we lost our best teacher. When she was leaving the schoolgirls all gathered round her and sang "going on a jet plane". After only four months on Glasgow-London flights she had enough and returned and told me that what I had said was correct. But the Department would not let her come back to Craigend.

SEE LEYLAND CARS...

When I was appointed Head Teacher and had that long journey from Muirend to Ruchzie to make – I made a huge mistake. After reading many car reviews I applied to the Muirend bank for a loan to purchase a car and was told in no uncertain terms by the bank manager that I was not a fit person to receive a loan from his bank. But only a few weeks later I was called back to the bank and told by the deputy manager that the manager was off sick, he was running the bank, and he thought it had been a disgrace that a worthy person such as myself (sic!) had been refused the loan requested and he arranged for me to have the money originally requested.. A few weeks' later I was called back to the bank – this time by the great man himself who was back from his sick leave. Angrily he told me that I had been refused a loan and would have to give back the money received. All a bit like Dad's army! Needless to say I did not return any money, for I had brought a brand new Triumph Dolomite to replace my Renault 1100.

Boy was that money wasted. First afternoon I parked outside the house with it, the old City Registrar opposite reversed out of his driveway and backed right into the side of the Dolomite. He denied having done it although I was standing watching the smash. I could never get the power out of the twin-carb engine that I should have been getting and even after five return visits to the dealer there was no improvement. As I left the last time their foreman said I should be getting much better performance! I asked him why he thought I had been returning repeatedly with the car. I decided to take matters into my own hands and removed the cylinder head and had a look-see and it was obvious that the crank-shaft had been installed some ninety degrees out of turn. That fixed, I had the power, but to get that engine to fit under the low bonnet of the Dolomite, British Leyland had replaced the normal cylinder head with one of reduced height and that continued to give over-heating trouble. Although I had had the body especially under-sealed, one day the whole under-body of the car dropped off. I made up my mind never to buy a British-made car again.

CHILDRENS' PANELS

One very foggy morning, on my way to Craigend, I had just turned from Shettleston Road on to Rigby Street -a favourite short-cut – when fortunately I spotted that a thick telephone cable had been tied at windscreen height from the railings of a scrappy's yard across the road to a lamp standard on the other side of the road..

I looked in my mirror and there was a primary school boy wearing a most distinctive pull-over peering round the corner of Beardmore's Howitzer Shop waiting to see what was going to happen. I knew that he had to be from my old school – St. Mark's Primary – the only school around. I phoned a friend who was Head Teacher at St. Mark's, and he knew immediately who the culprit was. He told me that he was hardly ever out of serious trouble and the school was at its wits-ends trying to cope with his nuisances. On one occasion they thought that they were going to get respite. The pest had fallen out with a neighbour in Dalton Street and had found the woman's baby sleeping in the pram. Getting a piece of wire he had put it round the child's neck and strung it up with the wire to the roof of the pram. The poor mother had come back and had discovered this and in her shock had collapsed and injured her head on a kerb and had to be rushed to hospital. My friend thought that his school was going to get a breather from the miscreant but he was back from the Children's Panel within two hours – the Children's Panel having decided to take no action.

Most of us, and particularly the Police, had no time for the Children's Panel and regarded the whole farce as a waste of time. A male offender would turn up in a nice suit. And be beautifully turned out. And the whole thing was obviously a mistake from the Panel's point-of-view – members of the panel coming from such refined areas as Bearsden or Newton Mearns.

I once checked all the addresses of panel members and only one came from a housing scheme, and I could never get any of our parents to join the panel as they were rightly afraid of reprisals being taken against them.

Year after year the head of the Children's Panel would be on the media preening himself about how successful the panel was as referrals were reducing each year. Referrals reducing, of course, because referring pests to the panel was largely regarded as a waste of time.

One morning at Craigend I saw the Dolomite had a flat tyre and intended dealing with it at lunch time. (Its Pirelli tyres were pretty duff and I often had a flat tyre.) But the Craigend unit policeman had spotted this, removed his tunic and replaced the flat tyre with the spare – all un-asked. I was staggered but very pleased at his kind action. One morning I was having the usual coffee meeting with the Craigend and Ruchazie unit men to discuss local affairs. (For obvious reasons the two unit men preferred to come on duty together at irregular times to keep a watch out on the local neds.) At the end of our friendly meeting one of the unit men went to say something but the other gave him a dunt in the ribs. After they had gone I did a quick think and went out to look at the Dolomite. Sure enough the road tax disc was months out of date. So at four o'clock I went straight down to Bothwell Street and bought a proper road disc. You could do that nae bother in those unenlightened days. I thought that a very decent "no-action-taken" by the unit men.

They always gave the school great service. On one occasion a local resident was handing out anti-Catholic leaflets to all and sundry. I showed one to our unit man and asked him if he could do anything about the perpetrator. The unit man said that would be no bother and that he would warn the pamphleteer for breach of the peace. And that did stop him.

Great action on a complaint unlike many years later when I was walking the dog at Uddingston Cricket Ground and two police officers were sitting in their police car watching the cricket. A mountain biker was making a great nuisance and disturbance on the public pathway along the banks of the Clyde. I politely asked the pair to do something about the nuisance but all the lazy blighters thought to do was hand me a load of guff about the biker being on private land etc., and they needed a complaint made by the land-owner. They must have thought they were talking to an old brainless fool. Later, early one morning, a police superintendent friend was walking his black lab past the Uddingston cricket pavilion and discovered two uniformed police officers both sound asleep in their police car. He wakened them and asked them why they were not properly carrying out their patrol duties. He was greeted with curses and the threat of arrest for breach of the peace. They soon discovered their mistake when they were disciplined, received the black mark on their record – which meant no possibility of promotion – and were posted to different police stations. I wondered if they were the same pair that had treated me with nonsense.

RED HAT IN THE OFFING

I became puzzled by the number of times Tom Winning came to visit me at Craigend. Then on one visit he came out with it. He said that he wanted all his Head Teachers to be married. The penny dropped. Obviously someone had told him I was a homosexual. I indignantly explained that I certainly was not one. He asked me then why I had not married. I told him that when I was seventeen I was accepted as a novice by the Society of Jesus, but that my father flatly refused to sign the necessary release form. I would have to wait until I was twenty-one, and although the Society had obtained a deferment from military service for me, I thought that I might as well experience the Royal Navy for a few years. But they were not taking anyone, so I went into the Royal Air Force instead. While doing my time at Kinloss I discovered that my father was dying of cancer and since my mother had buried five infants before I survived, I could hardly go away and leave her to fend for herself as she was now nearing seventy years old. The Archbishop listened with interest and said that if I still wanted to try for the priesthood after my mother died he would arrange for me to go to the Beda College in Roma.

Outside the school a double-deck bus hired for a school outing was being filled up with eager pupils. And some parents were standing alongside waiting to wave their children off. (No doubt heaving sighs of relief after they left!) But as we were doing this, a passing heavy road roller veered left and went into the side of the bus. Cue "stramash" again! It was revealed afterward that a steering chain had broken just as the roller was attempting to pass by. Fortunately no pupil was injured. But some were scared – as were the waiting parents. Me too! Me too! Then the fun really started. The bus company did not have another replacement bus available. So no outing for the fortunate/unfortunate children that day. The angered parents kept insisting that in Alexanders' bus garage in Stepps there were plenty of buses lying empty. In vain I tried to point out to them that when I phoned that Garage I was told what I had expected that these were service buses needed for Alexanders' duties and that in any case they would not be licensed for a day out hire with school pupils. All to no avail. Head Teacher to blame as usual.

PATIENCE REWARDED?

Then I heard that one of the two obdurate Head Teachers who had caused all the confusion over my first H T appointment was telling people that the Head at St. Margaret Mary's Primary was retiring and he was going to Castlemilk. I went to the Education Department and pointed out that for some time now they had a letter from our Doctor, Eugene Connolly, requesting that I might be transferred to a school nearer home as I was the sole carer for an aging mother. The appointments department looked through a huge thick file about me and said that they had no such letter. I assured them that it had been sent in. So we went down to the finance department and they too had a thick file about me. They were good enough to look carefully through that file too and sure enough buried almost at the bottom of the pile was the letter from our doctor. They were very decent and agreed that I should fill the Castlemilk vacancy on compassionate grounds.

HERE COMES THE BRIDE

We had a big laugh at a Shawfield match when a bridal party dressed in full wedding regalia came into the front row of the stand before the game started.

DOWNWARD SPIRAL

But things were not so happy at Parkhead. It was obvious that the disgraceful head-on accident on the A74 had badly affected Stein. And the Lisbon team had almost disappeared, apparently because poor mentally and physically sick Stein resented their making themselves better off as a result of Lisbon than he had done. And he was enraged about the Auld-led mutiny before the second European Final. He gradually dispersed the Quality Street Kids – who might have become even better than the Lisbon Lions. The Board felt that he was determined that no-one at Parkhead would emulate his great Lisbon achievements. One player, John Gorman- a superb left-back – alleged that he was transferred away against his will to Carlisle in order to settle a Stein gambling debt, and later a Director alleged too that that the club had never received a penny of the huge British record £440,000 Dalgleish transfer fee and Dalgleish himself was to say that he had not requested that transfer.

Sean Fallon was dismissed after a quarrel (not of his making) with the directors over disorganised arrangements on a tour abroad and Davie McParland had been brought in as assistant manager with a view to his replacing Stein as manager. Stein wanted nothing to do with that arrangement and many years later, in Tullibody, McParland's father told me, that in consequence, Stein had not spoken a single word to his son in two years.

BILLY'S BACK

After an excellent managerial stint with Aberdeen – where he had finished second in the League and reached the Scottish Cup final in his first season in charge – McNeil was brought back as manager. I always think when Ferguson gets all the plaudits for his Aberdeen stay, nothing is ever said about Billy laying the foundations there – just as McGrory never gets the acclaim he should get for signing most of the Lisbon Lions. Although Stein had made some remarkable signings in his closing years as manager – for example there was the strange Alfie Conn signing – allegedly because his father wanted to stop him marrying a Catholic and Stein took his part: Deans with his hat-trick against Hibs in that six goal thrashing in the League Cup Final: the fine footballer Stanton and the likes of strong man Icelander "Shuggy" Edvallson (on the recommendation of a Church of Scotland minister), there was much for Billy to do re re-trenchment when he took over the Parkhead reins. His first game in charge saw us lose 2 – 6 at home to Burnley (of all sides) in the then Inter-city Cup. Billy improved matters, however, by two great signings – Provan from Kilmarnock and McLeod from Dumbarton.

But my attention, of course, was largely taken up by my move to Castlemilk.

Poor Jock Stein refused a directorship – went as manager to Leeds for only a few months as allegedly their players did not take to his ways – and then he made that fateful move to become Scotland's manager. Requiescat in pace.

UP RA MULK!

"Up ra Mulk" being the local patois for living in Castlemilk.

After the war, instead of carrying out the pre-war intention of renovating and improving the old tenement flats, the politicians and planners decided in their wisdom to build three vast housing schemes miles out from the city. Financially it would have been impossible to connect the city tramway to each of the schemes, so the thought was only to connect Drumchapel to the tramway system, as Drumchapel was to be constructed a short distance across the Forth and Clyde canal from the tram terminus at Blairdardie. And there was also the disused line from Duntocher to Clydebank still there, so that trams could have gone thorough Drumchapel and down to Clydebank. (There is a good story about the replacement bus service that was put on from Duntocher to Clydebank. Ticket issue had become computerised and the driver just had to enter the required destination for the appropriate ticket and change to be issued. An old lady wanted to purchase a ticket and the driver told her that the computer had to know where she was going. She lent forward over the ticket-machine and shouted that she was going to the chemist for her prescription!) .

But agreement could not be reached about the costs of laying tram lines across the canal bridge – so no tram ever reached Drumchapel.

Castlemilk was to be served by means of a semi-circular trolley-bus line from Polmadie round through "ra Mulk" and down to

Rutherglen, and a little work had been started at Croftfoot in preparation for the projected trolley-bus overhead, when it was decided to abandon trolley-bus operation in Glasgow. Glasgow transport engineers and the Glasgow public had never wanted the "Whispering death" as trolley-buses were called – so Castlemilk never saw a trolley-bus as intended.

The result of the two transport fiascos was that the Corporation did not have enough buses to serve Easterhouse at all, though that was the scheme to be served by them. So transport for Easterhouse had to be devolved to private bus companies –who rubbed their hands and pocketed the cash.

Punters in Castlemilk were then supposed to bus down to Kings Park railway station and change onto a train to reach the city centre. They were not daft enough to take that seriously.
And, of course, the schemes nonsense meant that as their tenements were destroyed the former locally- living together-ness of the extended family was dispersed to the three miles-apart schemes indifferently and that led to the disappearance of the supervision formerly given to the young of a family and consequently a great increase in juvenile delinquency.

Even when first built (it was enlarged later) Castlemilk was size of the city of Perth. But hardly any amenities were provided.

All through my time there, there was not even a bank. More on that later.

No churches were allowed in Castlemilk. And this in the city of Kentigern which has the motto "Let Glasgow Flourish by the Preaching of the Word"! See politicians……. As enlargement took place the churches originally outside the circumference of Castlemilk became a little more enclosed by the buildings they were there to serve.

I always had a chuckle passing the splendid Church of Scotland kirk beside Carmunnock Road. A clever architect had designed it as large ark.

WHAT'S IN A NAME?

When St. Margaret Mary's Primary School (known in the patois of the Mulk as ra Wee Maggie – to distinguish it from the Secondary School of the same name) opened, its first Head Teacher was given a list of some four hundred likely pupils by the Department. When he had called that list of names, he found another four hundred pupils still standing in the hall. So hurriedly, another school for the district, St. Julie's, had to be built. Presumably that school was named after St. Julie Billiard – foundress of the Notre Dame nuns. Our Saint Margaret Mary Alacoque was known for her devotion to the Sacred Heart. Could never see why these two names were chosen for Castlemilk when there were many unused Scottish saint names. But there you go. Catholicism can be more than strange at times.

DOON TAE TROON

I heard an amusing tale from the daughter of that first Head Teacher. He and his family had planned to go for a fortnight's holiday to Troon in the Summer but on the strength of her father's appointment to a Headship they could now afford a motor car. And so they spent that holiday fortnight not staying in Troon as planned but by going up and down daily from Glasgow – every day for the fortnight. Most peculiar I thought?

THE PRESS STRIKES AGAIN

"Gestapo methods used in Catholic School!" was the head-line in the front page of the Daily Record. Editors will get up to anything to try and improve the circulation of their rag, and this farrago of lies was no exception. The unfortunate truth was that mother of one of the teachers from The Wee Maggie was slowly dying in a prolonged illness, and as if she did not have a big enough burden to carry, she started to get malicious abusive phone calls from a couple of girls along the lines of "Has the old so-and-so not kicked the bucket yet?" One night a colleague was visiting, and when another rant came in, she asked to listen to the abuse. She said that she recognised who one of the miscreants was. Unfortunately, as it turned out, the two concerned teachers took the matter into their own hands and the following day had the culprit out and quizzed her as to who the other pest was. She was from the neighbouring non-Catholic school. Much too late they gave the names to Mr. Docherty – the excellent Wee Maggie Head Teacher. He told me that he asked the mothers of the two culprits to come in and see him all he was interested in doing was to let them know what had happened. The mother of the girl from the non-Catholic school was ashamed and full of abject apologies but the mother of the Catholic girl stormed and raged and said she was going to make trouble for the school. Hence the Daily Record head-line. The Education Department were irate at that head-line appearing and censured Mr. Docherty for not better controlling the actions of his staff. Like me later, Mr. Docherty decided that he had had enough of suffering the slings and arrows, and forthwith resigned. Hence there was the vacancy "up ra Mulk" for me to fill. I had had the pleasure of having had his son, young Docherty, as a top-class pupil at John Ogilvie Hall. He was extremely, bright and intelligent and well-behaved and I thought he would have an excellent academic future. But the last I heard from his dad was that his son wanted to be a pop star. Never heard of him making it. But he was not the most intelligent pupil I had had. At Langside. Tom Burke was very keen on finding out just how bright the pupils who scored 140+ on the annual intelligence test actually were. One afternoon he came in all breathless and excited. He had taken one of my former class pupils to 180+ but did not know of any way of furthering out how high the boy's intelligence actually was. I was quietly pleased that may be I had had a pupil who became a High Court Judge or may be a Cabinet Minister or even a Cardinal. But one night after visiting my mother in the Victoria Infirmary after one of her four cancer operations, I stopped at the fish and chip shop in Mount Florida to purchases a fish supper, and there beaming and smiling a friendly welcome was the 180+ star. But I suppose that if he was happy – as he obviously was – that was the main thing. But I was a wee thing disappointed all the same.

LOOKS GOOD ON PAPER

The Wee Maggie building was another post-war monstrosity. It was situated on the side of a high-hill over-looking Glasgow and had stunning views to the mountains beyond the Campsie Fells, particularly when they were snow-capped in Winter. Ben More and Stobinian could be picked out in clear weather. And yet the wonderful architects had arranged that not a classroom had a window facing North. Every year we would be infiltrated by a large team of architects under training at Glasgow University and I would make the point of asking them about that omission. The standard answer always came back that the school windows had to face south to catch the sun-light. I would take them around the school and show them that over-looking the south-facing windows were rows of high tenement-style houses that blotted out the sun and that in any case the class teachers always worked with the window venetian blinds drawn to prevent dwellers in the over-looking houses seeing what was happening in the class-rooms. (These architects always wanted the blinds raise up and our school football pitch removed – their misguided theory being that there were some 500 in the school but only 22 could be on the pitch – which meant that the football pitch was a waste of space. Imagine me taking away a football pitch in Old Firm city? With as much patience as could be mustered, I would point out that I could use the pitch as a disciplinary measure. If there was any trouble among the pupils I would quietly spread the word that unless the matter was rectified, the football pitch would be placed out of bounds. That usually solved the problem without harsh measures having to be taken.) And they never had a word to say about there only being those four sit-down toilet seats for our hundreds of pupils. Another nuisance they caused was to turn down all the school thermostats and there would be an outcry about the lack of heating – particularly from the Infant teachers – Infant departments always seeming to be at the end of school heating systems. The annual phone call to the Heating Clerk of Works would get the annual reply. "Those so-and-sos again! I'll be up straight away to put things right." And he would be. The main building in the Wee Maggie had no class-rooms on the ground floor. (A boy lost the use of his legs after a road accident. His solicitor would not accept that we could not have the paraplegic back because of that, and had to come up and see the ridiculous situation for himself.) So in the main building all the class-rooms were one and two floors up but there were no upper floor corridors – so if I was in a top floor class-room at one end of the school attending to some matter and had to go to another classroom on the top floor at the other end of the school it was necessary to descend four flights of stairs run along the bottom corridor and then ascend another four flights. I suppose it kept me fit.

CANNY COONT, ME!

Every year some minion in the Scottish Education Department in Edinburgh would return the annual census form with the comment that it had been incorrectly filled in and would I rectify matters and not be so careless in the future. I would waste time phoning the accuser and point out that it was an actual fact that we had only four sit-down toilets for our 500 plus pupils.

JANITORIAL APPROVAL

"Our wee school's a rer wee school
The best joab is ra jannie's.
When we want tae play at fitba'
He's ra wan that says "Ye canny!"
He gets ra boys tae scoosh ra mulk
While he sits on his fanny!
A great wee job, a rer wee job!
The best job is ra jannie's!"

Or so the folk song put it. But it was not quite like that – at least in ra Wee Maggie!

When I found out who the janitor was when I took over at ra Wee Maggie I was very pleased. He was an excellent servant to the city. Perhaps at times a little too keen to do his best, and of course he liked things his own way. But I did not find that too irksome in view of his many other fine qualities. I had the devil of a job explaining to him that he should not be carrying on with his pride and joy, namely, maintaining such a wonderful polish on the gym floor. He found it hard to accept that the school would be liable for any injury caused through slipping on the polished surface. I was always bothered by the semi-circular huddle of some five hundred pupils packed together in front of the altar when Mass was celebrated in the school. So one morning when there was going to be a Mass in the school, I went up to ra Wee Maggie at around seven a.m. and sorted the 500 or so chairs into separated class groups so that each teacher would have better supervision over their own class. Imagine how displeased I was, when we started to fill the hall for Mass, to find the seats all re-arranged as before. The janitor thought the seating to be better as he had always arranged things.

AWAY FRAE RA MULK

For years we had had good rapport with various book selling businesses and never had any problems with them – always receiving excellent service. Then one year we were told that by an instruction from Bath Street that we could only order supplies from one firm.

That greatly puzzled us until very soon we discovered by accident what had been going on in the then ruling political party.

A friend had a younger sister who was receiving unwanted nuisance attentions from an older man. The annoyed family had an investigation carried out about the sexual predator. We were staggered by what they uncovered.

An individual from Pollok estate had joined the ruling political party and boasted that he had a double-first honours degree in Maths and Nat Phil from Glasgow University.

Without checking such an unlikely tale the political party running Strathclyde made him convener of education. Disaster followed. He put his most unsuitable and poorly-qualified pals into important school posts. No offence to woodwork teachers intended but can you imagine a run-of-the mill woodwork teacher being competent enough to adequately direct one of our most important large comprehensive schools? And suggestions of defalcations followed. It became only too obvious that he had to be removed from his position as convener of education. In return for not complaining about his sacking and keeping quiet about the political corruption he had been well aware of, he was rewarded by the creation for him of a company to deal with all the book requirements of Strathclyde schools. This is why our perfectly previously satisfactory book firms were left out in the cold – much to our dismay and annoyance.

Our friends investigation of the stalker revealed that he had gone to the Provost of the time and the Provost's good lady (clue – her Christian name is the same as the saint from Lucca who is a finder of lost keys for us) and told them he was homeless as his wife had left him taking with her their three children. The good couple took him in out of Christian charity and allowed him to stay with them in their home for two years before they discovered the truth of the matter. In fact he had deserted his wife and children. And a cousin of mine who was running the Housing Department was sent to prison for putting his mother at the head of the housing waiting list. His reward for keeping mum (no pun intended) was to be given the ownership of a dairy. See politics…

There not being any industry available locally, many of our "complete" families started to move away from "ra Mulk" to new towns such as Cumbernauld or Erskine or even far off Livingston, while a few emigrated across The Pond to Canada or the States. So much for the U.K.'s post-war brave new world – at least in the outskirts of "the fair green place" We consequently enrolled in one month twenty-four single-parent families – one after the other – and the school and local area went rapidly down-hill. The excellent janitor's wife saw this happening – and after all they lived twenty-four hours out of twenty-four in the deteriorating situation – and naturally she persuaded her husband to apply for a school in a more peaceful area. His replacement was an eye-opener. I had to be rid of that pest. Repeatedly he would be badgering me to order something expensive for the school and then he would sell it off for a profit to his mates and then we could share the gain between us. Really? It never seemed to occur to the thicko that I could do that by myself for my own profit – not that I ever would. The third janitor was one of the laziest blighters it has ever been my misfortune to come across. For starters he did not think that it was the janitor's job to sweep the school yards and keep the surroundings of the school clean and tidy. He was soon put to rights about that. And he never kept the school and classrooms secure, so that things continually would go missing – especially since in their wisdom, politicians had decreed that local groups of all kinds could make use of the school after the usual school hours. (In an effort to reduce crime and vandalism the police had started a policy of unexpectedly saturating ra Mulk of an evening. Three guesses who got that stopped.)

When the Papal visit to Glasgow was confirmed – despite the Falklands War – and urged to continue by Tom Winning flying with Worlock to Roma, all the Head Teachers of Glasgow's Catholic Schools were summoned to a meeting with a high-up member of our security service. His good news was that they had received information to the effect that in order to disrupt the visit, bombs would be placed in Catholic schools. And he also advised that the Police would not search a school for a bomb, but the search had to be done by the school's Head Teacher. He strongly advised that all school interior doors should be kept locked at all times and particularly those near to a school's entrance, as the placing of a bomb would probably be a quick in-and-out performance. So accordingly, on the following day, I called a meeting of everyone connected with the school – teachers, auxiliaries, cleaners, cooks, and of course the janitor, and told them what the security officer had to say and stressed to them that I was not particularly anxious to be a bomb disposal person. When I arrived at ra Wee Maggie the following morning, the four interior doors adjacent the entrance were all lying wide open. Suffering a high rise in my blood pressure, I asked that fool of a janitor if he had been at yesterday's meeting and had he not heard me say that all school doors, especially those near a school entrance had to be kept closed at all times? What was his reply? Did the instruction apply to him? I described him and his brainlessness in loud very un-Catholic language, Having been in the RAF I knew some rare choice words. I wished that Wotija had stayed in Roma – as did all the tree-lovers that crawled out of the woodwork to protest the removal of trees from Bellahouston Park. The same lot surfaced again when Celtic was thinking about constructing a new ground at Cambuslang. But a couple of jokes did cheer me a bit. Supposedly The Pontiff had said that he did not want more trees removed from Bellahouston Park, as he really had no wish to see Paisley. And, of course, Castlemilk humour surfaced the following day after his visit. I lost count of the number of pupils who asked me if I had seen the Pope's ice-cream van.

WHAT WAS THAT?

The school secretary was a proper headache. I often wondered why she had been given such an important position in the first place. She often just could not get things right. For example: a one-parent father phoned to say that he could not collect his infant son at the Infant Department lousing time and would the school look after his son until paterfamilias could arrive at the school to pick him up. The secretary went to a class and told the teacher the wrong name of the child concerned. So we had a wee boy wandering round ra

Mulk on his own, while another was crying his eyes out because he could not get out to his mother who was waiting patiently for him. Imagine the furore that caused, and guess who took the blame. And it could have been worse had there been a paedophile about. But the one that really shook me was when that secretary's father died and left her 190 Celtic shares. And she handed them back to the club! I felt I needed at least three Vallium and two Librium to recover from the shock. But she caused one amusing episode. We were having an interval cream cakes stuffing session, when she knocked on the staff-room door and said there was a book rep wanting to see me. I thought he might as well have a cream cake too, so told her to send him in. But it was the Director of Education, no less, who had the same name as the book rep. He took the whole episode with good humour and had a cream bun too. He said that he had just dropped in to see how things were going. I said I thought he had come in to see the latest fire damage. But he did not know about that and when he asked about the size of the damage repair bill and I said £14,000, he shrugged and said that was nothing to bother about. That made me wonder what size of a school fire would really have bothered him. During the very friendly conversation he told me that he always found the atmosphere in his Catholic Schools to be much better than in his non-Catholic schools and put that down to the fact that Catholic teachers were from the same environment as there pupils, while non-Catholic schools employed teachers from all over Scotland who did not enjoy that same rapport with their pupils. A very nice compliment indeed and of course I was pleased to be able to pass that on to the staff and Tom Winning. The secretary was such a pathetic soul that I did not have the heart to have her removed – though there were times when I was sorely tempted.

KEY GONE WEST?

But I could be a bit stupid myself. One week I searched for my school master keys and could not find them. I was on the point of having to have some sixty school locks changed when I went into a rarely-used storage cupboard and discovered I had put them down there while looking for something or other. That reminded me of the occasion at Craigend when the Infant Mistress lost her Master Keys but suspected that one of her class had stolen them. She was too scared to go to the home to get them back – so off I had to trot. There was no reply when I knocked on the open door of the house but I went in to a corridor that was packed about five feet high with coal. The boy's mother was in the kitchen and when I tried to say what I was about she did not stop what she was doing but just said "Have a look around – he is always taking keys". There must have been about fifteen sets of keys scattered about the living room – and sure enough, there were our missing school master keys. They did not tell us to expect that sort of thing at Jordanhill.

WHO DONE DAT?

One morning a kindly resident from one of the over-looking flats told me that on the previous evening a bunch of boys had been pushing one of our starter class boys up and through a small stock-room window and told me the name of the wee boy. I went along and called him out of his class. I put on an even more fierce expression than usual and asked him who did he think he was breaking into my stock-cupboard. Alarmed he called out "It wisnae me an' ah'll no dae it again!" I had to turn away convulsed with laughter. The episode gave me a good laugh for many a year.

MORE SPUDS, SIR?

Our first school cook was wonderful and I used to grab my lunch and race down to Muirend and give it to my mother. And she always enjoyed it. Then like the janitor couple she had had enough of the deteriorating situation in ra Mulk and retired to her native Lossiemouth. That was a disastrous loss because her successor was a dismal creature and the food was so poor that even my mother refused to eat it when I took it down to her for her lunch. That cook created mayhem by ordering our teachers (and me!) to stand in the queue with the mass of children. That was speedily sorted with a few kind words.

STAFF

Most of Mr. Docherty's team departed before I took over, but I was pleasantly surprised to find two former colleagues and a splendid University friend had moved in as part of the replacement. I admired my University friend's stamina as well as her marvellous rapport with her class. She had seven children of her own and adopted two more. The family would take up a whole pew in the church for Mass. On one occasion a small child crawled past paterfamilias who was engrossed in his Mass missal. Thinking it was one of his own, he smacked the child without looking, and told it to get back on to its seat. You can imagine the ruckus after Mass created by the real parents of that errant stray. The sister of Dr. Connelly – Celtic club doctor -was there as an assistant head teacher, and she had agreed to stay on to help me- and a great help she turned out to be. Nine probationer teachers arrived too on the first day – all excited – and straight out of training college. They turned out to be simply splendid and they had a great compassion among themselves and for the pupils and even for me. When I first gathered them together I asked them to put what they had been taught at training college to the back of their minds, because their first priority was to love the children and make the school a happy place for them. Came one Christmas Eve and some not-so-bright specimen had ordained that schools should be "in" until three o'clock. Three o'clock on the afternoon before Christmas. Quelle horror and stupidity! I told the staff that come noon they should airt rapidly off and do what preparations they needed to do for the great feast of Christmas, and I would hold the fort until the prescribed time of three o'clock. I reasoned that there would be no brass from the department daft enough to be prowling about that afternoon. After I had seen all the children off at lunch-time, I started to catch up on some tardy paper-work. Then about two p.m. there was a bit of a commotion in the corridor outside my door and I went out to see what it was all about. A group of excited girls was the cause. When I asked them why they were there they said that it was so much better being in the school than being at home and could they stay on in the school and enjoy themselves. Of course I had to send them away with great reluctance. But I went into my office and cried my eyes out. Imagine it being better in the school than at home on Christmas Eve. When we re-assembled after the holidays I thanked the probationers in particular for so successfully carrying out my request to make the school a loving place.

WHAT! CASTLEMILK!

I wanted to make Castlemilk a loving place too but had little success in that task. I tried to have the Scouts come, but the commissioner I contacted just about had apoplexy at the mention of Castlemilk. So no success there. Wonder if Baden-Powell stirred in his grave? Exploring the school I had found that, hidden away in a small cupboard. were eight violins – all in good condition. I had them valued and was told that two were quite expensive ones, and the expert was keen to purchase them from us at a good price. I tried every contact I could think of to try to obtain a music instructor. I always received the same answer. If I could find one then let them know as they too were desperate to fond a music instructor. Eventually I tried the musicians union and they told me that there was a musician living in Ralston who had a free Thursday afternoon. Of course when I managed eventually to contact him I received the disdainful comment to the effect that did I really expect him to give up his only free afternoon to go to a place like Castlemilk. How I blessed the planners who thought up those three monstrous housing-schemes. I should have known better than to have bothered. A music teacher in a Catholic comprehensive secondary went round all his feeder primary schools with an array of musical instruments and tested every pupil from Primary Five to Primary Seven, and worked out which musical instrument best suited each one. But when, after his mammoth effort, he applied to the Education Department for money to provide all the necessary instruments for the children, he was told he was not getting even a single penny. I wondered at the time if sectarianism was playing a part in that decision. So much for the Education Department loving the children under their care. There was no point in having our violins left unused in a cupboard, so I sold them for a good price, and we used the money received to provide breakfasts for the children whom we knew were coming to school unfed, and also to provide clothing for those in need – especially in Winter, and for First Communion dresses for the girls. I have always thought the First Communion dressing–up a bit of a nonsensical waste of money for poor people. I managed to have school uniform only for the boys, but the girls had to have an expensive fashion show. It got to the quite ridiculous stage. The priest was about to place a host in a girl First Communicant's mouth when her tiara lit up and played a tune. The poor priest was so startled that, as he told me later, he nearly dropped all the hosts. The various Parish Priests running St. Margaret Mary's parish took little interest in their schools. But my first chaplain at the Wee Maggie was a great benefactor for the school, assistant priest Fr. McKelvie, a member of a high-powered liturgy/theology commission. He could not do enough for us. Sometimes too, some of the other assistant priests would drop in to see how things were going. Arriving at the school one morning I found the splendid Father Tony Bancewicz already seated in my room. (I twice recommended him for a bishopric – but like life, promotion in the Church usually depends on who you know – not what you are. He always insisted that he was of Lithuanian extraction – not Polish!) To my dismay the poor man was surrounded by hundreds of souvenir pictures of Pope John Paul. I lamely managed to stutter the sad news that Pope John Paul had died. He retorted that that was not a joke to make about a Pope. I said that unfortunately it was only too true. He rubbished that, saying that he had been talking to the Pontiff only the day before. It took some persuading for him to realise that Pope John Paul had in fact died during the night. Oh! Dear! The great Fr. McKelvie's successor was of lesser calibre altogether. His first demand was that the Infant Department should not come to a school Mass celebrated by him. Apart from the damage that would be done to the children if they were excluded from Mass, did the brainless wonder really think I was going to tell the Infant teachers they could not participate in a school Mass? And did he not know Matthew 19:14 : "Suffer the little children to come to me for theirs is the Kingdom of Heaven"? Apparently not. He was soon disabused. Then we had another appalling request. He wanted anti-English sporting songs sung during the celebration of the Eucharist. Like me the teachers were staggered by this coming from a man with an Italian surname. So that was another no-no. There seems to have been a "we are not English" sentiment amongst Scottish clerical circles, and I had an extreme example of that thrust on me later by a Bishop – no less. For example we sit at the Sanctus where in England they stand and of course we arrange Holydays of Obligation differently too. That is just to show we are different from England. No appreciation seems to be there that in fact England preserved for Scotland the Valladolid Scottish property that Scotland had completely forgotten about in penal times.

MITRES IN ABUNDANCE

Then we had the Confirmation occasion when, for the first time, Tom Winning brought his two newly appointed auxiliaries Donnie Renfrew and Joe Devine. Donnie was an interesting visitor because he was a class-mate of mine. (As a boy he and his sister were well taken care of by the Scottish hierarchy. It was a very sad story. His father had been looking after the finances of the Edinburgh Archdiocese. A new archbishop- formerly abbot of Fort Augustus Abbey – came to the Archdiocese, and for some inexplicable and apparently unjustifiable reason, he had instituted criminal proceedings against Mr. Renfrew for embezzlement. The shock of it all killed Mr. Renfrew. The rest of the Bishops were upset by the whole affair and took to caring for Donnie and his sister (who became an excellent P T teacher). So I arranged for our wee choir to greet Donnie at the school entrance with "Ecce Sacerdos Magnus". The head at St. Julie's just about had apoplexy because he had not thought to arrange such a greeting.

Being a great believer in the Second Vatican Council I had always tried hard to promote ecumenism and to promote good relations with adjoining non-Catholic schools but it was hard going. Pupils would repeatedly come out with utterances such as "it was they proddies at that school that did it" and I would try in vain to point out that in fact not every pupil at a non-Catholic school was a Protestant. Tom Winning opened his schools to non-catholics who wanted to attend. This led to difficulties at a school Mass, for obviously, if they did not want to attend a Catholic School Mass, special arrangements had to be made for their supervision, and if they did go with the school for Mass, then, again, they should not have been going up to receive the eucharist. We had one little girl who came under the new arrangement and one day when I returned at lunch-time, I was told that her mother was being cremated at the Lynn Crematorium – which was just down the road. So I hurried down there and arrived in time for the cremation service. I was appalled and very puzzled. There was only a very fine young Church of Scotland minister, a middle-aged married couple and an old man present. I could not work-out what was going on.

Then, after the summer holidays, a social worker phoned me and asked if she could come in and see me about the wee girl. I was only too delighted for such a visit, and, when she arrived, I said I was puzzled at the cremation service at the Lynn crematorium and that I could not work out what was going on. Then came the startling information that it was the second foster-mother of the wee girl that was being cremated, her proper mother and a previous foster-mother having already died, and that the old man was the surviving foster parent. The social work department was in a difficult position then, but thought it would be best to leave the child in the care of the old man, and she – the social worker – would do what she could to replace a proper mother and the foster-mothers. She said that this was exactly why she had come in to speak to me, and to say that she was no longer prepared to carry on doing that. She had taken the wee girl to Edinburgh Zoo, and after about two hours, the wee girl had asked the social worker who the other lady was that was walking round the Zoo with them. This gave the social worked such a fright she was not prepared to take the wee soul out again. Was the apparition she was seeing the wee girl's proper mother? I tried to keep in touch for some time in my concern for the unfortunate girl. But nothing untoward ever seemed to happen after that, and the foster father was very caring father for her .I too have seen apparitions. The most notable being when I as walking my dog, old Jimmy the Woof, around the pond in Strathclyde Park. He had run on ahead to investigate a couple of dogs, and I was trying to keep an eye on him. I realised that walking towards me was a lady in what I can only describe as a very old-fashioned long brown coat. I was surprised that she was smiling so much at me, and after seeing Jimmy was O K, I turned around to further look at the amiable lady but there was no one there and nowhere anyone could have gone. Was it my maternal grandmother thanking me for a marker I had put on her grave in Leadville, Colorado?

WHO TOOK THE PARROT?

Edinburgh Zoo was a favourite destinations for a school outing. Sometimes our teachers would also visit the Camera Obscura as well as the Castle. On one occasion I had seen all our pupils from the Zoo aboard the bus for home (and counted them) when I realised that there was a small girl still sitting by herself in the Zoo cafeteria She wasn't one of ours but quiet questioning revealed that the poor wee anxious and upset child was actually from my very first school – St. Martha's, Balornock – and unfortunately had been left behind by mistake. Someone had not done a careful enough count! We took her back to Glasgow with us and my reward was for her to be violently sick in my Dolomite en route from Castlemilk to Balornock. Did not think my driving was as bad as all that.

One Summer I decided to organise a day out for the whole of the Wee Maggie to Edinburgh Zoo. This was over the objection of our neurotic Infant Mistress and to satisfy our upset Infant teachers who always complained that the poor soul would not let them take their Infant classes to anywhere worthwhile. (That Infant mistress had tried three times to become a nun but the three orders she tried would not have her.) Her brother was a Glasgow assistant priest who succeeded in having the hitherto traditional Wednesday afternoon bounce game between Celtic and Glasgow clergy abandoned. This balloon voiced it round Glasgow to the effect that the Celtic players were over-rated, since the priests could hold their own with them. The idiot never seemed to be aware that the Celts were holding back because they were playing priests. Of course the bombast got back to Parkhead, so the next Wednesday, the players rolled up their sleeves and ran the priests off the park. The fixture was never started again.

We had arranged lists for promised teacher-student support to take small groups round the zoo, but we should have known better. The promised students never bothered to turn up or even say they were not coming. We could not cancel the event, so when our extremely happy gang arrived at Corstorphine, we told the children where the school auxiliaries would always be stationed in case help was needed, and we asked the older pupils to take their younger siblings round with them while myself and the teachers would be patrolling round the zoo to keep an eye on things. We thought the day had turned out fine despite the non-attendance of the student-teachers and the forebodings of the fearful Infant Mistress. In fact the Parents Group was full of praise for the great day out and said it was the best the school had ever enjoyed. But! I went up to ra Wee Maggie during the holidays to see what mail had accumulated there and was horrified to read a letter from the Director of

Education enclosing a letter from a lady which accused the school of neglect that day. It went on at great length: some of the accusations were along the lines that our teachers had all gone off to enjoy themselves and left the children to run wild in the Zoo: she had seen a girl dangling her legs over the polar bear pit (quite impossible of course – even for someone from ra Mulk!): and much more to that effect. Of course the Director demanded an explanation. I explained the whole circumstances of the day to him and the arrangements we had put in place at the zoo, and added the fact that we had been so well congratulated by our Parents' Group. I heard no more about it, but later discovered that the slanderer was an English woman who had wanted to become a teacher in Scotland but who had been rejected by The General Teaching Council because of inadequate qualifications. She had several letters published in the press about this and that failure of our education system – so we were not the only target.

Oh! And we were not that Castlemilk school who pinched a parrot from the Zoo and taught it to swear at policemen.

YOU JUST HAVE TO GRIN AND BEAR IT

But days-out could have a bit of humour too. I personally prefer Stirling Castle to Edinburgh's and we had gone there on our way back from The Safari Park at Blair Drummond. I was standing in the excellent museum trophy room and was quite pleased at the way our boys were so interested and well-behaved. A grim-faced tube of a corporal in full regalia stamped up, stuck his nose in my face and bawled "Honour of the regiment, Sir! Honour of the Regiment!" I managed to keep my cool – which as readers will know is not easy for me – and quietly asked him what he was on about. It transpired that one of our stars was quietly chewing a sweetie as he went round. I thanked my stars I had been one of the Brylcreem Boys.

Another amusement was caused by a teacher comment. One of her class was a very disturbed and mis-behaved pupil who caused her endless trouble. One winter's day, the pest licked a bus stop, and his tongue stuck to the pillar, and the Fire Service had to be called to un-stick him. The teacher's bitter comment, when she heard the sorry tale, was a heart-felt one. She made us laugh by saying that it was a pity he had not licked the back of a moving bus. No pity there then.

And we roared with laughter at the tale of the three – not musketeers nor tenors – but lorries. There was only a small car park at the school entrance but an even tinier projecting addition had been added to accommodate the school dentist when he deigned to appear. His appearance was a rare event and he would rant and rage if he came and found a teacher's car occupying his precious space. One morning a lorry was making a delivery and had parked in that small space facing the school entrance. When the driver attempted to leave, he reversed off the tarmac and on to the very steep slippery grass slope that fell away down to our boundary fence at a wood. Despite his best attempts to retrieve the situation he slid backwards away down into our distant boundary fence – which did the fence no good at all. He phoned for another vehicle to come to his rescue and this one proceeded to do the same thing. There even was a third lorry stuck down at our fence before it dawned on someone that a fully-fitted rescue tow lorry would have to securely anchor at the top and tow all three miscreants back. I was splitting my sides at the carry on – as were pupils and teachers, – and I am afraid I did not help matters by saying to one of the errant drivers that it was just as well he had not been with the Eighth Army in the desert.

Then one of our less bright alumni later opened an account with a building society, and a few days later went in undisguised and held up the office concerned. It did not take the polis much thinking to solve that crime.

NOT ALL SAINTS IN CASTLEMILK

Then too, unfortunately, sadly, much later some of our alumni were involved in the Busby murder of a passing student and some of the girls hid the weapons used in the cisterns of the women's facilities in Lewis's Polytechnic. The Police were wise to that practice and recovered the weapons and accordingly were able to make the necessary charges.

On another occasion I was even more foolish and impetuous than usual. I encountered Shuggy Edvalson while I was shopping in Muirend Safeway. I asked him if he would be kind enough to give out the prizes at our forthcoming school prize-giving. (At that time there was a lot of do-gooders' nonsense – in my opinion – about equality, and that there should not be competitive events in a school such as sports day and football and so on, and certainly no awarding of prizes for school work But I have always believed that hard effort should be rewarded.) Edvalson said that he would be pleased to come and do that. But on the day before the prize-giving, he phoned the school and said that he could not manage to come to the prize-giving, as he had to pick up his girl friend at the airport that same evening. Nothing I said could get him to change that decision. And, of course, we had been selling tickets for the prize-giving on the strength of his appearance. His non-appearance meant that the school did not stand well in the opinion of the ticket buyers that night. All my fault of course. I should have arranged for a Celtic player to come by contacting the ever helpful and courteous Billy McNeill. One of the male teachers ran a fine and very successful football team and when they won the Primary School Trophy competed for by the whole of Glasgow's Catholic Primary Schools, Billy was good enough to have Packie Bonner and Frank McGarvey to come to the school and give out the trophy and medals won. But I was disappointed to find in discussion with them that neither player knew anything about Celtic's famous history.

Then a more knowledgeable person came to visit the Wee Maggie – Lillian Beckwith no less. What a joy that delightful lady was. The school sat fascinated listening to her.

OPPORTUNITIES MISSED

I covered myself in glory again over Celtic, though I did not realise what I had done at the time. We were going to Dundee for a match there, and friend Jimmy Gordon was going up to take part in a debate at Dundee University, and said, very decently, that he would run us up for the game and then bring us back after the game and debate were over. He picked us up opposite the Rex cinema at Riddrie, and there was another fair-haired chap in the back seat. On the way north Jimmy handed us some pre-election literature to peruse. It was for a candidate standing in a Fife constituency House of Commons election. My pal and myself had a great time ridiculing the likelihood of all the promises in the manifesto ever being fulfilled. It turned out that we were ridiculing the election manifesto of the lad in the back seat. His name was John Smith. Yes! The real famous John Smith. So no Labour party career would have been forthcoming for me. Not that I ever wanted one.

At that time Celtic thought that two Castlemilk brothers were going to come to Parkhead. But it was alleged that Revie turned up unexpectedly at the Castlemilk house, chatted about Leeds United, and then as he left, he put a wad of bank-notes on the table. The brothers' father counted the thousands there and told the brother that they were gong to Leeds and not Celtic.

About that time Celtic were adding hospitality buildings on to the old stand. Two of the labourers involved broke through a wall and into a manager's office. There was an unsigned player's contract on the manager's desk. And what did the not-so-bright pair do? They kept the contract and broke up that historic desk for fire-wood. Dear me!

TARGET PRACTICE

One sunny afternoon one of the men rushed into my office and proclaimed that a youth was down at the woods shooting at the school with an air-gun. I said I would come up and look as it was probably one of our former pupils. But it was not, and as we looked, he fired again, and the pellet hit the window right at the teacher's face. I ran back down the staircase and told the secretary to dial 999, but she dithered as was usual with her, so I did that myself and reported that we required urgent assistance as shots were being fired at the school. Now the Castlemilk Police Office was only ten minutes walk away from the Wee Maggie, but it took four and a half hours before any minion of the law bothered to respond. I repeat – four and a half hours to respond to a shooting. Of course I wrote a letter of complaint to the chief constable – and what was the response? I received a pathetic letter from one of his inspector minions saying that they did not have a unit available to respond to the 999 call, and had to get one to come from Hamilton, and that unit did not know the way to Castlemilk. Too bad for that thick inspector. You can see Castlemilk from Hamilton. And all this nonsense in the nineteen-eighties. There would have been a proper response if it had happened after the Dunblane tragedies. And a similar thicko Inspector could have prevented that happening.

SLINGS AND ARROWS

Things began to get too much for me to bear. For example: I could never get the replacement teachers I asked for. I would know of a first-class student who had passed out for a probation start and had qualities I wanted, but only got what the department wanted to send. So I could not put in the extended quality I wanted for the school. I had one very nice chap sent to us but he could not control his class and his pupils were not being taught at all. I went to the Department and asked to have him removed. And what was the disgraceful reply? They knew he was no use as a teacher but he was being passed round from school to school and it was my turn to have him for two years. Unbelievable but true. Then we were plagued with so-called advisers. What a pain and waste of time they were. Someone decided that they were not doing enough school visitations, so if one was passing he would just drop in for no good reason. On one occasion I had spent three years imposing a new arithmetic scheme on reluctant teachers – who like me did not see the point of it, and had just got it going in the school when a bright specimen of an adviser turned up and complained that the scheme was out of date and it had to be a new one that was implemented. Of course it was obvious what was going on. Back-handers were flying about. In my time we had to go through five – repeat FIVE different writing schemes –all from the same happy chappy. He must have been doing well financially. Several ways I had checked that unemployment in ra Mulk had reached the astronomical figure of 60% unemployed. One of the not-so-bright advisers dropped in and asked me what I would like for the girls in my school. I said I would be delighted if they all could at least get good secretarial jobs. I was told I was an obscurantist and did I not know about ballet, poetry and the arts etc. Too bad for the chump that my cousin was the celebrated Prima Ballerina millionairess Antoinette Sibley. And supposedly I did not know about ballet.

But I missed a trick just the same. My old university friend pointed out that there was a boy in the school who should be going to St. Aloysius' College and I had done nothing about him achieving that. So we arranged for him to sit for a Bursary to the College, and he passed with flying colours. I was astounded when the grandfather who was looking after the boy would not agree to the boy attending the College for four years as required by the terms of the bursary. Later I was attending a demonstration of how the Secondary School – "the Big Maggie" – St. Margaret Mary's Comprehensive – thought to help their more backward pupils and was sickened to find that boy who had sailed through the St. Aloysius' Bursary exam was included among the most backward pupils. Of course I blew up about that only to be told that they had done that to help and encourage the dunderheads. You will gather I was no admirer of Comprehensive education. Still. The "big Maggie" had its moments: a nun would drive up to the school on her motor-bike. She was known as Sister Evil-Kinevil! They could never get the girls to wear school uniform. But if one girl came in wearing a brown coat, then you could bet all the girls would soon be arriving wearing a brown coat.

DUCK! DUCK!

The boss of ra Big Maggie would come down every year at the end of term to give a supposedly welcoming spiel to our Primary Seven pupils who were going to his school in the autumn. Invariably when he asked for questions, he would be annoyed by excited boys who would ask was it true that there was a teacher at ra Big Maggie who taught IRA songs. (Unfortunately there was.) We had a troublesome family and in a heated dispute at ra Big Maggie, the father concerned had punched and knocked out that Head Teacher. The last of that clan was a poor soul who was no trouble at all and quite well-behaved – compared to the rest – but the poor soul could not control continuing facial contortions. On one occasion ra Big Maggie Head Teacher was delivering his usual talk when he became aggravated by the poor boy's continual facial contortions and roared at him that if he kept making faces at him he would sort the boy out when he came to ra Big Maggie. The irate head asked the poor boy for his surname. And when the boy told him that, and it was the same as the father's who had knocked the Head Teacher out. I have never ever seen anyone turn so white in shock as on that occasion.

But we had a very sad and upsetting case. I had admired a pupil for his excellent work and behaviour but noted that things had begun to deteriorate in his Primary sixth and seventh classes. I had his mother in and suggested that he might have a growing brain tumour. She listened to that suggestion and several times took her

215

son to the family doctor but each time was told that her son did not have a brain tumour. But then later when the boy was at ra Big Maggie, things got so bad for him that he had a brain operation, but the tumour found was so large that it could not be extracted and nothing could be done for him. All very distressing for everybody.

When a pupil had a head knock I would always insist on an auxiliary taking the child to be examined in hospital despite the same hospital repeatedly saying that I was continually wasting their time. To me it was not wasting time to have a head-knock carefully examined.

TROUBLE, TROUBLE, TOIL AND TROUBLE

Then I had a letter of complaint about me published in the then Glasgow Herald. The writer complained that I had unjustly sacked her from her job in ra Wee Maggie. And I had the Scottish Education Department asking me why I had sacked the complainant. Of course I had done no such thing. The woman concerned – an elderly retired teacher – had been sent to us as our Remedial Teacher. This was arranged not by me but by the School Psychologist. And one year the latter decided that the teaching was so good in the Wee Maggie that we did not need a Remedial Teacher, and so had not appointed the retired teacher to spend another year with us. And I had not even been consulted about that decision. Accordingly I told every teacher in the school to make a list of every pupil they felt needed Remedial support and the reason, and forwarded over two hundred requests for assistance to the erring School Psychologist. So we had another Remedial Teacher appointed. This appointee gave me an inward quiet chuckle. On the first day she arrived I was doing my best to give her a good welcome and make her feel at home. For some reason or other we started talking about football, and she said that her husband – a policeman – had only ever taken her to one football match, and her husband had been very angry that day because his team had lost seven goals in that match, and so had never taken her to football again.

WHAT WENT ON

Then we were puzzled. An instruction came in saying that we could only now order required books from a named firm. This was annoying because we had received excellent service from previous stockists and we saw no reason not to order from them. But the solution to the mystery came in an unexpected way. A friend of my assistant head teacher had a younger sister who was being harassed and stalked by a much older man. The young girl's family and friends got hold of the pest and in so doing uncovered the following scandal. This fly-man had surfaced in a Glasgow housing scheme, told the tall tale to the Labour Party that he had a double first-class honours degree in Maths and Nat. Phil. – a highly unlikely scenario – and of course he hadn't such an award. But the Labour Party in Strathclyde swallowed the tall tale and appointed him as Convener of the Education Committee. From this eminent position he appointed friends and cronies to high positions in schools for which they had no qualifications. Of course there was such an out-cry about this scandal that he was prosecuted eventually and in return for his silence on various corruption happenings involving the Labour Party he was given a new book company and all Strathclyde school book orders had to go to him. Another of his tricks was to tell the Glasgow Provost (Yes! He of Glasgow Smiles Better fame!) and the Provost's wife that his wife had deserted him and taken with her his three children – so out of pity they had taken him in to live with them for two whole years. Of course he in fact had abandoned his wife and the three children. I had a cousin who went to prison, for advancing his mother and some other family people to the top of the Glasgow housing list. He was imprisoned also but his reward for silence on Labour party corruption was only a dairy!

MONEY! MONEY! MONEY!

When I started teaching, for my sins I had to wait six years before I was earning what I had been earning for conducting a tram. In those days it took around sixteen years of yearly increments to receive a top teacher's salary. Eventually there was such an outcry about poorly-paid teachers that an important commission was set up which eventually awarded a quite large increase in the salaries of ordinary teachers. And who did that important commission forget about? Why Head Teachers of course. Depending on an expected high increase in her salary to come, one of my Head Teacher friends booked a passage to Australia and when the expected increase did not materialise she had to take out an expensive loan to pay for it.

FIRE! FIRE!

I had a good way of lifting my spirits when I felt despondent. It was necessary to have and record the happening of an unannounced school fire drill. And sure enough, there usually would be one teacher who had brought the children out but had not remembered to also bring out the class register as was a strict requirement. This small-minded person (me!) would quietly arrive beside the errant teacher and gently enquire had she not forgotten something and so ensure a bit if confused embarrassment. Small thing amuses small mind – I suppose. But I had a good chuckle too when we went through to Tannadyce for an evening game on a really miserable night. Climbing up the steep stand staircase, I was highly amused to see the whole of the Scottish Catholic Hierarchy huddled uncomfortably on the back row of the stand. No doubt Tom Winning had brought them all there, but they certainly looked extremely miserable and unhappy and not at all enthusiastic about being at the match.

CANDID CAMERA?

Then one very hot and sultry Summer night the staff were slogging away meeting parents on a Parents' Open Night, so I decided to nip down to the Italian ice–cream shop at Croftfoot and purchase some double-nuggets for them. I asked the unfortunate soul behind the counter for twenty-four double nuggets and she looked at me in amazement. I repeated the order. She asked me was it a joke I was playing on her. I said no, I just wanted to buy twenty-four double nuggets. She then asked me was I from the much-watched TV programme of the time "Hidden Camera". Eventually she had to exit from the shop to a backroom store and bring out an unopened box of the necessary wafers.

MEMORY LOSS

But the joke was on red-faced me one morning. It had been ordained that the teachers would be on primary school preparation duty for two or three days or so before the pupils arrived, and I had to arrange a preparation schedule for them – not that I had any real clue about what to do about that. So I thought, as a wee sort of treat for the excellent teachers, that they need only come in at nine-thirty on those preparation days instead of the usual nine a.m. kick-off. So in the first morning of the new deal after the summer holidays, I sailed in at nine-thirty, only to discover that the quite rightly annoyed teaching staff had been sitting impatiently waiting for me for half-an-hour or so. Before the Summer holidays I had completely forgotten to tell them what I had planned. Four hundred lines for me "Get a grip!" One time I gave an errant boy lines, and when he handed them in, the first few lines were in one hand-writing and the others were in a different hand. His soft-hearted mother had written the rest for him. What could I say?

QUID EST?

I also learnt one time that you had to be careful about setting a week-end task to win a competition. The task given was to write down the words on the side of a police car. In those days it was in very large letters, "Semper Vigilans". One of our more disturbed family-less boys from a care home, went in with the query to a police-station, and when the reply came that they did not know (really? – did not know about "Always awake"?) The disturbed boy, annoyed with that senseless reply, opened the door of a police car in the yard, took out the radio set – which was worth about eight thousand pounds in value – and threw it into the Cart. Very fortunately, no suspicion came my way. Phew!

FEELING FLAT

But I was becoming more and more exhausted by the continual slings and arrows coming my way. We suffered all the time from those cheap (?) idiotic flat roofs. At night a perpetrator would bore a hole on one part of a flat roof and water would come in somewhere else in the school. Workmen were for ever going around trying to help stop the leaks. Did the thicko architects who put in flat roofs not know about Scottish weather? Wisely a programme had started to put pitched roofs on all Castlemilk's flat-roofed schools. I was looking forward to our school being rid of the flat-roof menace. The programme had reached an adjoining school and the roofing contractors put their remaining stock of timber trusses etc. into a classroom there, ready to start work the following morning. But the not so bright Head had all that expensive timber removed from that classroom and piled up in the school yard. Ra Mulk had one of its finest bone-fires ever that night, and that was the end of the remedial programme and we never got our pitched roof solution.

One Castlemilk Week I thought to support it by arranging a Model Railway Show in our school hall. All our posters advertising the event were torn down – even in shops – and hardly anyone bothered to come, so that I was out of pocket refunding the Model Rail specialists who had arranged their displays to no purpose.

At first there would only be the occasional occasion when that excellent first janitor would be out waiting on my arrival at ra Wee Mulk with a horror story, but as the years went on, he would be there most mornings, and I used to pray, driving up the roads, that at least I would get into the office, have a cup of coffee, and be a bit refreshed before the bad news hit me. After all, I had spent an hour or so getting my old mother up and dressed and fed, before I could set out for work. The cruncher came when one morning he was there as usual. He suggested that I take a look at the large hut which had once been erected in past times to cater for an over-crowding of pupils. It contained two large class-rooms which were so superior to the ordinary class-rooms in our monstrosity of a school, that there was keenness among the teachers to have their own class installed in the large wooden building. I looked at the hut from the playground side and saw nothing wrong. The janitor advised me to have a look from the other side. The whole back wall of the large hut had been removed, and it was like looking into a doll's house. Not a thing had been taken from the two class-rooms. A craze for keeping pigeons had started in ra Mulk and this was the way for the clowns to obtain the wood they wanted for constructing doo-lofts. But the remains of the two class-rooms had to be removed – and this was the reason why we could not have that car-accident paraplegic back.

•

OPUS DEI. REALLY?

Like me, two of the excellent young teachers had had enough. One departed for Spain where she found herself working in an Opus Dei school with her class standing to attention every morning and giving the fascist salute while singing the fascist anthem. She was soon dismissed after her pupils had deleted her to the Head Teacher for her socialist attitude. And she was just an ordinary Glaswegian. I had to laugh one morning. I encountered the nice wee teacher in our long corridor and she blurted out, "Aren't the costs of taxis exorbitant these days?" I burst out laughing, and, indignantly, she wanted to know what I was laughing about. When I replied that I had never been in a taxi in all my life, she was perplexed, and asked what I did when I was young. This old man (of fifty!) told her that in those days there were things called tram-cars and I used to run two stops to get to the next fare-stage to save a half-penny. She stamped her foot and shouted that she did not believe a word of it and flounced off.

The other splendid girl went off to Luxemburg and became married there and involved with the European Parliament. We will meet her again later.

FOR THE HIGH JUMP

One of their replacements was a fine new probationer but there was a snag. She went parachute jumping at the week-end and resisted all my efforts to dissuade her from that dangerous practice, but kept telling me how wonderful it all was doing that. And of course the inevitable happened. On one jump her main parachute failed to open, but fortunately her reserve chute worked. She never went parachute jumping again. We discovered that she intended to get married to a fellow jumper and so the staff decided to obtain a puppy for her as a wedding present. I went through to Fife and bought a lovely wee Black Labrador bitch for the staff to present to her. How I wished I had one for myself. I had always wanted a dog since I saw the St. Bernards in Shettleston, but that had to wait for a later time still.

WRONG DECISION?

My mother died, and so, having had more than enough of ra Mulk, and no longer having reason to struggle on there against the odds, I put in my resignation, put my house on the market, and took up Tom Winning's offer of being sent to the Pontifical Beda College in Roma. I was sadly mistaken again if I thought I was going to get away from slings and arrows. After my mother's funeral the Department and the staff of ra Wee Maggie were most generous in allowing me to the some bereavement leave, and I used it to go on a Christmas Pilgrimage to The Holy Land. It was a little disappointing that the Christmas Midnight Mass for us was not held in The Church of The Nativity but in The Fields of The Shepherds, understandably so in view of the numbers of more important people wanting to attend the Church of the Nativity Mass. Of course we visited all the major Christian and Jewish sites. I was suitably awed by Megiddo, and the site of Armaggedon, and the ascent of Mount Carmel. But when we arrived at our hotel in Tiberias, I immediately ran down a narrow lane in the gathering gloom — as I was desperate to have a first look at The Sea of Galilee. A large building loomed through the darkness at the foot of the lane. It was emblazoned in huge letters with "St. Peter's Fish and Chip Shop". Very disappointing. Another time, again in the gathering dusk of an evening, more distraction from the spiritual level I was seeking to reach. We were going down the massive concrete steps to the River Jordan, and I was in awe about this, but a loud cry came in an Irish woman's voice, "Sure, now. Will there be water down there?" The pseudo-synagogue at Jesus' town Caparnaum was a bit of a disappointment. His synagogue was long gone when early Roman tourists would arrive in the Holy Land seeking to see it, so in that distant past they cobbled up a supposed synagogue out of whatever ancient bits of buildings they could find. Interestingly we were able to visit places that would be quite impossible to visit to-day. Gaza was a miserable and quite forlorn place, and we wondered why the Syrians had not descended with their tanks from the Golan Heights, so commanding were they. Even then it was risky to visit Hebron to see the Caves of Abraham, and it was a bit frightening to pass through the strong Israeli army presence which was there to protect the Ultra Jews who had persisted in re-settling in a large and hostile Arab community.

LAUGHING YOUR SOCKS OFF

We had a couple of very non-spiritual moments, but I suppose such amusing events will always occur on a pilgrimage. Our chaplain was a Redemptorist from Perth, and, as necessity required, we were taking off our shoes before entry to The Golden Dome Mosque, and we all roared so loudly in laughter that The Mosque guards came running up to investigate the commotion. Then they too laughed. The Perth priest was wearing two different highly-coloured socks.

One day the young coach driver dropped the coach into a trench that was being dug across the road. While we were awaiting the relief coach to arrive, three of us went for a walk down the road. It struck all three of us at the same time. We were a threesome walking down the road to Emmaus. Wow! (And I know now that there is some doubt about which Emmaus is the correct one.)

OUT OF THE ORDINARY

Then came a paranormal happening. In the party was a doctor from Market Rasen. We were sitting on a bench opposite the Knesset and I thought about asking her about a Market Raisen priest I hadn't heard from for a while. To my astonishment she sat down beside me and said, "You are going to ask me about Father Mike!" Now how on earth did she know that? Mind you I often used to know what my mother was going to say before she said it, and I have experienced dogs having a paranormal sense about something that lay beyond my senses. But I must have had a paranormal experience when I made that joke at my Head Teacher's interview.

Back once more at ra wee Maggie, I was looking forward to running down the clock, when one afternoon a semi-hysterical teacher burst into the office in tears and bubbled to me that she was pregnant but the man responsible would not stand by her. Of course we all stood by her, and we all pulled together to enable her to keep her salary and job despite repeated enquires about her from the Department. Later she had a good marriage.

NO ESCAPE

When I became a Head Teacher (they must have been desperately short!) a more worthy pal was made a Head Teacher at the same time. He was appointed to "ra Wee Rock" – otherwise properly called St. Roch's Primary School situated on busy Garngad Road. He was immediately concerned, because, right at the school entrance the road – widened to take tram tracks – immediately narrowed considerably to cross a railway bridge. He foresaw the possibility of an unwary motorist coming up on the inside lane of the wide part of the road, and being unprepared for its narrowing, to drive straight on onto the pavement where his pupils would be coming down to school, and so causing injuries or even deaths. My friend tried unsuccessfully for two years to have the necessary precautionary safety railings installed at the danger point. And of course, sadly, what he foresaw might happen, actually happened – resulting in the deaths of two of his small girls and injuries to others. He then had the sad task of going to parents and advising them of what had occurred. Needless to say, the much sought-after safety barriers were installed the following week.

I had nearly worked out my last year and actually was feeling grateful that I never had had to go to parents about a pupil's death – unlike my friend. But it had to happen. There was a splendid little cheery Primary Four boy who was always coming to ask me if he could do anything for me. I would think up some small thing for him to tackle – usually picking up litter etc. And when he had finished the wee job I would give him a little reward of some kind. That particular day there was lying on my desk a sheaf of stickers emblazoned "Keep death off the road!" so I gave him one of the sheaves. That night I was alone in St. Margaret Mary's church house when the door-bell rang. There were too very upset policemen standing there. They wanted someone to go with them to break the news to the parents because a small boy had been knocked down and killed on the dual-carriageway. The casualty was my cheery little friend. His dad drove the bus that shuttled between Central and Queen Street Stations and when the house door opened, he was standing there wearing his bus driver's open jacket, and stuck on his pullover was one of the "Keep death off the road" stickers. It was the last thing the wee fellow had done before going out to play. And he had actually said to his father as he stuck it on – "You be careful too on the roads". I was shattered of course. The tragedy account was that a car had been lying disused down on the dual carriage way on the other side of the road below the school, and a group of the children had run down to look at it. They then ran back across the dual carriageway, but, for some unknown reason, my wee friend had turned round and started to run back across the roads by himself, and so was knocked down and killed by a car driven by an unlicensed and uninsured youth.

Then, a few days later after the funeral, another hysterical teacher rushed in, and I thought, "Here we go again!" But this time it was more of an unnecessary hysteria. Some of the staff had arranged a summer holiday and the mother of a badly–behaved pupil had created threats about her badly-behaved off-spring not being allowed on the holiday.

OVER THE HILLS AND FAR AWAY

Because the children of ra Mulk were so deprived, I usually gave them a day on the Campsie Fells, thanks to the permission of an excellent sheep-farmer who allowed us to cross his lands, and who always was kind enough to send us framing pictures and literature for the day out. Usually we started from Queenzieburn and ended in Kilsyth. But on my last visit to the Campsies, I wanted to see once more the wonderful display of buntings I used to enjoy in Campsie Glen, so we made the longer trip to there on a very hot day. I kept encouraging the troops by saying that there was a great Italian Trattoria at Campsie Glen – but when we staggered down to the Glen, the ice-cream paradise had long been closed. I was not very popular as a result.

If the weather was really suitable we would have an even more adventurous day-out – taking Primary Sevens to Tinto – that strange prominent almost conical hill – usually visible from most of Lanarkshire. It derives its name from the reddish rocks abounding on it. On a clear day our east coast, Ireland, Arran and the very Cairngorms might be visible. On top is that large amazing Bronze Age cairn. We told our gang that it was a tradition there to carry a stone to add to the giant cairn. We would make it a really strenuous day by going right over the top and down the other side, having arranged for our bus to meet us at the other foot of the hill.

If the children (and teachers) of St. Martha's School had the time of their lives at Aberfoyle, the wee Maggie pupils hand staff had an even more joyous stay at an even better Glasgow Education Establishment down by Newton St. Boswells. And it meant a great day-out for myself as Head Teacher. Well! I had to visit and see if everything was going well, didn't I? It was great to get away from Glasgow for a day. And I went one-up on the charming Lady Head Teacher in charge of the holiday home. She had thought that she was the first former pupil of St. Mark's Primary to become a Head Teacher. I enlightened her that I had beaten her to that honour.

I had become so fed up with always having to drive around Glasgow with my mother, that after her death I started to walk up to Castlemilk of a morning and back after school though after school a staff member friend would usually give me a lift back down part of the way. The exercise fairly improved my wonky health. The shortest way up to Ra Mulk was through Lynn Park and its adjoining cemetery – a stiff climb. One dark morning a figure arose from behind a large tombstone. Of course I was startled but when the "ghost" asked me for the time I realised that it was only one of the grave-diggers trying on – for him – a joke.

Most summers the staff would give pupils a week at Butlin's Holiday Camp at Dunure, Ayr. I well remembered it as an RN camp during the war. In my final term at ra Wee Maggie, they decided instead to have a fortnight at Barry Island. This delighted me, as I could now go and see the Welsh railways at first hand, and I also wanted to pay a visit to Caldey Island, for I had devoured all I could find to read about Aelred Carlyle. Aelred was a devout Anglican who thought, against fierce opposition, that the Church of England should have an order of Benedictine monks. So he founded a small community of monks in London in 1895. His community moved to Caldey Island in 1905 and became a Catholic order in 1916. Unfortunately Aelred could not work as Abbot under Catholic auspices and he left, with his order moving to Prinknash Abbey and being replaced by a Belgian order of Cistercian monks. Aelred was the inspiration for several other Benedictine communities both Catholic and Anglican and of men and women foundations too. During the war he worked as a ship's chaplain out off Kamloops in Canada, and then much later had to be rescued as a starving hermit from Shepherd's Island. So I shot off one morning to drive to Tenby. Looking for the harbour, I saw a notice that a ferry was to leave for Caldey Island in about twenty minutes time. So I hastily found a place to park and ran all the long way down to the harbour. But the ferry did not leave until two days later, so I never achieved my long-awaited visit to Caldey Island. But it was a great fortnight. There were new railways to explore, especially round Barry Dock – the once great coal-exporting port, and we took the party for a steam ride on the recently-established Brecon Mountain Railway. The Mint was visited, and a splendid bird sanctuary, and I was taken back to my childhood pleasures with all the huge number of slot-operated machines in the various amusement arcades near the residential camp. What added to the pleasure was that everyone was so nice and friendly and helpful to us. On our return, still more unexpected slings and arrows awaited me. Tom Winning said that he would keep his promise and send me to the Beda College in Roma. During a very friendly conversation he advised me that he would never be able to offer me a parish in his Archdiocese and so I should think about going to a smaller diocese like Aberdeen or Dunkeld where they were known to be short of priests. I was telling my friend Hugh Harkins (R I P) about this conversation. Hugh at that time arranged for the Scottish Diocesan Pilgrimages to Lourdes, and he said that he was friendly with the priest who was in charge of the Dunkeld Pilgrimages, and that this priest was a late vocation – a former Dundee Art teacher – who had gone to the Beda College. Hugh arranged for me to go through to Tullibody where the priest had his parish – appropriately St. Bernadette's. In turn the priest arranged for me to see the Bishop of Dunkeld, Vincent Logan, who surprised me greatly by, without much ado, agreeing to have me for his Diocese. Accordingly I wrote to the Beda College for a reading list, but was astounded to receive a reply to the effect that they had never heard of me. The brother of one of my excellent assistant head teachers was the Vocations Director for the Glasgow Archdiocese, so I contacted her, and she was good enough to ask her brother what was going on. The answer came back that Tom Winning had washed his hands of me because I had decided to go to the Dunkeld Diocese. Of course I passed this state of affairs on to the Dunkeld Bishop who thought that I was making it up and that Tom Winning would never have said such thing. I had

227

difficulty in getting Bishop Logan to accept that what I was telling him was as it was. Eventually he said that he would be going out to Roma the following week on his ad limina visit, and that he would go along to the Beda College and see what he could do about having me accepted there. Meanwhile I insisted on a meeting with Tom Winning and complained to him about his attitude to me and said I thought the comment that he had washed his hands of me was quite disgraceful. He said that I had decided to go to another diocese. I pointed out that was a result of his own suggestion. He denied that he had said any such thing, and we had a right old up-and-downer about that – with him eventually reluctantly admitting it, but that he had only made the suggestion of going to another diocese "in passing"! Another fortnight passed, and I was becoming despondent, and since I had not heard anything from Logan I phoned him – only to be told that he had been in touch with the Beda College and they did not have a vacancy available for me. Why could he not have told me that bad news once he knew? So there I was – no job – no home – and depending on the kindness of the St Margaret Mary's parish priest for a living space. Then with only a week to spare before the start of the Beda year, Logan told me that the Beda had had an unexpected cancellation from an American applicant, so that they could take me after all. Phew! As I had no home, friends had suggested I purchase a Volkswagen Caravanette, and so I set off to Roma for a second time. My first stop was in Amsterdam on a camp-site next to the old National Arena and I was able to see Nicholas and McCluskey score the two goals against the great Ajax side that unexpectedly got us through the first round of the European cup – though we went out in the next round to Real Sociedad in a tie we might well have won. Present Everton manager David Moyes came on to replace Paul McStay in the Amsterdam game.

Then it was on to The Eternal City. Unfortunately by this time of year many of the listed camp-sites in the hand-book were closed for the Winter so some of the passages were quite lengthy, though the European motorways made the journey much easier than in 1950.

THE PONTIFICAL BEDA COLLEGE

A College was founded in 1852 by Pope Pius IX after Newman's entry into the Catholic Church, as it was hoped that there would be a "Second Spring" with more ex-Anglican clergy following his example. Then it was known as the Collegio Pio. But the expected influx did not occur and there were not many "late" vocations either, so it gradually just became part of the English College, that is until the time of Pope Leo XIII. He had a great devotion to St. Bede (whom he canonised) and in 1898 he re-founded a College – named after the great Jarrow historian – for late vocations, and situated near to the Triton fountain. That building existed for some time until it was demolished to make way for a Roma Underground line. There was a big increase in late vocations after the 1914-1918 disaster and a new four-year Beda comprehensive code of teaching was established by Monseigneur Duchemin in the early thirties. There was such a surge of late vocations after 1945, that a much larger brand-new establishment was created across the road from the great basilica of St. Paul's-outside-the-walls.

PEACE AND QUIET, PLEASE!

Hence it was that I was to find myself spending more of my existence in yet another post-war architectural monstrosity. The Beda so created in 1945 was an extremely large, and long in length, rectangular-shaped building. Its long terrazzo-floored corridors ran right the length of the building with absolutely no sound-proofing of any kind in the students' quarters. Some nights the racket got so mind-wearing that I would have to slip-out and obtain some much-needed refreshing peace and quiet in my Caravanette. (The Rector- of course – strongly objected to my having brought the Caravanette with me and ordered me to leave it in Glasgow. I replied that it was the only guaranteed home I now had, and that there would not be much left of it if I left it unattended in Glasgow.)

INTROIBO!

I first came through the Beda entrance doors with considerable trepidation, but was astonished when a Benedictine turned round from the large notice-board he had been perusing, and, pointing at me, exclaimed "Faith, Hope and Charlie Tully! And the greatest of these is Charlie Tully!" Honestly! Unbelievably these were the first words ever spoken to me in the Venerable Beda College. Derek Summers had been an RAF colleague in the Catholic Society at Coastal Command's Kinloss aerodrome.

(Shortly after my arrival at The Beda College, another friend from Kinloss days, Paisley's John McLean, sent me a letter in which he said that my decision to go to the Beda had inspired him to follow my example and try to go to the Beda too as a late vocation. But John, then teaching in Queen Margaret Secondary School in Ayr, had also been for a time a Jesuit lay-brother. When he too applied to Dunkeld, Vincent Logan had told him that as he had been a Jesuit lay-brother he could not become a priest. Nonsense of course. John told Vincent Logan he had contacted his old Jesuit head-quarters in Roma and the Galloway canon-lawyer – and other authorities – all of these had pointed out, quite correctly, that a former lay-brother could obtain a dispensation that would allow that person to become a priest. He enclosed the quite disrespectful letter he had received from Dunkeld in return. It was a one-liner that snarled "If you think you can do better elsewhere then feel free!" John came the following year to The Beda, became a highly-respected priest in the Galloway Diocese, and eventually retired as the parish priest at Stranraer.)

BELOW EXPECTATIONS

To say that I was disappointed with the Beda is putting it mildly. Repeatedly I had read in The Catholic Herald marvellous and remarkable descriptions of life in the Beda, and had long wanted to experience the excitement so described for myself. It was only later in my Beda spell that I was to discover that all the wonderful Catholic Herald Beda stories were pure fabrication made-up by self-amusing Beda students and fed to a very credulous Catholic Herald correspondent in Roma.

THEY JUST HAD TO PUT UP WITH ME

The Rector turned out to be Billy Mitchell – a very decent wee man from the Clifton diocese. Monsignor had had a seizure of some kind and I am afraid it showed. He seemed to me to be a bit scared by the whole business of running such an important College and treated the place as though he was running a small preparatory school instead of caring for real grown-up men. Additionally he was far too parsimonious. For example: only the cheapest and weakest Italian wine was provided at meals. Everyone was watched to see if they dared to take a second glass of wine. Guess who made a point of taking a second glass!

Irritated by this pain-in-the-neck parsimonious attitude, when in my last year I was acting college dean, and with the connivance of a splendid Irish nun cook we managed at least to repay the Irish College for some of the great hospitality we had received from them. I could not understand why there was no proper Beda bar so that we could entertain others without having to resort to an outside bar or to a near-by trattoria – where the food was passable but where we were constantly subjected to small itinerant children playing a few bars of music and then begging for contributions. Also a proper Beda bar would have clearly indicated those students who might have had an alcohol problem. And I strongly disliked the "horse-troughs" – as I called the long wooden tables where we had to eat. At least we moved along for each meal so that we had a change of conversationalist –which was a good idea. Try as I did I could not get the Rector to have small sensible four-to-a-table dining arrangement as we saw when we visited other Colleges.

One of the nuns put me off salad for life. She laid on "greens" (usually weeds form the extensive College grounds) for breakfast, dinner, tea. Because it was good for us. Ugh!

SEE STUDENTS...

On one occasion, two of the men had been out for a late session in Roma and on returning discovered that neither had brought the necessary gate key with them. They were attempting to surmount the tall boundary wall when they were arrested by the Roma policia. There had been a number of break-ins to religious premises around that time and the policia were being particularly vigilant around places like the Beda.

One of our year had been taken out by a group of older Welsh former Anglicans to celebrate St. David's Day. Having over-indulged, next morning my friend decided to absent himself from lectures and stay in bed to try to better remove his intense post-prandial headache. Unfortunately that was the morning when the Rector and the Sister Superior carried out their weekly room inspection. When Wee Billy came in and saw my friend still under the bed-clothes the decent man just said "Quite right to take life easy at your age Mr. --------!" And he and the laughing nun quietly left.

AND THEN THERE WAS THE STAFF THAT HAD TO SUFFER US!

And Monsignor could preach a marvellous sermon, but unfortunately had a bad habit. Right at the end, when we were all enthralled, he would throw out some challenge or other to us, which was very poor psychology (in my opinion!)

And we were not to indulge in tall stories either. That challenge I could not resist. When it was my turn to introduce newcomers to Beda and Roma life, I was walking a "starter" up from the Metro. Unfortunately he asked me why there was so much untended ground at the back of the Beda well-kept gardens. Wish now he hadn't opened an opportunity for me. I said that I would tell him if he promised not to tell anyone else. I informed him that that was where the married quarters were going to be constructed for the expected influx of married Anglican priests entering the Catholic Church. Sure enough, later, students would sidle up to me ad spin me that supposedly confidential yarn. Mea maxima culpa – yet again.

COME OUT! COME OUT! WHEREVER YOU ARE!

One morning two of the lads decided that they would forego another Rector challenge and skipped off to the local bar, a bar much-frequented by Beda students. They were enjoying their Camparis and blethers when they spotted the Vice-rector of the Beda heading for the bar. Immediately they ran round the bar counter and hid under it. Mgr. Molyneux sat quietly above them leisurely drinking his coffee. When he had finished he leaned over the bar and quietly said, "You can come out now". And do you know, they never heard any more about their escapade. Mgr. Molyneux was a dignified, kind-hearted, highly knowledgeable, good-natured and most helpful Christ-like man. He is the person I would have most-liked to have been (excepting Jimmy McGrory of course).

And then there was poor Ernie McConnon. This Monsignor had been one of the periti that translated Latin for the English Bishops at the Second Vatican Council.. (Imagine being a bishop and not understanding Latin. Dear me!) Monsignor certainly knew his Latin. He once gave me thirteen Latin nouns for a bat. He seemed to have taken on the role of Prefect of Discipline at the Beda. Having coped – often unsuccessfully – with Jesuit Prefects of Discipline, I am afraid I found him risible in his misbehaviour as did most of the students of my time. The poor man was an irritant more than anything else.

Manchester United supporter Richard Taylor was more to my taste in the high quality of his scripture-analysis lectures. I used to wonder why such an able priest had not moved on to higher things. But I did not like his always annoyed refusal to discuss interesting points he had raised in a lecture – after the lecture. I felt he had missed a trick or two with that attitude. But I suppose that was just my university background. Father Brian Noble was one of the tutors I admired. It was fairly obvious to me that he was going to be a Bishop one day, and so it turned out. Unfortunately as Bishop of Shrewsbury he suffered two serious illnesses and then became involved in controversy over his closure of the historic Wirral "Dome of Home" sea-farers church.

Fr. Cotter was another kettle of fish. His behaviour as a tutor was a real puzzle to me. I could never figure out what this man was up to. I did suppose that his erratic behaviour and observations were part of some deeper Beda ploy to see how students would react to it? During one discussion I made the mistake of opening my mouth and saying that I thought a married couple having difficulties would prefer to discuss them with a married priest instead of a celibate with no experience of marriage and its possible traumas. From then on he repeatedly annoyed me by saying almost every time we ran into each other, here is the man who wants married priests. Of course I had said no such thing. Although I think it is bordering on scandalous that Catholic priests of the Eastern rites are allowed to be married, but priests of the Western Church are not so permitted. It is a reasonable argument that if Western Rite priests were allowed to be married there would be less of a priest shortage around Europe and also less of the scandalous child abuses that have taken place and the scandal of many – even high-ranking priests having mistresses – as happened in the much-publicised Dunkeld diocese scandal for example. Rightly or wrongly – I suspect that too many in the upper echelons of the Western Church are scared of having to deal with wives.

OUR EASTERN RITE

I was having an after- Mass coffee with the parish priest of the "bocca" church in Roma – Santa Maria in Cosmedin – only a short distance from the Vatican. It is called the "bocca" church because of a large Roman drain cover with a face set into one of its walls, but it is a wonderful old building with one of the tallest and most fantastic towers in the eternal city and it has an altar to Hercules underneath. It was originally the port church for Greek merchants trading with Roma. The priest told me that his father and grand-father had also been parish priest there. Of course it was the abuse of this way of appointing successor Vicars Substitutes by land—owners that caused the Celibacy law to be introduced by the Western Church in the Twelfth Century. There is no real reason other than that for the celibacy law to exist today when there is such a shortage of priests. And it is well documented that in Scotland in the Middle Ages some Bishops and even some Archbishops had not only mistresses but wives as well.

LISTENING CAREFULLY

There were most interesting visiting lecturers at the Beda.

I particularly liked the top Vatican Canon lawyer who talked to us on Canon law and why it was there. It amused me very much to hear him emphasise that Canon Law was supposed to be treated with "epikeia" – the Greek word for "treating law with benignness and as much indulgence as possible" – Canon Law being there to be of assistance and not repression. I thought of that Ruchazie Irish parish priest who must not have heard that word in his Maynooth seminary days.

At the Beda, to begin with, there was a Jesuit lecturer who had been prominent at the Second Vatican Council. I thought at first he was up to best Glasgow University standards but shortly he started talking round in circles so his lectures had to end.

Two Carmelites were amusing. One wore traditional garb while the other was dressed Humphrey Bogart style. But they were both excellent and interesting lecturers and certainly could well put over their information.

The second one was giving me a viva voce exam and I thought to put off the difficult questions by telling him that his order had charge of St. Mary's, Abercromby Street in Glasgow's Calton, and that was from where Brother Walfrid had started Glasgow Celtic Football Club. But he torpedoed me in the end.

STAGED PERFORMANCE

Another of the ridiculous Beda non-senses was to have students up performing on the hall stage in front of the rest of the Beda body. Quite what that had to do with priestly formation escaped me, but with two other Dunkeld candidates we pulled the black soutanes over our heads and performed the old Scottish children chant "Three craws sat upon a wa'". Which, of course, went down like a lead balloon among the Sassenachs. But I suppose we had passed some test or other.

NO KEYBOARD FOR ME

I had long been keen on being a pianist but eventually found that my finger span was not sufficient to do Chopin's marvellous chords so turned to organ reciting instead. I wanted so much to get into the organ group for the Beda ceremonies but that was a closed shop. Instead I had the wonderful job of being in charge of the Beda window blinds – which I thought a bit of a come-down, but I suppose it was another of those pestilential Beda tests of character.

It turned out not to be such a pain-in-the-neck .I have always been one for delegation and I was astounded to discover that some of the Sassenach chiels were scared to go into Roma, so it was easy to find one of these obliging souls to look after the Beda blinds for me. I thank them very much for letting me have more time to explore Roma and particularly the remnants of its once great tramway systems.

A REAL STRAMASH

On one free day I travelled across Roma by ATAC motorcar (a tram but of course!) to the wealthy area around Viale Giuseppe Mazzini where I had been told that there was a great model shop. Well it was great – with great models but naturally great prices. Beyond my means unfortunately. But it was worth seeing. Then something else worth seeing happened. I was coming back on service thirty, sitting in a modified MRS bogie car from the Twenties. We halted at the traffic lights positioned on the complicated road junction below the beautiful Borghese Gardens. I saw on my immediate left – to my further delight – a brand new green and white Mini-Cooper with British number plates. Liverpool were in town that week and I was wondering if this was some rich Celtic supporter in Roma to see the game, when the smashing car did a smashing thing and suddenly raced forward and crashed into my tram immediately below where I was sitting. The heavy stationary bogie car hardly flinched – though I certainly did. One of the great Arthur Montford's "stramashes" duly ensued in true Italian fashion.

After a considerable delay, an eager excited crowd eventually pulled the ruined Mini out from under our MRS car and without any more ado our eager motorman set off on his lengthy journey round Roma for his far distant Via del Casaletto destination.

I was fascinated to see that what would have happened in Glasgow after a similar occurrence, being the first tram along for a while, happened in Roma. The motorman did not observe fermatas unless some passenger indicated the wish to alight, but waved to would-be boarders that other cars were coming behind. So I had one of my fastest ATaC rides ever.

PRESERVATION

I made contact with the most interesting Roman rail preservation group GRAF (Gruppa Romani Amici Ferrovia). They knew all about Glasgow tramways and had some interesting historical Glasgow documents I had not seen nor known about. They had been given the former military nine mile line from the Alban Hills down to Mussolini's then new resort at Ostia Lido. They intended to turn it into a working preservation tramway and had amassed historic trams and an enormous amount of discarded Roma track, point-work and overhead equipment. They most generously offered to supply to the Crich, Matlock U. K. Preservation centre one of the old A.co.Tral chopper-controlled single deck interurban cars that I had travelled on in 1950 and any amount of point-work (including maker-choice) and overhead material in return for help and advice about the Ostia project – but when I went to Crich with the great offer all that happened was I was told that I was making it all up, and I could not even persuade the Crich thickos to write a letter to GRAF to verify or nor the truth or otherwise of my information.. What a chance missed. Of course as usual I suspected sectarianism was about at Crich. Unfortunately for the eager Roman preservationists a Green Party persuaded the Italian authorities to declare a deep "green" belt inland from the coast at Ostia – so GRAF could not proceed with their intended preservation line. However they took Roman councillors – who apparently did not know of modern tramway development on a tour of the best Europe tramways and as a result the decline of the ATAC Roman system was halted and new replacement lines were built and modern trams introduced into Roma. I was promised a "go" of operating a works tram at night over the remaining Roma system – but of course that would not have been a possibility as The Beda would have been aghast.

PASS!

In the second year I still could not get into the exclusive organ group but only became one of the Beda drivers and accordingly was issued with a very useful Vatican pass. This also allowed me to join the throngs of Romans who also could get cheaper Vatican petrol. Amazing how many Romans supposedly worked for the Vatican – but then the Romans never miss a trick. (On one occasion the Roma authorities tried to reduce traffic congestion in the historic centre of Roma by requiring any motorist who wanted to drive into the historic centre to have a pass which was only to be available to residents of the historic centre. You have guessed it. So many "historic" passes were illegally obtained that then scheme had to be abandoned.)

The Beda had a twelve year-old very battered Volkswagen mini-bus and also a superb vintage Fiat swanky saloon car. The latter was used for only those and such-as-those such as Cardinals and Archbishops and of course the College Staff.

One of my driving duties was to take the rather pathetic Monsignor McConnon to play golf at the Aqua Sancta course. Yes! Acqua Sancta it was called. Wonder if the golf was Sancta. Doubtless you will be saying I should not be calling the Monsignor "pathetic". Well! Read on!

One time I dropped him off for his "gowf" – as it is known in Scotland; drove back to the Beda; parked the old crock of a van, and went off to enjoy the sights of Roma. Well! An uproar ensued. The golf course was closed and the monsignor did not know how to get back to the Beda by public transport. I was supposed to have taken the van sight-seeing round Roma. But I pointed out the true situation. Anyway who in his right mind would take a van on a Roma sight-seeing tour!

I often wondered how the good Monsignor managed to make his way to Killarney Lakeside for his summer golf holiday.

Then one day he surprised me. He thought it unlikely that I would know his uncle who lived in Glasgow – a Doctor O'Flaherty. I laughed, and said I knew him all right, as he was the Doctor who had brought me into the world. The good Doctor O'Flaherty once told me that he had brought 4,000 Catholic babies into the world before he got a non-Catholic baby to help. I caught a dose of the Spanish flu when it abounded but because we had been so short of teachers I only took two days off instead of at least two weeks, and so kept very unwell for a considerable time. Doctor O'Flaherty told be not to bother about playing golf in an attempt to become stronger as golf was a waste of time, but instead go for a five-mile hike. So night after night I would plod round the eastern outskirts of the dear green place for mile after mile. And what did the Monsignor say? He loved going to visit his uncle in Glasgow as his uncle would take him to play golf at Turnberry, Troon, Gleneagles or Carnoustie. So much for the advice I had received that golf was a waste of time.

R.I.P.

Then came a tragedy. My next-door student and very good friend had been an Inspector with the St. Helen's trolley-bus system and accordingly was the Head College driver. He died during the night following a meal with his Jesuit confessor friend. Requiescat In Pace.

It was suggested that he might have been over-indulgent? So I became the Head College driver, being called upon to drive dignitaries here and there and everywhere. So I got to drive that swanky Fiat. Various destinations were of peculiar interest. At Fiumacino airport were storage rooms full of mail-bags which lay there month after month unattended to. On one occasion the Rector was desperately waiting for an important letter so he asked me to go to the sorting office for our district of Roma to try to obtain it for him.

No wonder I got Christmas cards and letters from the U K in March or April. The Italian postmen would take a few letters off the top of the box for each address leaving a load lying waiting to be lifted out for delivery. Then more would be put in on top of those lying there and the process would be repeated and repeated.

I liked taking English bishops out to the English College summer residence at the beautiful Villa Pazzola across the lake from the Pope's Summer residence. If you are planning a visit to Roma that is the place to stay. Some years later I was asking my successor as college chief driver how he got on. (I had been surprised at his selection as a College driver as he had been involved in a serious road accident in Lucca as he was driving to the Beda for the first time. But there you go!) He recounted an episode that occurred when he too was taking a party of seven English bishops out to the summer residence. One of them asked him how he managed in the ferocious Roma traffic. He turned to say he managed all right and drove straight into another vehicle. Oh! Dear! Concentration! Concentration!

ROYALTY LOYALTY!

I wanted no part of Charles and Diana's visit to the Vatican and made my refusal clear when I was asked to take the Beda staff up to the Vatican for that occasion, stating that it was insulting in extreme that the Irish College were banned from attending. However I was firmly told that that was an order not to be disobeyed. So I ran the loyalists up to the Vatican in the posh old Fiat saloon. I was leaning on the wooden barrier where the couple were expected to exit after their visit and I suddenly realised that I would likely be the first person they would speak to on their exit. That would not have gone down well with me and would have made me a subject of ridicule and a laughing stock among my fellow Glasgow republican friends. So I quietly made my shuffle to the back of the expectant and very excited English loyalists. Sure enough my replacement was the first person Charles shook hands with and spoke to – uttering the unbelievable words, "I have never seen so many clergymen gathered together in the one place before." Where did he think he was, I mused, hiding my mirth at the stupidity of that utterance.

ASSISI BREAKDOWN

One driving order turned out to be not so amusing. The battered (not by me!) twelve year old Volkswagen had obviously seen better days. A Welsh vicar and his son had come to stay at the Beda – supposedly with a view to entering our Church. Wee Billy Mitchell had a great thing about Assisi. Of course we friends had visited it several times and had been a bit shocked at the grandeur of the basilica dedicated to the great man of humility.

The Rector had several peculiar notions about celebrating the Beda Centenary – apart from having wonderful Cardinal Hume and other Cardinals for me to bring to the Beda – and one of them was to make us all go off to Assisi for the day. It turned out to be a lashing wet day, and my friend Joe and I spent the whole day sitting blethering and eating (and drinking!) in a splendid trattoria. Great thing about Italian caterers –unlike in some Scottish places – you could linger as long as you liked and they never became upset or hassled you.

The Rector instructed me to take that Welsh visitor and his son to Assisi. I told the Rector that was impossible as the starter motor on the old Volkswagen had packed up. But he insisted on me doing it all the same. I was to discover that our Church was full of such inconsiderate commands. I dropped the two passengers off at the top of Assisi and told them where I would pick them up after they had wandered round sight-seeing – as I knew of a small hill down near the basilica at the bottom of Assisi on which I could jump start the Volkswagen. In the middle of Assisi the main street dips down into a hollow and then rises again. There are traffic lights at both ends of the street and system changes permitted direction on the main street as the lights change. I was going slowly down that main street when a woman tourist walked right in front of my vehicle. Of course I had to jam on the brakes and the engine stalled and I had no way of re-starting it. What I thought then of the Rector and his nonsense I cannot put in print. The lights changed of course and there I was stuck in the midst of the heavy traffic pointing the wrong way. I expected the carabinieri to appear anytime. I tried to get passers-by to give me a push up the opposing hill but was largely ignored until a group of young German girls came to the rescue and helped me push the vehicle up to the hill summit – over which I could jump start once more. I never did hear if the Welsh pair joined up. Whether the rector read my disgust about the whole business I know not – but "Alleluia!" Shortly afterwards a brand new Combi van appeared. It was much larger and much more comfortable and very tempting to drive. So of course I had to take it out – didn't I! I used to park the old Volkswagen between the Beda entrance pillars and when I came back with the new van I tried to do the same with the new vehicle. Of course I realised too late that it was too broad to go in between the pillars. Silly Tollan. I braked hard when I realised that but the front bumper struck both pillars. Mea maxima culpa. Fortunately no-one was about and I had time to run upstairs and grab the black shoe polish with which I hid the revealing collision marks on the bumper. And, do you know, I never heard a word about my stupidity. Phew!

UP IN THE AIR...

One of my former teachers from the Wee Maggie was by this time living in Luxemburg and that charming, delightful girl used to let me stay in their Luxemburg villa to break the road journey to and from Roma. She wrote to me that she was coming to Roma so I drove in my camper van out to Fiumicina airport to await her arrival. I got into a terrible quandary at the airport parking barrier. Because of my camper right-hand drive, I could not work out how to purchase a ticket and get back into the camper to go through the raised barrier before it closed again. Two kind men in the following vehicle saw my dilemma and came to my rescue. Lo and behold! They turned out also to be friends of my Luxemburg teacher friend and they were at the airport to meet her too. They were the most friendly pilots of the illuminated advertising airship that would float over Roma at night, and though I was made most welcome at their airship base outside Roma, and taken over the interior of the airship – just as not managing to operate that works-tram at night, I never did get a much-sought-after flight over Roma – as the waiting list was much too long.

MORE FITBA! BUT OF COURSE

I had another visitor, my old school chaplain Fr. McKelvie – and he was accompanied with the celebrated Father Fitzsimmons of later Radio Scotland Sunday record-request playing fame. Fitzsimmons was not interested but McKelvie and myself went to the Olympic Stadium to see Roma playing Pisa. At centre-half (as it was in those days) for Pisa was Eliot – who later came to Celtic and then ruined his career by being badly injured with Chelsea. The tickets were very expensive and there was no stewarding help to assist us find our proper seats, so we spent most of the match sitting on the access steps. The Roma ultras were anything but friendly and I made up my mind that I was not going to attend any game at the Olympic Stadium again. That was a pity because I could have had free tickets to see Dundee United and Liverpool play in their famous matches there.

When Roma won their League – for only the second time – the city went mad. It was impossible to sleep for over a week as motorists continually sounded their horns night and day. All the road markings and traffic signs were changed into Roma's red and yellow colours -hence the AS Roma nick-name "Yallowrossi" though sometimes "I lupi". In English pronunciation that would be very appropriate for their often erratic performances.

Fr. Fitzsimmons unfortunately ruined his clerical career later on. When appointed as Rector of the Scots College in Roma he was strongly disliked by the seminarians there. He had a habit that greatly annoyed them. When introduced to a visiting cleric from forth of Scotland, he always said "I have been to your Cathedral!" and "I have met your Bishop!" So the seminarians introduced him to a student from the North American college who had been coached to say that he was from a non-existent Diocese and to name a non-existent Bishop. Poor Fr. Fitz fell for it – hook, line and sinker. So that was his clerical credit destroyed – once and for all – and he had to be removed from the position of Rector of the Scots College with no advancement to the hierarchy taking place.

YOU CANNOT KEEP THE SCOTS DOWN

At the Scots College I met up with Monsignor Charles Burns – Curator of the Vatican archives. Of course I jumped at the possibility of seeing the famous archives, but that could never happen as only bona fide researchers were allowed to do that. But Monsignor Burns was extremely kind to me. He told me that he was from Busby outside of Clarkston, Glasgow. His father, as was so often the case in those sectarian days, could not make a decent career for himself in the dear green place, so he joined the Canadian Pacific Steamship company, and eventually became Commodore in charge of their great liners. Monsignor recalled that once, during the war, his father suggested that he might like to be at Renfrew Ferry at a certain day and time. So the young Charles cycled over to the Renfrew Ferry, and was there at the appropriate time. During the war the name of ships were hidden by wooden baffles hung over them. Soon a large liner came down the Clyde and there was his dad on the foredeck. His father leant over the side and lifted a baffle board to show Charles that the liner was The Empress of Canada. Quite a tale. When Charles Burns had finished his seminarian training in Roma and had been ordained to the priesthood, the Bishop of Paisley said that Charles should go back to Roma for a holiday. Charles said that he did not want to do that as he had just returned from Roma, but the Bishop persuaded him to go back to Roma -ostensibly for a holiday there. But Charles was never to return to serve in the Paisley diocese. He discovered on going to Roma that it was for an appointment to the Vatican Archives. Monsignor was most interesting, of course, about the Archives. Apparently they extended then for two miles under the Vatican. They were still recovering from all parts of Europe material stolen from the Vatican by the plundering troops of Napoleon when he occupied Roma. In the archives were a dozen or so large "forsicles" each containing thousands of unclassified documents. There was not the staff available to sort these huge bundles out and it was not likely that there would be enough staff appointed to do that huge task. A new Cardinal Protector of the Archives had been appointed and asked

Monsignor Burns what he could do to help. He was shown the mass of unclassified material and was informed that even if the existing staff did nothing else it would take them at least thirty years to sort the documents out. No additional staff was forthcoming. An additional problem was caused by the nationality of John Paul the Second as now staff fluent in Polish had had to be obtained to classify his documentation. Monsignor Burns was very generous to me. He took me several times for lunch at one of the very expensive ristorante adjacent to the Vatican. I would never have dared to go there myself. We Beda men soon discovered that the trattoria/ristorante around the historic Roma area had two menus. One was for the tourists but the better one was for the Romans. Additionally certain quality meals in these places were only available on certain days of the week. So a good memory was needed. A good place to take our visitors was to pizzerias by Trastevere. Here one could see ordered pizzas being prepared and then cooked within sight in blazing ovens. We discovered one trattoria that provided pasta Scozzese – pasta flavoured with salmon and whiskey. And it was opposite the wonderful Jesuit church – San Ignacio. in Via Seminario – just along from the Pantheon. In our first year we would take visitors into that superb church to see not only a wonderful trompe-d'oeil on the ceiling but the huge dragon on the sanctuary with Luther and Calvin emblazoned on its tail. But these two names were eventually removed when ecumenism became the order of the day. Monsignor Burns saw that I was upset at the cost of a meal in his favourite dining spot (usually about £20 – a lot of money in those days before euros). He explained that he had to eat out three times a day for a week and that if he went to the cheaper, more tourist-orientated places, he would have to spend a lot of time suffering requests from visitors to Roma to order for him, and that became very wearing when happening time after time, day after day. He had barely finished explaining this problem to me when an American family sat down at the next table, and, surely enough, when he heard us pattering the Scottish lingo, the husband asked Monsignor to order for them. You should have seen the look Monsignor gave me. I had to chuckle inwardly. Monsignor Charles Burns was generous enough also to give me two signed gratis copies of two of his historic books "Golden Rose and Blessed Sword" and "Papal Gifts and Honours for the earlier Tudors." I highly commend these fascinating books to any reader with an interest in history. The first was published by John S. Burns & Sons, and the second is "Estratto da Miscellanea Historiae Pontificiae Vol. 50".

FELLOW STUDENTS

When I observed things at The Beda I was extremely disappointed at the calibre of quite a few of the students there and as I said earlier, I had been eagerly looking forward to being there as I had avidly read great stories in The Catholic Herald about the remarkable previous careers of students here. Alas! As indicated these proved to be merely far-fetched fairy-tales that had been fed to a credulous Roma correspondent of The Catholic Herald and he had swallowed them hook, line and sinker without any follow up to see if they were indeed true. Of course there were excellent men there in my time, and I still keep in contact with some of them. But! I was shocked at the obviously active homosexuals, the alcoholics, and even one of two who were almost semi-literate. Dealing with the homosexuality: it was so obvious that I was quite disgusted that the powers-that-be in the Beda allowed it to continue. I went to the then Rector of the Scots College and asked for advice from him – but he just did not want to know, which made me wonder about what went on at The Scots College too. It wasn't until an irate Roman mother ended up at the Beda and read the riot act to the Rector and named names, that a very few of the active homosexuals were sent packing.

By some mischance I had become acting student dean of the place and it fell to me to remove a quite violent drunkard from the College as it appeared that the Rector could not cope with doing that. This individual had tried to hide his propensity for alcohol by swallowing large amounts of garlic. I got him packed up after a struggle and delivered to Fiumicino and booked on a flight to the U. K. and his parting words to me were, "I am going to join the Jesuits because they always know a good man when they see him" Really!

The academic side of the Beda was not too onerous. Basically one had to write an essay on a given subject every ten days. This was a bit of an annoyance to me because the Beda had a simply splendid library and I would be immersed in following up the set topic but then have to give up the interesting study to stop in order to dash off the required essay in time. One or two of the students could not even write a short essay and usually their essays were written for them. One not so bright specimen tried jogging across the main Roma high-speed eight-lane motorway with obvious consequences. It all rather made me wonder why some students at the Beda had been selected for progress to the priesthood by their Bishops (including me!)

To celebrate the Tourist Mass in St. Peter's Basilica was an ambition for a lot of the men – especially those from North America. It was a Mass celebrated in Latin, of course, and I had to do a fair bit of Latin teaching for these hopefuls in consequence. A Beda practice that all detested was the requirement by the Rector that from time to time we had to undergo viva voce examination by external examiners. This of course was not a required thing – but no doubt Wee Billy Mitchell had his own reasons for it. (Having been appointed Rector of the Beda, Monsignor's next step would have been to become a member of the hierarchy. Unfortunately at one of the annual week of meetings held by the various rectors of the English-speaking Colleges Monsignor discovered that he could not rise from his seat. Presumably that was the result of a small stroke? May be Monsignor still had hope of further promotion by insisting his men suffer these viva voce exams?) It was a perfect pest having to struggle through the Roma rush hour traffic to get over to the Lateran where, for some unknown reason to me, the viva voce exams were held. A consolation was that they were held in the magnificent salon of the Lateran in which Mussolini signed the Lateran Treaty of 1929 acknowledging Vatican independence with the creation of the Vatican City State and solving at last the whole tumultuous Roman question re the position of the Church in Italy and making reparation for lost lands and revenues. So at least it was of great historic interest to be allowed to be in that salon. Most of the viva voce examiners were cool and friendly and I had the impression that some too were, like us, not too enamoured of the whole proceeding. That is except for one. He was a sour-looking and very small crabbit Belgium Jesuit. A most unpleasant person. No-one wanted to have him as examiner and I had managed to avoid him with all the cunning I could muster until my very last time at the Lateran exams. I knew what he was going to ask me and I had prepared a good answer- as I thought. Here it came: "You are celebrating Mass for ninety nuns and at Communion time you go to the tabernacle and find there are only a few hosts in the ciborium there. You then see that you did not notice a full ciborium of prepared hosts sitting on the Credence table. What do you do?" Of course the answer he thought correct was to turn to ninety nuns and say that they were not going to receive Communion. I replied I would not be doing that as before each celebration of Mass I would make the resolution that I would consecrate whatever had been prepared for consecration. "But that would be no use if the hosts are not on the Mass altar." he snarled back. "Then how come last week I was standing some two hundred yards from the Papal altar in St. Paul's-outside the walls and the Pope consecrated the hosts in the ciborium I was holding?" I queried. "He is the Pope and he can do that." came the daft reply. No wonder the Church in Europe is in such a mess. And I never heard of any Beda man being failed at the Lateran viva voce exams. What a waste of time they were.

I thought it a bit of a let-down that after four years of supposedly higher study no-one leaving the Beda received a certificate to say what he had studied and/or obtained. Certainly as far as I was aware. (I knew of a fellow parishioner/organist from St. Gabriel's parish, Merrylee, Glasgow, who had not completed his course of study at Glasgow University, but, after attending the Gregorian University in Roma, submitted a certificate re what he had studied at the Gregorian and this was accepted by Glasgow University and so he completed his degree from there) .

The normal starter number at the Beda was 32. I knew that in my time the number that went on to ordination usually varied to only between eight to twelve so presumably the rest had nothing to show for their four years at the Beda College? But there was an astonishing (to me) exception to the average number going on to Ordination. Of our 32 starters one good friend died as I related – R I P – but twenty eight went on to be ordained. I still continue to be perplexed as to why our year was so wonderfully exceptional.

WAS IT AN OMEN?

We had to make a private self-supervised, self-examining retreat before the official supervised one. So our group decided to head out to a Redemptorist House in the lovely countryside near Nemi. And what happened on the day before we were going to leave the Beda? Nothing less than a great blizzard accompanied by tremendous thunder and lightning. The roads and streets piled up with snow and to our amazement every Italian motorist had safety chains fitted round their tyres; and we could not find any that fitted our U K wheels. (I had once had chains for an earlier car but when in the U. K. roads began to be swept and properly treated when there was snow and ice I had no need to use them.) I gave up the search for tyre chains, put a film in my camera and set off on an old MRS tramcar for the tramway hub of Porta Maggiore. As used to happen in the good old days of the Glasgow Corporation Tramways, the tram had no bother in navigating the snow-filled roads and streets and we were swiftly and smoothly at the great tramway hub. I intended to alight there and take some pictures but a large, muscular and rain-coated Inspector came out of his Inspector Box and ordered the poor thin and unwilling and un-rain-coated motorman to take his place in that Box while muscle-man took over the operation of the tram. I was delighted and highly entertained when the "new" motorman began to sing operatic numbers in a tremendous and accurate voice and interspersed his great musical performance with proclamations of how unusual and marvellous it was to be operating an electric tram through the great snow. . Despite "Vietato Parlare Guidatore" above his head, soon an admiring group of young beauties had gathered round him. I was highly amused when he began to announce to them how dangerous it was to be operating this electric tram in the snow. That did not worry my dad and his motormen friends in the dear green place. The fine opera singer was soon silenced when we reached the large tri-angular junction at Via Flaminia. All the points and track-work were covered in about a foot of snow and I bet that Inspector was now wishing he had not changed places with his motorman for he was almost up to his knees in the snow as he fished about with only his point iron to see if the points were set to take us up to Risorgimento terminus. You have guessed it. In my haste to get to Porta Maggiore I had not properly wound on the new film in the camera and I had not in fact taken all the marvellous pictures of trams in snow-bound Roma that I had thought I had taken. Worse was yet to come. On the day we had arranged to set out on our self-controlled retreat there was a repeat performance of a second great thunder and lightning terrifying blizzard. So we had a most frightening and slip and slide crawl to Nemi. I wondered if Someone-up-there was trying to tell us something – just as I wondered about the great thunderstorm in Glasgow on the day of my Gilmorehill graduation. The media were to proclaim in amazement that there had never ever been two blizzards in one week in Roma since the days of Julius Caesar no less.

MORE TREPIDATION

,And then another big worry for me came. It was whether I had been properly ordained as a Deacon that bothered me considerably. For Diaconate the rector brought back a retired bishop who had been a Beda man. To my puzzlement he carried out the Diaconate ordination verbage in Latin and then in English. I have always been bothered as to why a repetition was necessary.
There had been a time when Beda ordinations to the priesthood had been carried out while the ordinands were still resident at the Beda but because so many could not be bothered to work after Ordination that practice was discontinued and Ordinations were then carried out in the particular Dioceses when the candidates had returned home. That was a great disappointment too for me as I would have been delighted to have been Ordained in St. Peter's by the Pope.

But of course I had suffered another great disappointment after reaching the problematic (for me) Diaconate. Usually the Beda student Dean had the great privilege of being Deacon at a Papal Mass in St. Peter's and I thought that privilege would happen to me – even though I was only acting Dean by default. But the Rector had other ideas and wanted to show off his African Prince student rather than the argumentative bit of scruff from Glasgow. Reverse discrimination of course.

But a surprising thing and another of life's little mysteries happened. The American priest who lectured (very well) on Moral Philosophy, called me aside after a lecture and said that he could not manage to come for next week's lecture and would I do it for him. I was staggered and even more shocked when he said it was to be on Logical Positivism. Now how earth did he know I could do that? Of course A.J. Ayer's thoughts on that philosophy had been discussed at Gilmorehill so I knew how to confront it. But I made the mistake of doing what had never been done at The Beda before (or so I was to be told). Before the lecture I festooned the lecture room with philosophic definitions, data and info re personalities involved from The First Vienna School onwards. (I had once previously given a slide show on trams and tramways and apparently that had never been done at the Beda before either. What an archaic place.) On the week after my attempt at demolishing Logical Positivism, the aforesaid American lecturer said to me that I had wasted my time putting up all the definitions etc. round the lecture room walls as most of the students would not have understood any of it anyway. Now there was a comment on the standard of men being sent to the supposedly esteemed Beda College.

And that did not only apply to the students. Near the end of my time an additional member of staff appeared. (I suspected that he was meant to succeed Wee Billy Mitchell.) A most pleasant personality, Fr. Brendan Soane was from an up-market family but in discussion Jim High (A former Dundee teacher) and myself discovered that he had never heard of Quantum Mechanics. Amazing to us. An oak statue of St. Bede's stands in The Beda entrance now in commemoration of Father Soane.

In the Beda there should be two other donated statues (from a German sculptor working in London). Wee Billy asked my friend Joe his way back Roma to go via to North London to collect one and bring it to the Beda. Fortunately I had accompanied Joe with my vehicle in order to take him to stay with my Luxembourg teacher friend en route and in fact there were two statues being donated to the Beda. So we travelled across Europe bearing a statue each. Unfortunately the Channel was so rough when we attempted to go across that ferries were badly delayed and we did not have time to detour via Luxembourg.

FREE DAYS

But it was an interesting life at the Beda College. Once a month we did not have to attend the Beda Sunday Mass so with some fiends we would make a point of going to one of the Roma Eastern rite churches to give support. A wee problem was that when we would go into an Eastern Rite Church wearing clericals almost inevitably we would be invited to come onto the sanctuary and participate in their Mass. I particularly liked going to the "Bocca" church, more properly Santa Maria in Cosmedin. Thus is well worth a must visit if in Roma. The church there was built over a temple of Hercules in the Sixth Century and the crypt has great mosaics and a collection of relics salvaged from the catacombs. The Eastern rite priest was always very friendly and would have coffee for us after he had celebrated Mass. He once told me that his father had been the parish priest there and his grandfather before that. This family succession to parishes caused great problems, so two thousand years ago the celibacy rule was established – with a great deal of protests and difficulty in the Western church. Of course the rule of celibacy does not apply to the priests of the Eastern rite. Adherence to the Western Rite celibacy rule is regarded by many as one of he main reasons for grave shortage of priests in the Western church and as it is only a disciplinary rule it could easily be rescinded – as it is for married Anglican priests becoming Roman Catholic., My own theory as to why the Vatican obstinately refuses to rescind such a disciplinary rule is that bishops and cardinals and even the pope are all scared of having to consider wives and family situations when dealing with priests. Certainly most wives would not stand for the way celibate priests are sometimes treated like glorified altar boys. On one occasion I had sat down to have the usual after Mass coffee at the "bocca" church when a pleasant lady asked if she could join me. Not being adverse to pleasant ladies I agreed. We had a long conversation during which she asked me where I came from – and of course I told her the dear green place of Kentigern. She told me that she had uncles who were Clyde shipyard engineers. As we were leaving the church one of my Beda friends asked me did I know with whom I had been having that conversation. He explained that she was Princess Doria Pamphilia no less. The Scottish connection had arrived via a war-time romance. And I just loved walking in the Pamphilia Gardens and watching the large goldfish swimming in their huge pond.

Another Eastern rite church which was even more fascinating was the large Ukrainian church – Santa Sophia on the Via Boccea. Their swirling, engaging, lively, liturgy puts our rather mediocre one to shame.

We had many excursions once a month and at holiday time. At Christmas we would tour the churches of Roma admiring their astounding variety of crib scenes. What an industry St. Francis started by arranging for a friend to first construct a crib. In the great basilica of Santa Maria Maggiore there were even two.

EXPLORING

One of our Edinburgh men would go off and research day tours to unusual and spectacular and most fascinating places.

Unfortunately some of his spectacular destinations were so remote that on the day the hired coach could only negotiate with great difficulty the narrow roads with their twisting bends. On one occasion we were stuck for too long a time on an awkward level-crossing. By some miracle we had just managed to get across the line when a diesel unit went hurtling by. Phew!

One place visited drew us back several times. Montefiuscone was fantastic. There is a splendid castle on a crag overlooking beautiful Lake Bolsena and a lovely adjoining forest alongside the castle. I thought the little village by the lake was charming and very peaceful and that it would be a wonderful place to retire too. But on one occasion I was strolling along admiring the village when in the other direction a youth came slouching towards me followed by an irate middle-aged woman who was hurling bottle after bottle at him. May be the village was not so peaceful after all, and as a native Glaswegian I had never seen a bottle thrown in earnest there. Montefiuscone of course is famous for its wine.

"EST EST EST"

The story goes that in the twelfth century a Bishop was journeying urgently towards Roma and would send a manservant ahead to see what the wine was like at the bishop's next proposed stop. If the wine was good the servant would send back EST (for vinum est bonum!) The servant thought the wine at Montefiuscone was of such excellent quality the he sent back "EST, EST, EST"! Supposedly when the bishop arrived at Montefiuscone he so indulged himself with the excellent wine that he over-drank and died. Who said that they did not know of good publicity stunts in the Middle Ages?

We visited the great Etruscan excavations – the mysterious Etruscans are supposed to be the fore-bearers of the early Romans and of course have given their name to the much-loved region of Italia called Tuscany. Fortunately- or unfortunately – since we had nuns with us in the party we were not allowed to see some of the more extreme mosaics excavated there. And of course we were at the amazing Pompeii, Herculaneum and Ostia excavations too.

BENEATH

Pius XII had arranged excavations under St. Peter's and St. Paul's basilicas and as Vatican members we were given the privilege – when a suitable qualified guide was available – of going down into the original Vatican cemetery under St. Peter's and getting, after passing amazing and interesting sarcophagi, to the reputed very burial place of St. Peter with some of his remains. (The normal tourist visit under the high altar of St. Peter's is a level above that.) Visiting early Christians had obviously believed that to be St. Peter's burial place as they had carved their visitor graffiti saying that alongside.

Unfortunately nothing of St. Paul's remains were found under his basilica when a similar excavation was made there. And it is believed that Viking raiders coming up the Tiber might have plundered his remains.

Unfortunately too that excavation is now inaccessible. Above it was a tram turning circle and the weight of the Roman articulated cars, caused the excavated entrance passage way to collapse.

And Roma has many, many catacombs to visit. I doubt if even in a life-time you could explore them all. But we managed more than one varied catacomb visits.

SOUTH OF ROMA

We combined visits to Napoli and Sorrento with crossings to the magnificent island of Capri. At the time when to be a homosexual was not acceptable in the best of European society, Capri became a refuge for practising homosexuals. I had read Axel Munthe's remarkable book "The Story of San Clemente", and visiting that astoundingly beautiful villa was a must. Gracie Fields had a splendid villa nearby to see too.

But unwittingly we caused some amusement on our first visit by hitching a ride on a tractor to get from Lower Capri to Upper

Capri. We did not know on that occasion that there was a bus service available to do that.

I had wanted to visit Napoli to ride on their trams. But on the first occasion I tried that there had been an earthquake and since much of the main route ran through tunnels the tram system was not operating

On one occasion I had made the mistake of taking my camper van down to the Naples area. But never again. If I stopped in a lay-by to make a brew, large threatening youths would appear bearing cardboard boxes supposedly containing TV sets etc. The only way to be rid of them was to show my Vatican pass and say I was a priest. Mea culpa! I asked if it was safe to go up to the top of Vesuvius and was assured that it would be fine if I parked outside the ticket-office. (Tickets needed so that officialdom could be sure that no-one who went up to the rim of the crater did not come back safely.) Muggins did that. Took the few minutes to go up to look into the smoking crater and come back down and the van door had been jemmied open. Obviously someone in the ticket office was the guilty party. I knew it would be a waste of time challenging them or contacting the carabinieri. But nothing had been stolen from the van. They had obviously spotted my Vatican passes. But it was over fifty pounds to have the door re-fixed when I returned to the Eternal City. And fifty pounds was a lot of money in those days. . A Canadian friend with a Stornoway aunt was anxious to see a Napoli suburb called Barra.

We went to Barra on the wonderful narrow-gauge line The Circumvesuviana which, as well as obviously having a circuit of the volcano connects Napoli with lovely coastal places down to Sorrento such as Castellamare. On one occasion we were in a retreat house near Sorrento on the self-catering pre-Diocanate retreat supervised by an admirable North America College professor. A couple of us were despatched to purchase some spaghetti and we wandered into a small grocery store in a near-by small village. In the middle of the floor was a large open sack of pasta. We asked for a kilo of that pasta and the store owner and some customers were pulverised with laughter. We gave embarrassed smiles too when we were told that pasta was there to feed dogs. You cannot win them all.

When we alighted from the Circumvesuviana at Barra and strolled down the main street I felt more afraid than I had ever done even in the notorious gang areas around Baltic Street in Glasgow. Inhabitants started to some out of buildings and stared at us in a most hostile manner. We came to a large church and that frightened me even more. It was surrounded by enormous thick black railings about fifteen feet high. And waiting patently outside the church entrance were six beautiful plumed black horses in front of an enormous black hearse. We plodded on towards the sea front and I found there was a turning loop for the Napoli tramway, but a service to this Barra branch did not seem to be working. Eventually even my Canadian friend had had enough and we made a quick retreat back to the Circumvesuviana.

The next time I tried to have a look at the Napoli rete tramviaria the trams were on strike!

When I at last managed a ride on the Napoli tramway I was astonished to find that Napoli motormen operated their vehicles in the crowded city centre with their air-brakes continually applied. Brake shoe wear must have been appalling.

A LENGTHY MASS

On another occasion we were exploring the back streets of Napoli on a Sunday morning and had just discovered an interesting-looking large and very crowded market square when an old lady appeared on the outside veranda of a huge church and via a megaphone shouted that Mass was about to start. We thought that we might as well join in the Mass. The large church was packed – with a huge congregation. A shock came with the Prayers of the Faithful. We counted fifty-two persons going up in turn to announce a bidding prayer. That took long enough but then the celebrant realised that he had not made the any of the necessary preparations for the coming Offertory and Canon of the Mass. In all that Mass took two hours and ten minutes to complete. I for one was glad that I did not have to attend a Mass there on a regular basis. But the Italians did not seem to be bothered.

ST. PAUL'S OUTSIDE-THE-WALLS

Our Beda parish church was, of course, just across the busy road – namely the Benedictine basilica of St. Paul-outside-the-walls. (At one time when Roma was a smallish place, there was a covered walk-way from the city out to St. Paul's.) We sometimes went to the public Mass there – apart from when we were having our own liturgies in the basilica. At a public Mass I would be was amazed how many locals refused to participate in offering the sign of peace. I was amused however to fond that there was a door in the apse behind the high altar. This was there for WC use for aged celebrants if they were participating in a liturgy that was too long for their bladders. Another amusement came thus. A poor small Italian – not quite the full shilling – was a usual sight by a huge multi-story building even bigger than Lewis's department store on Glasgow's Argyle Street which was reputed to be necessary to hold all gifts presented by visiting dignitaries to the reigning Pontiff. Gifts had to be stored there to be available for show in case a particular dignitary paid a return visit to the Vatican. During one Sunday Mass the poor wee soul had managed to dress up as a Benedictine monk and came on behind the assembled Benedictine altar party and performed Abbott and Costello antics as the proper Abbott was giving his homily to the parishioners. And do you know – the Abbot and monks did not turn a hair. Great men I thought. No doubt someone had put him up to it.

John Paul II was (like me!) dissatisfied with the quite inadequate information given to tour parties by poorly-informed tour party guides. So we were asked to volunteer as guides (who knew what should be told to visitors). It was quite amusing to find that many of the visitors could not appreciate that they were getting a free fully informed tour of St. Paul's Basilica. The poor souls were so used to people trying to rip them off. As a reward participants in the volunteer scheme like me were rewarded with a personal audience with the Holy Father in one of the splendid vast Vatican interior reception salons. Unfortunately here was a cause for some joking. When John Paul II was shaking your hand he did not look directly at you but at the person coming behind. The sick joke went the rounds that the poor man was looking for the next assassin.

BEDA GUESTS

As well as meeting the Pope we met other prominent churchmen. Cardinal Hume, as is always recognised, was humble, friendly and most approachable.

A strange fellow was Archbishop Couve de Mourville. (The then U K Papal Nuncio had the habit of appointing members of his higher society to top positions in the Church.) He was friendship itself when I drove him around Roma but twice staggered most of us during the two occasions he celebrated Mass for us in the Beda. On the first occasion he stopped in the middle of .his Mass celebration and advised us to have nothing at all to do with Jesuits. They were not to be trusted. This was shocking for many of us who, like myself, were products of a Jesuit education. Later this puzzle of a man expelled all Jesuits from his Birmingham Archdiocese. On the occasion of his second Mass he again told us to have nothing to do with charismatics. Their movement was much too dangerous also. Again staggering shock to many present as they were at the Beda as a result of charismatic activity. Later in the real world of parish work I was to find that if anything needed to be attended to as a matter of urgency, charismatics were always the first to respond. My only worry about them was a practice of having open general confessions. In vain I would point out to them that that was a dangerous practice.

Other interesting visitors included a very gentlemanly and friendly Tonypandy – former Speaker of the House of Commons. The most entertaining and friendly visitor we had was renowned singer Dana. Twice we welcomed Moderators of the Church of Scotland. And then a new friend with whom I still try to keep in touch – though she now lives widowed outside Chicago. One of the aforementioned College lecturers (clue – a strong Manchester United supporter with relations in Bailleston of all places) liked to have his afternoon siesta. So if he had brought in a visitor for lunch, he would do his best to pass that visitor on to one of the students. I realised one Sunday that I was going to be a victim of this manoeuvre and tried to dodge – but I was too slow off the mark. He said that here was someone from Glasgow so we would have a great deal in common and then promptly vanished from the scene. Trying to be friendly, I asked which part of Glasgow she was from. Coatbridge was the reply. I laughed and said that that most Catholic of Scottish towns was never part of Glasgow but that I had worked on the trams through Coatbridge. Then I was truly amazed at what followed. She said that her father had been a motorman in Coatbridge depot, and that her surname was Cantwell, and I replied that my father, a motorman in Parkhead Depot, had, through the Glasgow Catholic Transport Guild, been a firm friend of her father, and that her brother Jackie had been a

Celtic centre-forward when he came out of the navy after war-time service. She said that her brother received a few pounds if he played and a few pounds for each time he trained. So we have got on fine ever since.

REJOICE AND BE GLAD

But even more wonder was to follow. There was usually much more television of Scottish Football on RAI TV than I had ever seen in Scotland, but of a Saturday afternoon I would be glued to the BBC World service trying to find out how the Bhoys were doing. On the 3rd of May came the astonishing 5 – 0 thrashing of St. Mirren at Love Street and that – what with the Jambos unexpectedly losing at Dens Park – gave us our 34th League Title on goal difference. I ran excitedly all over The Beda College but could not find anyone with whom to share my unexpected great joy and happiness. I always felt David Hay was never properly appreciated or well-treated by his then Parkhead Board.

ACTIVE DIACONATE

My appointment as an active Deacon in the Diocese of Dunkeld was to St. Matthew's in the Dundee suburb of Whitfield. This was to be a great disappointment for various reasons, most of that by my own poor performances. Originally Whitfield had meant to be a giant new suburb with a multitude of Swedish style multi-storied blocks to help clear the terrible Dundee slums, and the Diocese had accordingly constructed a very large church building for Whitfield, fully expecting there to be a large Catholic population in Whitfield. Previous generations of Catholics in Dundee had had to live in very crowded unsavoury tenement conditions because, as mentioned previously, the prominent jute mills owners of the past would not employ Catholics, leaving Catholics to take lowly-paid employment if they could obtain any at all. The Whitfield plan turned out to be a disaster as the Swedish-style blocks of housing erected thee turned out to be quite unsuitable for Dundee conditions and really nobody wanted to live in them. So only a few of the wretched miserable blocks were constructed leaving the Diocese with an impossible-to-finance and pretty useless large church building. The priests' accommodation was awful and completely unprotected to burglary and unwanted invasion. There were two priests attached to a parish with hardly any parishioners to serve. I was greatly disturbed and puzzled. There seemed to be little point in my being there. I think the kind parish priest Fr. Gallagher provided an answer. The very friendly and helpful priest from Lanarkshire was a late vocation like me – though a lot younger. He indicated that among too many of the priests in the Dunkeld Diocese late vocations were not very welcome. He gave me permission to travel down to pay my last respects to Jock Stein when the latter's funeral was taking place at Linn Park Crematorium.

Later, one week when staying at Whitfield, it was obvious to me that my good friend was having a succession of small heart attacks. I could not get him to go to Ninewells hard as I attempted to persuade him to do that. I contacted the bishop but he would not act and later Fr. Gallagher took yet another heart attack that killed him. The other priest who was at St. Matthew's had once been a high-flyer marked out for promotion to the hierarchy but in the then isolation of Kinross had succumbed to alcoholism. The bishop had just recently rescued him from a recovery situation in an English monastery. He was an excellent type – very fond of a small motor-scooter. In fact he was to make a complete trip on it right up the Outer Hebrides – brave man. A number of times at a concelebrated Mass he would ask me to consume the remains of the consecrated wine as he dared not even take a sip of the wine in case he restarted his alcoholism.

Shortly after my arrival at St. Matthew's, a fellow Beda deacon and myself were invited to participate in a concelebrated Mass elsewhere in Dundee. Unfortunately that turned out to be a bit of a disaster. We stood about on the sanctuary and were given not a thing to do. And then after Mass no one at all even spoke to us in the house where a buffet had been laid on. This lack of courtesy proved too much for my fellow Beda friend and nerves got the better of him. He said to me that he was going to be physically sick and did not want to disgrace himself in the house – so would I quickly take him away from the house in my van. I rushed round the place but could not locate our host to thank him and make our apologies for leaving. But I did not know where he had got to and could not find him at all before rushing off to the rescue of my fellow Beda man. Later that priest spread the word around Dundee that I had been thankless and ungrateful and was a very ill-mannered person.

However the Chancellor of the Diocese – Monsignor Hugh McInally, a very highly qualified Chartered Accountant – went out of his way to welcome me by inviting me to dinner. It was a wake-up call, as I discovered that he lived in an adjacent block of flats, and not to the house attached to his Church. Safety for priests in the Diocese did not seem to be good.

Travelling home for Diaconate Service had been a nightmare. Every time I took one of the Beda brethren home in my van they refused to help me with the driving. This time it was even worse than that. Previously the Rector had dumped large loads of the Beda magazine on the van, This time the Benedictine student practically filled the van with all sorts of luggage other than his own. It never seems to have occurred to these chumps that the camper van was my living space. I had wanted to go home via Trieste to ride the trams there but that was now impossible. The Benedictine's payment was to go home via Benedictine monasteries scattered throughout Europe that he wanted to visit. I had once toyed with trying to become a Benedictine but this trip sure made me glad I hadn't. Each monastic community was most welcoming – of course – as is the Benedictine tradition. But at every meal I found that I was still munching away slowly – as I had been taught – but all the monks would be finished and sitting impatiently waiting for me to finish. My digestion is not great at the best of times but that speed of eating would have been far too injurious to my wonky digestion. But I have to admit that apart from one, the Benedictine monasteries where we stayed were most impressive.

I had been to Muri Gries Abbey at Bolzano before, but only on a flying visit, as then I was heading for the impressive Sopra-Bolzano mountain tramway. (Both well worth visiting.) This time the interior of the vast monastery was staggering (as is the huge building's history – which would need a book on its own). The monastery owed its great wealth to one of its Abbots who took the community very successfully into the wine-growing industry and he is commemorated with a huge impressive twenty foot bust of him carved into one of the enormous wine vats in the Abbey cellars. And, believe it or not, that monastery has a very large heated indoor swimming pool. Gosh! In a monastery – but I suppose why not, if you have the money, as the Muri Gries monks obviously have.

Our next monastery was also vast and impressive but for a different reason. Kloster Andechrs is on a hill adjacent to the city of Munich with marvellous views especially over a lake, and, while we were staying there continuous great crowds of visitors came to it from the city. It brews a dark brown beer but what was of more interest to us was a splendid museum of the missions. That monastery had sent members out to the Central African areas when Germany started to have outposts there. We were wandering through that mission museum quite enthralled at what was on display, when one of the Benedictines came along, and, seeing our interest, started to tell us in detail about what we were looking at and why it was there. He pointed to a large replica scorpion and said that on one occasion he had gone out to celebrate Mass and a similar sized scorpion had, unknown to him, been sleeping inside his alb and it bit him. Brave fellows, missionaries I thought. Ugh! And we Scots worry about wee midges.

Then we stopped at the Kornelimuster on one side of a grim street in a most run-down area of Aachen. I wondered why we had come to such an unwelcome spot, but apparently the Benedictine I was carting home knew someone there. I was glad to leave Aachen. Not a lovely place from what we saw of it though of course once so historically important when it was the Capital for Charlemagne – the ruler of the German Franks.

More to my liking was St. Andre near Bruges. It is set in splendid parkland and has a boarding school to which the Belgian royal family send their children. The monastery church has a restrained quiet beauty and is very restful and prayerful – except when a young probationer monk comes into that church to toll their loud bell.

Then my Benedictine passenger gave me a good laugh. I parked the van at the front of a lane on the Zeebrugge ferry. But as the ferry loaded, the loading master wanted to move me to the front of another lane. To do that he directed me to move forward on to the front loading door that was down over-looking the sea and then to reverse back into the approved different lane. I wondered if he supported a certain team, but, having worked on the Glasgow caurs, carrying out the dangerous move did not bother me too much. However as I started to move forward the Benedictine let out a scream of terror and leaped hurriedly off the vehicle. I found that most amusing but thought it showed little confidence regarding my control of the van

At last he reached his destination – his home monastery of Ramsgate. It was a fantastic place to see. It had been designed in the great revived- Gothic style of Pugin and indeed then the Abbey owned Pugin's own Gothic revival house. Both places made up a bit for the misery of that crowded continental journey. But last I heard the few remaining monks cannot afford the upkeep of even the church building itself despite selling-off Pugin's wonderful house. So another Fort Augustus style loss of an impressive important holy place.

After a few days of recovery from the cross-Europe hassle, I headed north but covered myself in glory by getting into a no-change lane at the Dartford tunnel by mistake and causing a bit of a rush-hour traffic jam. Sorry London commuters.

NOT SUCH A GREAT DAY

The final journey home for Ordination was a much more civilised affair. By that time I had exchanged the Volkswagen camper van for a Polo Estate, (a decision I regret to this day) and had arranged for other friends going home for the last time to have a celebration part of the way in a very up-market Swiss hotel. After a tremendously enjoyable dinner we gathered round a magnificent grand piano and started to rattle off all the old well-known Parkhead ditties. We could not have been too bad, for instead of objecting to our use of their expensive piano, hotel staff started to assemble round us and cheered and clapped after each rendering. Just as well we had that happy time, for things were not so comforting after that. Our excellent pianist was to die suddenly after his appointment in Orange County, California, and my Ordination Day, instead of being the happiest day of my life as it should have been, was an upsetting disgrace – to put it mildly.

It was appropriate that the parish priest of St. Bernadette's, Tullibody was Father John Nolan. May he rest in peace. As I have said Fr. Nolan was Lourdes mad. He would go out there for the important seasonal pre-pilgrimages conference that arranged the times for pilgrimages to come, then go with the Dunkeld Diocesan conference to Lourdes, and then later go to Lourdes for a holiday.

Quite amazing. He had another great idiosyncrasy. If you were on a car journey with him he would stop at every garage we came to and ask what price they would give him for his car!

But I liked him very much and he was very good to me. An ex-Beda man himself (he had been a principle art teacher in Dundee and indeed made the stained–glass windows for Dundee municipal town hall), he was responsible for me and three others from the Diocese going to the Beda College. The trouble descended on my head because of that Beda College English ex-referee who could get me tickets for the Olympic Stadium matches. He had started his religious odyssey in the Salvation Army and then went through several religious establishments before coming to the Beda. Cheekily I used to tease him by asking him where he was going next – stupid me being a cradle Catholic. But he took the poor joking well. Unfortunately it did not go down well with the hierarchy that after his ordination his friends held a grand top-drawer full-dress celebration ball in his honour. Accordingly, former Cardinal Gray's secretary Bishop Vincent Logan decreed that after my ordination in St. Bernadette's, Tullibody, (always thought that name a good joke for a Celt like me), I could not celebrate the occasion with my friends (some of whom were coming considerable distances) but only after the Ordination ceremony with the parishioners of St. Bernadette's. Fr. Nolan and his parishioners thought that a stupid, nonsensical decision (me too!) and decreed that I should celebrate with my friends after the Ordination and with them the following night, although I strongly opposed their plans several times – as I had come to know a bit about Logan's personality by this time. I strongly believed in Pope John Paul's wish that developing ecumenism should be a priority for the Church, so I had asked my High-Anglican priest friend and a lady Church of Scotland minister to say the readings chosen for the Mass but these choices were summarily dismissed by His Lordship.

Then came further disaster. Father Nolan had not wanted to have Communion under both kinds – but I persisted and he gave in. At Communion, a Scots College pal was standing next to me holding a full consecrated Chalice and when the first communicant tried to receive The Blood of Christ, my amigo dropped the full chalice. No need to say what Father Nolan said afterwards. But I thought he had taken it rather mildly after my obstinacy.

A happier occurrence at that Ordination was the sight of my father's old tram conductor and family friend –Jimmy Kelly – among the congregation.

One of Bishop Logan's comments had raised my eye-brows considerably and I still fail to understand why he made it. For some reason unknown to me, this man from Bathgate – of all places – said that people like me who came from Glasgow thought that the Catholic Church in Scotland stopped at the Baillieston traffic lights. And here was me thinking – as I have indicated – that the most Catholic place in Scotland was Coatbridge and district.

I knew that if I did what the parishioners wanted there would be retribution from Logan for the parish. And of course there was. St. Bernadette's was down-graded from its parish status. But I am eternally grateful for the enormous kindness shown by the parishioners of St. Bernadette's to this stranger from Parkhead. I tried to repay that great kindness in vain later, as I will relate. Still! I suppose not much common-sense about realities of life was to be expected from a man who as a priest had only experienced being a parish priest for six months – in Roslin of all places. And comments about him from my friends were not at all favourable either. Of course it only came much later that the bishop was in fact a mentally sick man.

FIRST PARISH APPOINTMENT

Bishop Logan sent me to St. John's Parish Perth as an assistant priest. The use if "curate" has long gone out of date. All that happened there would need a book in its own right. The parish priest was a genial enough Irishman who had recently had a prostrate cancer operation. When he told me about that I was upset for him as it was well known then that such cancer sometimes returned after about six years. That illness probably explains why he was truly under the thumb of one of the Marist nuns who lived next door in what had been the first priest's house in Perth. I was amazed to see her unpack and pack the parish priest's baggage when he came and went! (I was told that when ground was needed for church extension work the body of the first Dunkeld Bishop had to be exhumed and moved. It was found that the Bishop's coffin was extremely long – so long in fact that when the body was re-interred in the cemetery, the grave had to be extended under the gravel cemetery access road. It was thought that the extreme length was occasioned by the Bishop being buried wearing one of the very expensive and magnificent mitres which had been presented to the first Scottish bishops by the Marquis of Bute after the restoration of the Scottish hierarchy in 1878. An attempt to see what the mitre was like was thwarted by Health and Safety forbidding the coffin to be exhumed.)

When I arrived, Fr. Durkin asked me where I would like to stay in the house. There was a self-enclosed wing on the west end so naturally I opted for that. But as I started to move in, the domineering nun put her foot down and told Fr. Durkin that had to be kept for important visitors and not for a lowly assistant priest. I next started to move into the ground floor accommodation next to the dining room, but, in the midst of doing that I was told to vacate that space as the recovering-alcoholic priest from Whitfield was coming and he took priority over me. So there was little point in the St. John's p.p. asking me where I wanted to live. In fact I ended up in the loft in a long very narrow space – to enter and leave which I had to make my way through a mountain of large packs of paper. Fr. Durkin complained when I started to move that huge amount of paper away from the loft entrance and asked me what I was doing. It should hardly have been a problem for him to understand why I was doing that. Patiently I expressed my desire not to be trapped in a narrow loft space if a fire occurred.

Yet another problem came my way from that Irish priest. In the "drawing room" I would set my TV and video-recorder ordination presents to record a Celtic match and later would find that he had been in and used my TV and recorder for his own purposes – destroying my carefully chosen settings. I had a few choice words to say about that and despite that, even had to paste sealing requests on the equipment to get him to leave it alone. I was mystified why he did not have his own TV and recorder repaired or restored as it could easily have been done at the parish expense. However on the plus side of being in that large house was the fact that there was an excellent cook employed so dining was first class. I ate well too because to my surprise and pleasure an American sister and brother living in Glencraig "adopted" me and would take me to the most expensive restaurant in Perth.. I knew it could not be because of my wonderful personality (non-existent!) And before long I discovered that it was because I had been to The Beda

College. Their father had heard about me being a late vocation there and was interested in going there himself and had wanted to find out what being at the Beda involved. Eventually I met him when he came to Perth and was dismayed that he was a giant of a man who could only hobble with the aid of a stick. I thought of that Beda monstrosity of a building which had staircases to surmount to reach any living accommodation, there being none on the accessible ground floor. (Amazing how some architects are happy to design a building that looks well on their drawing boards but give no thought to how it will work for the poor humans who have to make use of it – monstrosities like Cardross, the new John Ogilvie Hall addition and Whitfield.) Sadly the poor man only lasted a few weeks at The Beda College – as continual use of those staircases was beyond him. Another plus point about being in Perth was the astonishing vibrancy of the Perth Celtic Supporters Club. They would take me along to games singing their hearts out on the coach carrying them. Their favourite anthem to belt out was:

Aye! Aye! Aye! Aye!
Lisbon Lions were smashing!
Simpson was better than Yashin!
Murdoch was better than Eusebio!
And Johnstone was better than anyone!

Aye! Aye! Aye! Aye!
We are the Glasgow Celtic!
We'll be full of hope
And cheer for the Pope!
For we are the Glasgow Celtic!

I was in agreement with those sentiments at the time but had to change my mind about one of them later – as I will explain later.

SAD EVENTS

But there were the usual life's sad happenings. One of the early things Fr. Durkin asked me to do was to visit a couple of parishioners who were celebrating 60 years of marriage. I protested that I did not know them at all and that really he should be going, but he insisted that I was to make the visit – which I duly did. No doubt he was more anxious to get to his golf. Four days later both had died. When he discovered this Fr. Durkin flew into a rage and asked me what in earth had I said to them. I had just given them the congratulations of the parish and spent a little while on inconsequential chatter. Doubtless he was now wishing he had bothered to make that visit and knew that the parish would be critical of him for not having done so. The elderly couple had probably just died through being over-excited about the occasion? Requiescant in Pace.

OFF TRACK

Later I was to become involved in yet another death through over-excitement. I discovered that one of the parishioners had a non-Catholic husband who was the signalman at Errol station. I had always wanted to see inside a railway signal-box so I was grateful for a most kind offer to visit him there and went along at the agreed time. I discovered that he was ex-Royal Navy. He told me that Errol station had just closed and that there was an intention of setting up a railway museum there. I already had already prepared for the visit by reading up on Errol village and knew it had a kirk that had been a centre for the Free Church disruption and that reeds were gathered from the Tay for thatching purposes there, but when the Errol signalman told me that Errol to have a railway museum in its recently closed station that was a new one for me. (Actually Errol station became a railway heritage centre but apparently that did not work out and the station is now a craft centre.)

My kind host showed me his track-diagram and how things worked and which levers did what, and explained that he had two level crossings to control – one besides the Errol box and one further towards Dundee before Longforgan. Mention of Longforgan occasioned him to tell me that a communist signal man working there had once been run over and killed by a train and that the true story of the unfortunate man's death had nothing to do with politics as had once been suspected, but the real reason was that the dead signalman had been having a dalliance with someone's wife and the insulted husband had gathered a group of his pals together to extract revenge. The Longforgan signalman had seen them marching towards his box, realised what was going to happen, and had tried to escape them by running across in front of a train, but had badly misjudged speed and distance, and so had unfortunately been run over and killed by the train.

My new friend had just finished that dreadful story, when he was offered a Dundee express form Perth. Accordingly he closed his two level-crossings to road traffic, cleared the appropriate signals and accepted the express. He duly noted the red tail light at the end of the express and opened the Errol level crossing for road traffic again. He stood and watched his track diagram and then began to become agitated, exclaiming that the Dundee express had not cleared the section controlled by the box, so that he could not open the other level crossing for its road traffic. Two track workers were outside the box so he went out on to his veranda and asked them to walk along the track towards Dundee to see if they could find out what had happened to the express as it had not cleared the section. Then an empty two-coach diesel was offered from Perth, so the agitated man cleared the level crossing for it but kept the Errol home semaphore at danger. When the diesel pulled up, he then went out onto the veranda with his red flag and asked the motorman of the empty coaching stock to proceed slowly and with great care to see if he could find out why the express had not cleared the section. While all this was going on he was constantly also on to control to keep them informed of what he was doing to find out why the express had not cleared his section. The poor man was becoming more and more flustered and red-faced with anxiety, so I quietly took myself off out of the way.

Some years after I had moved from Perth, I had occasion to travel to Dundee. The Errol signalman had told me that his hobby was model-making and a friend had given me a very large cut-out cardboard model of a Glasgow Coronation tram, so I thought that by way of showing him my sincere thanks for receiving the privilege of a visit to his signal-box, I would let him have the cardboard model to construct. So I turned off the A90 and went down to the Errol box. The Perth signalman friend was not there and when I explained to the duty signalman the purpose of my intrusion and asked him to excuse it, there was a significant pause. Diffidently that good man courteously explained that because of over-excitement caused by an express not going out of section as it should have done, my Perth friend had suffered a heart-attack from which he was never to recover. Requiescat in pace.

That kind duty signalman explained that the AWS shoe had fallen off the diesel locomotive of the Dundee express, bounced on the track and had come up and penetrated the engine's diesel fuel tank. The driver had seen diesel fuel spraying out of the punctured tank and had accordingly stopped his train in section. Nowadays, of course, with modern radio communications the necessary information would have been passed quickly and freely and the unexpected stoppage would not have caused such bother, puzzlement and consternation. Needless to say I will always remember that first visit to a working railway signal-box and I remember in my prayers – for what they are worth – that friendly railwayman and his widow who had arranged it.

A JUMP TOO MANY

Another less serious happening was to affect me for the rest of my life too. I always enjoyed hill-walking – and while not up to "collecting Munros" standard, I always tried to cover as much high ground as time and opportunity afforded. Schiehallion, only ten miles away, beckoned from Perth. On the way I stopped to admire the glorious view of the conical mountain as seen from the Queen's View beauty spot – a tempting picture which made me more intent on trying to assail the mountain. Then, starting at the Braes of Foss car park, I puffed my way to the Munro summit from which Astronomer Royal Maskeleyne measured the mass of the earth in 1774. Eventually I thought, with relief, that I had reached the summit, but was deceived by the first of several small cairns, the summit consisting of a long narrow ridge covered with a mass of boulders. I stopped to watch an RAF fighter performing manoeuvres hundreds of feet below, and then decided to do some of my own by leaping from quartzite boulder to quartzite boulder to get to the true larger summit cairn. Silly old me. I should have taken my time and zig-zagged through the quartz field. Eventually one of the boulders gave way as I landed on it, and so I badly wrenched both knees. Somehow I made the painful descent. I should have gone into Perth infirmary to have my knees seen to, but I did not want to start my Dunkeld Diocese career by way of being an absentee passenger. The wretched knees have handicapped me considerably to this day.

DRINK DISGRACE

I did not help matters by continuing to do an early keep-fit morning walk to celebrate Mass for Kilgraston School. This was an onerous daily duty that Bishop Logan insisted on his St. John the Baptist priests carrying out – despite our protests that we had enough to do in Perth itself. For example: on every third week one of us was duty chaplain to Perth General and Bridge of Earn hospitals. One evening I was not supposed to be on this duty rota when an emergency call came in for a chaplain to come to Perth general. One of the other two men was supposed to be duty chaplain but they were not to be found and had not troubled to say how they could be reached. It was a sad affair and later quite a notorious court case was to follow. A family was proceeding down the A9 towards Glasgow. Mother was holding a young baby in her lap when their car was viciously rammed by an intoxicated driver who had been part of a Gleneagles Hotel company conference. The unfortunate baby was flung out of the mother's arms and hurled on to the windscreen of the family car. I rushed to Perth Infirmary and found the Emergency Ward crowded with surgeons, doctors and nurses and attached to the poor baby were numerous pieces of medical electronic equipment. The chief surgeon took me aside and quietly said that the baby was not going to survive despite all the efforts they were making to try and save it. I asked the weeping mother if I could baptise the child and briefly administered the Sacrament of Baptism when she urged me to do that. I also administered the Sacrament of Confirmation – as a priest may do that in a case of emergency like this one. Sobbing she managed to tell me the name of her parish in Airdrie. But when I contacted that parish and then all the other Airdrie and District parishes, no-one had ever heard of her or her family. I waited for some hours to see if I could offer any further comfort but when I returned to our church house the chief surgeon telephoned to thank me for all that I had attempted and of course to say that the poor wee soul had just died. Needless to say I never heard from the family again.

SPIRITUALLY DESTROYING

I think that one of several reasons I left the priesthood was the year I spent in Perth. I continually read statements that at the altar the priest is really "in the Image of Christ". After months of trying as best I could to well-celebrate the what should be the grace-giving Sacrament that is the Sunday Mass four and even five times each week-end, I ended up in spiritual and mental and physical distress.

Sometimes I had to celebrate Saturday Vigil Mass in our St. John the Baptist church and then early on Sunday morning go out to Kilgraston, next Mass would be at Perth prison, and then came the long trek to Dunkeld, and more often than not an old parish priest in one of the subsidiary Perth parishes would be in absentio and I would have to add on a Mass there.

Eventually it just became an effort to survive the Sunday strain. Hardly spiritual strengthening for me. And regularly a Catholic teacher at Strathallan School would be wanting me to come and say a Sunday Mass there. And, of course, much to my regret I just could not do that. An added burden was that a different more suitable homily was required fore each different place.

The worse place to try and give a homily was of course at Kilgraston Boarding School. Apart from disliking the upper-class Sacred Heart nuns (one of my old teachers had a niece there and she would repeatedly ask me why I had not spoken to her niece and this was simply because the Kilgraston nuns always refused to let me do that), I disliked the way in which the older young ladies would be lying about stretched out on the organ loft floor making it quite clear that I bored them to death.

Next came the problem of what to say that would be of value to some hundred Perth prisoners? (I was convinced from the manner in which they disported themselves at Mass that quite a number of the prisoners were not Catholic at all but had said they were to make the number of Catholic prisoners appear larger than it should have been in order to further denigrate the Church they hated.)

Then it was the long journey up the dreaded A9 to Birnam by Dunkeld. The Birnam/Dunkeld area is most wondrous and beautiful and historic territory. As well as having the partly restored remains of the Cathedral on the spot to which Columba's remains were brought from Iona in 850 AD (out of concern about the dangerous Viking raids of the time), and which gives its name to the present Catholic Diocese, across the river Tay, and linking Birnam to Dunkeld, stands the magnificent. Telford Bridge of 1808. A bridge that is home to hundreds of wonderful bats.

Architect brothers, the Fairlies, from Fife, (try to visit Kelly Castle!) who worked on such splendid great projects as Fort Augustus Abbey nave and the Catholic churches in Troon and St. Andrews – all commissioned by the Marquis of Bute – had a brother – Gilbert Thomas Ogilvie Fairlie who became a Catholic priest. The architects built for him the attractive little church and house which stand in their own magnificent grounds by Birnam and the Tay. Father Fairlie was to spend most of his priestly life in this idyllic situation and was very well liked in the area. A university friend told me that during the war he had been evacuated to the Birnam house and consequently had the time of his life there. Apparently there were two staircases in the mansion – one for the servants use only -and consequently the house was great for "hide and seek "games.

STOP GRINNING!

The Birnam church proved most attractive for up-market weddings. On one unfortunate occasion I could hardly properly witness the Sacrament for inward laughter. The groom party consisted of four extremely large and brawny Kerrymen. But they were all kitted out in full Highland Dress. Oh! Dear!. Mea culpa!

And St. Columba's Church was up-market for another reason too. A non-Catholic father bequeathed his three Catholic sons several thousands of acres of Perthshire each. One of them was from a near-by castle owned 28,000 acres, and on my first Birnam visit I was upset to witness a practice that I thought had long been vanished from a Catholic Mass. This laird would take a Communion Plate and stick it under the mouth of a Communion recipient. So on one visit I took away the unnecessary Communion Plate. On my next visit this giant of a man was standing crying tears – yes, crying tears – because he could not find his beloved Communion Plate.

On another occasion I was at the back of the Church after the Sunday Mass and he approached me. He took out a wad of notes of a size that I had never seen in my life, peeled off a five pound note and said to his wee girl – "Go to the Collection Plate and get me change so that I can give Father a Pound for a Mass". Of course a Mass stipend is not the price of a Mass but merely meant to be towards a priest's sustenance. This same laird later installed a new £22,000 organ in his castle for a daughter's wedding. So he was not exactly hard-up. I told him I would celebrate a Mass, gratis, for his intention.

WILD LIFE AND WILD MAN

Dunkeld was convenient for a visit to see the ospreys at The Loch of the Lowes, Loch Garten. And, of course, silly me got himself banned from what was left of Dunkeld Cathedral. On my first visit there, I could not miss in the nave a superb Grand Piano. I could not resist sitting down to it and trying it out with my attempt at playing "It's a Grand Old Team etc." Someone was watching and so permanent expulsion followed. May be I missed out too many black keys in my poor playing!

INCARCERATION

There were two prisons to serve in Perth. As well the main grim fortress there was also an "open" prison on the outskirts of the Perth. The warden here told me that he had been the policeman who had taken the first 999 call about The Great Train Robbery. He said that he thought the call was a hoax – until his switchboard starting lighting up with a plethora of 999 calls. We were on a friendly basis – especially when I was able to respond successfully to his request to have some of our lady parishioners visit approved prisoners in need of visitations.

When there were new arrivals in the prison since my last visit, I was required to inspect all their documentations and some of their documents were very thick indeed. One morning I was ploughing through a vast appoint of paper work for one prisoner, when, hidden carefully near the bottom of the pile was a Police Warning Notice that this man must not be kept in an "open" prison. Obviously my warden friend's entrance officials had not been doing their job properly – or had they?. I said nothing to them when I returned the file of documents but slipped along to the warden's office and told him that it was imperative that he requested to see that prisoner's file personally– and why. That made him even more friendly towards me.

I got on well the warden and staff at the main grim pre-Victorian prison (originally built to house French prisoner-of-war) although I had always been bothered by the fact that I had never been given any instruction from the Church about how to carry out my prison chaplain duties. I did know that I was not supposed to ask a prisoner what he was in prison for.

I would wander through the prison corridors just to let the men see that I was there and available if they wanted to talk about anything. On one occasion I was passing a kitchen and three men were inside drinking tea and they very politely asked me if I would like to come in and join them in a cup. They were only "in" for a short stay and I later told Lord Wheatley – Sheriff as he then was – that these short-term prison sentences of a few weeks were a waste of valuable time and money as many of these unfortunates seemed to see a wee spell in prison as a welcome break from the cares of their outside worlds. To make conversation I asked one where he was from. "Salamanca Street, Parkhead, Father." came the – to me – surprising reply. The next man said he was from Helenvale Street, Parkhead, and the third was from Janefield Street, Parkhead no less!. And there was lucky old me from nearby Westmuir Street, Parkhead. My Guardian Angel must have been working overtime!
And then I was completely taken to the cleaners. A prisoner asked me if I would take a complaint to the Prison Governor. The complaint was that there was not a Bible in the prison library. The top man laughed and laughed and told me that they had to stop putting Bibles in the Library as the pages were torn out and used for rolling cigarettes. He also told me on one occasion – after a prison disturbance – that he should have known better than to have allowed a certain two of his warders to be on duty together because when they were on duty together they were known to deliberately cause trouble among their charges.

There was a PFR scheme running at the time, PFR standing for Preparation For Release. St. John's would try to help the scheme by having PFR men down to work around our church. On one occasion one of the PFR men – a convicted murderer – would not do the work requested in the church because there was a body lying in front of the altar preparatory to a Requiem Mass.

But there was a truly funny happening concerning another of the PFR men. One came to me in a highly agitated state. The PFR men were not supposed to leave the church premises. That was a condition for their being allowed out of prison. This chap had broken the rules and gone into Perth and entered a cake shop to buy some cakes. He was waiting to be served when an excited policeman burst into the shop, stood beside him and shouted "There has been a serious break-out from the prison. If you see anyone wearing what looks like a prison uniform let us know at once!", and then ran out of the cake shop. And the blue-coated minion of the law had been making his important utterance right next to my friend who was standing there wearing his prison uniform. When he told me the tale my prisoner friend was still white and trembling and exclaimed, "I thought I had blown my chances of an early release." Guess what I said to him. The parish priest asked me to supervise one of the PFR men clean out some archives under the church. I came across a souvenir bulletin issued to mark the fiftieth anniversary of the parish. Of course I could not avoid taking it away to read through it, and what did I see? In a description of the church was the sentence "The church contains two original Old Master paintings." Wow! What a discovery I thought. But of course I could not persuade either the Irish Parish priest or the Bishop to take any interest in what I had come across. I carefully scoured the church and house and examined every picture I could find but there was no sign of an Old Master original. Then I realised that at the time that souvenir brochure had been produced what had now become the convent had been the church house and there was no hope of looking through a convent. The thought also crossed my mind that perhaps a previous parish priest had not known what he possessed and had given them away, and somewhat uncharitably I thought it possible it might have been the case that a parish priest of the past had known what he possessed and had sold them and pocketed the money. Years later there was somewhat of a sensation in the media. A hitherto unknown Old Master original painting had turned up in Perthshire and had been sold for a very large sum of money indeed. I wondered which of my theories had been correct.

HEAR THAT WHISTLE BLOW!

There was a superb Railway Historical Group in St. John's Town and they made me extremely welcome as a new member. I learned an enormous amount about the coming of railways to the Perth area and what happened on the lines after that. One of the members knew a great deal about the history of Perth station. He had graphic descriptions of the panic that had happened when it was discovered that Queen Victoria, no less, was unexpectedly coming down the lines from the North on one of her very first railway journeys ever. He had a great deal of interest and knowledge concerning Perth Station history and I wondered why he was so concerned about the re-building and enlarging of the station. He was particularly bothered by the fact that when the General Station was enlarged and re-built the original foundation stone was lost. I wondered why his concern for a piece of stone. Later I read that at the opening of the original Perth Station there had been a huge majestic Masonic procession to the laying of the first foundation stone which was embossed with the usual Masonic symbols. When Perth General Station was being rebuilt was that Masonic foundation stone just carelessly covered by the new building or had some Irish navy realised what it was and knocked it into small pieces?

BACK TO SCHOOL AGAIN

As if it was not a heavy enough burden being a chaplain to two prisons and two convents and being a hospital chaplain to Perth Royal Infirmary and Bridge of Earn Hospital I would visit St John's large Secondary School and take a class of leavers there, trying to get through to them what they might well be facing as they grew older.. The Head Teacher at that time was from good old Baillieston – so we got on like a house on fire – having family connections. Thanks to him (and the school) I was able to have the wonderful uplifting experience of celebrating Mass for them on Columcille's isle – Iona. A great memory. The Irish parish priest said that I was appointed chaplain to St. John's Primary School. Oh! Sure! Except when he would take over and oust me out of that position without warning. In the days when Ireland had a surplus of priests, (it was the belief that the third son of an Irish family had to be a priest whether he liked it or not – and a lot did not like it at all!) the Irish Bishops would take their pick of the best and the rest were foisted off on Scotland. And clearly this was one of the latter. I was concerned that the two starter classes in a Catholic Primary School were being taught by two non-Catholic teachers. I could get nothing done about it from my supposedly responsible parish priest and took my complaint to the Bishop. I should have known better by that time. Bishop Logan lamely said that he could not obtain Catholic teachers to take the classes. I politely – I hope – said that was rubbish and contacted no less than six Catholic teachers who said that they would be only too willing to take the classes. Stupidly I went back to the Bishop with their names' only to be peremptorily bounced out of his presence while he declaimed that the appointment of Catholic teachers was nothing to do with him but was a matter for the Monsignor in charge of Diocesan Education. This was the later great-scandal-creating Monsignor Creagan, who, when I took the matter to him said that teacher appointments were to be no concern of mine. I was a bit disappointed by the whole Education situation in the Diocese as every other Beda man of my time who had been involved in Education before going to the Beda had at once been given Education responsibilities on going to his diocese.

UP, UP, ON HIGH!

And then I really went and did it. For some reason that puzzled me – O K so I am easily puzzled – the Irish parish priest decided to put on a light opera version of Joseph and his multi-coloured coat. (Of course Joseph never had a multi-coloured coat – that was a mistranslation in The Vulgate – he only had a long-sleeved coat on which his brothers rubbed blood to fool Israel.) To stage this production a web of scaffolding was erected over the High Altar – quite a ridiculous nonsense of course – and when I went out to celebrate Mass on Ascension Day I had to clamber up and over and thorough the scaffolding mess to teach the altar. Trust me. I could not resist saying to the congregation that I knew it was Ascension Day but my having to make such an ascension was quite ridiculous. Again I should have known better. My sarcastic remark – meant as a bit of dark humour – was reported to the Bishop and there were words from him about me and about the Parish Priest's quasi-desecration of the church.

YOU CAN HAVE A LAUGH

But I enjoyed other much better bits of humour. On Assumption Day I answered the door-bell and there was a worried puzzled gentleman. He asked me if he had gotten it correct and that this was Assumption Day. I reassured him on that point. He then asked me if Assumption Day was not a Holiday of Obligation in England (in England!) I said it certainly was – inwardly chuckling as I realised what was coming. "But Father," the poor fellow said, "there is no Mass in the church." I could not resist telling him that he was in Scotland and not in England. I wonder how many days in Purgatory such bits of fun will get me. As I said previously I got on well with the prison authorities and I was always able to have prisoners down to our church for special occasions – even though there had been the time I arrived back at the church house only to be followed at once by a prison van. I quite had forgotten to hand back the master key for the prison. So I had a group of prisoners seated in the church on Holy Thursday and I was delighted to see that the very last person – by a distance – to approach for the reception of Holy Communion on that day of days, was none other than my own great hero Davy Hay. The excited group of prisoners almost stood up and cheered when he passed them and afterwards they genuinely thought that I had arranged that especially for them. Nice to be well-thought-of for a change. Then unexpectedly came a phone-call from the Bishop. Would I like to take charge of Kinross parish. Would I not!

SAINT JAMES' KINROSS

Way back when I was posted from the RAF Signals School at Yatesbury, I had never heard of Kinloss and had mistakenly thought I was going to Kinross. So I made Kinross after all. In my time there Kinross still had a huge radar dome and a vast underground complex, though its former air-field was out of use. Huge US Air Force four-engine jet bombers would regularly come over from the east carrying out some sort of exercise with the radar dome as a target. As well as the giant U.S. Air Force bombers, in due season thousands – and I mean many thousands – of geese would appear and settle in the fields surrounding Kinross. It was fascinating to see how time after time the leader of a huge triangle of geese would slip to the side and another immediately take its place to lead the squadrons.

In the past Kinross had been known as "sleepy hollow" but had now been discovered as a commuter place to live so that spouses and families could diverge to work in Glasgow, Edinburgh and Dundee. But a bit of the old "sleepy hollow" remained. In the general hardware store, for example, the old overhead cable system whereby customer's cash and bill was sent to a central teller was still extant. This system had been introduced in times past because only the central teller was reliably numerate whereas the counter servers had not been so reliably numerate. And the old them-and-us attitude could still prevail. A resident was knocked down on the busy road outside the general store and the staff came out to look at the casualty, shrugged and went back inside muttering "He is only an in-comer". The unfortunate casualty had been resident in Kinross for some twelve years or so.

Near by Loch Leven, once famous for its Winter Curling Bonspiel – it even had its own railway station in North British Railway days – had become a nature reserve and on it there was still the island with the castle in which Mary Queen of Scots had been imprisoned in 1567 – 1558 and forced there to abdicate in favour if her son who then became James the Sixth of Scotland and later in 1603 James the First of England and Wales as well. Mary had been rescued from imprisonment by means of the then parish priest's boat – so I was but an unworthy successor to that brave man. A more up-to-date house now stood on the site of what had been the priest's house and was widely reckoned to have paranormal occurrences. There certainly was one in my church house as I will relate later.

There probably had been a Pictish fortification on the island in the 6th century AD but parts of the present castle have been dated to the 13th century with towers added in the 15th century. It is believed that there was once another St. Serf living on the Loch Leven Island and he is thought to have been an Israeli. There was a Culdee establishment in the island as late as 1248 and the Celei-Dei (servants of God), being the great Hospitallers that they were, the island group had their hospital across the loch at Portmoak. The castle on Loch Leven island was to prove a bit of a nuisance for me. Several times I was asked to preside at wedding ceremonies on the island which somehow had an attraction for some parties trying to arrange their wedding. Fortunately the Diocese had a rule that the Sacrament of Marriage could only be carried out in a consecrated church and only elsewhere by the Bishop's special permission and I certainly was not going to pursue that permission – as the island was invested in summer by huge clouds of one of Scotland's 37 varieties of midgies.

One of my perturbations re my status as a priest was that the Bishop never once inducted me officially as a parish priest though apparently he carried out that ceremony for others. I found that omission troublesome. But I had to try to shrug and bear the disappointment.

BEWARE OF THE DOG

I had always wanted to have a dog since the days when as a boy in Westmuir Street I had been friendly with a neighbour's Yorkshire Terrier. My mother too liked dogs but because she would be in our house all alone we were frightened in case she tripped over the pet and might not be able to rise again without assistance. Shortly after arriving in Kinross I saw an advert for Black Labrador pups. They were on sale in Dunning, and I had always wanted go visit the historically ancient place where Kentigern's mentor St. Servan was reckoned to have slain a dragon. Wonder what the basis for that myth was? I took away the runt of the litter, wishing that I had had the money to take one of his brothers with us. But of course I had not the necessary cash. On the way down to Kinross the wee black fellow was in a cardboard shoe-box on the passenger seat and I was alarmed to see him upside down with his paws straight up in the air. But, of course, he was just having a contented snooze. I had no sooner placed the wee boy – still in his box – on the kitchen table, when the kitchen door-bell rang and I welcomed in the wife of the chairman of the parish council. Being wildly excited about having my first doggie friend I urged her to come and see the wee pup. Haughtily she drew herself up and snarled – yes snarled: "I thought that you would have more to do with your time taking on a parish than taking on a dog.!" Yet! Later on, in the wee small hours of the night, the front door bell would ring and her two teen-age girls would be weeping and asking me to take them in and give them shelter – alleging that mother and father were being upsetting protagonists again. This happened more than once and I realised that it would be the cause of considerable scandal if teenage girls were being seen coming into the church house at that time in the morning. And the local Police Office was but next door. Eventually I arranged for a decent friendly retired couple of parishioners living near to their house to give them shelter instead of me. On one occasion the front door bell rang frantically and continuously yet again in the wee small hours, and I was determined I was not going to have teen-age girls coming in at that time again. So I ignored the commotion. Next thing I knew Police were going round the house shining torches on everything, so I dived under the bed with the wee pup. I wondered what crime I had supposedly committed. The Parish had first been established in Kinross as a satellite of Alloa in order to cater for the spiritual needs of what we used to call – a bit scandalous in our child-hood ignorance "the tattie-howkers" – Irish immigrant farm-workers who had stayed on in the area. Of course they had had a gang-master and it was this fairly well-off man who was slowly dying in his big house on the outskirts of adjacent Milnathort, and it was an understandable but misplaced panic that had caused some of his family to come seeking me in the middle of the night, and so causing such a frightening brouhaha. In fact I had been up to the mansion the day before and had quite properly administered the Last Rites of the church on his behalf. Had they contacted me that night there was really not much else I could have done except perhaps read the Psalms for the Dead by his bedside. After their failure to contact me they brought a fellow Beda friend of mine down from Perth in the middle of the night and he too administered the Last rites. A quite unnecessary journey as I explained to him afterwards and he shook his head in agreement. I had never seen any of that family attend our church in Kinross and even after the Requiem Mass and funeral, only one female relation bothered to come to our church – though she started to be a fairly regular attendee.

But early on I nearly lost Jimmy the Woof through my customary stupidity. A friendly non-Catholic farmer contacted me and said he had noticed that there was no gate across the entrance to the Church House small driveway. He had a spare wrought iron gate that he would come and affix gratis to the drive entrance if I would like him to do that.

Of course I agreed to that generous offer and after he had completed his task and we had a smashing gate affixed, I went out to his farm to thank him for his great kindness to the parish. As I was speaking to him the new wee pup was sitting behind one of the two lovely Clydesdales belonging to the farmer. After a bit the big horse became annoyed at the wee fellow sitting so close behind him and swung a great back-heeler which just missed the head of my new friend by only a few inches inches. Silly me of course. I should have had the Lab on a lead and well away from annoying the big horse.

AND ANOTHER BIG MISTAKE

One of the many things I got wrong at Kinross was my effort to have the retired Irish community back taking their part again in the running of the parish. They had been ousted from their parish efforts by some of the better-educated and more affluent commuters who had moved into Wimpey land. I should have just let things be and followed Walpole's advice "Let sleeping dogs lie!" I just alienated both parties.

WHAT'S IN A NAME?

I had to name my new friend – and a great friend the black lab turned out to be – after he eventually realised I was his friend too. My parents had had a cat they named Patsy Gallagher after their great Celtic hero. Apparently Patsy would follow them on their walks from Westmuir Street up and around that pleasant Glasgow lung, Tollcross Park. So, to follow that tradition, I named and blessed the newcomer Jimmy Quinn, McMenemy, McGrory, Delaney, Johnstone. At first he would fight to escape from the church house and grounds and try to make his way back to Dunning. It took brainless me too long to realise that their really was a problem for him in the church house apart from me. I once asked why our church houses were constructed on such a monumental scale when, from the small size of the parishes, only one priest need be accommodated. The ridiculous official position was that regardless of expense, extra rooms had to be there for two or three priests who might have to be accommodated when they might come to preach the old-time mission week. Eventually as he hardly ever barked, Jimmy gained the joke nick-name of Jimmy the Woof.

PARANORMAL

I just could not get the new arrival to go upstairs in the St. James' too large church house. I would carry him up to the top floor but as soon as his paws touched the ground, he would flee down the stair-case again at top speed. When I would close the door and then put the poor wee fellow down, he would turn to a wall, face it, and quite unusually, loudly bark and bark at it until the staircase door was opened for him to speed back down stairs again. Too much later the penny dropped, and then I quietly made enquiries about the construction of the post-war house. I worked out – thanks to the good will of parishioners- that during the construction of the building, no fewer than three workers had died on site. That shook me. Later when I was trying in vain (thanks to the Bishop) – to expand the church that was becoming overcrowded – because of the continued increase in house-building in the area, I personally took a sledge-hammer and demolished the brick-wall that so upset Jimmy the Woof. And do you know? After that demolition Jimmy went up and down the staircase nae bother and would sit or lie contentedly on the top floor! But that is just one of my unexpected experiences of the paranormal.

WHAT HAPPENED TO VATICAN TWO?

When I arrived in Kinross some things surprised me greatly. I felt I was moving back quite a bit in time. Despite the fact that my predecessor had been the Vicar General, the Parish Council I inherited did not know Eucharistic Ministers existed. I had to take them up to Dundee and show them Eucharistic Ministers at work there to convince them that I knew what I was talking about. After I held the great Easter Vigil ceremony I was told that they never had had such rubbish before I came. The Easter Vigil rubbish! And this some twenty years after the Great Second Vatican Council.

WHERE TO PARK?

A calamity for me was that that Vicar General – just before he left for Dundee to be nearer to his sick mother, had established a Saturday Evening Vigil Mass – and I was told that this was because the St. Andrews and Edinburgh parish of nearby St. Joseph's, Kelty had started one and he did not want to be outdone. This made it extremely difficult for me to get back in time for that Vigil Mass after attending to a Celtic Saturday home match at Parkhead, the A977 being a slow and even then quite crowded road down to the M876 Though I obviously knew only too well all the side-road short-cuts through the east end of the dear green place, by the time I could get down for a match it was sometimes difficult to find a good place to park which would get me away quickly to start the return journey. On one occasion I had just found a space to park outside the Calton Church of Scotland building in Helenvale Street and thankfully stepped out of my Polo when a young lad stopped me and asked me did I not think it was quite improper to park outside as church. Oh! Dear! He was right of course. Flustered, I bluffed that I thought that parking outside a church was a safe place to park. He asked me where I had come from, and, of course, I told him Kinross. He then asked me where that was. I explained that it was about sixty miles away and roughly halfway between Edinburgh and Dundee. "That is all right, then!" he said and strode off. Phew!

That Helenvale Street Calton Church of Scotland church was descended from the original old Calton church that once stood in Tobago Street and was a subsidiary of Glasgow Cathedral itself, and the present Helenvale Street parish was formed from an amalgamation of several Parkhead Presbyterian parishes. One of its Minister's wives was the celebrated Dr. Dorothy Chalmers- one of the first lady doctors in Scotland who was once arrested for setting a building on fire in a protest about Women's Rights. So, having my own Parkhead ancestry, I always felt I was being on very historic territory in parking there. And across the street from the church used to be the Glasgow Corporation Transport Sports Facilities where I could sometimes watch a world champion athlete competing and where on one remarkable occasion I saw the much-media-lauded Sir Alec Ferguson playing in a very modest match – having been demoted to that side after an alleged incompetent display in a Hampden Old Firm game. How the mighty can be fallen. Bet he does not say much about that to the media, nor about his dismissal from managing St. Mirren after he was accused the defalcation of some £24,000 – a great some of money in those far off days.

On one Saturday I was late getting down to Parkhead for the match and the only parking space I could find was in distant and ominously named Macduff Street. After the game I ran all the way back to Macduff Street, jumped into the Polo and hastily started the return journey to Kinross. As I shot out, a small car came racing down the other way and I side-swiped it. Of course I stopped and gave name and address as required and said I would pay for the damage. And though I twice tried to obtain cost of repair for their car, they twice said they would not let a priest pay for the damage. I feel rotten about the whole affair to this day. However, my Parkhead parking problems were going to be solved in a most unexpected and delightful way.

LUCKY OLD ME

We had been instructed at the Beda never to make a joke or bit of humour at the end of Mass. I thought that a bit off. After all, Mass is called a celebration. And all too often with certain supposed "celebrants" is more or less a thoroughly boring almost funeral-like dirge with a long-winded uninspiring homily thrown in. I would always try a wee bit of light humour at the dismissal with the object of perhaps encouraging young people to come back the following Sunday to hear what the clot might say next. One Sunday I made a crack about Celtic needing St. Jude's assistance- as they were performing in hopeless fashion. Then as I was performing the customary farewell shaking of hands with departing parishioners at the back of the church, a tall young man whom I did not recognise, asked me if I was a Celtic supporter. I admitted that I was – for the sake of my sins. He then surprised me by asking if I was going to the game on Wednesday evening. I said that I sure intended to. Imagine my further amazement when he said in that case that he would take me down to Parkhead, and we arranged a time to meet outside the church house. After he departed I asked a friend who the big man was. He gave me a look of great pity and told me that the big man was Gerard Eadie who was the owner of Celtic sponsors CRSmith. Wow! Holy mackerel; and all the other fishes. So there I was of a Wednesday evening standing on the pavement of Kinross High Street and coming up from the cross was a huge Bentley. I had gone to matches in Hugh Harkins Jaguar but a Bentley ride was even better. Then until Fergus killed off the CRSmith sponsorship, I would have a reserved parking space, a four-course lunch and refreshments in the CRSmith lounge before a home game, seat in the Directors' box with refreshments in the Directors' room at half-time – and then refreshments and meeting all sorts of players after the game – if time permitted.

So for a sadly only too short years, there I was with a nice wee town to live in, splendid surrounding scenery for walking the much-wanted dog, a most friendly Celtic sponsor, and some very helpful parishioners.

ECUMENISM RULES O! K!

Good and most friendly ecumenical relations existed with the Church of Scotland Minister and the Episcopal Canon. I greatly admired them both but thought that Mr. Barr – the Kinross minster – was a marvellous exemplar of Christ. We three used to meet regularly once a week for a coffee and a blether and about arranging happenings in Kinross. For example we were kindly given the lovely grounds of Kinross House for large ecumenical events – such as the joint celebration of Easter and Pentecost. And the local large mill would allow us to put a large life size Christmas crib in its large display windows facing the in-coming A977, and we held joint services and many other little events.

At one of the joint services I had a complaint from one of the Episcopal parishioners that we Catholics were quite wrong to be only saying "The Gospel according to Matthew" instead of "The Gospel according to Saint Matthew!" I hastily made up the probably inadequate reply that we omitted "Saint" before "Matthew" because we regarded him as one of us. Hope that he was!

But it was a bit sad that in the Summer months English Anglican visitors would attend our Mass in St. James and not go to St. Paul's Episcopal church on The Muirs – some of them saying that the Episcopal church in Scotland was not a proper church. What rubbish of course.

One morning during our clerical coffee chat one of them observed that there were three different dog collars in the room. I quickly corrected him and pointing to Jimmy said that there were "Four!" As well as our local friendly three-some weekly get-together there was a monthly gathering of a larger group of local clergy for morning coffee and rolls at the Cleish Presbytery – and it too was all very pleasant and friendly except when I tried to have us all recite some of the Psalms together. That effort did not go down well and I have often wondered why.

I noticed that the superb Baptismal font from a closed Kinross C. of S. kirk was being used as a litter bin in the Kinross Parish Church Hall. So, with permission and gratitude from The Parish Church we had it brought into our wee church and there it was restored to its proper use.

CLEISH

The name comes from the Gaelic for "trench" and it is believed the Mary Queen of Scots fled through the village of Cleish after her escape from Loch Leven castle.

The first time I was conducting a funeral service in Cleish cemetery, I found myself reciting the necessary prayers etc, alone by the graveside on top of a small hill while the group of mourners remained gathered together down below me on the red gravel access road. I thought this strange and peculiar and after the burial I asked the funeral director – a Catholic friend of mine from Perth – why had this happened .He burst out laughing and explained that on one previous occasion the group of mourners had gathered round a grave site on that hill, and without warning the soil had given way and some of the grieving mourners had found themselves down in the grave beside the coffin of the person for whom they were grieving. No laughing matter I thought and wondered if I should think of wearing my hill-walking boots next time I conducted a funeral in Crich cemetery.

Crich village occasioned another surprise for me. I was trying to get round on my parishioner visitation. And one of the addresses I had seemed to be for a large medieval castle on which flags were flying and with an enormous beautiful yew approach avenue. Could not be there I thought – but as usual I was wrong. The celebrated architect Parr and his family were living in the castle and always made me very welcome. Mr. Parr showed me all over this interesting 16th Century castle and its superb terrace gardens. The family used the vast central hall as their main living quarters. Mr. Parr laughingly explained that if they needed another cupboard they simply carved into the nine foot thick walls and hung on a door. Wow! Then there was the occasion when a grandchild was baptised in St. James and we took ourselves down to the castle for the celebratory meal. The father of the child asked me did I not remember him from St. Conval's School. He remembered me all right. Apparently when he was a pupil there, we had been watching our pretty-poor school team playing and he had made a derogatory remark about the school goal-keeper and I had immediately retorted, "Then you go into goal and see if you can do any better." That opened a long forgotten can of worms.

SAD BEREAVEMENT

On my very first day in a teacher promoted post as an assistant head at St. Conval's Primary School in Pollokshaws, the head teacher dismissed the school at 2 p.m. instead of the normal time in those days of 4 p.m. This caused the pupils to have two hours without supervision, and a large group of them went down to the banks of the fast-flowing White Cart River where a considerable amount of horse-play ensued. One pupil was pushed into the river where he drowned. It was two weeks before the body was found miles down-stream near Crookston Castle. Day after day for the two weeks of searching, the grieving parents were in the school. There was no psychological counselling available in those days as there is now. It was a terrible fortnight for us all. I resolved then that if I ever became a head-teacher, I would never, ever, dismiss a school early without first warning parents in advance. How the St. Conval's head teacher got away with it, I, to this day, cannot understand.

HITTING THE HIGH NOTES

One morning I was walking up Kinross High Street when a very excited young male parishioner came running towards up to me, and, rather breathless, he exclaimed that the Pope's organist was at Edinburgh University and wanted to go to an Old Firm match and could I arrange that for him. I just laughed and said that I had once been a University student too, and had tried such tricks too. But it turned out that it was not the Pope's organist that was at Edinburgh University but rather the Pope's Master of Music who supervised seven organists at St. Peter's Basilica. For some reason the papers and manuscripts of Giovanni Paisiello – a Neopolitan who had been the Court composer for Napoleon and then after Napoleon's abdication became the Prussian Court composer – were at Edinburgh University, and the Master of Music had taken a sabbatical in order to study these manuscripts and papers. The material must have been of significant interest for he took a second sabbatical to complete his investigation into the material. The great Master of Music could speak five languages and knew far more about Scottish History than myself. Of course Gerard Eadie was proud to be able to take the celebrated musician to the CRSmith lounge for an Old Firm match on two occasions. Before setting off for Parkhead's Sunday games the maestro accompanied on our wee organ my celebration of Sunday Mass in St. James and played for me as he would have done for John Paul the Second himself. And I am not making this up unfortunately. On both occasions parishioners (women sic!) complained afterwards about the way the Bolzano maestro played the organ. I suppose critics will always exist – but that to me was incredible. Of course we kitted out the Vatican maestro in Celtic tie, scarf and blazer, but he rather shook me by telling me that he had a monthly conversation about football with the Pontiff but that John Paul the Second had never heard of the Celtic. Of course I joked that in that case that was me out of the church. But he arranged for papal blessings to be sent to two of Celtic's much-loved players – great left back "Shuggie" alias Darius Wdowczyk and that fabulous striker "Jacki" alias Darius Dziekenowski.

BACK TO SCHULE AGAIN!

Among my Kinross tasks as well as weekly visits to St John's Secondary in Perth, I visited Kinross Primary,. Milnathort Primary and Kinnesswood Primary, and was always given the most hospitable welcome in the non-Catholic Schools and in each I would be given a period to assemble our Catholic Children and give them religious instruction. One of the Head Teachers usually had her two lovely friendly dogs with her in her Office and it made me wish that I had thought about doing that in Glasgow. I was also asked on occasion to take the then compulsory morning religious assembly in both Kinross and Milnathort Primaries. I always expressed my great appreciation for the privileges and great courtesy shown to me. But! On the first occasion I accepted the invitation to take Morning Assembly for Kinross Primary, it was the week after Bishop Logan had administered the great Sacrament of Confirmation in St. James' Church. The good ladies of the parish had gone to great lengths to find out what his favourite food was, but he had turned up his nose at every thing prepared for his expected delight. He had shown such an unfriendly and unsocial attitude generally that parishioners were very upset with his visit. Indeed one non-Catholic husband who had seen the rudeness of the Bishop at first hand (he was a former RAF jet fighter pilot married to a Catholic former air-line hostess) and whose surname was in fact Mason, said to me later that if that was Catholicism at work then he was glad he was not a Catholic but a Mason. Good pun I thought but a very sad justified comment. So the Bishop's visit was still in my mind when I took the assembly at Kinross Primary and I thought to make it a relaxed atmosphere by starting with an old (for me) chestnut. I said that our Bishop had been in our church for Confirmation and a boy had gone home and said he now knew what a crook looked like. I should have known better. The joke went down like a lead balloon and even Catholic teachers present did not crack a smile. So I frantically had to explain that a Bishop was supposed to be the shepherd of his flock, and as a symbol of that he carried a crozier or shepherds' crook. Oh! Dear! That was not the relaxed start I intended.

EPISCOPALIA

You will have gathered that Bishop Logan bothered me in many ways and of course much worse was to come. Every year he would instruct me to represent him at the annual Episcopal General Diocesan Synod to which he had been invited. Talk about passing the buck. The Synod was always held on a Saturday and on the first one I attended I waited for the whole day of their Synod and so missed out on the Celtic game. I then discovered that the Bishop would not accept any remit from me on the Synod activities and so

I thought therefore that there was no point in waiting at the Synod for the whole day and would leave after their morning programme of events so that I could get to the Celtic match. Their top bishop of the time was the media celebrity Hare-Duke and he and all the others were most friendly and welcoming to me. One time in friendly conversation the good Bishop sighed and said that he wished the Episcopal Church had the Catholic rule of celibacy for priests. I replied that it was discriminatory and applied only to priests in the Western Rite of the Catholic Church and not to those belonging to the Eastern Rite of the Catholic Church and after all some of the very Apostles themselves were married. He explained that he had great difficulties over the handling of his married priests. For example if he had a vacancy in one of his parishes for a priest and that vacancy urgently needed filling, there would be great difficulty in moving a priest there, for the intended priest for such a move would have a wife who did not want to leave her present highly-paid employment or there would be children whom he did not want to have their schooling disrupted. Hare-Duke was a most likeable highly-educated man and it was a pleasure to know him.

Our not-so-pleasant and well-educated man had strange (to me) behaviour. Just a few examples: as if a competent and busy parish priest did not have enough on his plate to keep him fully occupied Bishop Logan followed the trend from elsewhere and introduced that terrible and complicated American "Renew" programme. Of course renewal is always necessary, there is no disputing that. But it was pretty impossible to carry out the difficult and lengthy Renew programme with much success in Kinross. Apart from the disruption it caused to our already prepared and undertaken local ecumenical programme, the great difficulty I had was that if I left the parishioners to take on some part of Renew by themselves then I was told I was not interested in it or their efforts and if I tried to handle a part of the programme I would be told I was too much hands-on and did not trust my people.

Then there were the Bishop's appalling attempts at looking after his priests. An example that dismayed me was in one of the usual one-pager that came annually re a priest's sustenance and travel allowance. There was a minimal increase in the sustenance allowance but there was to be no increase in the travel allowance "Ha! Ha! Ha!" Unbelievable from a so-called leader of the flock. I was not to be allowed any increase for petrol expenses and I had a parish territory of some 200 square miles to cover. I will contribute something about the problem the size of the parish created later.

The St. Andrew's Cathedral in Dundee's Nethergate was an 1836 architectural monstrosity and nightmare, with its large raised sanctuary incredibly sitting above some of the actual church house accommodation. Something certainly had to be done to improve matters if the heap had to be continued in use as a cathedral but the Bishop exhausted the million plus cash reserve he had inherited by commissioning some pretty inadequate attempts to improve the old antique. Yet St. Joseph's Church in Wilkie Lane was a large and most impressive building only a short distance away, and it would have made a splendid Cathedral. Having exhausted the Diocesan funds quite unnecessarily, the bishop imposed a tax on each Parish's Sunday collection in order to try to retrieve the financial situation of the Diocese. I made myself very unpopular with the three-man dictatorship that ran the Diocese viz. Bishop Logan, the later to-be-disgraced Vicar General Mgr. Joseph Creagan, and the supposed financial wizard Chancellor Mgr. Hugh McInally, by pointing out several times that these Diocesan Administrators were not exactly entering into the spirit of Canon Laws numbers 1284 and 1287 by never annually rendering a public account re the handling of the Diocesan finances. Eventually Mgr. McInally (I presume!) insulted us with a miserable barely A4 size of paper, on which was scrawled untidily in red Biro only a scant few items of the Diocesan financial situation.

REALLY?

You will have observed that my predecessor in St. James' Kinross, Mgr. Donachie was no longer Vicar General. The amusing allegation that went the rounds was that there had been a meeting of the Vocations Committee held to decide to which seminary intending seminarians should be sent. We still had several Scottish Seminaries then. When it came to one candidate's name, Mgr. Donachie shouted "Drygrange!" Someone asked Wee Ben why he was suggesting "Drygrange" for the candidate. Back came the response, "He is a thicko! And that is where all the thickos go!" Supposedly there was a stunned silence round the table and then Bishop Logan leant forward and said quietly "I went to Drygrange". Comes back wee Ben, "I was the Rector at Blairs (formerly our Junior Seminary) and I know where all the thickos go!" Guess who was no longer the Vicar General in the following week? But was it the true reason for Mgr. Donachie being replaced? Bishop Logan had been the private secretary to Cardinal Grey and it was said that he had been sent to the Dunkeld Diocese as a step towards replacing Cardinal Grey when the latter retired. But that was never to happen. Perhaps someone in the Vatican was on the ball? Poor Bishop Logan only ever had six months experience as a parish priest and that in the hardly exhausting parish of Roslin. Led by the redoubtable Mrs. Parr, an enthusiastic team had infused the hitherto unknown tax-envelope refund scheme into the Sunday collections. Eventually we should have received an almost four hundred pound rebate from the Inland Revenue but a clown of an Irish Parish Priest had grossly over-claimed for his parish rebate, the Revenue had observed the clear discrepancy (I nearly printed cheating!) in the claim, and were conducting an exhausted investigation into the whole tax rebates scheme running in the Diocese – so we never got the money back in my time as parish priest at Kinross and we badly needed it. I advised Logan several times that with the housing increase occurring in Kinross and there being more schemes planned to come, that the church building was becoming far too small for the growing congregation. He said that he would buy Kinross a replacement church if I could find one available. Obviously he knew full well that there was no such thing in the area – and anyway there was not the money in the diocese to do that. I wanted to double the size of the small church by duplicating it lengthwise in the available garden space but he would not grant me permission to do that – so much for buying a new church. So there was nothing else for it but to push an add-on extension into the large house itself, and I had started to do that on my own – which was when I resolved Jimmy's problems by knocking down that interior wall with my sledge-hammer.

And then there was the amazing expectation from Bishop Logan that one priest in the diocese should gather in and accumulate a file on all the extra pious works of devotion etc. each priest in the Diocese was performing. Unbelievable. No one with any commonsense could come up with that one. Sadly of course it was too many years later when it came out that Bishop Logan had had serious disturbing health problems for many years.

WHO IS THE BOSS?

As if I did not have enough on my plate – no doubt as any conscientious parish priest might feel these days – I had an over-excited phone call from someone unknown to me – apparently the parish priest of Our Lady and St. Bride in Cowdenbeath. He sternly (sic) advised me of dire consequences if I agreed to a request from two of his parishioners to have a son make his First Communion in St. James. Sure enough the request came and I had to tell the parents of the ban applied through the refusal of the Cowdenbeath parish priest to allow that to happen. (Have always been surprised and upset by those clerics who seem to think that clinging on to a bit of authority and power is supposed to be what matters to a representative of the Good Lord.) Anyway, through a serious illness – probably measles – I had not been able to make my own First Communion with my school-mates in St. Mark's Shettleston and actually made it in the recently built fine modern church of St. Quivox while recovering in Prestwick. So I could not really see what all the fuss and bother was about by the Cowdenbeath parish priest. And then came an astonishing surprise. I received an instruction. It came from the Archbishop Keith O'Brien of St. Andrews and Edinburgh saying that I was to allow the child to make his First Communion in St. James. "Que faire maintenant?" as my old Garnethill French teacher Fr. Lakeland S.J. used to propound. I felt that I had to consult Bishop Logan about my dilemma, and, as I expected, he said to me that I had to obey a mandate from an Archbishop and not a request from a parish priest. So the boy made his First Communion in St. James and I later received and hung up on a mouthful of such abuse fortissimo that beat anything I had even heard in the RAF when a fitter fell of the engine of a Lanc he was trying to repair.

And this from a supposed representative of Christ!

I made discreet enquiry and found that the Cowdenbeath parish priest was a late vocation and had previously been a baker – which obviously explained his large, loud and extensive foul vocabulary.

294

COULD REPAIR A NUCLEAR SUBMARINE BUT NOT OUR HEATING

I was never able to work out how the peculiar heating system in the St. James' complex worked. I could not discover how to save much needed money by separating the house heating from the church heating. Then I discovered that a former pupil who had just retired from being the engineer-commander of a nuclear submarine had moved into Kinross – so I thought he would be the man to explain the heating system to me. My friend spent the best part of three days toiling under house and church and even he was stumped as to how the heating system had been set up and worked. And from that and later experiences I believed that unscrupulous tradesmen took Diocesan clergy to be soft options and easy to defraud with poor workmanship and second-rate material. I recalled how at the Beda a friend had commented that prospective candidates for the priesthood should be given a course on Domestic Science but that there would never be any one among the clergy capable of running such a course.

CHARISMS

But good things were happening too. We had a large and active charismatic group (frowned on by Bishop Logan of course) and if I needed anything urgent doing they immediately responded well. My only problem with them was that I could not stop them having open "confessions" with the dangers that might have. I pointed out to them that the Church had insisted on private secluded individual reception of the Sacrament of Reconciliation for that reason.

In my first year a boy played the trumpet at Mass very well in my opinion but much to the annoyance of the usual ever-moaning women parishioners. He went off to become an army bandsman. As I have said, like the poor, critics will always be with us.

Then two most accomplished and gifted and talented lady teachers started to accompany the Vigil Mass with great guitar playing – and I took that opportunity to make it a Youth Mass – again to the usual disgruntlement of parishioners who could not see over their noses. The youth certainly started coming to the Vigil Mass and I told them that after Mass they could have free use of the small hall and that they could bring along their non-Catholic friends to the hall too if they wanted to do that too. However this ecumenical venture failed – as the youth of Kinross preferred obtaining money for stacking super-market shelves. No stacking supermarket shelves for Shettleston Co-operative Society in the long-gone days of my youth.

Thanks to great volunteer helpers, for three years running we took young people from the parish for an annual week's holiday. Our first attempt turned out to be the best. We travelled down to York and stayed with the nuns of The Bar historic convent in which we had daily in its very ornate chapel. The convent had its origin in the terrible persecution days of 1686 thanks to the heroic Mary Ward who also founded its order of nuns. The present magnificent building was deliberately designed in the 1760 era to conceal the splendid chapel we were privileged to use. I was doubtful about a couple of stories told by the present Mother Superior. The first claim was that Mary Ward was the only woman Jesuit, and the second was that the convent had been protected by the appearance of St. Michael during one of the anti-Catholic riots. Wonder what the latter story was all about. Very upper class, she did not like my criticism of the way The Beda College had been run in my time.

The weather was so good that we put off visiting the great Minster until a wet day which never came during our York stay. And imagine my annoyance when I discovered on the last day of our holiday – too late to do anything about it – that in a most generous ecumenical gesture – a visiting Catholic Party may celebrate their Catholic Mass in the historic crypt of the Minster. The good nuns were careful not to tell us about that.

Of course I was in my element in York. There was a great model railway running at the entrance to the huge curved York Station, and of course York Station itself and its expresses was a magnet for me as was the near-by National Railway museum. The young people loved walking round via the city walls if we were visiting one of the many York attractions and The Shambles – the old butchers' alley – caused wonder with the shrine to Saint Margaret Clitheroe and its many modern shops great magnets for them.

1812 WITH REAL ARTILLERY

The first evening of our visit we had decided to refresh the party after its long journey with a quiet evening stroll round Rowantree Park. But it was not to be a quiet stroll at all. We discovered that an English regiment in full regalia was there and their magnificent military band rendered the 1812 Overture with some of the regiments' artillery pieces firing blanks at the appropriate moments to accompany the stirring music. The children thought we had arranged that wonderful treat especially for them.

THE HOLY WELL OF WALES

The following year we betook ourselves to Wales – to stay at Holywell where a former Beda friend was now in charge .The Holy Well was where Caradoc beheaded St. Winifred. and has been a continuous centre of pilgrimage since the Seventh Century – the evil Henry the Eighth having spared its destruction because his mother had gone there to pray for his forthcoming birth to be successful.

Apart from wanting to see my old Beda pal and the Lourdes of Wales, I had another compelling reason for visiting Holywell. The story of that eccentric homosexual rascal Frederick Rolfe – alias Baron Corvo – had always intrigued me. He had caused so much trouble for the rectors of Oscott and the Scots College in Roma but then went on to design and make a series of magnificent religious banners and had also become a prolific writer of pseudo-historical novels. I had supposed the famous banners to be still in Holywell but apart from one remainder all the others had "Walked" at some time or other. So that was a great disappointment. My Beda pal also added that there had once been a priceless collection of expensive-crockery-equipped Welsh dressers in the church house but that they had vanished too – allegedly taken by a previous parish priest who left the priesthood to be married. He had organised that great Liverpool Conference and was disgusted that the hierarchy had totally ignored its consequences and of course he had received no recognition for all the hard work he had put into organising the huge conference. Oh that stupid celibacy routine.

A trip to nearby Llandudno was an obvious choice and on the way we stopped at little St. Asaph's Cathedral – Kentigern having been Bishop there too after he had had to flee his dear green place for a time in the days when Strathclyde really was Strathclyde. Llandudno was an attractive place for retirement days for Merseyside. As a result four funerals a day was the norm that had to be attended to from the appropriately named Our Lady Star of the Sea church. Accordingly the assistant priests there had to be changed every four months and my Beda buddy had done his four month stint there. He told me that while he was there the very wealthy parish priest had purchased a brand new large Mercedes saloon and on the first day the Monsignor had had it he took it out to go round visiting parishioners – as all good parish priests ought to do. Unfortunately he parked the new vehicle too close to the rails of the Great Orme cable-car system and the new Mercedes was wrecked on its first outing by a cable-car – as the cable-cars cannot stop for obviously they are attached to a moving cable that only stops for loading and unloading at the termini.

I was astonished at the costly items on display in the securely locked Llandudno church, church and parish priest being wealthy owing to the numerous large bequests received.

We ascended the stupendous Great Orme headland on the cable-car system, changing cars as required at the half-way stage. After enjoying a couple of hours on the summit with its great refreshment facilities and magnificent views I decreed that we would go back down on the associated chair-lift system. This suggestion terrified one of our lady helpers and she did not want to do that but I told her that she would enjoy an unusual experience and that anyway nothing untoward ever happened on the Great Orme dangle- bars. Oh! Dear! We were only ten days back in Kinross when there was head-line news. The Greta Orme chair-lift system had been shut down in error while there was still a family up on one of the cars. The unfortunates were marooned for two and a half hours before the errant operators of the chair-lift could be found and brought back to restart the system. Was my name mud! I will not repeat what the parishioner called me. And quite right too. And I had had another disaster. Coming off the Llandudno beach, Jimmy the Woof decided to relieve himself on the back of an unsuspecting nun who was sitting dangling her feet off the promenade edge. Crawl, crawl and much abject apologising by me – but to be fair, she took the mishap quite well. My great regret about Llandudno is that its once famous tramway system was abandoned with no attempt made to have some sort of preservation group working a bit of it: though a group have produced a replica Llandudno tram at Bodafon Fields. As we did too, my Beda pal found the people of Holywell very friendly, and I was quite amused when he said that he had been having an evening meal with a local family and a very pleasant and intelligent professional footballer had been there too. He could not remember his surname but thought his Christian name was Ian. It was the great Liverpool forward Ian Rush of course but my Beda man was not into football.

Being not too far away and myself being a Festiniog Narrow Gauge Railway "anorak" we went over to Ffestiniog and took a train up to Blaenau Ffestiniog. It is usually an enjoyable ride with great views but on the day we picked it was very warm and the train was packed out and it worried me that we could not keep the children seated together for safety sake, so for once I did not enjoy the historic old slate narrow gauge line as I usually did.

MORE HOLY PLACES

For the third year outing bully old me decided we would go to Lindisfarne. Apart from showing the young people a bit of important Catholic history I was looking forward to celebrating Mass on Holy Island. We discovered that there was at Alnmouth Gardens an Anglican Friary run by an Order of St Francis monks which welcomed visitors. So we booked in there. Oh! Dear! The good monks were excellent and treated us extraordinarily well and some even attended our Masses but we scared stiff when we found that their hospice was open house to all and sundry who wanted to come in and that there was no security for us. We prayed that no paedophile would come in to stay in the hospice. And we had trouble on the A1. A well-meaning parishioner had hired a large mini-bus for our party. It was comfortable enough but going along the A1 it got slower and slower and I could not get speed out of it. The honking of irate motorists at us grew in intensity and I decided we would just have to get off the main road. A suitable exit appeared and I thought it was going to be all right as it took us down to a neat-looking cafeteria by a lovely loch. But when we started to disembark a furious attendant from the cafeteria rushed out and shouted at us that the cafeteria did not allow people off a mini-bus to come there and we would have to leave immediately. I tried to reason with the irate individual. I pointed out that we had young children with us who needed refreshments on such a sultry hot day but the blighter would not even allow us to disembark on to a grassy bank even when I told him the vehicle had become horse-de-combat. I phoned the Police but they were not at all helpful saying that they could not get involved and that what the cafeteria decreed went. So I ignored the cafeteria employee and we took the children off the mini-bus despite his loud remonstrations and settled them down on a grassy bank where at least they could get some fresh air during the hour and a half time it took a mechanic from the bus hire company to arrive. Of course when we returned to Kinross I wrote letters of complaint about our treatment to the owners of the cafeteria and to Northumberland Tourist bodies but never receive an apology from any of them. So much for encouraging tourism. As with the Llandudno dangle-bar fiasco my name was mud again.

We had Mass on Lindisfarne and visited Seahouses to view the famous Farne Island rocks. We visited the great and historic Bamborough Castle – perhaps the largest in England. Very impressive. Naturally we stopped in at the St. Andrew's Priory at Hexham and went down into its still extant 7th Century Saxon crypt of St. Wilfred. We could not miss out on this priory as it was from Hexham that an eighth century bishop of the time, Acca, fled to Scotland with relics of St. Andrew. Though he may have been Bishop of Whithorn after his exile, it is believed his relics of St. Andrew were deposited in present-day Fife at a place of worship established by Columban missionary St. Regulus and later a Culdee holy place – Kilrymont – and so the place was later named St. Andrews and accordingly once had the largest cathedral in Scotland and perhaps the finest in Europe. The majority of St. Andrew's relics were known to have been stolen from Constantinople in the days of "relic hunting" and are now supposed to be in Amalfi but when Keith O'Brien was made a Cardinal, the pope gave him some relics of St. Andrew which are now displayed in St. Mary's Cathedral in Edinburgh, the present day cathedral of our Catholic Archdiocese of St. Andrews and Edinburgh, so things may be said to have completed a full circle?

When you visit Hexham there is a delightful riverside walk along a bank of the River Tyne. Jimmy the Woof found it even more refreshing than we grown-ups by diving in and swimming about in the slow-flowing water. We eventually – Jimmy came out with great reluctance – moved on to have a look at Vindolanda – one of the best excavated forts on Hadrian's customs' wall. Unlike on previous visits I was annoyed that Jimmy the Woof was now banned from entry. After our return to Kinross the ruling opinion among the party was that next year's outing had to be back to their favourite place York. That was fine by me but marvellous Bishop Logan – whom God preserve – was to ensure that that was not going to happen.

FAR OFF PLACES

One of my Kinross problems was that I was never given the official boundaries of the parish. Families would move into the extensive hinterland and I would wonder if they should be parishioners of St. James. An obviously wealthy Canadian family asked me if they were in our Kinross parish or that of St. John Vianney's in Alva. I did not really know as they were so far out in the countryside. Since there was obviously going to be money involved I thought it only fair to consult the Alva parish priest on the matter. (He had been a teacher in next-door Castlemilk Primary St. July's when I had been boss in the Wee Maggie.) Immediately he replied that it was quite straightforward. Anything on the east side of the River Devon was mine and everything on the other side was his. I said that was fine with me but I had been attending to a nursing home on the west side of the Devon at Rumbling Bridge – so with that decision made by him he better start attending to it instead of me as it was in the territory claimed to be his Well! Did not the roof fall in on me. He voiced it round the Diocese that I was a lazy so-and-so and others agreed with him without bothering to consult me.

A Polish regiment had been disbanded in Perth and a lot of people of Polish descent were around. Most of them had changed their surnames to good old Scottish names like Stewart or McGregor etc. Once I was invited to a Burns supper and just as I had been highly amused at the Kerry men at the Dunkeld wedding being outfitted in Scottish regalia – so I was highly amused at all the diners at that Burns supper being Poles with Scottish names. One of the ex-Poles was palsy-walsy with the Alva priest who would give him ample ammunition to fire at me, and of course he caused upset in the parish with his remarks about me. And this was the bloke who could not have cared less about writing off three motor-cars in ten days. As he boasted "After all, I am in the Insurance business!" With clowns like that in insurance no wonder our premiums are so high. That Pole was to have serious problems with a son later – which did not surprise me at all. It was easy to see that was coming.

Then there was the chap who, with his wife, owned a prosperous shop in Milnathort. After my arrival he started to come to the church house regularly with large sums of money instead of using the offertory collection basket, and eagerly became an excellent Reader. He was into gliding, and wanted to take me up for flights in his own expensive glider which he kept with the Scottish Gliding Club at Portmoak on the other side of Loch Leven from Kinross. This was a most generous offer, as a single flight at that time was around fifty pounds – if you wanted to have a glider experience. He told me that the gliding conditions at Portmoak were ideal and apparently the club thought that a member had made the longest-ever U K glider flight on record by reaching France form Portmoak, while another pilot had claimed some kind of altitude record. But I had seen too many flying casualties at Coastal Command's Kinloss, so I respectfully declined the offer. And some time later there was in fact a fatal glider and tow-plane accident at Portmoak. However his services to the church had to be brought to an end following a complaint from a parishioner that they were selling pornographic magazines in their Milnathort paper shop. When I tackled him about it, he asked if it would not be all right if they kept the pornographic material under the counter! Well! You do not need to be told what I said about that misguided suggestion.

LEADVILLE AND COLORADO

I had always longed to see Colorado and my mother's Leadville birthplace and to find my maternal grandmother's burial place there. The Royal Navy Catholic Chaplain at Rosyth was always willing to look after Kinross if I wanted a vacation, so I pestered

Rod Bronstein, the parish priest in Leadville, Colorado until rather unwillingly he let me take over his parish for a month. To be fair, what most concerned him was my ability to stay well and healthy and fit at Leadville's ten thousand feet altitude. I thought that with my Scottish hill-walking endeavours that would not turn out to be a problem, and I never had the slightest bother with altitude – even when –as I will later relate- I went over the much higher continental divide. Leadville got is name when in the 19th Century many prospectors had come into the area looking for gold discoveries. Disappointed prospectors left huge mountains of discarded excavated material round where they had been attempting to find gold. A Geology Professor from Chicago was visiting the area and was astounded to see these huge mounds lying abandoned, for he realised that the unwanted material was in fact extremely valuable silver ore and it was there just for the uplifting. So he hired transport, gathered in the silver ore, and became a very rich man indeed. When the fact of his discovery became known, parts of Colorado filled with prospectors now looking for silver rather than gold. Several silver-mining towns started up round the silver mines and one of them was the fabulous Leadville, which with its multitude of mines and rail connections, for a time became extremely rich indeed. The silver boom collapsed with closure of the silver mint in India.

Mining towns such as Aspen and Vail gave up on the silver mining industry. When I visited Aspen there was not an American motor-car to be seen there. Aspen was full of Mercs, Jaguars, Ferraris and every other make of exotic non-U S car, for it had become a film-star and millionaires' play-ground. The Aspen priest told me that he had recently had a very well-known Holywood celebrity visiting him to try to arrange a Catholic marriage. When it was pointed out to the celebrity that there were too many matrimonial irregularities and impediments in the star's life to' permit that to happen, the big-head had stormed out shouting, "I see that you do not `know who I am!"

Vail had become the war-time training camp for the U.S. army's mountain divisions, and, when the war ended, the commanding officer of the base had had the fore-sight to turn Vail into the world-famous ski resort that it has become to-day.

Poor (now!) old Leadville is still waiting for the silver boom to return – as two-thirds of the silver ore is still under the ground.

First time I celebrated a Sunday Mass there I was staggered when one of the Eucharistic Ministers was dressed as an old-time mining engineer. But he was a great parishioner and this was his outfit for taking visitors down a tourist mine. One poor old lady who had been told by her husband before he died to keep hold of the mine, would walk every Spring over the high and very steep Mosquito Pass to distant Denver in a vain attempt to obtain employees for her mine. And of course the unsinkable Molly Brown of Titanic fame had also once been a Leadville mine owner and had become quite rich as a result.

NEVER THE TWAIN SHALL MEET!

I discovered that up until a year or so before my arrival, Leadville had had two distinct parishes with their separate churches only a short distance apart. Annunciation Church is a vast and superb building easily holding a thousand worshippers with, supposedly, the highest church spire in the world. The spire is some four hundred feet in height and after all the church itself stands at least some ten thousand feet above sea level – so that might well be the case. (And Leadville also claims that its nine-hole golf course is the highest in the world.) Annunciation was the church for Spaniard/Mexicans and Italians, and St. Joseph's was the one for the Slav inhabitants of Leadville. I was told that in the years previous to my coming, there would never be a marriage between a parishioner of Annunciation and one from St. Joseph's.

St Joseph's was a greater attraction than Annunciation to tourists arriving in Leadville, because they wanted to see the large colourful murals a long-living old-time Slav priest had hand–painted on all the church walls. Just as well that it was a smallish building!

They told me that the aforesaid energetic priest – even in his old age- would take a Sunday afternoon stroll up one of the adjacent Rockie Mountain peaks. And here was me thinking I had done well when I reached the summit of the Galloway Merrick. It was the church house of St. Joseph's I had to stay in. I was amazed at its size and the quality of this wooden house's fittings. For example: it had a fridge that I could have walked into. The house-keeper could not do enough for me. This friendly African/American had an incredible little dog that always greeted me by standing upright on its back legs, then doing a wonderful high backward-somersault and then landing upright on its back legs again. I asked the good lady had she obtained the wee marvel from a circus but she said no. And apparently she had not trained the wee marvel to do the trick either. It had just begun to do the somersault of its own accord. This great house-keeper gave me a very large dog's bouncing ball for Jimmy the Woof when I was leaving Leadville. I carried the expensive gift all the way back across The Pond and even was stopped by the fine Customs Officer at Prestwick who wanted to know what was in the large box, and, would you believe it. Jimmy the Woof just did not want to know about his generous American gift.

But there was a big snag about staying in the St. Joseph's church house. St. Jo's had a huge bell arrangement which loudly sounded Westminster style Big Ben chimes every quarter of an hour, twenty-four hours out of twenty-four. Once, when exploring London while on RAF leave, I had stayed in the welcoming Methodist Central Halls' forces accommodation adjacent to Big Ben, and could barely manage a good night's sleep there. So it was – next to the Slav church.

It was quite common in the Leadville area for the large wooden houses to be moved about on trailers. During the war the molybdenum mine at the top of the Platte valley at Climax was of utmost importance and was extremely busy. The narrow gauge remnant of the Denver and South Park line up to Climax was changed to standard gauge, because of that mine's importance to the war effort, and in fact was to become scene of the last commercial steam operations in the United States. After the war when the Climax mine ceased to be profitable and closed, many of the employees who had moved their wooden homes up to Climax just moved them back down to Leadville. Later still the Leadville-Climax line saw a preserved diesel operation for tourists. (Of course I tried it,)

One wooden house move took a family close to the Slav church. Having endured its loud every quarter-hour chiming for a continuous forty-eight hours or so, the house-owners went to the Leadville Police and lodged a complaint about the disturbance. They did not realise that the Leadville Police were Catholic, and they received the reply that St. Joseph's had been ringing its bells for over a hundred years, and the complainants had been in

Leadville but two days. So why did they not just move their wooden house away from the church as there were many vacant lots in Leadville.

The unexpected problem I had with the two "parishes" was that everything had to be performed twice. It was clear to me that the kind priest who had allowed me to be there in his parish – Don Bronstein – was not at all happy about being there but would father have been in Colorado Springs where the Diocesan headquarters were situated. Father Bronstein was obviously of Jewish extraction and appeared to have been fostered by a Catholic family. One of the Catholic family's sons had become a Catholic priest and Don had decided to follow his example.

Unlike him I loved Leadville and its people. They appealed to me by being exactly like those of my own families' mining background. They could not do enough for this intruder while I was there. I was written up in the local paper. The splendid librarians dug out old census documents and went out of their way to take me to the empty site where my grandfather had had a general store. That he had been a store-owner was news to me.

A parishioner – like me a retired primary school head but unwell unlike me – he was to die just after I returned to Scotland – requiescat in pace – went to enormous trouble to assist me in finding my grandmother's unmarked grave where she lay among some forty thousand others. That involved a great deal of his time and efforts – freely given. I was extremely disappointed to discover that the grave was unmarked – not even with a cross of any kind – but the Leadville undertakers were to put a splendid headstone on my grandmother' final resting place at very reasonable cost.

Many times I was invited to eat with families – both in their houses and at splendid dineries. Their tastes usually ran to Mexican food which I quickly learned to enjoy.

FOUR WHEELS THROUGH THE ROCKIES

A retired couple who had an enormous (to me!) Cherokee Jeep, discovering through the librarians that I was a rail nut, took me over all the lengthy old railway track-beds around Leadville – especially the track-beds of the amazing very lengthy narrow gauge lines. The Victorians were fearless engineers, and even thought of linking Denver to the far off Pacific coast with narrow gauge railway lines.—all constructed in the times of the search for mineral wealth. We crossed the continental divide several times in the jeep – much to my delight, including several times crossing the famed Tennessee Pass by Holy Cross mountain – which once had had the highest main-line tunnel crossing of the continental divide in the United States.

Another of the highlights of these arduous cross-continental divide trips along the old track-beds was going up and down and up again to both sides of the astonishing narrow-gauge Alpine Tunnel which was bored out at some 12,000 feet to link the then bustling prosperous mining towns of St. Elmo and Pitkin. There even were the remains of the high Alpine station and m.p.d. shed which allowed engines to be changed at that astonishing height. Part of the track took us along the Palisades – track-bed cut into the side of a giant mountain and giving fantastic views down to the bottom of the valley and the track-beds down there. Excursion trains would be run all the way from Denver to allow the citizens of that city to enjoy the amazing Palisades spectacle. That thrilled me to bits as well as seeing some of the highways still snowed up in July.

But a most thrilling and amusing day-out took us to follow the track of the old standard gauge Colorado Midland Railway line up to the Busk tunnel – another wonder 600 yards in length at some eleven thousand feet again. And this was built to replace the lower Hagerman tunnel and its lengthy wooden viaduct which had been proved to be unsatisfactory as the Colorado Midland tried to serve Colorado Springs, Leadville, Aspen and Grand Junction. After reaching the Leadville side of the Busk tunnel we drove a long way round to reach the other side of the tunnel – which by that time only carried a water main. What a pleasant surprised greeted us on the Aspen side of Busk tunnel. We found ourselves in a most delightful, pleasant and peaceful large Alpine-style meadow land beside a beautiful loch called by the appropriate Scottish title of Lake Ivanhoe. But it was in strangely named Frying Pan Valley! There was a little house at the end of our road and a friendly man came out to greet us and have a little blether with us.

When I was dealing the strain of trying to cope with the woes of Castlemilk, I would say to my splendid assistant head, "Why could I not have had a quiet job at a water-works miles from anywhere. All I would have to do would be to get a message to turn the water wheel six turns to the right and some weeks later to turn the wheel back the six turns". And here was a Coloradian with that very job I coveted so much. He controlled the water supply down to Pueblo – some two hundred miles away – and he would come up from there when the snow relented to inhabit this lovely place. How I envied him his peace and quiet in such a lovely beauty spot.

SO DIFFERENT FROM SCATLAND!

What a surprise awaited me when I was about to celebrate my first Sunday Mass in the great Annunciation church. I was vested and quite apprehensive, waiting at the back of the church. It was bad enough that I was totally awed at having the great privilege celebrating The Sunday Eucharist in such an enormous church before a huge congregation and with four beaming smartly attired teen-age altar-girls to assist me. I came to realise that there was also a compere – complete with microphone – sitting behind a desk in what was once a large side-altar. I was totally shattered when out she came with over the loud-speakers in a broad American accent: "Welcome to all our visitors: the celebrant this morning is Father Bill Tollan – all the way from Scatland (sic!): give Father Bill a big hand!" Wow! And then I had to try to gather my wits while making the lengthy journey up the central aisle to the sanctuary accompanied by thunderous applause. And this was to be repeated on each of the following Sundays.

In some ways it was a relaxation to celebrate the follow-up Sunday Mass in the little St. Joseph's church.

HERE COMES THE BRIDE

Another wow was when I had to preside at a wedding in the Annunciation church. To start with the couple and their relations made it clear that it was Father Bronstein they had wanted to preside at the sacrament and not me. But eventually they came to realise that I did not have a tail and two horns and all went well. First evening there was an ice-cream nosh-up between the close relatives of the couple. Being an ice-cream fanatic I did enjoy wiring- in at that. Next night there was a large and lengthy meal attended by most of those coming to the actual Sacrament. The following afternoon was spent with a never-ending lengthy wedding rehearsal. I write "never-ending" for no fewer than ten best men and ten bridesmaids had to learn their parts and places. I had the utmost mental praise the very fine organist who had to stay through the lengthy proceedings during which this and that hymn was chosen after trial while others were discarded. Phew!

After the Sacrament of Matrimony was over on the chosen day (and the proceedings seem to have gone well and been much appreciated), I was waiting to lock the church. I had to wait for no less than two hours because everybody – repeat everyone of the congregation – had their picture taken with the bride. Then it was off to The Elks for a mammoth wedding feast. I have never before or since seen a wedding cake with a water fountain playing in the middle of the cake. (The Elks being a huge philanthropic society open to all except atheists.)

MORE UNUSUAL HAPPENINGS

Then on another day there was a great and very friendly and enjoyable parish picnic in some lovely shaded woods.

The next startling event was not so friendly. I was asked to go to the jail to see a murderer who wanted to speak to a priest. Although I had been in Barlinnie and Perth prisons, it was quite an experience to be locked in behind several sets of bars by gun-toting police. As I was not wearing clerical clothing I had a time of it convincing the young man I really was a Catholic priest from Glasgow. He admitted he had killed another young man with a heavy tree branch. Sadly he showed little remorse for his action but was more very much afraid that his victim's family and friends would be waiting to take revenge on him if he was ever freed.

One night I was startled out of my few remaining wits. I was only told that someone's remains would be coming to Annunciation church preparatory to a funeral Mass and burial next morning. As I entered the partly darkened church there were four large fully hooded figures in black kneeling across the front of the sanctuary. It transpired that the deceased had been a member of the immense American Catholic charitable organisation called the Knights of St. Columbus and this was the local Leadville council showing their respect for a deceased member. I wish somebody had thought to warn me beforehand. I knew, of course, of our own

Glasgow-founded Catholic charitable organisation Knights of St. Columba but this was something else to discover.

To get the hundred or so miles from Denver to Leadville I had of course pre-booked a hire car in advance. It was amazingly smooth running with only three cylinders and automatic drive. It was so new that it did not have number plates attached but instead had a large folded-paper arrangement sitting at the rear window with car registration written on it in large letters. One afternoon I had been up at the splendid Leadville library and driving carefully back to the church house I saw in my mirrors that a large police vehicle was following me. Eventually on came its sirens and blue flashing lights. I wondered what offence I had committed despite my care, so I stopped and went back to the police car.

I was told afterwards that to go back was just not the done thing in the States. However the decent town cop gulped when he realised who I was and somewhat apologetically explained that he had stopped me because my car had no registration plates. I took him to the car and explained that it was so new that the Denver hire people had not had time to attach proper registration plates to it but that the registration number was displayed on the back ledge of the vehicle. But no it was not. I had not noticed that the paper device had fallen down in front of the back ledge – so no number was in fact being displayed as the law required. But the embarrassed officer accepted my explanation and took no further action.

That is only the second time I have been "pulled-over" by the police. The other occasion was when I was driving in Italy to Roma in my Volkswagen caravanette. I thought I would change my normal direct A1 autostrada route and see what the more coastal way was like. Going down the A 15 I saw that there was quite a steep gradient ahead to reach the coastal A11 austrada. The heavy caravanette did not do well on gradients, so, although I knew the speed signs decreed a speed of 60 kilometres per hour to the junction I put my foot down on the accelerator and went for it. Oh! Dear! Ahead a carabinieri stepped out on to the autostrada ahead of me holding a red stop disc. I was mightily relieved that the customary poorly braking Volkswagen managed to stop only a few feet in front of him. But the young officer was very polite and after asking to see my papers he contented himself with wagging a finger and saying "piano!" "piano!" I still occasionally remember to pray for him as a way of thanking him for not taking more serious action.

POOR MUTT

There was a large splendid English sheep dog that used to lean over a Leadville backyard fence and be friendly every time I walked past. The sad story was that the Annunciation parishioners had bought it as a present to help a widow who was running a sheep ranch outside Leadville. The said sheep ranch comprised thousands of acres but the stubborn widow refused to take the smashing dog. I would have loved to take the unwanted friend back with me but in those unenlightened days even if I could have afforded the air flight for it, there would have been the statutory six months of quarantine to pay for and that of course would have been well beyond my financial ability. That was very sad.

More amusing was the occasion when Bronstein asked me if I would like to go with him and a priest friend to fabulous Glenwood Springs. When we arrived at the motel he asked me how I was going to pay for the stay! And I thought it was only up the Scottish east coast that the question was "You will have had your tea!"

More parsimony followed as I was heading back across the big pond. I was awarded the princely sum of 24 dollars for my month's supervision of the parishes including a presiding at a wedding and a funeral. And as I hinted, Aberdonians were supposed to be the mean lot. (Of course they are not.)

EAST – WEST! IS HAME BEST?

When I returned to Kinross I was disappointed that Jimmy the Woof was not exactly enraptured at seeing me again. The great mutt had obviously been having a more enjoyable time during his stay with a kind parishioner at Glenfarg than I had been able to give him. Said parishioner was so impressed with having a dog about that she bought a Rhodesian Ridgeback – bred up a tenement close in Parkhead – of all places. You cannot keep a good Parkheidian down!

IN DUNKELD DIOCESE AGAIN

The first day back in Kinross I received a phone a call from a Redemptorist friend in Perth. When I heard what he had to say I went up a few points in my usual low scale of self-approval.

Sadly there was a Catholic couple out in the country-side about whom I had not known about. The wife was suffering badly from leukaemia and the grieving husband wanted her to be attended to by a Catholic priest but not by one of the usual "clod-hopper" coarse secular priests. This was why he had contacted the Perth Redemptorists. My friend had told the worried man that he would find the parish priest in Kinross a quite suitable priest to attend to his wife's needs as he certainly was not of the "clod-hopper" coarse variety. Jings!

When I attended to her, I discovered that the dying woman had four smashing large and friendly white wolf-hounds. Unfortunately I had been trying to get a young would-be organist to come back and play at the church. He had been sacked by my predecessor and I wanted to give him a second chance. Oh! Dear! He completely messed-up the timings of the chosen hymns at the deceased lady's Requiem Mass and, in fact, played "All Creatures Great and Small" twice and on both occasions at inappropriate times. Guess which organist was sacked for a second time.

I made my customary follow-up visit to see how the grieving husband was faring and expressed astonishment that I was not greeted as usual by the marvellous dogs. "Glad they so-and-so nuisances are not around anymore!" loudly shouted the stricken man. When the poor lady had been told that no further treatment for her leukaemia was possible she had put her lovely friends down by her own hand. Had I known how things stood I would have been more than happy to have them stay with Jimmy the Woof and myself. One of life's saddest moments.

OUCH!

I once had had a not so happy encounter with a dog that I thought was a true pal. Because the owners of a Cocker Spaniel left him alone in their house all day as they were both teachers and so out all day – and also because they put such great effort into organising the splendid music for St. James, I would take him out with Jimmy the Woof and myself when we went out for our daily exercise in the lovely countryside round Kinross. I was a bit late for their Christmas party because of the customary parish crisis occurring as usual at the inappropriate time. When I opened the outside door to their house, the wee Cocker was standing there. Unthinkingly I stupidly put my hand down to greet him as usual and he replied by jumping up and seizing my right arm firmly in his mouth. I could not make him let go. Eventually I had to have a tetanus injection and then two other injections at frequent intervals in the arm. A friendly parishioner who was a top-ranking Edinburgh consultant who had treated me because of the injury, said that he had not wanted to say it at the time but he thought I was in serious danger of losing the arm. Certainly I could not use my right arm at all for three weeks and had to be driven around to enable me to do the necessary parish work for that length of time. Apparently the Cocker had taken it upon itself to be standing keeping guard on the Christmas presents on a tree in the house corridor. The distressed teachers wanted to put their dog down but I was not for having that – though I never again took it out for a walk with Jimmy the Woof. So that was a wretched Christmas, but, as I hope to relate later the next one was to be even worse.

ORTHODOX OR UNORTHODOX?

The Consultant who saved my arm was a very involved parishioner. We had had to have an "event" as part of that dreadful "Renew" programme ordained by Bishop Logan. The Consultant told me that thee was a very interesting priest who ran (sic!) about Edinburgh University and we should have him over to perform in St. James. From the description the Consultant gave it was clear to me that this was in fact a Greek Orthodox priest, and while I personally would have had no objection to his coming to Kinross, the Orthodox man would probably not want to come to a Catholic parish, and in any case, remembering his objectionable attitude to my intended participants in my ordination ceremony, I knew that Bishop Logan would have had kittens at the very idea of an Orthodox priests participating in a Catholic Kinross event. And all this is supposed to be about Christianity. As Chesterton said, "Christianity is a great idea – just a pity no-one has tried it."

I explained the situation to my Consultant friend and parishioner, and said that instead of inviting the Greek Orthodox priest, I would send an invitation to the Catholic Eastern Rite Ukrainian chaplain for Scotland. We were delighted when he accepted our invitation to preside at a Eucharist in St. James. It was even better when the good man came, because he brought with him his wife (no celibacy intimidation of priests in the Catholic Eastern Rites) and a superb all-male choir. What a joy it was to listen to their magnificent joyous chant. The good man said it was an all-male choir because of the shortage of Ukrainian women in Scotland at that time. (Needless to say the usual parish grousers about everything did not accept the great gifts they had freely received.) Apparently it was customary for the Ukrainian priest's wife not to participate in any post-Mass meal. But we insisted that she should join us for that – and rather reluctantly she did.

ONE CAN BUT TRY

Among other things intended to gee-up the parish, we had started a monthly magazine. One of the contributions was immensely sad to read. A retired naval officer related how he was on his warship off Anzio during the landings there, when an adjoining Canadian Hospital ship was blown up by a Luftwaffe radio-controlled glider bomb. Only later did he discover that his fiancée nurse had died in that tragedy.

Having been a bridge fanatic I thought to get a bridge club going as a parish activity and I asked a known Kinross bridge-player parishioner to come along and try to get it started. Unbelievably he came alone and did not bring in any of his customary bridge partners – so that idea died the death.

For two years running I had organised a parish treasure hunt (as I had done when in the Wee Maggie), and a parishioner complained that the clues I had produced were too difficult to understand so she would do it next year. Of course the following year she denied that she had ever said such a thing. Hard to understand the thinking of some people?

As the next Christmas came near we prepared a great ecumenical concert to celebrate Christmas and to participate in it I had worked on a comedy duet routine with a former Roma Scots College friend. One corny patter from our "Vatican News" routine has always stuck in what passes for my mind: "Following a domestic strike at The Vatican, the Pope swept down the staircase and then Polished the door knobs." I was never to find out how that sort of rubbish would have gone down in Kinross for a week before Christmas I was summoned by the Bishop and he told me that since I had been so incompetent in Kinross he was moving me to a different parish so that I could start to learn how to be a proper parish priest. So poor old incompetent me had only − − with the great assistance of all the helpful parishioners − had somehow, in three years, managed to treble the mass attendance at St. James, double the weekly collection amounts and take the bank balance from three hundred pounds to three thousand pounds. The latter being accomplished without the tax refunds that the Chancellor in his wisdom had refused to return to us. And of course, as I previously said, this supposedly incompetent priest had somehow managed to run a couple of parishes in Colorado to the apparent pleasure and satisfaction of their parishioners.

I thought it a great pity that the rule that insists on a priest remaining with a Diocese for six years had prevented me from going to the Colorado Springs diocese and asking to be posted to Leadville.

So there were all my own plans for celebrating Christmas with my own personal friends all ruined. What a great Christmas present I had received from Bishop Logan. Now I realised why I had never been properly inducted into St. James parish as I ought to have been. What really lay behind my enforced transfer had nothing at all to do with my supposed incompetence but the situation that the parishioners of St. Margaret's, Montrose had been strongly agitating for a while over the fact that they did not have a permanent parish priest in place but only temporary priest appointments from various Orders who were trying to help out. The bishop had brought into the Diocese a priest from the English midlands who was presently at Arbroath and he had refused to move from Arbroath to Montrose − so I became the fall guy. And so I was sold a pup. As I had been before by that Jesuit Head.

But I did have a laugh out of the personal disaster none the less. On the first Sunday he was in Kinross my successor did not appear for the early Sunday Mass. Worried sides-men could get a reply from the church house bell and so eventually decided to break into the house. And what did they discover? My worthy successor snoozing away comfortably in bed. So I was not the only one who had to learn how to be a parish priest. I did have a chortle when Kinross friends told me the tale.

And I received a phone call about my coming to Montrose asking me what my plans for Montrose were. Thinking it was a friend making me a hoax call I breezily replied that I wanted to have a tramway running between Montrose and Brechin. But it was no hoax call. It turned out to be from the editor of the local rag (owned as I was belatedly to discover by one of the Montrose parishioners). So there was the headline across the front of the paper "Priest wants trams between Montrose and Brechin!" Oh Dear!

And it was to be "Oh Dear!" again when the headline appeared "Priest says he cannot walk on water!"

I usually took Jimmy the Woof for a run on the Montrose links before many golfers were awake. One morning when I came back to the car-park I discovered a flood of the most filthy dirty water surrounding my Polo. Next morning I waited and watched and discovered it was a drain-cleaner who simply disposed of his lorry's surplus mess by the annoying solution of simply emptying it over the car-park. Try as I might with every authority I could think of, I could not get that unsanitary practice stopped and so had to go elsewhere for Jimmy's early trot. The local paper had heard of my complaints – so hence that head-line.

ST. MARGARET'S MONTROSE

As usual that triumvirate "running" – "ruining" the diocese were not to be trusted. And they had the cheek to call themselves Christian! I asked the Chancellor about the state of St. Margaret's parish and was told that every thing was in good order – the finances were as good as if not better than in St. James' and the house had been redecorated etc. Really?

The church – built around 1886 was in a perilous state. Apart from having hardly any worthwhile heating, only two things were keeping it from collapsing completely. A concrete choir loft had been put in at the back of the church (without any planning permission) and it was holding the exterior walls together, and a corner of the church was tied into the church house. The church house had been painted on the exterior but inside was just a filthy slum. In the kitchen extension the paint was peeling off the walls in shreds.

For some unfathomable reason the Bishop had had an excellent small wooden hall erected in the extensive grounds behind the house. Why on earth he had not made that wooden hall (excellently constructed) of a size to replace the decrepit church baffled me. And as a result of the erection of that hall the debit in the parish account was some £16,000. So much for the Chancellor's honesty, and of course, the Sunday collection in Montrose and Brechin was not up to Kinross's later standards, so there was little hope of paying off that debt the bishop had incurred for the parish.

As there was a high-up bank employee as an active parishioner I left the money side of things entirely to him.

ST. NINIAN'S BRECHIN

Then there was the problem of Brechin. Old records I discovered showed that Brechin had once been a Catholic parish in its own right. (And the records were of such a vintage that there were notices of the Sacrament of Matrimony being performed in hotels and inns.)

But of course Bishop Logan would have none of that and insisted that it was only part of the Montrose parish. What rubbish.

I discovered that our St. Ninian's church in Bank Street, Brechin was, in fact, a quite splendid former Church of Scotland building that could have accommodated several hundreds of parishioners quite comfortably. With its fine tall church tower the upkeep of such splendour was financially quite impossible as there were only about forty regular Brechin Catholic attendees at Mass, with another score of United States servicemen usually coming along too. They were from what was nominally R A F Edzell but which was in fact an American Navy listening post with only a solitary R A F Group Captain nominally in charge.

I never met him but worked in harmony with the American Chaplains and in fact was to receive a much appreciated U S Navy commendation for that co-operation which I thoroughly enjoyed of course being half-a Yank.

WHERE AM I?

There is a funny (at least to me) story re RAF Edzell. Bishop Logan carried out Confirmations there only to receive a rebuke from the Bishop of Aberdeen (then Bishop Conti) who enquired why Logan had carried out Confirmations in another Bishop's Diocese without having the courtesy to seek permission to do that. Ignorance of the Dunkeld Diocese boundaries was also shown by the Dunkeld Diocese Parish Priest of St. Columba's, Cupar, who built a Catholic Primary School for Cupar but in the diocese of St. Andrews and Edinburgh! See Scottish seminarian training.... Geography was not a top subject, was it?

The first US Navy chaplain at RAF Edzell did not impress – though his successor certainly did. The former seemed to be more interested in going to the Montrose Auction Rooms and bidding for loads of antique furniture which, along with his superb expensive sports limo was freely shipped back to the States for him on a giant aircraft carrier – no less.

NOT "AYE READY"!

When we prepared our candidates for Confirmation in our Glasgow schools we were always aware that one of the questions the Bishop administering the great sacrament of Confirmation would ask, would be if the candidate could tell him anything about the saint whose name the candidate had chosen as the Confirmation name. The first time I was invited to take part in an Edzell Sacrament of confirmation ceremony, Bishop Conti asked the first teen-age girl for her intended Confirmation name. "Catherine" came the bored reply. And Bishop Conti then asked, of course, "And who was Saint Catherine?" "I don't know!" came the weary reply. And of course I knew what was going to happen. The good Bishop asked ever one of the candidates who was the saint they had chosen and everyone of the fourteen teen-agers gave the same monotonous answer – "I don't know!" And sadly the response was always in a voice that suggested each one could not have cared less about the whole business.

BEST BEDSIDE MANNER YET AGAIN

As well as Montrose and Brechin to try to cope with I now found myself once again as a hospital chaplain looking after the patients in Strathcathro and the Royal Infirmaries of Montrose and Brechin. On my first look in to Strathcathro hospital I discovered that it was based round an old large mansion house and behind the house was the lovely North Esk river. So after doing the necessary rounds I took good old Jimmy the Woof for a ramble along the river banks. Next time I visited Strathcathro there were numerous signs erected all round the driveways saying that dogs were not allowed. Charming I thought. Bureaucracy! Bureaucracy! The signs must have cost a fair bit of money. All authority really needed to do was to have a quiet word with me.

A CLASS OF ITS OWN

There was a good Primary School attached to St. Margaret's with a fine Head Teacher and I was very pleased when she agreed at once to my suggestion that he take part in the Preparation for Reception into the Church scheme. St. Margaret's had a large piece of green land behind the Church House but I was told that planning permission had been refused for the erection of bungalows on it. That would have been a means of raising some much needed money for the combined parishes.

A DUMPING GROUND

On one occasion I rose and went into our attached kitchen to make the customary porridge and found a member of the constabulary at the kitchen door with others looking around on the grass-land. The fine constable exclaimed that our grass land was a known dumping ground for thieves discarding what they did not want and on this occasion it was an empty safe. I told the blue-coated member of the law that I could have done with a full one. Of course the culprit was one of our ex-Glasgow fly-boys. Later he was to appear in the wee small hours drunk to the eye-balls on the grass and yelling loudly to be allowed into the church.

WHAUR'S THE KEY?

Upstairs in the decrepit old house I had seen that there was a large closed safe in one of the rooms. I could not fund a key for it. So I had a locksmith come out from Dundee open it. He said it would be no bother to get it open. But after five visits – no less – he ended up by drilling through the safe door. And, but of course, the safe was completely empty.

DO NOT TIDY

The sacristy in St. Margaret's was in my opinion a total mess, unlike the neat and tidy one in Brechin, so I started to clear it up. Oh! Dear! What a mistake. What I took for absolute junk was in fact objects gathered by old parishioners for some mysterious religious purposes. An elderly parishioner was most distressed that I had "evicted" her favourite large piece of driftwood. I went down to the beach and found a similar piece but that did not, but of course, sort the problem.

Then there was the mystery of coinage appearing round the altar tabernacle. (No one having gotten round to follow the advice of Vatican Two to have the tabernacle elsewhere other than behind the altar which is supposed to be the sole centre attraction of the sanctuary.) Eventually I discovered that because in their wisdom the politicos had closed down most of the once large Montrose Asylum (first of its kind in Scotland) a poor mentally-retarded lady would come into the church and climb up over the altar to give Jesus in the Tabernacle some money for food. Very distressing. It reminded me of the occasion at The Beda College when a mentally disturbed Asian student had climbed up to the Beda tabernacle and started to bang on it demanding that Jesus be released.

U S OF A – AGAIN

One morning a fairly tall woman appeared from the back of the church. Unfortunately she was wearing a sort of deer-stalker's bonnet with the ear flaps sticking out. Poor Jimmy the Woof took fright and for once barked loudly in alarm. It turned out that the "strange" lady and her non-Catholic husband were multi-millionaires who were normally resident in Manhattan but came to

Scotland in the summer months because they owned the fishing rights on both of the Esk rivers as well as a nearby range of hills about the size of the Cathkin Braes. When in Scotland they lived in a large expensive flat on a Kinnaird estate castle. Repeatedly I would be asked there for an evening meal. I did not enjoy travelling there and back in poor light because cataracts were beginning to affect my eyesight – never very great at the best of times. But I thought I better oblige in case some much needed money-benefit might accrue – not to me – but to the two parishes. In fact all I ever received from them was a small can of soup. No wonder millionaires are millionaires. And for the only time in my life I got to wear an expensive Barber jacket/coat. The good lady had asked me to accompany her on a walk along a bank of the South Esk river. It was quite a lengthy walk on a rain-filled miserable night and I was wondering what it was all about. Eventually we came to a pile of large stones obviously taken out of the river and arranged in a rough circle. Then she dropped the bombshell. "This is the site of a pre-Reformation chapel and I am going to build a new one here and you will come and celebrate Mass in it!" Holy mackerel! I hastily pointed out to her that my parish ended on the other side of the river and that in any case the bishop was hard-pressed as it was to find an adequate number of priests for the existing needs of his Diocese and he certainly would not allow that to happen. (And of course I later warned our man in Forfar what was afoot in his parish.)

Years before, the good Catholics of Tillicoultry had bought a piece of ground and were about to build their own church on it when they were banned from doing that great work by the Bishop. Not much Christianity in that decision and it certainly was not encouraging nor promoting ecclesia – the preparation for The Final Coming, that the Church is supposed to be about. Like many others I have often pondered about how Bishops are chosen and appointed. Certainly the lay members of the Church have little say in that. In truth it was surprising that the couple tried to be so nice to me because on an earlier occasion the woman had asked me what I thought about Medjugorje. Now I knew that the Franciscans in their Roma headquarters had told me that they thought it was all a bit of a con because the local bishop had been taking back parishes from religious orders and that the Franciscan parish of Medjugorge had been the next one on his list.

Additionally one of my Beda buddies had gone to the Adriatic coast and had taken the Ancona-Dubrovnic ferry in order to visit Medjugorge. When he returned he said to me that he had spoken to one of the girls concerned in the supposed apparition scenario and that she had told him that Our Lady had just told him that we were keeping Her birthday on the wrong date. We both thought that ridiculous. But there you go. So I told the millionairess that I thought that Medjugorge was a lot of nonsense. She replied that she was a Croat who had come into the church at Medjugorge. Me and my big mouth. It was a wonder that she ever bothered with me again.

WALK-DOGGING

On an afternoon I had the habit of taking Jimmy the Woof for his afternoon stroll along Montrose's West End Park. In truth this so-called park was just a narrow stretch of cultivation running alongside the main Dundee and Aberdeen railway line and of course my object in going there was also to see if anything of interest was happening on the line.

One afternoon I discovered that the bit of the park reserved for dog-poo had been removed and there was a poor dog-lover who complained to me that it had taken him two years to train his mutt to use the dog-poo spot and just as he had achieved that after much effort the dog lavatory had been closed. Instead the authorities had erected the now familiar dog-poo reception bins on top of tall poles.

On one occasion – just for a laugh – I asked another dog walker how my dog was supposed to get up the pole to use the dog bin. The sombre man took me seriously and carefully explained that I was supposed to lift the excrement with a bag and put that in the receptacle myself by hand. Silly me as usual. Me and my daft jokes. Fr. Bately S. J. (R.I.P.) – better known as "Baldy" for obvious reasons – told me several times I was far too frivolous. Reckon he was correct.

But on one occasion that West End Park nearly proved disastrous for me. A couple of very friendly and supportive Montrose parishioners had told me that they were going on a much-needed holiday (he being a University lecturer and she a secondary school teacher) and that accordingly they were putting their Springer Spaniel bitch Bracken into kennels while they were away. The Springer and myself and Jimmy always got on fine. (Unlike Jimmy with one of their two cats which would sit on the middle of their large kitchen floor wagging its tail until poor Jimmy, trying as usual to be friendly, would get within range and then it would lash out violently at him. Poor old Jimmy never learned.) I said that we would look after Bracken while they were away. At that time Stagecoach were trying the experiment of attaching one or two coaches to the night mail train from Aberdeen to London and occasionally I would go down to The West End Park at night to see the long train climb on to that long single-track viaduct over Montrose Basin. (Strange piece of single line as no staff seemed to be employed but reliance placed only on drivers obeying signals.)

One night I was standing in the Park watching proceedings in Montrose station while the Jimmy and Bracken were doing what dogs do – sniffing around. Too late I realised that Bracken had sniffed a trail important to her and was off running and following it up and onto and along the single-line viaduct and heading towards Arbroath. Nothing I could do but watch helplessly and say a quick prayer to St. Bruno. The night mail started to leave Montrose station and there was no sign of Bracken. I wondered if she had fallen into Montrose Basin. The train started to accelerate along and just when I thought all was lost, Bracken came racing back down happily wagging her tail. Phew! Perhaps she had felt the vibration of the rails and knew danger was coming towards her?

But a bigger and better joke was to happen in The West End Park. One afternoon I was sauntering along there behind Jimmy, dressed in my usual scruff-bag way when dog-walking. (We were allowed in the Diocese to dispense with Roman Collar etc. when not on duty.) I was trying to prepare my next sermon in what passed for my grey matter when I suddenly realised that an apparition was approaching me. (I was to meet a real apparition much later!)

This apparition was a real toff wearing top-hat and tails and in his right hand were a pair of kid gloves and an expensive looking cigarette holder. His left hand was holding a long lead to which was attached a little Mr. Jigg's dog. (Mr. Jiggs was a Daily Record rich cartoon hero of my youth. I always looked for Jiggs first in the morning before taking the paper home.) The two dogs did what dogs usually do and started to have a good sniff at their back-sides.

I was about to pass by, chuckling inside at that apparition, when the toff stopped me by waving the cigarette holder in my face, then he asked the sixty-four dollar question. "Excuse me!" he said. "Do you know why dogs sniff each other's arses?" Inwardly I was immediately thinking what a shock he would get if he knew what I was. So I replied with a mumbled "No!", while trying to suppress my laughter and thinking I might as well hear what was coming next. A bit of Theology came next!

The well-heeled gent said "God was doing (sic!) Creation and while he was doing It there was a fire in Heaven. The Archangel carrying the dog's arses got such a fright that he dropped the dog's arses and they all got mixed up. So every dog smells every other dog's arse to see if it has gotten the correct arse." I nodded and passed hurriedly on before exploding with laugher at the thought of how he would feel when he discovered he had been using such crudity to a Catholic priest.

ECUMENISM – ECUMENISM

I did not have long to wait before he had that come-uppance. Just the following week I was courteously invited to participate in the Installation of a new priest in the local St. Mary and St. Peter's Episcopal church. As I have said it had always bothered me that Bishop Logan never took the trouble to "install" me as a parish priest and I often wondered why not. I had to have the presumption that he had a poorish opinion of me. But later I was to find out that was not what he thought about me at all. Strange man Bishop Logan.

So there I was in all my glory participating in the introit parade down the central aisle of the splendid Episcopal Church – which put our poor building to shame and there to my unexpected delight near the end of a pew was the dog-walking toff!. I assure you that his jaw dropped a few inches when he saw me all dressed up in the procession. I gave him a wink and a cheery smile. At least I hoped that it was a cheery smile.

Another surprise awaited me. The installing Episcopal Bishop turned out to be none other than an old pal. Bob Halliday – or to give him his full nomenclature Robert Taylor Halliday. We used to sit and suffer together in Christian J. Fordyce's Latin class at Gilmorehill. In those days he told me that he was heading for the

Church of Scotland ministry – yet here he was now Episcopal Bishop of Brechin.

After the service I could not help myself making the jokey comment that he had succeeded to climb high up in the world while I had only managed to be a humble parish priest in a poor parish.

I thought my second-rate humour had not gone down too well and to make it worse someone informed me that the Bishop's wife was probably dying of cancer. No wonder the poor man was not in the mood for a joke. Me and my big mouth. Yet again.

BRECHIN SURVIVAL

In Brechin is the much altered and restored Cathedral once dedicated to the Trinity but now controlled by the Church of Scotland.

Kenneth the Second (971- 995) had founded in Brechin a monastic community for the Celi Dei (Culdee) monks who taught Christianity in the area. Then in the twelfth century, under David the First, Bishop Samson replaced the Culdees with a more modern monastic community and work for their monastery on the present cathedral site started. This work lasted through to the 15th Century. Through the subsequent ages there were several attempts made at reconstruction of that building – some very misguided –as frequently happened to ecclesiastical sites during the Victorian era. But a better reconstruction of the building was made around 1900.

It also has a celebrated historic round tower adjacent to it – the Irish style tower obviously dating from the 11th Century, This tower was a great attraction to Jimmy the Woof during his sniffs around it – unfortunately I did my best.
But I definitely kept his nibs well away from the magnificent Brechin Castle gardens – well worth a visit if you are touring up there as they are possibly the finest and most extensive in Scotland.

The Castle, too, obviously has its history – with Edward the First meeting Balliol there. And it had its involved history dating from the Norman Maules and Ramsays through Mar to the present Dalhousie family.

The Countess was extremely friendly to me – for some unfathomable reason – and was always suggesting that she could organise various activities to assist the Brechin parish financially.

But the Catholic parishioners wanted nothing to do with her or her assistance, which I found strange – but it was their parish after all. I liked the Brechin parishioners a lot, but never got to the bottom of that dislike for the Countess.

On one sad occasion I was summoned to make a sick call to the Castle. I was most courteously greeted at the Castle entrance (no draw-bridge!) by a butler attired in full regalia and shown to the very sick relative. After I had administered the Sacrament of the Sick, that gracious butler led me into what I suppose was the Castle drawing–room where as I was having a friendly chat with the Countess, the wonderful butler served me excellent coffee and cakes. Wow! That sure beat the fish and chip shop in Westmuir Street nae bother.

SCRAPE AND BOW!

But I was to have an entirely different style of encounter with Stourton – the Premier Earl of England – as he was in those days. In fact for some reason inexplicable to me he was also the third ranking Earl of England so a Baron twice over. He would be at Sunday Mass in Brechin when he was up in the Summer months visiting a shooting estate he had nearby. One Sunday after Mass I asked him if he would be good enough to arrange a day's shooting for friend Gerard Eadie, explaining that Gerard did a lot of unpaid expensive work for the Church. Big mistake! Stourton glared at me and snarled quite red-faced that he left that sort of thing to his estate manager and almost ran off.

Some time later I was relating the story to a Holy Ghost Father friend in Dunblane and he said that I had been lucky. I asked how could I be lucky when I had been so rudely insulted. Then came a tale. Allegedly that Stourton had fallen out with his father- the then Baron at Knaresborough Castle near Leeds – so the old man had left all the money necessary for the running of the estate and castle to a grandson though he could not prevent the titles passing to his son. But the latter had no money for castle and estate. The Bishop of Leeds had forbidden any priest to serve Knaresborough Castle and estate because that obviously mentally-disturbed old man had been seen thrashing a priest out of Knaresborough grounds with a horse-whip. Another allegation was that a keen young constable had given the old Baron Stourton a ticket for parking his vehicle in disobedience of the pedestrian crossing rules and regulations. The old Baron had been seen with a rifle searching Leeds for the young constable – who had to be transferred away from Leeds for his own safety. So no wonder my Holy Ghost friend said I was lucky only being treated with rudeness. May be my Guardian Angel was on the mark that Sunday!

OH! DEAR!

Ecumenism did exist in Montrose but not as comprehensively as in Kinross. A gathering of the clergy usually amused me. When I would enter the room for a chat or so, a poor wee soul would hunch himself up, mumble something, glower at me and rush from the room. I always resolved not to let my horns and forked tail show next time. You cannot win them all.

But, au contre, two of the Presbyterian ministers could not have been more welcoming or friendly. One in fact was to later marry a widowed parishioner as I will relate. The other I remembered as being the minister at Busby Church in Church Road, Busby.

Holy Week services were not very well attended in St. Margaret's. One Good Friday only nine people attended the important three o'clock service. One of them was a tremendous singer and I was truly thrilled. After the conclusion of the service I asked her was she new to St. Margaret's parish. Me and my big mouth again. It turned out that she was the wife of the former Busby minister and she had come to the service with a friend because they knew that I would not have many there to support me. That was true ecumenism I thought.

One year I attempted to improve Holy Week attendances by bringing up a priest friend from Glasgow to conduct Holy Week in Brechin while I concentrated a bit better on Montrose. But during that week we received an urgent call from Stracathro Hospital. (Stracathro was where Baliol was deposed by Edward the First.) There had been a car crash on the A90 in which a family were involved. The mother had been killed and father and sons injured. Of course we both rushed to the hospital and did what we could spiritually. The family belonged to a Catholic parish near Southampton so on return to Montrose I had the sad duty (as with the Airdrie baby) of notifying another parish of a fatality. But this time the priests at Southampton knew the casualties to be active parishioners.

After he had somewhat recovered later from his severe injuries the grieving widower explained the circumstances of the terrible accident. With the Easter week-end coming on the family had decided to use it to visit relatives near the Moray Firth. Quite a journey to make without an over-night stay. The husband had driven all the way from Southampton and naturally after passing Brechin he felt tired and wanted to stop for a breather. But unfortunately his wife had decided instead that they should change places instead. But, unaccountably, just after that happened she crashed the car through a hedge and into a field just after the Edzell turn-off. Requiescat in Pace.

Later came another sad business. The owners of a top-class hotel in Montrose had always been fine supportive parishioners and had me and Jimmy the Woof in for lunch any time I wanted to be there. But after fighting off a second cancer attack the husband lost his second battle and I was told that he had expressed a dying wish to be buried in his native Cockermouth and had wanted me to preside at the Funeral Rites.

I made the long journey to Cockermouth with heavy heart. My sadness deepened when on the way over from Carlisle I realised I was passing a milestone into which a once so cherry and uplifting pupil at John Ogilvie Hall had crashed and died while later in life delivering a new car. It was believed the poor lad had fallen asleep at the wheel.

I found Cockermouth an interesting enough historical place with the poet Wordsworth and mutineer Fletcher Christian being from the area. The residents were extremely down-to-earth and most courteous and friendly. I was greatly intrigued by a large toy museum (never ever having quite grown-up!) and also the River Cocker flowing into the Derwent and dividing the town. Cardinal Basil Hume liked to have a break and fish there.

The parish priest was also quite friendly. He told me that his greatest headache in Cockermouth was having highly-educated parishioners who were high-flyers at Sellafield and who would listen carefully to his homilies and then dispute with great detail what he had said. I thought lucky old him. I only once ever had a known reaction to something I said and that was in Kinross High

School when one of the school musicians blew me a raspberry at the end of my diatribe on St. Paul.

I soon realised that the Cockermouth self-important parish priest had no intention of allowing me to preside at the Funeral Mass. He was the parish priest after all and it was his duty to preside etc. Fair enough. I had no intention of having an up-and-downer on such a sad occasion so I went along with being an assistant in The Funeral Rites. Moreover one of the friendly Presbyterian ministers from Montrose had turned up and I twigged the reason for that. He and the widow were later married – which I thought was a good thing to happen. Unlike at my Ordination when Bishop Logan refused point-blank to have my non-Catholic clergy friends participate, the decent Cockermouth priest was most agreeable that the widow's Minister friend should have a speaking part in the proceedings. Pacee Bishop Logan: the Spirit is free to roam where it wills.

DIES IRAE

Despite being sad occasions for relatives and friends, funerals can occasionally be of interest to the presiding celebrant. The mother of a very prominent Scottish architect had asked that I be the priest to conduct her funeral. Why she wanted me to preside was a puzzle to me. After the Funeral Rites we all went to a brand new hotel in Dundee for the communal meal. I disliked the building and the way it was laid out. (Me and my Gothic tastes.) I was on the point of saying that I disliked the place when the Scottish architect asked me what I thought about his hotel design. Near miss. Near miss. I remembered the Garnethill Jesuits telling us that there can be certain occasions when it is not sinful to lie. So I uttered my admiration and hoped that was one of the permitted occasions.

I regularly visited an old Irish labourer living out his lonely life in Brechin. On one of his walls was a large marvellous picture of the great John Thomson. When he died and I was preparing to conduct his Funeral rites a nephew turned up out of the blue and he claimed that prize. Drat! When we took the remains into St. Ninian's Church I did the usual honour of placing a Bible and Crucifix on the coffin. Discussing the details of the next morning's funeral with my Funeral Director friend, he nudged me to turn round. Without so much as a courteous request, that know-all nephew had removed the Bible and Crucifix from the coffin and replaced them with the Irish Republican tricolour. I tried to be as reasonable as I could muster at Weddings and Funerals, so I simply replaced the Bible and Crucifix on top of the flag. The Funeral Director later was full of laughter and said that he thought that a black beret and gloves were going to go on to the coffin as well. I was not so amused at the insult to Crucifix and Bible. Then at the graveside I had to stand and listen to a woman wailing Danny Boy. Not that at my graveside please. "Going Home" hopefully then.

Brechin continued to be full of surprises. A man – only in his forties – had been a very active and helpful parishioner especially in the work of the St. Vincent de Paul Society. He had a long lingering death from cancer and I had paid many visits to his bed-side in Ninewells hospital. After conducting his funeral I went along to the family Brechin house for the customary pos- funeral meal and I was inwardly perplexed by all the nicotine-stained walls in a house where a lung-cancer sufferer had lived and was wondering why nicotine addicts sometimes cannot see the health problem nicotine can cause, when to my astonishment presentation was made to me of a Queen's Farrier product – namely an expensive large hand-tooled dog collar for Jimmy the Woof on which was beautifully engraved his name. This was to thank me for my services to the family. Wow! I never expected that.

Another grateful show of thanks was made to me in Montrose. A bereaved family came to me with the sad news that a young man belonging to the family had committed suicide. He had never appeared in St. Margaret's church in my time there but despite this the family members expressed their regret that a suicide could not receive a Catholic burial but asked if I at least could come to their house and say a prayer over his body. I explained to them that I would gladly give him a full Catholic burial, because the theological thinking about such a tragic occurrence as a suicide had advanced to the certain belief that there is a moment after death when everyone has the opportunity of deciding whether to say "Yea" or "Nay" to Christ.

Every week after that tragic funeral I received the family's thanks via a parcel of fresh herring.

Just as in the case of that disturbed young man it was always a sad disappointment to discover that there was an unknown-about Catholic in the parish who had died. This time it was back to

Brechin again. A widow wanted her deceased husband to have a Catholic burial. Because the deceased would have so many non-Catholic friends attending the obsequies it she did not want the funeral rite to be held in our fine St. Ninian's Church but only in my Funeral Director friend's parlour. I found that sad, but, as I have said previously, I never tried to increase a person's grief if I could avoid doing that, so I agreed to conduct the funeral rites in the Funeral Parlour as requested When I arrived at the Funeral Director's premises my friend apologised to me and said that he did not have an individual room where I could prepare for the funeral but did I mind doing that in his coffin room. That did not bother me. When I had vested in the coffin room there was still time to spare before the service. In front of me was a large expensive-looking coffin and I wondered what it was like inside, so curious me lifted the non-screwed down lid to have a look. I do not mean to be insulting about what I unexpectedly saw but I was shocked to be looking at a little man dressed cow-boy style with stetson, red neckerchief., cow-boy waistcoat, vest, chaps and boots. And this in Brechin not Leadville. Standing in that shock and amazement I suddenly realised that my Funeral Director friend was coming back to that room, so I hurriedly put the coffin lid back down. Then I was even more shattered. As he hurriedly screwed down the coffin lid, the Funeral director told me that the coffin contained the man I was to bury. I could have done with a large whisky after that but I dutifully followed the coffin into the Funeral Parlour to find it absolutely packed with mourners. That sight did not help my nerves at all. But I did my best to pull myself together, and thought that possibly the best way to introduce myself was to tell that my mother was born in Leadville, Colorado and that my grandmother was buried there, and this was at the time when Wyatt Earp, Doc Holliday and co. strode the Leadville side-walks, so may be it was appropriate that I was presiding at this funeral. There was no reaction to that. All I could see was a sea of faces staring blankly at me. Now it might be hard to understand, but when conducting a Catholic Funeral in a Catholic Church, I always felt a rapport between myself and the congregation. In that cold Funeral Parlour I had no such comfort. Anyway I just got on with it and did the usual best I could. Afterwards I thought that that was the worst funeral I had ever conducted and that I never wanted to go through that awful experience again. Later I was recounting my experience to a Montrose parishioner and saying how staggered I had been when I had opened that coffin lid. To my further shock/horror that parishioner drew himself up and gave me a cold look of disdain, saying proudly that his father had been buried in his Confederate Lieutenants' uniform. Me and my big mouth again! I wondered what went on behind the scenes in that neck of the woods.

And then a few weeks later I was informed of yet another death in Brechin of a Catholic I had not known about. That news distressed me as usual. I went to visit the bereaved husband to explain that I had previously agreed to conduct a Funeral in St. Margaret's on the same date and time (Funeral Directors tend to arrange Funerals at a time that suits their purposes not the presiding clergyman) that he wanted his wife buried but that the American Catholic Chaplain from Edzell would gladly conduct his wife's funeral for him. Then more surprise and astonishment for me. He said that his wife would be most disappointed about that because she with others had been so impressed with the way in which I had conducted that previous Funeral Parlour funeral that she had said to him "That is the man I want to bury me!" Wish I had been told after that previous funeral that I had been so impressive!

ARS GRATIA ARTIS

I discovered that I had a parishioner who was a wonderful artist but seemed to be a recovering drug addict. I did my best to help him. The local paper took him on as a sketch/cartoon/headline artist. To find out more about his past so that I might better be of assistance to his continued recovery I travelled all the way down to Paisley to obtain information about his past from a priest he had said he had known there. That lengthy journey was a complete waste of time and effort for although the priest concerned confirmed that he knew the artist he could not or would not tell me anything of my parishioner's past. I wondered if he was concealing something rather serious or if it was the case that he had not bothered to find out more about a person needing help. Once when a guest at Celtic Park, I had noticed that there was a very fine large coloured picture of the White Star liner "Celtic" hanging on a wall of the board room.. I knew that the London and North

Western Railway engineer Webb had constructed a class of his compound engines named after the White Star liners and that one of them was called "Celtic". To help my recovering parishioner I commissioned him to do an oil-painting of the L.N.W R compound. But an artist being an artist he would not do exactly what I wanted but insisted in putting me in its cab as the engine driver. Oh! Dear!

I had a plaque attached to the frame of the picture informing that it was in memory of my father and mother – great Celtic supporters. Sir Robert Kelly was kind enough to receive the painting from me and I know it was hung in the Celtic Park boardroom where I saw it. But in later days after the McCann take-over I never saw it again and I have often wondered what happened to it. Does anyone know?

ENVOI

I liked Brechin and Edzell and the countryside surrounding both parishes quite a lot. I just loved going with Jimmy the Woof to Lunan Bay or Buddin Point or following the disused railway track bed along the coast to Johnshaven and Inverbervie. And of course Jimmy delighted in swimming in sea and river estuaries. We thought about having a replacement narrow-gauge tourist railway to Inverbervie but, with little forethought, housing-developments had been allowed to take pace on the old right of way.

Who wouldn't love the Angus countryside after Beardmore's Parkhead noisy smoke-filled Forge and the east end of Glasgow.

But I thought Montrose itself to be a quite wretched, depressing place. Unlike the great people of Girvan, Montrosians, by and large, had no time for our tail-wagging friends.

On the narrow winding streets of the old-part of the town, youths would drive, chasing each other at top speed and scaring me and Jimmy stiff when I was trudging around trying to do some parish visiting. The local Police kept well clear of that offensive behaviour but did not mind booking a parishioner on the way from the countryside for Sunday Mass for doing a few miles over the speed limit. That happened more than once. I suppose it was much easier to carry out their required quota of stops that way instead of tackling unruly and cheeky youths.

In the centre of Montrose was what could have been a really attractive large market square but unfortunately its boundary shop-frontages had been allowed to develop in an ugly higgledy-piggledy fashion and it looked positively unpleasant. The golf-links were pretty dreary too, leading away to some un-removed derelict buildings from the once supposedly – haunted First World War air-field. Neither Jimmy nor myself detected any presence and he for sure would have known if anything untoward was about. (As I suggested when writing about Kinross, I have always been certain that dogs have an extra sensory dimension unknown to humans.)

There was, distant from the town itself, a lengthy forlorn beach surmounted by a long high cliff of sand. Two children were killed when the part of the sand-cliff they were tunnelling into collapsed onto them.

Then there was the almost continual stench, dirt and obnoxious smoke from the daily operation of a North Sea oil fire instruction site. And as if that was not enough there was the stench and continuous sea pollution coming from the Glaxo-Cline chemical complex along Cobden Street. And its beer-house was on a corner adjacent to our church property and that was a continuous nuisance too with the intoxicates that would noisily stagger about coming from it.

MORE ATTRACTIVE PLACES

Across the South Esk was the small place of Ferryden. This too disappointed me because I knew that one of the great heroes of my youth, Peter F Anson had retired there. Mr. Anson produced great literature on places of historical Catholic interest and I would eagerly devour the sketches of Catholic places made while travelling round the United Kingdom by horse and caravan. Peter Anson was a founder member of Stella Maris – The Apostleship of the Sea. He had only died in 1975 and though there was a group of very active Catholics living in Ferryden I could not find anyone who had the remotest memory of my wonderful hero. That was extremely puzzling. (If you can lay your hands on any of his forty-plus books you would find it as rewarding as I once did.)

The road through Ferryden continued on to the magnificent Cruden Bay lighthouse. By my time this had become a family dwelling. Still. I could see (water-spouts permitting!) the far-off even more stupendous Bell Rock light. So although I knew that I would be leaving a town steeped in past history (Douglas leaving there with Bruce's heart: participation in both '15 and '75 risings: and so on) when I saw something I would prefer doing I took that opportunity. But, as life often has it, events did not work out as I had expected.

The kind-hearted parishioners of Tullibody had been so generous and good to me at the time of my Ordination there, that I always, and still have, had a soft spot for them – especially as it seemed to me that their defiance of what Bishop Logan wanted to happen after the Ordination had caused Tullibody to lose Parish status.

I knew that there had been a great tragedy there. At a parish youth evening there one of the participants had managed to kill himself by sniffing too much of the contents of a gas canister. Obviously after that sad happening the parish priest responsible for the youth club would have to be replaced. So I travelled to Dundee and most politely asked Bishop Logan if I could be the replacement for him. The Bishop surprised me by immediately agreeing to that request. I travelled back to Montrose a very happy man, delighted that I could in some little way thank the Tullibody parishioners for their superb kindness to me.

I should have known better. Instead of receiving a letter appointing me to Tullibody, I received an appointment to Whitfield. Presumably Vicar General Creegan had had Logan by the nose again. I never received any reason or apology for that change. But I think I discovered the reason later.

IGNORANCE OF HISTORY

Before leaving Montrose – with a great sigh of relief – I was privileged to celebrate an Ecumenical Mass in Brechin which was very well attended by our separated brethren as intended. It was great to see St. Ninian's fairly full for a change. To mark the occasion – as I mistakenly thought – I included in the Eucharistic Prayer the names of many of our Scottish Saints – Sts. Ninian, Columcille, Fillan, Serf, Drostan, Thenog and Kentigern and Donnan being obvious ones. But to my astonishment and dismay, after Mass a knot of Presbyterians gathered round me and asked me what I thought I was doing praying to their Saints! Well! I think the Saints themselves knew better than that piece of ignorance.

ANOTHER ATTEMPT

Then just as I was getting prepared to leave, an old friend turned up. I was going round the parish making my farewells when the well-known burglarising villain attempted to break into the Church House. Little did he realise that some of the excellent women parishioners were cleaning the church. (Why do men rarely become involved in church cleaning?) The good ladies heard the noise he was making in his attempt to break into the Church House and rushed out to confront him. In his haste to be off he abandoned a rather costly smart bicycle. On my return I contacted the local Police, told them the tale, and asked them to retrieve the bike in case someone was looking for his property. A large and well-built young constable eventually arrived and when he had examined the bike he radioed his Police Office and asked his sergeant for a van to be sent to collect the machine. I have the occasional chuckle yet because of the Sergeant's reply to that request. Leaving out the unprintable words he responded "You are a big young fit man. Get on the bike and ride it back to the Station!"

GIRL TROUBLE YET AGAIN

And then I had again to avoid having a teen-age girl in the Church house. A fine couple of active and helpful parishioners had adopted young coloured girl into their existing family of children. But as the coloured girl grew older she began to play up. The only reason the parishioners could work out for the increased misbehaviour was that the adopted girl resented the colour difference between her and the Montrose original family. To try to resolve their difficulty, when the adopted girl came of the age to do this they bought and furnished a flat for her in Montrose. A nasty critical rumour that they had just thrown her out on to the street swept through Montrose and my parishioners had to threaten legal action to have the canard halted. But the coloured girl proceeded to wreck the flat and furnishings bought for her and ran a bit wild in the town. A Presbyterian minister's daughter tried to befriend her and persuaded her minister father to take her into his Manse. But after putting up with her still violent and unpleasant behaviour for a week or so the minister phoned me and tried to make the point that as her parish priest I should be taking her into my house.

No need to write what I replied to that suggestion. Imagine the scandal that would have caused – an elderly priest living with a teenage girl.

Sadly, later, even greater scandals were to sicken the Bishop and Diocese of Dunkeld and our Church in Scotland.

The good news is that I have since heard that the girl concerned had sorted out her life and had done quite well. Deo gratias.

Do not tell me that prayer for a good cause does not work. Memorare! Memorare!

We had two quite similar tragic cases of ex-railwaymen dying of throat cancer. And they both put it down to the same cause. Both had been steam engine firemen. One had been the regular fireman on the Inverness-Helmsdale heavy night goods and the other poor soul had fired on trains from Manchester up through the many long tunnels on the old Lancashire and Yorkshire lines that climbed through the Pennines. Both fine men blamed the smoke and soot conditions on steam engines for their disease. Requiescant in pace.

A parishioner was on the Parole board for Scotland. Regularly he would boast to me that he had arranged for this prisoner and that prisoner to obtain early release from prison. Being a former prison chaplain I found that a bit wearing but eventually I asked him did he never think of asking the victims of crime or the neighbours to whom a prisoner would be returning what they thought of him obtaining an early release. His prim and self-satisfied reply was that that was not part of his remit. To which I retorted, too smartly perhaps, that, but of course it ought to be.

NO LUCKY STARS, PLEASE

I had wanted our parishioner-owner of the local newspaper to replace his pagan Astrology feature with a local Christian ecumenical column but got no-where with the good idea. Then later I heard him boasting on a radio "Thought for the Day" programme that it was his daughter who produced the Astrology feature. No wonder I got nowhere with him and no wonder I was glad to leave Montrose. Before leaving I had offered to purchase a house in Brechin (a place I liked very much) and serve Stracathro Hospital and RAF Edzell from there but Bishop Logan and his cohorts would not have that.

WHITFIELD

I went off to Whitfield – a place I had know as a Deacon and knew to be entirely unsuited to me and especially Jimmy the Woof as the few large Swedish type blocks did not allow dogs in. The over-ambitious plan intended to relieve some of Dundee's housing over-crowding problems, was to construct a vast estate of tall Swedish-type high-rise blocks. Unfortunately for the plan, after only a few blocks had been constructed for one of the U.K.'s last high-rise projects, it was realised too late that the Swedish type of housing was not acceptable and was not liked by those who had moved in originally and so the rest of the scheme was abandoned. (In apparent desperation and in order to have someone living in what had been built, the Dundee Council seemed to have been ready to ignore a frequent tax and compensation racket that I observed. A couple, happily married and living together in down-town Dundee, would have one of the couple taking a flat in Whitfield and then claiming with that address to be separated from partner etc. Wonder what that cost the tax payer?)

Unfortunately too, the Dunkeld Diocese had anticipated the needs of what was expected to be a vast housing complex and had constructed a large church holding about a thousand seated. Some time after I had been there as a Deacon and the completion of the huge scheme was abandoned, St. Matthew's Church was divided into a hall and a church. Even the smaller church was still far too large. I was to discover that we only had a smallish number of Whitfield residents attending Mass – with some outsiders coming in.

There was also a self-contained Christian community that had to be served on request – though they too occasionally came to Mass in St. Matthew's.

The almost war-time pre-fab style single-story church house was frightening to inhabit. I soon realised that it was impossible to have the usual evening devotions in the Church itself without a house burglary taking place.

So in that apology for a house I could not re-erect my large model tramway (24 trams!) nor decorate the walls with any of my greatly revered and very valuable collection of tramway pictures and Celtic memorabilia collected over many years.

To save my "treasured" possessions I had to make several trips to the dear green place where friends and relatives were kind enough to store them for me in their lofts.

I envied the Chancellor who was wealthy enough to decline the use of his equally unsafe parish church house but had chosen instead to live in a protected private house. No such luck for me. Did not have the Chancellor's wealth – he having been a prosperous chartered-accountant. My predecessor had been allowed to spend what he needed but I was put on a strict financial budget of a set grant from the Diocese – which was far from adequate.

For example: the church was freezing cold in winter – especially when the quite inadequate church hearing boiler broke down. Quite the opposite to the Kinross heating problem! When I complained to the Chancellor he insisted that a new boiler had been installed. Even when I had him in to see that it was in fact a second-hand used boiler I still got nowhere with him. So myself and the few attending parishioners just had to shiver.

Hard to understand that the Diocese – as I often found to be the case – could let dishonest tradesmen so easily take them to the cleaners like that. (And as I have said before, at the Beda my pal Joe – also a former H T – from Lancashire – said to the Beda Rector in a general discussion re what could be improved in the Beda, that the College should have a course on Domestic Science but unfortunately that there would not be any cleric available with the knowledge to carry that out.)

But of course in the good old Glasgow Education Service we took it for granted that we always had three good boilers attached to each building – one for normal use, a second one for very cold weather, and a third as a stand-by while one of the others was being serviced.

And I could not get the heating system supply changed from oil to gas -- the unsecured oil-storage tank being wide-open to thieves too, as was the flimsy exterior garage.

To try to give more comfort to Mass attendees I wanted to celebrate week-day Mass in the biggest room in the Church house.

But my predecessor – no doubt for a good purpose – let someone fill it with a family's furniture. So it took a while to get the furniture out. For to start with I could not find out whose furniture it was. Then I had a job having them take it away.

Our church hall was the objective of the local fly-boys for their own nefarious money grabbing purposes – false reasoning like wanting it for birthday parties etc. – for requisitioning the hall were made, and it took them a while to realise they were dealing with a Glasgow fly-boy who was well up to their nefarious tricks.

WHERE WAS THE LAW ENFORCEMENT?

On one occasion a local ned pulled a gun on a parishioner working in the Whitfield grocery store but she calmly named him and told him not to be so silly and to put the gun away.

I was very simpatico with an AA group that we allowed to use our premises but they had to stop coming as their cars were frequently broken into or damaged when parked outside St. Matthew's.

Complaint to the Police from me was a waste of time. All I had back from Dundee Police was a visit from an obviously over-weight desk sergeant who said that complaints had to come from the car owners by themselves and the Police had never had had one from them. I asked him did it never occur to him that AA members would not want to draw attention to their problem in that way. But I got nowhere and I never ever saw police presence outside our church premises. The extensive grounds had its edges filled with litter and rubbish, so I kept watch and sure enough there was the local road-sweeper dumping material over our boundary fence instead of properly removing it. Though I complained to the Council the practice did not cease and with the small parishioner numbers I could not have a proper cautionary watch kept on the miscreant.

Our grounds too were used by residents as a short-cut to the Whitrfield's small row of shops – which caused me to worry about the safety of Jimmy the Woof when he was outside in the grounds as the trespassers would carelessly leave our gates wide open.

CONGREGATION OF THE GOOD SHEPHERD

In one of the blocks of flats there was a tiny convent with a compliment of three nuns. They had to be attended to of course but were never a problem – except that I could not take my faithful friend into that building. Well! Not officially anyway. Two of the nuns were "retired" and I had great admiration for the younger third one who was in Dundee at night trying to improve the lot of the usual ever-present female night-life. The good nuns helped to look after a sad and tragic parishioner who was obviously dying. The saddest of all the sad cases I ever had to deal with had been an A B sailor wounded on a destroyer sunk during the famous Warspite and destroyer raid up a narrow Narvik ford. He had to be breathing from an oxygen bottle at all times and occasionally when his caring wife could not find an oxygen bottle replacement for him, then myself and one of the nuns would go scouring Dundee and district for the urgently needed replacement. But then we went to the invalid's house one morning and the house was empty. It transpired – after a bit of detective work – that poor sufferer had died as expected: a brother had arranged for his body to be removed: and another priest had carried out his funeral without having the courtesy to let us know. Requiescat in pace.

There were several old parishioners attending St. Matthew's who had been priest-house-keepers and I immediately recognised one who had refused me entrance when I had needed to speak to her Alloa priest on a matter of some urgency. Of course a few of the old dears – who had been house-keepers to Irish parish priests working in the Dunkeld Diocese – thought that they knew more about the liturgy and running a church than myself. But I very much respected one old dear who had given fifty years of her life to be a priest's house-keeper and was left high and dry when the last of her parish priests died. I went to Bishop Logan and tried to have him award her a "Bene Merenti" medal at least. But he flatly refused and just was not at all interested in doing anything for my parishioner. Yet that same week he obtained a high Papal Honour for the diocesan lawyer. No need to put into print what I felt about that hurt.

PRESENCE FELT

A family moved into the district and came to me to complain that there was an apparition appearing in their kitchen. I immediately remembered the story of my aunt and cousins living in a Shettleston tenement flat and their bathroom door mysteriously opening in the night. It was only when they had moved to Ardmillan Street in the decent pre-war Carntyne housing scheme, that a visitor asked them how they had managed to survive the bathroom presence in their Shettleston abode. Apparently it had been well known about locally that that bathroom had been the scene of a man's suicide.

The Whitfield family wanted me to carry out an exorcism but we had been well-warned by a Vatican expert on such matters that under no circumstances were we to attempt to do that. He made it quite clear that carrying out an exorcism could be quite dangerous and should only be attempted by a thoroughly well-trained exorcist. The Vatican Monsignor advised us that every diocese would have an appointed specialist exorcist who would be kept anonymous for obvious reasons. So I approached Bishop Logan to obtain the services of such a specialist, only to be told that the Diocese did not have one and he ordered me to carry out the exorcism myself. There was no way I was going to obey that command, justifying my disobedience on the strength of The Vatican expert's strict warning

GOOD OLD BRYLCREEM AGAIN

The parish priest of St. Fillan's, Newport-on-Tay, was quite ill and I was delighted to be able to cross the Tay to help out there because it also meant celebrating Mass for RAF Leuchars. Being back in an operational RAF station gave me a great thrill, but, having to collect keys from the guardroom etc. I cracked the old joke about not being in the Guardroom on a fizzer but that AC2 did not get y poor attempt at a joke.

NEAR MISS

As I said before the ground access gates would be carelessly left open and on one occasion I went out to bring Jimmy the Woof into the house and was just in time to see him almost run-over by a double-deck bus. That was another of the causes that made me realise that Whitfield was not a place I wanted to be long-term.

I went to Bishop Logan and said that I intended to leave his Diocese and go back to Glasgow as Cardinal Winning said I could do since I was entitled to change Dioceses after six years in a Diocese.

The Bishop appeared concerned and for once his side-kick the Vicar-General was not with him. He said that since Whitfield did not suit me he would send me to St. Joseph the Worker parish in Callander if I would like that. I certainly had not expected that consideration. I accepted the suggested change with delight as both Jimmy the Woof and myself were avid hill walkers and Jimmy would also have the choice of Lochs Vennachar or Lubnaig to pursue his delight in swimming as well as the Endrick.

But as usual I should have known better. Next time I had occasion to meet the Bishop I asked him how my projected move to Callander was going. Abruptly he denied point-blank that he had ever mentioned such a move to me. (Much later in life I was to be told that the priest in Callander – a former Franciscan- had refused to accept a move away from Callander – not that I would have wanted him to do that if he did not want to do so.)

Next I heard on the grape-vine and not directly – as was more than usual with Bishop Logan – that he intended me to go to a parish where I would have had two other parishes to attend to.

As I had found – with my deteriorating eye-sight – that driving around Montrose and Brechin was scary, I certainly was not going to attempt that scenario with three parishes to look after. So I arranged a visit to Bishop Logan's headquarters to make my fare-well. Again I should have known better. I was kept kicking my heels for nearly two hours while he conferred with Vicar-General Creagan. Being admitted at last to the esteemed presence his Lordship kept waving his sheet of paper in my face (as usual – he was a great believer in single sheets of paper) to inform me of my next appointment. As I have written I already knew what it was. I just sat and said nothing. But when the Vicar-General had temerity to ask me what was wrong with being in Whitfield, I suggested that if he thought it was such a great place then why was he not going there himself and at that point I just stood up, went out the door and left the Diocese next day. A very sad end to what I had hoped would be a good stage in my life – being useful to others.

NO HELP ELSEWHERE

On the way down to the dear Green Place I had a thought that perhaps the Motherwell Diocese might be a better habitat for my dear friend Jimmy the Woof than the busy streets of Glasgow. So again not knowing better – though I should have done by this time – I arranged an appointment with the Bishop of Motherwell. I was sadly mistaken in thinking he would be friendly, because his very first duty after being appointed an Auxiliary Bishop for the Archdiocese of Glasgow – along with my school class-mate friend Donnie Renfrew – was to assist at Confirmation for The Wee Maggie. I was to discover that Joe Devine and Vincent Logan had had a confab during which then Bishop of Motherwell was informed that I was just some kind of flibbertyjibbet – always wanting to change parishes. Really? Judge that for your good selves. Asking for two appointment changes with reasons is always asking for appointment changes?

And then came a disclosure quite revealing to me. Bishop Logan had told the Bishop of Motherwell that he had put me in the "rotten" – repeat "rotten" – parishes because I was a "hard man"! Obviously being from Bathgate and not the East End of Glasgow, Bishop Logan really had no idea of what a "hard man" really was. I certainly never ever thought of myself as being anything other than a run-of-the-mill person. I certainly would stand-up for what I thought was right or indeed my right – but nothing more than that. I was thoroughly horrified that a supposed Bishop of the Flock could describe three of his parishes as "rotten". And I had described Kinross to Bishop Logan in glowing terms and had no impression that Montrose/Brechin was a "rotten" parish either. Quite the contrary. Shocked, I immediately said a prayer for them. Then I thought that perhaps that belief of Bishop Logan was the reason why he had never gone to the bother of properly installing me in any of the three parishes? That had always been a worry to me.

But it was obvious that Bishop Devine wanted nothing to do with me and I road-journeyed back to Glasgow thinking that I should have had the courage to go to the Diocese of Colorado

Springs and tried to get an appointment to dear old Leadville – which was certainly not a place with two "rotten" parishes.

So I then went to see Tom Winning who had said that I would always be welcome back in his Archdiocese. Well that was true except that all he could offer me was an appointment as a Hospital Chaplain (after I had made my peace with Bishop Logan). Since I had spent so many months of my life attending a sick mother in hospital and had already twice been a Hospital Chaplain (Perth General with Bridge of Earn and Stracathro with the Royal Infirmaries of Montrose and Brechin) and since it was also a no-no for Jimmy the Woof, I respectfully declined the offer and no other was made.

UDDINGSTON

The name Uddingston originated with the Angles who arrived in the area around AD 700. The original spelling of the name was Odistoun, meaning the homestead of Oda. It gradually evolved into Evison and later to Udiston.

St. Molaise was Uddingston's own Saint and a church dedicated to her existed until 1852 when it was covered by the Caledonian Railway's embankment coming from the Clyde Bridge. Not many saints there these days but plenty of sinners.

St. Molaise (AD 566 – 736) was a protégée of Pope Gregory the Great and for a time Molaisec dwelt in a cave on the Firth of Clyde's Holy Island. At one time Holy Island was part of the Duke of Hamilton's Arran estate – hence the Saint's Lanarkshire dedication.

Certainly there was a bronze-age settlement at Kyle Park by the Clyde. And there was a Roman road that passed by to the East of the present M74 motorway.

Uddingston was once famous for well-made ploughs. But these days its fame rests with Tunnock's masses of marshmallows and other pastries and it is a noted Call Services and cable TV centre. In the pre-motor car era Celtic followers from Glasgow would take the tram to Uddingston and then walk all the way through Bothwell and over the Covenanters' Bridge to Old Douglas Park and of course return that way after a match. People were quite used to long walks in those days.

In my younger days our families just loved taking that tram out to the then quiet, peaceful and picturesque village of Uddingston – perhaps to visit the historic Cricket ground or the more historic Bothwell Castle. As I have described in my book of reminiscences of Glasgow Corporation Trams, when I was but ten years old, my dad let me operate his brand-new magnificent Coronation car the miles from Mount Vernon to Uddingston. So I thought retiring to Uddingston would suit me fine and let me relive my nostalgia .So I made yet another of my life's mistakes by retiring there. It had now become gang-ridden (including arsonists) and crowded and the district was now home to numerous highly-paid professional players of the Old Firm. Paul McStay lived just across the road and I would have – it has to be said – also pleasant encounters with personalities such as Archie McPherson (whom of course I knew from my Garrowhill days); Alex McLeish with his wee Scottie; Tom Boyd and so on.

When the Lanarkshire Tramway Company's rails reached Uddingston from Hamilton and Bothwell, the honour of laying then last sets between then rails went to the then Mr. Tunnock of bakery fame. The same honour was given to Mr. Tunnock when Glasgow tracks came up into Uddingston Main Street from Tollcross and Mount Vernon. I had once seen the Mr. Tunnock metal commemorative plaque that had been laid between the rails at the Glasgow cross-over. With the trams all sadly gone from Uddingston (at one time it was possible to travel from Newmains to Loch Lomond by tram!), I presumed that that commemorative plaque would be preserved in Tunnock's bakery, so I went in and asked the present Mr. Tunnock if I could be allowed to take a picture of the plaque for fellow tram preservationists. Mr. Tunnock was most friendly and agreeable but search as he did the plaque had disappeared, obviously stolen by a half-baked preservationist – as so many transport relics have been stolen in the past.

After chatting to me about my interest in tram preservation, unasked, that fine gentleman gave me an unexpected wonderful £500 cheque to help with the restoration of GCT's ex-Paisley school car 1017.

Another prominent confectioner I encountered was not so open-minded. A friend said that his father was looking for a partner to play in a weekly bridge tournament at Drumpellier – so I obliged. We won the tournament for two weeks running (boast!

boast!) and were awarded second place for the third week' event. Going round the tables during the fourth week a friendly lady opponent expressed the view that she felt sorry for the way we had been cheated at the third week's event. We expressed some surprise and replied that we had come in second. Not so came the reply. You were first place winners again, but the committee decided that they were not having two visitors come in and win the tournament for three weeks running and changed you down to second. And who was the chairman of the committee that allowed – or wanted – that to happen? He owned that Coatbridge firm famous for its excellent mouth-watering slabs!

When I would find Jimmy the Woof missing in Uddingston I just had to walk round to Tunnock's. The old boy would be happily sniffing around the large bakery.

And some talk about dumb animals...

WHAT A SURPRISE!

Then unexpectedly Bishop Logan gave me a big chuckle for a change. He sent me a hastily scribbled note which informed me that I could not practice as a priest in Glasgow! Once again the Bathgate lad did not know his geography. News to me that Uddingston was in Glasgow. And I also wondered if that instruction meant that I could practice as a priest outside of Glasgow. But no matter. What really tickled me pink was his last sentence which said I would be welcome back in the Dunkeld Diocese any time I wanted to return. And this from a Bishop who had told a fellow member of the hierarchy that I was some kind of a pest. And me that I needed to learn how to be a parish priest. When Italian club Chievo of Verona had aspirations for greater things it was said of them that for them to reach Seria A "pigs might fly" and so when they achieved Seria A status their nickname became "The Flying Pigs". I too uncharitably thought of flying pigs when I read Bishop Logan's last scribbled sentence.

Later, sadly, came the great public scandal of his retired Vicar General having his two mistresses squabbling over him. Thankfully, although I suspected as well that some other priests in the Diocese had mistresses, I genuinely never heard a word about that other great modern Catholic priest scandal – "child abuse" – occurring in the Dunkeld Diocese.

FLASH-BACKS

At one Celtic game I had a real-up-and-downer with a fellow standite about interpreting an incident on the field. After I had calmed down a wee bit, I discovered that my father could scarcely contain his mirth. I asked him what the joke was. He could hardly get the words out for laughing. "You have just told the one-and-only Tommy McInally that he knows nothing about football." O.K. Big mouth struck again! Tommy had been a great favourite with the Celtic fans but not with Maley and some of then players who did not look favourably on his irrepressible sense of fun and humour unlike the supporters. Although he had scored 127 goals in his two Paradise spells he was sold on to Sunderland. Dad told me that once an opposing centre-half had shouted at Tommy "I'll eat you!" Supposedly McInally's reply was "Then you would have some football in you!"

CELTIC AGMs

A great pal who was in the revenue and was posted to Workington said he would give me his proxy vote to attend the Celtic AGM.

On one occasion chairman Desmond White ranted about the huge number of stand passes that were being given out and so costing the club much-needed cash. Jock Stein said nothing at the time but went to the season-ticket gateman and asked him to write the name of the donor on the back of every stand pass that was presented to him. Jock collected a huge wad of stand passes and at the next annual general meeting pulled the passes out and told us all that by far the greater number of stand passes had been given out by White himself. No doubt such an incident would be one of the factors leading to the worsening deterioration in relationship between the two.

One year season ticket holders like myself had to pay admission to the stand in order to be able to buy tickets for cup matches. I complained about this at the next A.G.M and white had the cheek to reply that it had never happened. But I had written down chapter and verse and quoted the facts back at him. I then noticed Bob Kelly having a good smile and realised that relationship between the two was not too good.

TOLLCROSS

One Saturday afternoon Dad was taking his tram along Tollcross Road when he realised that McGrory and trainer Dowdalls were walking along the pavement at three-thirty with a match on at Celtic Park. Of course he stopped his tram and went over to ask them why they were there and not in attendance at the game. They bitterly complained that they had carefully selected a team for the match and had put their team sheet up on the dressing-room board. But just before kick-off time **B**ob Kelly had come in and had taken down their team selection and had replaced it with his own. So they had left in anger and disgust – leaving Kelly to it.

CATHKIN

It was a snow-swept Glasgow day but the good old trams took me cheaply and efficiently and safely to Cathkin Park. We fans stood in the snow for some time, and, very late, a game kicked-of in the snow. Of course we did not realise it was just agreed to be a friendly. Amazing how folk-lore can sometimes come true. Just it was said that Jambos would not win a trophy as long as trams ran along Gorgie Road, sure enough when then trams sadly stopped running on that route Hearts did win a trophy. So it was with Thirds. The credo was that if they ever renewed their decrepit old stand, then that would be the end of the club. George Young, – as great a manager as he was a player – had an excellent red-shirted team playing excellent football that was a treat to watch. There was a neat new stand erected. But the club was bought by a quick-buck merchant who closed it down and sold the ground for a housing development that never took place while he airted off to a hotel he bought in Blackpool with the proceeds.

GREAT RIGHT HOOK

Around 1948 I managed home from Kinloss for an Old Firm battle. And battle it turned out to be. The Celtic goalie of the time was Lucca born Ulando Ugolini, Badly fouled by one of their forwards, Ugolini rose to his feet and swung a perfectly-aimed right hook that left the offender lying out cold on the turf. Ugolini then turned and retrieved his cap from the goal-net and calmly walked off the pitch. Of course that made him a great hero of mine, but not to the Celtic Board who quickly transfered him – like so-many other Celts – to Middlesborough.

PITTODRIE PAIN AGAIN

There I was – dressed in business suit and traversing peacefully along the narrow pavement outside the Pittodrie stand intending to reach the gate for my ticket when a large policeman turned and hurled mouthfuls of foul language – such as I had never heard since my RAF days when a Fitter fell off a Lancaster engine. I kept my cool – for once – and walked steadily on past. But when I was ensconced in my Pittodrie stand seat I wondered why I had been subject to that abuse. Then the proverbial penny dropped. Was he in fact that bully who had yanked me off the Kinross train that night and had he re-recognised me in my civilian suit? Anyway, he was no credit to the Aberdeen Police Force – but I suppose they were not bothered about something like that?

It was one night at Pittodrie too that I was thrilled by then display of wonderful Davy Hay as he took on the might of Aberdeen single-handed and won. That reminded of the time that one and only individualistic and great Willie Fernie did the same to Hibs one day at Easter Road.

F'R'IL FOR THRILLS!

I was late in getting to Firhill for the Jags game because I had spent too much time investigating details of the circular Queens Cross turn-back overhead recently erected for the trolley-buses ("whispering death" to Glaswegians!) I was shocked to find – not tidy impatient turnstile queues for ground entrance – but a huge milling crowd filling and jostling in the street outside the ground. I was thinking of walking away round Firhill to take a place on the "Aberdeen stand" – that is the canal bank over-looking the terracing, when to my astonishment I found myself actually inside then ground without moving at all. Later it became obvious that someone had unbolted the large exit doors from inside and the mob had just swarmed in taking me with it. Of course I later sent a postal-order to the Jags but that was frightening in the extreme.

TIMS GET TO-GETHER

The school was due to have the Glasgow Education Department "high-heid yin" in charge of Sewing/Handwork coming to us to se if we were properly doing what we ought to be doing in regard to Sewing and Handwork. I was not worried abut that, being very interested in the "hands-on" approach to life following on my RAF "hands-on" position. It soon transpired that my visitor was non-other than a sister of fabulous inside-forward Sammy Wilson who, coming from St. Mirren (on a free transfer!) had that great and still fondly remembered partnership with Billy McPhail, and was scorer of over forty goals (including the famous one that set the unforgettable seven-one day alight) before Billy decided he would rather be a restaurateur than a great Celtic hero. Well! You know what happens when two died-in-the-wool Tims get started to talk fitba' together. There was not much Sewing and Handwork inspection carried out that afternoon.

A REAL JERSEY LOVER?

Then there was the case of the reserve team player that I had imagined might be a second Jimmy Johnstone.

Suddenly he was no longer playing with the reserves.

I wondered if he had been badly injured. So on the next occasion the club doctor Eugene Connelly came to chat with my mother I asked him what was the injury that had stopped my favourite from playing with the reserves.

There was a bit of a silence. Then the good doctor asked me not to repeat what he was going to tell me. (I suppose it is kosher to say it now?) That reserve team player had to be asked to quit Parkhead because he had been stealing hooped jerseys from the ground. What a way to lose a promising career.

NO SAT-NAV THEN

A friend was driving us to a Tannadice match and said that he did not know how to get there. Muggins told him it was dead easy. I advised him to take Dundee's dual carriageway Kingsway until he came under a railway bridge and then turn right. So there we were almost in Carnoustie and no railway bridge. Probably marvellous

Beeching had had the line closed and that landmark bridge removed.

I covered myself in glory too after a game at Fir Park. I thought I remembered a traffic-avoiding detour back to Glasgow. It sure was a detour. I mistakenly drove through Ravenscraig steel-works twice. Tollan's name mud as usual!

BUT WHY ME?

Celtic Football club were changing their original floodlighting system and kindly offered the old lights for Old Aloysian Rugby Club use at Millerston.

I was at Parkhead with Mr. Brogan who was talking the lights away to Millerston in one of his potato lorries. Naturally I took the opportunity to blether with some of the then first team regulars who were there at the same time. Suddenly there was a rumpus and commotion coming from the corridor leading to the Manager's office and a youth came storming out of the passageway with an adult trying in vain to restrain him. Later the story emerged. The teacher in charge of football at one of Glasgow's Comprehensive Schools had kept urging the rest of the teaching staff to come and watch this player he had discovered, telling them this boy was the best he had ever seen in his school team. Eventually the reluctant teachers agreed to watch one of the school team's games and agreed that this player was indeed quite remarkable and that he should be recommended to Celtic as soon as possible. The commotion I had witnessed had happened because as Stein was signing him the youth had said to the great man that he was a right-half. Stein had replied that at Parkhead he would play where Stein decided. At that the youth had shouted out that he did not want to sign and had stormed out.

Yet much later after playing for various teams in England he was back at Parkhead as an assistant coach – or so I was told. Certainly meeting me at Parkhead he asked if I could put in a word for him to get the then vacant Celtic manager position. I was flabbergasted and wondered then and have wondered ever since why he thought I would have the influence to do that. I believe that he went on to become an assistant coach at various clubs but certainly never became the Celtic manager.

TOUJOURS LA POLITESSE!

At Uddingston Cross there is on Main Street a fabulous Italian ice-cream shop replete with Serie A emblems, badges and memorabilia. Make sure to savour their delicious product if you are in the area. Celtic French left-back Stephane Mahe stopped his car opposite to the ice-cream shop at the Cross traffic lights. A bunch of neds on that corner directed a tirade of foul abuse at Stephane accompanied with the usual crude hand signs. Mahe came out of his vehicle and stood in front of them on the pavement. Brave monsieur indeed. He told them in no uncertain terms that they were a disgrace to the club they purported to support and that they ought to remember that every human being on this planet is due respect and courtesy. He must have thoroughly bemused them for he went back into his car quite unharmed and drove off to Bothwell. Vive la France!

SEE BRITISH CARS...

I was driving with my mother through to a game at Dunfermline. The nearer we got to East End Park the more worried I became as I thought the old car was not going to get there. Reaching their car park – and giving big sigh of relief – I told the sergeant there who was directing traffic that my car was about to pack up and could he please let me be somewhere where I would not be blocking others trying to get out After the game.. But oh no! He talked on about how capable he was at directing traffic on the Forth Road bridge – whatever that had to do with it – and I just had to park like the rest of the arrivals. Getting my mother into the stand I realised that we were sitting next to a very prominent Travel Agent of the time, so I tried to explain my difficulties to him and politely asked him if he night be good enough to take my mother back to Glasgow with him so that she could get there safely that night. He just totally ignored me and did not even have the courtesy to speak in reply. After the match – which we won three-two – getting the old banger started (with considerable difficulty) I managed to leave the car park and then good old St. Christopher came to our assistance. I was delighted to see an AA van waiting by the side of the road, so I stopped the car, showed the AA man my AA card and asked him if he could see what the problem was with my ailing car. He had the bonnet up and was working on the engine etc. when a large expensive up-to-date saloon pulled up alongside and the driver came out to see if he could also be of any assistance. And at my request he took my mother with him down to Glasgow. Phew! As they drove off the kindly AA man remarked that I sure had a rich friend who had a posh car like that one. I blurted out with some indignation that he was no rich friend but the blighter who had sold me my dud car in the first place.

COUTHY RIDING BUT UNCOUTH SPEECH

Much later my friend with the brand new expensive Jaguar started taking me to away matches. What a way to go to a game. When I used to go in my ordinary vehicles to an away game, the police would never let me get near to the ground to park. Now his Jag would be swiftly waved on and on almost to the grandstand of the club we were playing. After one away match we were cruising along smoothly and very comfortably and listening to the Scottish Radio Four match summarising. Finn Mixu Paateleinen had just started playing for Dundee United and one of the summarisers – a very prominent former Internationalist and no friend of ours – came out with the following immortal words which deserved to be carved in stone (or marble!): "Wae a' they foreign yins noo playin' in ra Scottish gemme, us commentators will hiv fur tae start learnin' foreign languages!" We roared in delight and Hugh said "Us commentators should first hiv fur tae learn how tae speak ra English!" I was to have a close personal encounter with that semi-illiterate commentator later in a most surprising place. I have often wondered why the media persist with employing poorly-educated commentators as football summarisers where they are no exemplars for our youth, when perfectly literate scholars would be available to do a better job. Just listen to the excellent grammar used by Cricket summarisers, both British and foreign.

HOSPITALITY LOUNGE

But being a frequent guest of Gerard Eadie in his splendid and spacious CRSmith hospitality lounge, I did meet some vey literate and well-educated players. It was a surprise to meet Paul Eliot – whom I had seen playing for Pisa against Roma in the Roma

Olympic Stadium. He was educated and talkative and friendly but of course had his career cut short when he moved on to Chelsea.

One who impressed me very much was Malky Mackay. I was fortunate to have several meals with him and his friendly bank-clerkess mother, and found him each time to be courteous, well-mannered and highly educated. I was saddened and disappointed that the club let him go as he was an excellent centre-back in my opinion – as he proved with his subsequent career. At time of putting this together he is the manager of Watford FC though being interviewed for the Cardiff job,.

Then came surprise. I found myself dining with Craig Levein and John Robertson, both Hearts players at the time. Both were well-spoken, courteous and good company. But they confounded me by saying that they both wanted to play for Celtic. Who would have thought that?

Then a fellow guest who was an engineer at Rosyth Dockyard invited me there into the sanctum of sanctums and I was given a comprehensive and detailed tour of the dockyard facilities and its history, and shown carriages that were being furbished at that time for the East Coast main-line. Being an avid reader of Royal Navy histories and of the times when the Home Fleet was based there that delighted me no end.

COURTESY! COURTESY!

Being Gerard Eadie's guest meant sitting in the Directors Box and being a guest of the Directors at half-time and so meeting some distinguished sporting and business people when we were courteously invited into the Directors own room to view the Club trophies and have half-time refreshments. The directors had a pair of private urinals for their use and the use of their guests, and at an Old Firm game I was relieving myself at half-time in one of them when I realised that the person using the adjoining urinal was non-other than that BBC sports' commentator who had once given myself and my Jag friend such amusement. Being a guest of the Directors I knew I had to be as polite as possible so I thought to ask him what he thought of the game so far. Confused "mumble, mumble, grumble, grumble!" "We are losing two – (bad language!) – one and you are asking me what I thought of the game so far?"

More confused mumble, mumble grumble, grumble. Well I tried my best. But be sure I had another good laugh at him afterwards.

But I was not laughing when I was nearly being arrested in the Celtic stand. The present Lord John Wheatley was a parishioner of St. James' Kinross and at the time Sherriff in Perth – now a Senator of the College of Justice. The sheriff and his son were keen Hibs supporters (failed in my mission there did not I!) John Collins was their favourite Hibs player and when Hibs came to Parkhead, Gerard took them to the match as his guest so that they could meet Collins. We were having pre-meal refreshments when the sheriff said to me that he would like to see the rest of the Celtic Stand, so I led the way out into the corridor and I was startled to find a steward rushing up calling out "Police! Police! I am having you arrested!" Cue panic stations. It turned out that the good sheriff had carried his glass of wine out with him as he came. Alcohol was not allowed in the stand outside the hospitality suite. I quickly turned John Wheatley back into the CRSmith suite, shouting to the alarmed steward "He is a sheriff! He is a sheriff!"

A SAD TIME

Then there was the occasion that the then celebrated Liverpool team came to Glasgow for a friendly to raise money for the victims of the Hillsborough tragedy and their families. They were subdued but conversed well. I found myself blethering to that world-renowned but eccentric goal-keeper Bruce Grobbelaar. To my considerable amazement he told me that he had often played table-tennis in a South African Catholic church hall with one of our Beda year – Eugene Patten. I then wished I had gone to play table tennis with him in South Africa instead of trudging round wet and cold Dunkeld.

I was beside Tommy Burns (R I P) and Fergus McCann when a tearful Burns thanked McCann for saving the club. I was nearly in tears myself for McCann's arrival meant the end of my enjoyable times via the CRSmith lounge.

REMARKABLE HIGHLAND OCCURRENCE

One New Year, in my student days, a pal and myself hitch-hiked up to the Glencoe youth hostel. Hitch-hiking was no bother in those immediate post-war days.

On the Saturday we were on Bidean. There was no snow at all – though it was stiff-going. On the Sunday we tried to walk to Ballachulish for Mass. There was a great gale against us. We struggled on to where the narrow road climbed between two great slate quarry bings but could get no further. Slates and other debris were flying over our heads. I was scared stiff. Just then small car pulled up and the driver asked us where we were going. We explained that we were trying to get to the Catholic church for Mass. He said that they were going to their own Wee Free service but that they would drop us at the Catholic church first. And they did. Right at the front door of St. Mun's.

Now that was true ecumenism, not like the Christian J. Fordyce Glasgow sectarian bigotry.

GREAT PALS

My first pal – Jimmy the Woof was a great find and a real character. On parish visitations he loved quietly pinching anything he liked from the unsuspecting houses visited. Later that night he would regurgitate socks or scarves or gloves which no-one would admit to having lost. One evening he was under the table at a large dinner gathering and I was amusedly aware that the bold fellow was amusing himself by quietly snatching table-napkins from the dinner guests. I was on the point of doing some correction for that when he suddenly let out an enormous bark of complaint – presumably because he was not getting the expected tit-bits. And this was a Labrador that no-one had ever heard bark – including me. Well! Knives, forks, cups and bits of food flew in the air from the startled eaters. Was my face red – as usual. Another time the choir were giving it big licks in their practice at the back of the church when he decided to join in. They thought it was their priest mocking them and expressed their annoyance. I had hastily to come out and explain to them that it was not me.

On a Sunday Mass occasion Jimmy sometimes liked to stand at the porch entrance wagging his tail to greet parishioners.

Sometimes he just preferred to have his Sunday snooze in the sacristy. But if my homily bored him by being tool long and tedious the bold fellow would come to the front of the sanctuary and look accusingly at me. A least that would cause a snigger or two among the cognescenti and accordingly I would apologise to the parishioners for being so boringly long. An exception to that behaviour would take place at Mass in good old Brechin. He seemed – like me – to be fascinated by our large church there, and he took himself into the habit of joining in the lengthy Introit procession round the church to the sanctuary, where the saintly fellow would peacefully lie lengthwise on the sanctuary floor quietly and attentively watching proceedings. I did not stop him from that practice as I thought, rightly or wrongly, that it might be an encouragement to youth to come again to Sunday Mass as they are so reluctant to do these un-enlightened days.

Kinross Golf Club had bought additional farms and was in the process of making another eighteen-hole course. So one nice day I decided to take Jimmy the Woof for his amble away across to see how things were going with the second course. One of the Kinross hotels had a big dog that was notorious for attacking other dogs. Jimmy was a good distance ahead of me as usual doing his customary inspections of territory when I was horrified to see the notorious large dog come bounding across the fields from Kinross and making a bee-line for Jimmy. A great battle ensued ahead of me and I could see a large cloud dirt and stones and dust flying up into the air. I thought it looked bad for my dog, but then to my amazement I saw the bully dog slinking off dejectedly back to Kinross. When I eventually reached Jimmy I found him completely unharmed and looking pretty pleased with himself. Later I was telling the local friendly vet about that happening. (Jimmy would not pass that vet's without going in for his usual treat.) The vet told me that black Labs are usually very calm and well-behaved but when attacked they can become extremely ferocious to defend themselves.

I was staying with my Beda pal at Oxford University Chaplaincy where he was assisting the redoubtable Oxford Chaplain Ian Ker – the great Newman scholar and postulator. I had discovered a near-by large piece of waste ground to which I would walk with his nibs so that he could carry out his necessary evacuations without being a nuisance. One morning I was strolling there as usual when an immaculately-turned-out young policeman – obviously going on duty – changed direction and came over to me. I thought it was just going to be the usual practice of a stranger admiring Jimmy the Woof but the young policeman announced that he was going to arrest me. (Afterwards I realised that there must have been an Oxford Bye-Law requiring dogs to be on leads.) As he made that pronouncement Jimmy wagged his tail and took the bobbie's immaculate white gloves into his mouth. That horrified me. But the young constable started crying – yes crying – spluttering that he had lost his gloves. I hurriedly explained that it was but a friendly gesture on behalf of the dog and had Jimmy give the gloves back. As the blue-coated minion of the law stood tearfully examining his gloves, Jimmy and myself made a hasty retreat round the first available corner. I had a great time in Morse country. My friend played the organ in many Colleges and he would take me beyond where tourists normally went, explaining that I was a visiting organist from Scotland.

If I managed to get down to Parkhead in time, Jimmy and I would have a wander round exploring the haunts of my youth. Occasionally we would examine the remains of the old Caledonian Parkhead terminal station just across the London Road from the ground and if there was time wander down the disused railway down to Rutherglen's triangular man-line junction. Fergus once went public on the lack of good transport facilities for Parkhead and I pointed out to him that there were three closed Parkhead railway stations (the old Caley terminal, LMS's Parkhead Stadium station at adjacent Springfield Road, and of course the closed LNER one for Beardmore's at the Duke Street/Shettleston Road junction), and I suggested he should get one of them back into use – but of course I had no acknowledgement from him. (I suggested to the people trying to improve the transport facilities for their Commonwealth Games that they use the line from Rutherglen which came into Dalmarnock – but instead they took away the remaining connecting Baltic Street bridge.)

Parkhead once had seven useful tram services and when the last scheme to have a Glasgow Light Rail service was planned, the depot was to be in Parkhead. Of course that great and marvellous scheme was scuppered by the Conservative government as they had grossly over-spent on the construction of the Jubilee line. London coming first as usual.

During the match Jimmy the Woof would be walked around for me by the most helpful and generous Parkhead stewards – so he did not mind coming to Paradise too much.

Because of his all-black colour I had a flashing red light which I would attach to his collar when we were going out at night. One night I was trudging down a long dark lane and James was doing his usual sniffing everything performance way behind me. As I reached the bottom of the lane I was horrified to see a woman clutching pale-faced to a garden wall. Of course I went over to offer assistance and asked should I summon an ambulance. Her reply that came back still gives me a laugh to-day when I think about it.

"I saw that red light zig-zagging down the lane and I thought that it was Old Nick himself coming for me!"

When helping to operate preserved trams at Summerlee Heritage Park, Jimmy would lie peacefully on the driving platform enjoying the ride. (And he knew about changing ends too.) At one terminus I was assailed by an irate passenger wanting to know why my dog was inside the Heritage Park when she had not been allowed to bring her dog in. I gently and politely tried to explain to her that if I could not have brought my woof in, then there would not have been a motorman to operate the car she had just ridden on. That did not calm her down. So I said to her – when I managed to get a word in – "Your dog is a hearing-aid dog, isn't it?" "No! No!" she shouted back – not appreciating that I was giving her a way to get her dog in. (Assisting dogs not being barred from coming in with owner.) I repeated the hint to her three times but the poor woman still did not get it. I had enough of the continued abuse and eventually just notched up and accelerated the car away from the tirade.

Sadly, his nibs met a young Bull Mastiff from a neighbouring house and loved going round to play with her. She proved to be too heavy for the old pal, as one night she playfully jumped on his poor old back crushing his vertebrae column – and that was my great friend gone.

FRECKLES – ALIAS FINDERLIE SNIPE

When I went through to Milnathort to bury poor old Jimmy, Gerard Eadie insisted on replacing him with a very young Springer

Spaniel pup. He was so small I could easily hold him on one hand. I renamed him "Freckles" because I did not fancy shouting "Snipe" for him in public because. I remembered a story that when the family lived in Barrachnie they had a dog named Caesar. Supposedly on one occasion in the street, a family member shouted "Caesar" to recall him and a passer-by went to the Police and complained that their dog had been told to "seize her!"

But the Springer Spaniel sure could spring straight up in then air if he needed to do that to get on top of a wall. He was smart and amazingly intelligent and not at all self-willed like Jimmy the Woof. He always understood everything that was said to him and never forgot instructions given to him. He could count as well and always gave a quizzical look if something happened more often than usual or if I worked too long on the computer...

His great delight turned out to be having his wee ball thrown for him and then running to find it and bring it back. I know most dogs like doing that but Freckles just loved running up to complete strangers and dropping the ball at their feet to have it thrown for him. Once we were perambulating along Dalrymple Street and as we passed by the Girvan Pet Shop he dived in and ran out with a brand new ball. And they say animals are dumb. Freckie certainly wasn't. The old dog belonging to a neighbour friend died and the good lady – despite her loss – came over and brought a large box full of her dog's now not needed toys. Then first time I gave one of the toys to Freckles he immediately ran across the road and left that toy in the dead dog's garden. How did he know to do that? Quite amazing.

He would have made splendid hearing-aid dog. He always ran to either the land-line phone or the mobile to tell me which was ringing.

One Christmas afternoon the wee fellow became extremely distraught and agitated. I could not find anything physically wrong with him nor think what was causing his upset. He was not himself for a few days and I took him to the Vet but he too could not find any reason for the continuing distress.

Then I had a thought and called Gerard Eadie to see if anything had happened to one of Freckie's family. The little brother that I had seen with him – when I first saw Finderlie Snipe – had been given to a farmer as a family pet. That farmer had run over Freckie's brother with a piece of farm machinery and the brother had died of his injuries on that very Christmas afternoon when my wee friend had become so distraught. That sad event strengthened my previous belief that dogs can use an extra para-normal sense that we usually do not participate in. Sometimes too in the house it was apparent that he was watching some presence that was not apparent to me.

But I have had paranormal experiences if you like to call them that.

I sometimes knew what my mother was going to say before she came out with it. When operating a tram for the first time I would realise that I was not operating the tram but someone was doing that through me. I would wonder if it was my father or one of the old Dennistoun Depot gang? Then sometimes when driving on roads I would find myself applying the car brakes or changing down gears without having thought at all about doing it and then those unpremeditated actions would prevent me from having an unexpected smash.

The most curious peculiar experience I had was when walking Jimmy the Woof alongside the man-made loch in Strathclyde Park. Jimmy had raced away ahead to investigate a group of playing dogs and I was trying to keep an eye on him to see if everything was safe for him. I glanced up and was surprised to see that there was a tall slim attractive-looking lady walking towards me and giving me a warm friendly smile. I was puzzled because I did not recognise her and wondered at the big -old-fashioned- looking buttoned-up light brown coat she was wearing. My attention went back to safe-guarding Jimmy and then I thought about turning round to see if I could speak to the lady but was staggered to find that there was no-one there. Being a completely unenclosed footpath there was nowhere she could have turned off into.

I have sometimes wondered if it was my maternal grandmother's way of thanking me for putting a tombstone on her unmarked Leadville grave.

Sadly I lost my greatly-loved brilliant and so-loyal and friendly Freckles when he was just coming into the prime of his life at six years of age. He had been poisoned by weed-killer – according to the vet who had tried hard to save him.

I was never able to establish the source of that killer poison.

CONNIE

When, broken-hearted, I went through to bury my great pal at his Milnathort birth-place, my friends said that they knew of a Springer relation who had gone to a ghillie but when she had given the ghillie the pups he wanted he had just kept her in a cage for four years. Well of course I had to give her a home.

Connie- alias Finderlie princess – proved to be entirely different from the previous two friends. She was quiet, patient, obedient and never angry or bad-tempered – unlike her boss.

The first morning I had her in Girvan, I took her down the cemetery steps to the beach and then stood in amazement. I had never seen anything like it. She raced along the wave front up right up to the Girvan pier turned and raced back along the great distance to the Ainslie Horse Rock. And kept on doing that time and time again.. I thought that she would never stop. Poor thing had obviously never been in an open space in her four years. For the first three weeks of her Girvan stay she did not want to come into the house or meet people but gradually she became accustomed to life outside a cage and has proved to be another great friend but not thrawn like her boss.

She always tried to please me by bringing me things – amazingly a herring out of the sea: a hare she captured on the disused railway line embankment – and many a bird or a hedgehog. But then on the Queen's jubilee week-end she just became agitated and died – for no reason I could discover. I could not obtain the services of her usual vet – though Girvan vet Allan Jeans came eventually when it was just too late. Then I had the sad business of burying yet another dear friend at Milnathort.

ZAK

Gerard came to my assistance with one more Springer, Zak, kindly brought all the way to Girvan for me. The lad is highly nervous about adults but perfectly well-behaved. I have discovered that he loves to frolic like the mad March hare round the paths and bushes on the old disused goods yard. He sure likes doing that. And walking with him helps to keep me fit.

FINITA EST

In my younger days there were two great authors I greatly admired Hilaire Belloc and Gilbert Keith Chesterton.

I managed to emulate Belloc, by like him doing military service and yacht sailing. Chesterton has gone badly out of favour these days, being judged by some to have been anti-Semitic. But at least we had that Distributist Club in his honour at Glasgow University.

I also had great admiration and wonderment about the Irish monks who so admired the desert hermits in their quests to become closer to God through isolation from worldly cares and accordingly sought to emulate them by making their coracle journeys across from Ireland and up among the various islands off the west coast of Scotland where they set up many hermitages and eventually even small monasteries – Iona being the best known. Unfortunately after some four centuries the devastating Viking raids were to destroy most of their great achievements.

Perhaps it would have been better for a lot of people if I had become an isolated hermit instead of too urgently trying this that and the next thing trying to serve God.

NOT THE FULL SHILLING?

I had often wondered why I had done something offensive and then wondered afterwards why I had done it without thinking about it first. When I asked my great school pal, Arthur McQuade (who became a Harley Street specialist), about my puzzling mis-performances, he suggested that perhaps like the great Mozart I had a touch of Tourette's Syndrome. I suppose that at least put me into great company.

MEA CULPA, MEA CULPA, MEA MAXIMA CULPA

May I take this opportunity to thank all those good people who assisted me in my wandering through life and those who are still there doing that?

My gratitude is also unbounded to the eminent Doctor Hutcheson, the great Ayr Hospital cataract removal expert. He restored my vision to how it was as a young boy.

I only wish I had known him earlier in my life. I might have been a better footballer.

But most of all I offer my prayers and apologies to the too many I have annoyed and upset with my mis-behaviour and attitude.

Say one for Zak and me occasionally.

LAUS DEO SEMPER